God Bless

WE SHALL BE Changed

To order additional copies of *We Shall Be Changed,*
call 1-800-765-6955.

Visit us at **www.reviewandherald.com** for information on other Review and Herald® products.

WE SHALL BE Changed

A Devotional From
Quiet Hour Ministries

Christy K. Robinson, Editor

REVIEW AND HERALD® PUBLISHING ASSOCIATION
Since 1861 | www.reviewandherald.com

Published by Review and Herald® Publishing Association, Hagerstown, MD 21741-1119

Review and Herald® titles may be purchased in bulk for educational, business, fund-raising, or sales promotional use. For information, e-mail SpecialMarkets@reviewandherald.com.

The Review and Herald® Publishing Association publishes biblically based materials for spiritual, physical, and mental growth and Christian discipleship.

The author assumes full responsibility for the accuracy of all facts and quotations as cited in this book.

This book was
Edited by Kalie Kelch
Copyedited by James Hoffer
Cover designed by Trent Truman
© iStockphoto.com / proxyminder / superseker / Pingwin
Typeset: 10/12 Bembo
PRINTED IN U.S.A.

14 13 12 11 10 5 4 3 2 1

Library of Congress Cataloging-in-Publication Data

We shall be changed: a devotional from Quiet Hour Ministries / Christy K. Robinson, editor.
p. cm.
1. Devotional calendars—Seventh-Day Adventists. 2. Seventh-Day Adventists—Prayers and devotions.
I. Robinson, Christy K., 1958-
BV4810.W39 2010
242'.2—dc22

2009039420

ISBN 978-0-8280-2505-8

FORGET ABOUT THE FUTURE?

Forgetting what is behind and straining toward what is ahead, I press on toward the goal to win the prize for which God has called me heavenward in Christ Jesus.
Phil. 3:13,14, NIV.

Did you make any New Year's resolutions? Maybe you've decided to lose weight, learn a language, find a significant other, start voice lessons, stop bad habits, exercise more, or clean the garage. Most people forget or break their resolutions within two weeks of making them.

Recently a song, which had been background noise, arrested me with the line "Forget about the future, let's get on with the past."

That's pretty anticommittal and unwilling to face the uncertainty of the unknown. But how many of us have done that? (again and again?) Don't raise your hands—we're all pretty obvious.

That never-say-die apostle wrote, "Forgetting what is behind [the past] and straining toward what is ahead [the future], I press on toward the goal to win the prize for which God has called me heavenward in Christ Jesus. All of us who are mature should take such a view of things. And if on some point you think differently, that too God will make clear to you" (Phil. 3:13-15, NIV).

Straining toward the future! Every morning at 5:30 a.m. my border collie acts like a Siberian husky, pulling me along, choking in her eagerness to sniff the next tree in the parkway. There's high tension in that leash as I drowsily stumble along behind, mumbling, "Slow down, doggie! It's too early to be enthusiastic."

The thought that God wants me to strain toward what is ahead is hard to learn. We all tend to "think differently," but God intends to make it clear that instead of our being a reluctant Jonah, He wants us to take the path of least resistance to Him. God will lead us toward the goal and its prize. And it seems clear from His Word that He wants us to forget the past and get on with the future. If there's no tension on your spiritual collar, you're not really straining. Where is God leading today? Get out there and pull like a working dog!

CHRISTY K. ROBINSON

JANUARY 2

FINDING WEALTH

"I know the plans I have for you," . . . "plans to prosper you . . ., plans to give you hope and a future." Jer. 29:11, NIV.

Plans to prosper." I thought that initially meant to make a lot of money. Prosperity as defined is "a successful, flourishing, or thriving condition, especially in financial respects; good fortune." I would change it slightly to be "a position of good fortune, with a successful, flourishing, and thriving condition." I have changed my perspective on prosperity and wealth—not because I accept poverty as a lifestyle but because I understand that money is a small factor to true wealth.

After I completed my master's degree, my expectation was to work for a business and/or develop a successful enterprise that generated lots of money. It would provide me (I thought) the opportunity to live and play where and when I wanted as well as give me the necessary prestige required for a teaching position at retirement. Little did I know what God had in store for me.

His plans included humbling experiences through setbacks in business and relationships, yet with each challenge He provided a silver lining. Through each experience He taught me about true prosperity. What is true prosperity? A life of service! What I do today is all about serving others. The money, as a secondary issue, is always there, but a fulfilling life of giving delivers the prosperity promise.

Serving has benefited me in several ways. I have more time than I would have if I was a corporate individual. I met my wife through the transition, and I now have physical and mental well-being through exercise, nutrition, and diet. Best of all, as she is my best friend, I am able to work with her to make future plans for life and the training of our two children. We plan to homeschool and travel a bit more. Prosperity is a direction that includes our love for Jesus Christ and each other. His philosophy has opened a door and provided a new perspective of what He means when He says, "I know the plans I have for you—plans to prosper you, to give you hope and a future."

Do you want to find true wealth? Allow God to teach you to serve.

CORDELL J. THOMAS

A NEW SONG

And he hath put a new song in my mouth, even praise unto our God: many shall see it, and fear, and shall trust in the Lord. Ps. 40:3.

For some 35 years it was my responsibility to choose music for the Voice of Prophecy broadcast. Listeners would write, "Why can't we have more of the old songs?" And if we did too many old songs: "Can't you find any new material?" We had to keep adding interesting new songs to our repertoire.

"A new song" can have several meanings:

* A song not heard or sung before, or not appreciated on the first hearing. Any musician worth their salt must learn new pieces to keep the skills alive.
* A new arrangement of the same old song. I think I made five different arrangements of "What a Friend We Have in Jesus."
* A fresh excitement to the rendition of the same old song. Professional singers have to find new energy for the song, new enthusiasm for its message, new nuances. Singers have to recapture the same thrill as the first time the song made their hearts beat a little faster with its beauty.
* A new song is not music at all, in the strictest sense. It is the work we do, the objects we make with our hands, the influence we have on other people, the personality we show to others, the selfless service we perform. The list is endless. Almost everything we do or say can be a new song that will brighten someone's life.

Each morning as you go to work, say, "What a privilege it is to be able to work." (Many people don't have a job.) Or "What can I bring to this job today that is exciting?" Or "How can I improve the quality and quantity of my work?"

The new song given to David by the Lord was "even praise unto our God." How long has it been since you said out loud, "Praise the Lord!" What kind of new song are you singing with your life so that others will see it and fear and trust in the Lord?

WAYNE HOOPER

WILL THE BEARS COME?

Unless you . . . become like little children, you will never enter the kingdom of heaven. Matt. 18:3, NIV.

Traveling across Wyoming on a freezing midwinter night, we missed a turn and found ourselves stuck tight in a snowbank. Fresh from years in a tropical mission field, we had flimsy mittens, light jackets, and one pair of boots between us. We were miles from anything on the map.

We kicked and clawed at the hard ice packed around the car's wheels, making not even a dent. "We can't get these chains on," my husband said. "I have to find help." I handed him my jacket and shivered my way back into the car. Thankfully, the children were asleep in the back seat. I revved the engine and turned up the heater. The gas tank was one-fourth full. How long would it last?

I worried about my husband. Would he get lost? How long could he hold out? With these concerns weighing heavily on my mind, I noticed the children stirring. They sat up, puzzled, surveying the scene around them. I didn't want to betray my anxiety.

"We're stuck in the snow," I said. "Daddy's getting help."

A long minute passed. "Mommy, will the bears come out of the woods and get us?" the 5-year-old asked.

I had to smile. I hadn't noticed how close we were to the forest.

"No, darling. Angels are guarding our car. No bears can hurt us." Satisfied and trusting, the children snuggled down again and went back to sleep.

Dear God, I silently prayed, *You said it long ago, "Unless you . . . become like little children, you will never enter the kingdom of heaven." I am Your child. I, too, can trust those angels.*

As the first streaks of daylight fingered the horizon, a large farm truck bumped into view. We were quickly out of the snowdrift and on our way. And we still had one eighth of a tank of gas.

AILEEN LUDINGTON

GOD'S PROVISION

You will drink from the brook, and I have ordered the ravens to feed you there. 1 Kings 17:4, NIV.

Ragged gray clouds covered Mindoro's mountaintops. Breathing heavily, Tim Holbrook and I stood on a ridge of rapidly rising terrain as we peered through the mist toward the central highlands of the Philippine island.

Pointing northeast, Tim identified Alangan villages that had yet to hear of a loving God whose power could break their terror of the spirits. "What difference would air support have made in your work?" I asked.

"Oh, it would easily have cut the first church-plant time in half," Tim responded. "Without an airplane to support us in the mountains, we started on the tribe's perimeter, where the gospel must compete with materialism. The message spreads faster the deeper we go into the mountains."

Tim swung southeast. "Up there live the most primitive of the six tribes on the island. Eight to twelve thousand people have never had contact with the outside world. They refer to themselves as the 'true Batangan,' proud of their mastery of the spirits and skill with blowguns and poison darts. Even rebels armed with rifles are afraid of them. My dream is to plant a church there. It will take someone willing to live in a crude shelter, wear at most a loincloth, and stay up to nine months when rains prohibit hiking in and out of the steep mountains. It is impossible to carry enough supplies to last more than a few days, necessitating regular air drops of food and medicine."

Have you accepted a divine assignment requiring tremendous sacrifice? Elijah did. "Then the word of the Lord came to Elijah: '. . . Turn eastward and hide in the Kerith Ravine. . . . You will drink from the brook, and I have ordered the ravens to feed you there'" (1 Kings 17:2-4, NIV).

Like Elijah of old and the person whom God will call to reach the Batangan, you may rest assured—God will sustain you today.

DON STARLIN

JANUARY 6

WE'RE ALL ELLA HERE

All the believers were one in heart and mind. No one claimed that any of his possessions was his own, but they shared everything they had. . . . And much grace was upon them all. Acts 4:32, 33, NIV.

Three-year-old Annika has no problem making up her mind. Whether it's her favorite colors (purple and pink) or her favorite food (strawberries), she is always ready with a swift, sure decision. Her favorite flower? The tulip. Her favorite name? Definitely Ella.

Annika has a trio of eight-inch baby dolls. When her grandmother came to visit, she asked what their names were. Annika replied, "Ella."

"Which one is Ella?" Nana inquired.

"They are all Ella" was Annika's answer.

Later on we discovered that not only were the triplets all named Ella, but her Barbie dolls and all other assorted dolls were also known as Ella.

Playtime took on a whole new dimension as each character in the scenario became Ella. When making one doll speak to another, you no longer had to stop and think of the right name—you simply said, "Ella." Although that did make things quick and easy, it was a little more complicated figuring out which Ella was being spoken to!

Although we each have a different name, as believers we all share the name "Christian," one who believes in Jesus Christ and lives according to His teachings.

The apostles and early church members took the name "Christian" to heart. "All the believers were one in heart and mind. No one claimed that any of his possessions was his own, but they shared everything they had. With great power the apostles continued to testify to the resurrection of the Lord Jesus, and much grace was upon them all" (Acts 4:32, 33, NIV).

The name Ella means "all" or "complete." Certainly in Christ we as Christians are a complete body. Paul describes this in 1 Corinthians 12: "The body is a unit, though it is made up of many parts; and though all its parts are many, they form one body. So it is with Christ. For we were all baptized by one Spirit into one body—whether Jews or Greeks, slave or free—and we were all given the one Spirit to drink" (verses 12, 13, NIV).

Although we are all different, we are all "Ella" here.

LAURA WEST KONG

UNDER HIS WINGS

O God, be merciful to me! For my soul trusts in You;
and in the shadow of Your wings I will make my refuge. Ps. 57:1, NKJV.

Crowds applauded as 17-year-old Manuel Pajón Torres dodged a charging bull at a ring in southern Mexico. *Luck has always been on my side,* he thought. *I just wish my old grandmother would stop praying for me. She keeps begging me to leave the profession I love and become a Christian.*

Seconds later the angry bull tossed Manuel high in the air. He landed in a heap on the ground—the bull headed for him again. The crowd cheered when he managed to get up and run. *That was a close one,* he thought. *When I walk out of the ring today, they'll give me more money than most men make in a month.*

He faced the mad bull again. *Either this bull dies or they haul me off to the mortuary,* he realized. Walking home that afternoon, he felt proud of the professional pay he received. Only one thing bothered him. *I just wish Grandma would stop bugging me.*

He rushed into the house, not realizing his grandmother was suffering a severe heart attack. In spite of terrible pain, she sang softly, "'Under His wings, O what precious enjoyment! There will I hide till life's trials are o'er; sheltered, protected, no evil can harm me; resting in Jesus I'm safe evermore.'"

Manuel moved close, listening to every word. The old woman kept on singing: "'Under His wings, under His wings, who from His love can sever? Under His wings my soul shall abide...'"

Before finishing the song, his godly grandmother was gone. The brave bullfighter fell to his knees. "Father, I've resisted You too long. Right now I give my life to Christ. Please forgive my sins."

Today Manuel fights the good fight of faith, sharing his love for Jesus with others. You can make this your prayer: "O God, be merciful to me! For my soul trusts in You; and in the shadow of Your wings I will make my refuge" (Ps. 57:1, NKJV).

It's true. "He shall cover you with His feathers, and under His wings you shall take refuge; His truth shall be your shield and buckler" (Ps. 91:4, NKJV).

WELLESLEY MUIR

THE MAGIC BOX

By wisdom a house is built, and through understanding it is established;
through knowledge its rooms are filled with rare and beautiful treasures.
Prov. 24:3, 4, NIV.

The new TV set was unwrapped with care, and family members gathered around to see its crisp, clear picture. But 2-year-old Annika cared little about the large gleaming black box that her grandparents displayed prominently in their living room. She did not clamor to be the first to watch her favorite programs. She could do that anywhere on just about any TV. Instead Annika was drawn to the empty brown cardboard box, which had previously housed the new acquisition. Instinctively she knew this box was where the real magic lay.

This ordinary-looking cardboard box became her playhouse, an oversized jack-in-the-box to jump out of, a mountain for dolls to climb, a diving board for toy dogs, a candy shop, a restaurant, part of an obstacle course, a bear's cave, a princess's castle, and a beauty salon.

Annika filled her "house" with all the enchanting treasures she could imagine and inspired everyone who played with her there. Each day in the box was a new adventure.

Our lives are like that empty box. We fill up our "box" by the everyday choices we make. As Christians we have the opportunity to fill our "house" to overflowing with the incomparable treasures that Jesus offers, with potential to bless not just ourselves but every person we come in contact with.

What are you filling your house with? Where does Christ fit into your house? Is He the cornerstone of your life? Think about these things as you consider Solomon's sage advice.

"By wisdom a house is built, and through understanding it is established; through knowledge its rooms are filled with rare and beautiful treasures" (Prov. 24:3, 4, NIV).

LAURA WEST KONG

EYES OF FAITH: BELIEVING IS SEEING

Jesus saith unto him, Thomas, because thou hast seen me, thou hast believed: blessed are they that have not seen, and yet have believed.
John 20:29.

In a conversation with a friend, I mentioned that I had not experienced a miracle that I could without doubt attribute to God's direct intervention. My friend seemed shocked, claiming that she experienced things daily that she attributed to God's leading. She seemed to pity me, which made me feel insecure—as if I had an inferior spiritual life.

It's not that I haven't had an experience with God. I feel a strong connection as a result of a daily relationship nurtured by prayer. I've been given peace, a clear mind, and strength when I've called upon Him. Though God feels very real to me, I simply haven't had a there's-no-other-possible-explanation-for-this experience.

After my conversation with my friend I talked to God about my feelings. I told Him about how the situation made me feel. Then it occurred to me: perhaps the reason God had never shown Himself to me in that manner was that I'd never asked Him to! So I prayed, "God, reveal Yourself to me. If You are moving and changing things, make it obvious to me. Remove any doubt that clouds my vision, and give me eyes of faith to let me see You working in my life."

Since that prayer, amazing things have happened. Many prayers have been answered in ways I never expected. Unavoidable disasters have turned out to be not only manageable but successful. Individual instances may not be convincing evidence to anyone else, but the cumulative effect on my spiritual life has been indelible. With each answer to prayer, my faith has grown. I have begun to understand that God works through us when we make ourselves available to His Spirit.

It's said that seeing is believing. With God I've discovered that it works the other way around. Until we express our belief, we cannot see Him at work in our lives.

LORELEI HERMAN CRESS

JANUARY 10

TRANS-SPECIES MORPHING

"Come, follow me," Jesus said, "and I will make you fishers of men."
Matt. 4:19, NIV.

The last time I cast a line into Minnesota's Rainy Lake, I was 9. My uncle baited the hook with something squishy, and I caught a northern pike, which my aunt cleaned. We ate it for dinner, and I choked on a bone. Ever since, I've disliked fishy-tasting food.

Recently I attended a professional development seminar on fishing. It wasn't about trout, bass, or salmon. It was about marketing. So often we drop a line into the water and expect fish to fight each other for the honor of taking the hook (the hook being our product, donating to our ministry, or joining our cause). That's absurd!

Christians who want to share the gospel and motivate others to join in service to humanity should think like the fish we're targeting. Go where the fish are. Use the lures the fish like, not what the anglers like.

My pastor once taught that fishers are hunters, not agriculturalists. They know how to prepare nets, where to cast them, what kind of lure is needed, and where and when to expect the best results. They cooperate with other fishers. They know how to harvest and process the catch. After those skills were mastered, Jesus transformed His disciples from aggressive fish hunters to protective, providing shepherds, and called Peter and His disciples to feed His sheep.

A church sign said: "Be ye fishers of men. You catch them—He'll clean them." That's right. Catch new people for God's kingdom. But don't even think about reforming them to your image of a proper Christian. Let the Holy Spirit have His way with them and transform them from fish to sheep!

I've created some strange metaphors—fishers morph into shepherds and fish morph into sheep—but it points to our inability to change anything or anyone. Only the Creator can do that work. By the way, where are you on the road from fish to sheep?

CHRISTY K. ROBINSON

VITAMINS

Now faith is being sure of what we hope for and certain of what we do not see. Heb. 11:1, NIV.

Pharmaceutical companies go to great lengths to make their medications appealing to finicky children. There are fruity syrups, chewable candy tablets, and even gummy bear vitamins. When Annika was little, she took baby vitamin drops. However, the baby vitamin formula was not sweet and fruity. It was thick, brown, and gooey. It smelled bad and tasted even worse. (I know; I tried it.) Getting the stuff down her throat was a nightly challenge.

My routine was to shake the bottle to mix its ingredients well, open the child-safety lid, and fill the dropper. Then I would put it out of sight while taking Annika in my lap. Next I would hold her down and maneuver the dropper into her mouth, aiming it at the side of her cheek far enough back that at least some of it would go down her throat and not dribble down her chin. We all looked forward to the day she could graduate to a big kids' vitamin without it being a choking hazard.

Once, when Annika was about 1½ years old, during the evening's vitamin ritual she squirmed out of my arms and knelt down on the kitchen floor. Clasping her tiny hands together, she bowed her head and squeezed her eyes shut. She then prayed her very first prayer: "Dear Jesus, thank You for all-done vitamins. Amen."

Annika, in her simple prayer, demonstrated what many of us never fully grasp. When God promises to help us through our trouble, whatever it may be, that trial is as good as over. She didn't pray "Dear Jesus, help me get through the vitamins" or "Please take away the vitamins"—it was "Thank You that with Your help the vitamins are as good as done."

We also face daily struggles in our Christian walk. Although the situations taste unpleasant, we grow stronger and healthier from facing them. When we encounter trials, may we have faith in God—a faith that with God the trial is as good as over, a faith that says "Thank You for all-done vitamins."

"Now faith is being sure of what we hope for and certain of what we do not see."

LAURA WEST KONG

January 12

THE EBENEZER STONE

Thus far has the Lord helped us. 1 Sam. 7:12, NIV.

My memory is not particularly outstanding. I forget so much. I forget birthdays, luncheons, my loved ones' favorites, and a host of other important things. But there is something else I forget that I want with all my heart to remember: all the times God has delivered me from trouble.

In 1 Samuel 7 the Israelites experienced a true revival. They were completely repentant of their sins and poured out their hearts before God. They got rid of their false gods and began in earnest to worship the one true God. As the Philistines drew near to invade Israel, the Israelites begged Samuel to pray for them. Samuel took a lamb and brought the sacrifice before the Lord in prayer.

It is so amazing to know that God, our intercessor, never ceases. He, in a thundering response, gave Israel victory over the Philistines. Samuel then brought out a stone to be a memorial and named it Ebenezer to encourage Israel.

"Then Samuel took a stone and set it up between Mizpah and Shen. He named it Ebenezer, saying, 'Thus far has the Lord helped us' " (1 Sam. 7:12, NIV).

How often do we forget divine delivery? We get so wrapped up in our busyness that we often neglect the One whose hand is with us. We focus on what is seen and not on what is unseen. Today I encourage you to focus on what is unseen.

"God is our refuge and strength, an ever-present help in trouble. Therefore we will not fear, though the earth give way and the mountains fall into the heart of the sea, though its waters roar and foam and the mountains quake with their surging. . . . The Lord Almighty is with us; the God of Jacob is our fortress" (Ps. 46:1-7, NIV).

Bring out the Ebenezer stone in your life so that you may be reminded that you serve the God of our help.

Stephen Robertson

ANSWERED PRAYER

You faithfully answer our prayers with awesome deeds, O God our savior. You are the hope of everyone on earth. Ps. 65:5, NLT.

When my father, a physician, was diagnosed with prostate cancer, I prayed that God would make the right treatment obvious. After consultation, Dad announced his choice to undergo surgery.

Since I trust my dad's knowledge and judgment, it was out of character for me to second-guess his decision. But I did! I researched treatment options online.

One of the first Web sites I found directed me to a surgeon who operates via laparoscope. I e-mailed the surgeon and asked if my father would be a good candidate for the surgery. Within a few hours he assured me that he'd gladly review and discuss Dad's medical records. Dad faxed his records, and the surgeon called Dad almost immediately. Dad was so impressed with the information that he elected to undergo laparoscopic surgery. Dad said that although laparoscopic surgery was the wave of the future, not many physicians were doing it.

Then, an obstacle. Dad's insurance company covered less than 10 percent of the surgeon's fee. Embarrassed and disappointed, he explained that he'd have to cancel the surgery since he could not afford to pay the difference. The surgeon responded, "Don't worry about it—we'll take care of you." How many surgeons are willing to forgo more than 90 percent of their fee?

The surgery was successful, and Dad recovered nicely. A few weeks later he received a check from his insurance company. Nearly all of the surgeon's fees were paid! Dad's happiness was complete, knowing that the surgeon would be compensated for his skill and his kindness.

While these circumstances may be attributed by some to chance, my father and I believe that God led us to this surgeon. God wants to reveal Himself to each one of us and to use us to reach others. If we open ourselves to His Spirit, He will not only give us what we need to cope with our challenges, but show us how we can be a blessing to others.

LORELEI HERMAN CRESS

January 14

THE TROUBLE MAGNET

Yet man is born to trouble as surely as sparks fly upward.
Job 5:7, NIV.

Haven't we all known people who seem to gather trouble to themselves? Murphy's Law seems to dog their footsteps. We shake our heads in wonder that they get through life in one piece. Recently one of my friends was described as a trouble magnet. He personifies Job 5:7, which says, "Yet man is born to trouble as surely as sparks fly upward" (NIV). Good thing he is married to an organized, forgiving, and loving wife!

There are a few women who are attracted to "bad boys," magnetic, rebellious, free-spirited men who wear ponytails and shirtless leather vests and decorative chains on their boots. (I'm not criticizing—but my taste is for Clark Kent cerebral types!)

If you look at an online Bible concordance, you'll find pages and pages on "trouble." Many of the verses fit into this niche: "A kind man benefits himself, but a cruel man brings trouble on himself" (Prov. 11:17, NIV). An ungodly person is a trouble magnet!

Again and again, we find Abraham, Jacob, Moses, David, and a parade of other very real humans, not at all different from our generation, bringing trouble upon themselves by poor planning, shortsightedness, lying, trying to save their own skins, worshipping at the altar of spontaneity, or (to use a modern term) flying by the seat of their pants.

But would we call these people ungodly? No! Because they realized their fundamental sin problem and its inevitable consequences and asked God to rescue them. We all bring trouble to ourselves at times. Some of us remain chronic lifelong trouble magnets!

But when life's nails, thumbtacks, garden rakes, and wrecking balls are flying around, there is an antimagnetic force to rescue us. Our all–powerful God repels evil and its effects.

"Who is like you, a people saved by the Lord? He is your shield and helper and your glorious sword" (Deut. 33:29, NIV).

Christy K. Robinson

RECEIVING CHRIST

So then, just as you received Christ Jesus as Lord, continue to live in him, rooted and built up in him, strengthened in the faith as you were taught, and overflowing with thankfulness. Col. 2:6, 7, NIV.

I have often heard Christians talk of "receiving Christ," but I never considered the implications of the word "receive." Reading an online dictionary, I was struck by the way each definition reveals something unique about our experience with Christ.

Receive: "To come into possession of," as in "to receive a gift." Receiving Christ means that we come into possession of eternal life through the greatest gift ever given—His sacrifice. "Christ is the mediator of a new covenant, that those who are called may receive the promised eternal inheritance—now that he has died as a ransom to set them free" (Heb. 9:15, NIV).

Receive: "To act as a receptacle or container for" or "to assimilate through the mind or senses." When we receive Christ, our souls act as a receptacle for His Spirit to dwell within us, and His love is assimilated through our entire being. "Don't you know that you yourselves are God's temple and that God's Spirit lives in you?" (1 Cor. 3:16, NIV).

Receive: "To permit to enter." In order to receive Christ, we must first invite Him in! He says, "Here I am! I stand at the door and knock. If anyone hears my voice and opens the door, I will come in and eat with him, and he with me" (Rev. 3:20, NIV).

Receive: "To accept as authoritative, true, or accurate." When we receive Christ, we accept the truth of His sacrifice. Paul states, "I want to remind you of the gospel I preached to you, which you received and on which you have taken your stand" (1 Cor. 15:1, NIV).

Receive: "To take a mark or impression from the weight of something." Paul illustrates this in Ephesians 1:13: "You also were included in Christ when you heard the word of truth, the gospel of your salvation. Having believed, you were marked in him with a seal, the promised Holy Spirit" (NIV). When we receive Christ, He leaves a mark on our hearts—His Holy Spirit.

And we are forever changed by the knowledge and acceptance of His grace.

LORELEI HERMAN CRESS

JANUARY 16

WORTHY OF THE CALLING

Our God will make you fit for what he's called you to be.
2 Thess. 1:11, Message.

In the late 1960s my mother let me ditch fourth-grade classes to attend a lecture by Maria Augusta von Trapp, the woman who inspired *The Sound of Music.* Baroness von Trapp was promoting a newer edition of her 1949 book, *The Story of the Trapp Family Singers* (still available with online booksellers). She struck me as a strong and determined personality but one who had twinkling eyes and who encouraged me to continue my piano lessons. She autographed my EZ-Play *Sound of Music* piano book while sternly warning me that the Hollywood movie was not the true story.

Maria and her family dedicated themselves to God's will and His calling. Her book was not written to be "religious." It's a story of a God-fearing Catholic family who made a huge difference in the world by their faithful service to the Lord. Their dedication to God, their commitment to daily family worship, and their loyalty to each other and to fine sacred music is phenomenal and exemplary. After emigrating to the United States, the Trapp family founded an international relief organization to help rebuild lives in the wake of World War II.

Being willing to work hard, submitting their discomfort or inconvenience to God's will, and have Him turn it into great blessings and lessons for the family and the world are building blocks of faith, hope, love, and encouragement. Maria was a peasant girl who achieved nobility as a daughter of God long before she was assigned the title of baroness at her marriage. She proved to be worthy of God's calling.

The apostle wrote in 2 Thessalonians 1: "Because we know that this extraordinary day is just ahead, we pray for you all the time—pray that our God will make you fit for what he's called you to be, pray that he'll fill your good ideas and acts of faith with his own energy so that it all amounts to something. If your life honors the name of Jesus, he will honor you. Grace is behind and through all of this, our God giving himself freely, the Master, Jesus Christ, giving himself freely" (verses 11, 12, Message).

Do you recognize Jesus' call to be godly? Do you have faithful acts planned for today? The Lord loves to give—open your hands and accept!

CHRISTY K. ROBINSON

JUMPING IN

Come near to God and he will come near to you.
James 4:8, NIV.

My husband is a world-class skydiver. When we were dating, I decided that I should try skydiving as a way to share experiences with him. The first jump I made was preceded by a day of training. The instructors would be jumping with me. We practiced standing in the door of the plane; it was just a doorframe safe on the ground. I felt pretty silly "pretending" in this way, but it was important. We practiced the voice commands they would give me in the door of the plane. They would say "Ready?" and I was to nod yes if I wanted to go. If I decided not to go, I'd shake my head no, and we would come back into the plane and ride it down to safety.

The decision was mine, but once I said yes there was no turning back. It isn't possible to turn back once you're out the door.

"Good things as well as bad, you know, are caught by a kind of infection. . . . If you want to be wet you must get into the water. If you want joy, power, peace, eternal life, you must get close to, or even into, the thing that has them," wrote C. S. Lewis. *

Knowing Jesus is like that. We can shake our head and ride the plane of our humanity safely down, or we can nod yes and be immersed in the power and wonder of living a new life in Christ.

James 4:8 tells us, "Come near to God and he will come near to you" (NIV).

If we want all He has to offer, we have to get close enough to Him to experience it. For me, it means saying yes every day. Yes when I'm worried about money or illness or security, yes when I have joy and opportunity, yes when I feel like it, and yes when I don't.

PAMELA MCCANN

---

*C. S. Lewis, *Mere Christianity* (New York: HarperCollins Publishers, 1952).

LIFE'S PENALTIES

If you are tired from carrying heavy burdens, come to me and I will give you rest. Matt. 11:28, CEV.

I have four brothers and no sisters. You can imagine what our home was like when we were growing up. No Barbie dolls! No *Glamour* magazines. Deprived? Not! We had baseball bats and gloves, footballs, and other sports equipment. As the years passed, we have retired most of the toys, except our golf clubs.

A British golfer, Ian Woosnam, began a tournament by making a birdie on the first hole. On the next tee his caddie informed him that he had an extra driver in his golf bag. Regulations allow a player to carry only 14 clubs. He had to take a penalty, though it was his caddie's fault. This two-stroke penalty cost Woosnam thousands of dollars and jeopardized his victory. He hadn't even used that extra driver. He was unaware that he was carrying "too much baggage."

Many of us go through the game of life carrying extra baggage that penalizes us and weighs us down. We are busy and are under too much stress and debt! Jealousy and envy and fear of failure consume us. The cost? It penalizes us in our relationships with God, family, friends, and associates.

Ironically, many people keep putting more and more into their bag of life until it can hold no more. The result? Major penalties: failed marriages and relationships, failed health, physical and emotional trauma, wandering in a spiritual wasteland.

What's in your bag? We are all involved in an eternal match—a match between good and evil—for our souls. We have total control as to who the winner will be.

"God cares for you, so turn all your worries [baggage] over to him" (1 Peter 5:7, CEV).

Jesus Himself bids, "If you are tired from carrying heavy burdens [loaded with baggage], come to me and I will give you rest" (Matt. 11:28, CEV).

Tired of the load you are carrying? Jesus will be more than happy to be your "caddy" for life. He will carry your load, your baggage, and pay your penalties. Are you ready to let Him carry your bag?

JOEDY MELASHENKO

IGNORANCE DOES NOT EQUAL BLISS

He didn't make it easy for himself by avoiding people's troubles, but waded right in and helped out. Rom. 15:3, Message.

How often we use ignorance as an excuse to avoid unwanted responsibility! Take my husband, for example. When asked to contribute to the household chores by dusting, he responded, "I don't know how!"

Needless to say, my reply, "This is not rocket science," did not go over well.

As my husband discovered, avoidance and procrastination often backfire, and you usually end up with more problems than you started with. Solomon describes it this way: "Understanding is a fountain of life to those who have it, but folly brings punishment to fools" (Prov. 16:22, NIV).

Claiming ignorance to avoid responsibility for our actions is an increasingly popular trend. We blame the media for negative influences on our children and teachers for not instructing them in moral values, rather than accepting the responsibility for providing discipline and moral instruction ourselves.

By avoiding responsibility we not only wrongly accuse others but rob ourselves of the opportunity to strengthen our character, our relationships, and our faith. Scripture makes it clear that we can overcome this weakness through a relationship with Christ and adherence to His teachings: "The fear of the Lord is the beginning of wisdom; all who follow his precepts have good understanding" (Ps. 111:10, NIV).

Human tendency is to do what takes the least effort. Paul offers Christ's behavior as an example for us: "Those of us who are strong and able in the faith need to step in and lend a hand to those who falter, and not just do what is most convenient for us. . . . Each one of us needs to look after the good of the people around us, asking ourselves, 'How can I help?' That's exactly what Jesus did. He didn't make it easy for himself by avoiding people's troubles, but waded right in and helped out" (Rom. 15:1-3, Message).

"Be very careful, then, how you live—not as unwise but as wise, making the most of every opportunity. . . . Do not be foolish, but understand what the Lord's will is" (Eph. 5:15-17, NIV).

LORELEI HERMAN CRESS

I WILL EAT WITH YOU

I will not drink of this fruit of the vine from now on until that day when I drink it anew with you in my Father's kingdom.
Matt. 26:29, NIV.

"The chief wants to see you. And bring that pineapple top."

Clifton Brooks and the teacher in the Philippines' Palawano village of Tag Biao Biao made their way down the trail. Arriving at the chief's hut, Clif noticed several villagers gathered. The chief greeted Clif and made a plea for him to bring his family and live with them.

Not wanting to offend the chief, who held a very large knife in his hand, Clif explained that he could not service the tribe adequately. The village needed medical assistance, but he was an airplane pilot/mechanic. The village needed someone who could live with them, and he had responsibilities elsewhere. Clif explained that he needed to recruit sponsors for workers the village needed.

Begrudgingly the chief countered that if Clif would not stay, then he must promise to return. The chief bent over and carved a hole in the earth with the tip of his big knife. He ceremoniously planted the pineapple top. Straightening up, he reached out to take Clif's hand and asked, "Do you promise that when this pineapple is grown you will come back and eat it with me?" Realizing he was about to make a covenant with the chief, Clif hesitated and replied, "Yes, I promise to do everything I can, but it depends on the response of God's people."

Wouldn't it be fantastic if the Palawanos knew Jesus? Isn't it wonderful that God's plan of salvation employs you and me?

Like the chief and his village of hurting, dying people who are waiting for Clif to return with help, we are all waiting for Jesus to come. Even more than Clif wants to eat that pineapple with the chief, Jesus longs to fulfill His covenant: "I will not drink of this fruit of the vine from now on until that day when I drink it anew with you in my Father's kingdom" (Matt. 26:29, NIV).

What a God!

DON STARLIN

PERSPECTIVE

It is plain that if Absalom were still alive and all of us dead, you would be content. Now go at once and give your servants some encouragement.
2 Sam. 19:6, 7, NEB.

When General Joab told David, who was wailing over the death of his son Absalom, to quit his bellyaching, he demanded a change in perspective: "It is plain that if Absalom were still alive and all of us dead, you would be content. Now go at once and give your servants some encouragement" (2 Sam. 19:6, 7, NEB).

Candace Pert's research on the function of neuropeptides in bodily changes, described in her recent book *Molecules of Emotion,* reports that a positive perspective change affects every cell in the body; likewise, a negative perspective produces perceptible bombardment of every cell of the body.

An example of this perspective was demonstrated by three prisoners of war who were confined in a cell. Faced with dire circumstances, they determined to maintain their sanity by changing their perspective. To the puzzlement of the guards, the prisoners would always prepare for dinner. Sometimes they said, "Let's go to the Boar's Head to eat after our day of hunting." At the Boar's Head they would discuss the hunt—the one that got away; finding a taxidermist. Another time they would dine in Queen Elizabeth's court, exulting over the Spanish Armada's defeat, arguing over whether the queen would marry or execute Edward DeVere. For formal occasions they helped each other fasten studs and straighten white ties. At a restaurant they were not above sending back a rare steak if they had ordered it well done. Their choice of perspective, they said, kept them sane in their miserable prison.

One of the world's best-known stories describes the perspective change wrought in a young man who came home ready to be a servant. Dad covered him with a fine robe, put a gold ring on his finger, and threw a party for his son, who had recently been eating corn with the pigs. I think our Lord told this story with great passion because it demonstrated an all-encompassing idea that we can possess a God-given perspective and exert a health-producing perspective on each other—if we so choose.

EDNA MAYE LOVELESS

SHE'S RUTHLESS!

But you, O God, are both tender and kind, not easily angered, immense in love, and you never, never quit.
Ps. 86:15, Message.

People say I'm a ruthless editor, which I take as a compliment. For this book I cut many a 900-word devotional essay down to 325 words without blinking an eye. Whether it's a book manuscript or a magazine article, my computer leaks virtual red ink at deadline times. (Red pens are so 1970s.) The trick is to maintain the integrity of the content and the writer's style while fitting it to the editorial and design format. Lose the adjectives, activate the verbs.

Ruthless means without mercy, pitiless, and as Dictionary.com puts it, "a monster of remorseless cruelty." Whoa! Just doing my job!

Loving words and linguistics as I do, I had to look up "ruth." You never hear anyone say ruthful. (In fact, my computer spell-checker accepts ruthful and rejects ruth!) I guessed that ruth might be an Old or Middle English word, and it is, derived from the Old Norse *hrygdh*. Its primary meaning is sorrow, regret, compassion, or pity for another.

Ah! God is ruthful. Every book of the Bible, and nearly every chapter in it, describes our Lord's ruth for you and me: His mercy, compassion, grace, pity, undeserved love, tenderness, faithfulness, forgiveness, caring, mothering and fathering, sharing, redeeming, shepherding, protecting, tending, growing . . .

"The Lord, the Lord, the compassionate and gracious God, slow to anger, abounding in love and faithfulness, maintaining love to thousands, and forgiving wickedness, rebellion and sin" (Ex. 34:6, 7, NIV).

That's how the Lord described Himself to Moses. Instead of physical characteristics (eyes, hair, limbs), He spoke of who He is and what He does. How much more precious is that knowledge!

People can say what they like about my editing style, but I pray that the words I put on paper will demonstrate God in actions, attitude, and demeanor. Should we bring back the old word ruthful? Shall we start a trend? When you encourage others in their godly attributes, tell them they're full of ruth, and then explain away the puzzlement you'll cause!

CHRISTY K. ROBINSON

RELIGION AND HEALTH

Dear friend, I pray that you may enjoy good health
and that all may go well with you.
3 John 2, NIV.

Not long ago Harold Koenig of Duke University's medical school published a book, *Is Religion Good for Your Health?* His answer was a resounding yes; religion is very good for your health. His research, based on two 10-year studies, parallels the work of Dr. Gary Frazier at Loma Linda University, who published the results of the Adventist health study in *Diet, Life Expectancy, and Chronic Disease.* The findings of these two long-term research projects demonstrate religion's strong positive effect on a person's sense of well-being, serving for many as a buffer against mental and physical adversity.

Consider the mental health conditions—depression, suicide, anxiety, panic, and alcohol and substance abuse—that are positively affected by church attendance, prayer, and a system of beliefs that provides individuals with coping skills and life satisfaction. Dr. Frazier's study found that in a system that promotes adherence to natural health principles—diet, rest, exercise, water, and trust—as a Christian obligation and privilege, because the body is the temple of God, people experience a lower onset of diseases such as cancer, obesity, heart disease, diabetes, arthritis, and rheumatism.

Good health and good religion travel together. Why not? There is life-giving potential in the belief on the part of religious people that God is a personal God who loves them, that something good can come from every situation if the believer puts trust in God, that anyone can at any time and any place talk with the sustainer of the universe, and that there is no sin or mistake that cannot be confessed and forgiven.

Wow! Talk about a healthy religion that generates healthy believers. I think this proves that religion is good for your health.

WILLIAM LOVELESS

LITTLE THINGS ADD UP

For if you possess these qualities in increasing measure, they will keep you from being ineffective and unproductive in your knowledge of our Lord Jesus Christ.
2 Peter 1:8, NIV.

Growing up in Saskatchewan, we were poor. We lived in a one-bedroom house with no running water, electricity, or plumbing, and we had only a wood stove for heat. But we were happy. We loved going into town with Dad. We boys would look for discarded soda and beer bottles that we could turn in for deposit money (one cent for beer bottles; two cents for soda bottles). We'd spend our income on jawbreakers and licorice.

One day Dad convinced us that we ought to save our money to buy something that would last longer than an "all-day sucker." Soon we had the garage stacked to the ceiling with soda and beer bottles.

We finally received our reward on Christmas morning in 1955. Under the scrawny Christmas tree, in newspaper wrapping, were two huge gifts. One contained a five-man toboggan; the other held a brand-new train set with real smoke and extra tracks for a figure eight. We were speechless! We hugged and then jumped on Dad, thanking him for the gifts. He said that the deposit money from the bottles was enough to make the purchases. Those tiny deposits added up to some serious money!

There is a great spiritual lesson in this childhood experience. In life the "little" things add up. Kind words, helpful hands, prayers for someone in need—all of these activities can make a huge difference in someone's life. The opposite is also true: "white" lies, unkind words, insensitivity, snide remarks, and cheating lead to bigger patterns in life that can spell trouble.

The little things we do in life, noticed or unnoticed, are the things that add up. They give a true picture of who and what we really are.

What kinds of little things are adding up in your life? Paul reminds us: "Make every effort to add to your faith goodness; and to goodness, knowledge; and to knowledge, self-control; and to self-control, perseverance; and to perseverance, godliness; and to godliness, brotherly kindness; and to brotherly kindness, love. For if you possess these qualities in increasing measure [if you keep adding these to your life], they will keep you from being ineffective and unproductive in your knowledge of our Lord Jesus Christ" (2 Peter 1:5-8, NIV).

JOEDY MELASHENKO

LOOKING FORWARD TO ETERNITY

Trust in the Lord with all your heart; do not depend on your own understanding. Seek his will in all you do, and he will show you which path to take.
Prov. 3:5, 6, NLT.

Recently a neighbor said sadly, "I have nothing to look forward to." That didn't exactly surprise me, because almost everything that comes from her mouth is negative. She is known for pessimism, and she seldom says anything positive. My heart ached for her, and I sent up a prayer that God would use me to show her a brighter side of life.

I remember what it was like to have nothing to look forward to and to wish I could close my eyes and never wake up. As a child I grew up in a one-parent home. Mom was a Christian, but she raised my older brother and me by herself and had to be gone most of the time—even on Christmas—just to keep food on the table and pay our bills. She didn't receive any help from my father.

So I looked for happiness in parties, movies, and dances, but I found nothing but emptiness and shallowness. I understood the wise poet who wrote in Ecclesiastes 2:1-3: "I said in my heart, 'Come now, I will test you with mirth; therefore enjoy pleasure'; but surely, this also was vanity. I said of laughter—'Madness!'; and of mirth, 'What does it accomplish?' I searched in my heart how to gratify my flesh with wine, while guiding my heart with wisdom, and how to lay hold on folly" (NKJV).

I dated a Marine whose Methodist mother had come to California from Ohio to see him. When she was in downtown Oakland, the home of the Quiet Hour at that time, she saw their sign, was curious about the name, and went in to see what it was about. She told her Marine son, Bob, about this wonderful ministry and urged him to check it out. He did, and he was so impressed that he started begging me to go with him.

At the time I was not one bit impressed by the name the Quiet Hour. If he had said it was called the Noisy Hour, that would have appealed to me more! But he prevailed—and my life has never been the same. I heard the founder of the Quiet Hour, J. L. Tucker, talk about heaven, and I decided that heaven would be my goal. J. L. Tucker baptized me, and that's the best decision I ever made! An eternity in heaven is something to look forward to, and I am guided by the Lord with every step.

DEL DELKER

WILL I LOSE OUT?

There is a way that seems right to a man. Prov. 14:12, NKJV.

"You can stay at Hotel Panama. It's on us," the woman at the airline counter smiled.

No way, I thought. *She wants to save money and put us in a cheap hotel.*

"Ma'am, here's a letter saying that you will put us up at Hotel Roosevelt."

"That's fine, sir, but you don't have to stay there."

A taxi driver tapped me on the shoulder. "Are you Mr. Muir? I came to take you and your wife to Hotel Roosevelt. You'll like it."

The woman at the counter looked at me. "Sir, you don't have to go with him. There's plenty of room in Hotel Panama. I'll arrange for a taxi to take you."

"No! No!" the cab driver insisted. "Come with me."

I turned to my wife. "Let's go to Hotel Roosevelt."

The airline agent gave me a strange look. Forty-five minutes from the airport, the cab turned in through an archway in a poor section of the city. "Hotel Roosevelt!"

I looked at my wife. "This may have been a great hotel in its day, but it sure looks run-down now."

We were the only guests in the hotel. Meals were included in the deal, but they said, "We don't have any food." Our room was hot and humid, with no air-conditioning. Open windows had no screens. The bed felt like a rock. All night long we turned, tossed, and fought mosquitoes. In the heat a cold shower didn't seem too bad, but there wasn't much water.

Ten minutes from the airport the next morning, we passed Hotel Panama—the Panama Hilton. We laughed, but we really wanted to cry. Because I failed to trust the airline agent, we'd just spent one of the most miserable nights in our lives. We could have stayed in the Hilton with a good bed, air-conditioning, hot showers, and all the food we could possibly eat.

Solomon wrote, "There is a way that seems right to a man, but its end is the way of death" (Prov. 14:12, NKJV).

We lost a perfect night in a great hotel because I chose to listen to the wrong voice. Will I lose out on eternity with Jesus by listening to Satan? Will I lose out on Jesus' plan for this very day because there's another way that seems right to mortal man?

WELLESLEY MUIR

WHERE IS MY STRENGTH?

This day is sacred to our Lord. Do not grieve, for the joy of the Lord is your strength. Neh. 8:10, NIV.

I was out of breath again, panting as I reached the top of the stairs. When would my strength return? Was I doomed to live this way the rest of my life? I was weary of my weakness while recovering from open-heart surgery to repair a heart valve defect.

I had been a hard worker, never shirking responsibilities or depending on others to do my work. I was very independent. Suddenly I felt like an invalid, having to pace myself and take frequent rests. I was frustrated and exhausted most of the time.

"Lord," I prayed daily, "I can't live like this. Please help me. Please restore my strength and ability."

But I continued to struggle and made little progress. I pleaded with the Lord to help me. One morning after I finished my devotions I was showering, and I heard a voice in my inner ear: "The joy of the Lord is your strength." I was warmed by these words and encouraged to know that the Lord had heard my earnest petitions.

The joy of the Lord becomes our strength as we realize that we can come to God only from where we are. As these people in ancient times stood there with their lives in shambles, they were not told, "I told you so. You should have known better. Look what a mess your life is in. Next time you'd better do better."

Instead, they heard, "'Go and enjoy choice food and sweet drinks. . . . This day is sacred to our Lord. Do not grieve, for the joy of the Lord is your strength.' The Levites calmed all the people, saying, 'Be still, for this is a sacred day. Do not grieve.' Then all the people went away to eat and drink . . . and to celebrate with great joy, because they now understood the words that had been made known to them" (Neh. 8:10-12, NIV).

No matter how bad things get, the joy of the Lord will forever be our hope and strength—we can return to the Lord to be restored.

BARBARA MOEN

THE HEALING TOUCH

The prayer offered in faith will make the sick person well.
James 5:15, NIV.

I keep a prayer list in my Bible cover that helps me to remember God's fulfilled promises. It's not a list of requests. It's a list of pray-ers, more than 40 people who promised to remember me daily in their prayers until my request was granted.

I had just been traumatized by one of life's blows and was in emotional and spiritual pain. My sisterly neighbor held me in her arms as I wept, and her husband, the priest of their family, anointed and blessed me with prayer. My pastors gave wise counsel and a sympathetic ear. A friend halfway around the world comforted me with an e-mail.

The apostle James wrote: "Is any one of you in trouble? He should pray. . . . Is any one of you sick? He should call the elders of the church to pray over him and anoint him with oil in the name of the Lord. And the prayer offered in faith will make the sick person well" (James 5:13-15, NIV).

I was in trouble and sick at heart! I invited some Christian friends to my home on a Saturday evening and served strawberries and sparkling cider to lighten the mood.

We gathered in a circle, and each person in turn offered a prayer for my situation, to strengthen my Christian growth and reliance upon God and to heal me. As each person left, I accompanied them down the walk. Each one hugged me and, amazingly, thanked me for being included! I had forgotten that when helping others, we are God's instruments and His healing touch. My friends were feeling the anointing of the Holy Spirit as they prayed for me and were thrilled to the core, knowing that the God of the universe had chosen them for His service. They were awestruck.

God loves you so much. He has gifts to give you, even in your time of trouble, and He wants to work through you to love others. Let the Great Physician heal you, and let Him use you to heal people with His gentle, loving, and powerful touch. There's no feeling like it in the world.

CHRISTY K. ROBINSON

COMING HOME

But while he was still a long way off, his father saw him and was filled with compassion for him; he ran to his son, threw his arms around him and kissed him.
Luke 15:20, NIV.

In Chinatowns across the United States crowds gather for spectacular parades of swaying dragons and dancing lions on the Chinese New Year. This dazzling display, however, is a mere shadow of the celebration that takes place in China during the Spring Festival or Chinese New Year.

The Spring Festival is the most important holiday in China—New Year's, Thanksgiving, birthday festivities, and more all rolled into one! Houses are decorated, feasts prepared, gifts given, and everyone, regardless of their actual date of birth, celebrates their birthday. All this fun cannot be squeezed into a single day. The Spring Festival lasts two weeks! However, during the two Spring Festivals I spent in China it was neither the firecrackers I lit nor the scrumptious delicacies I tasted that impressed me. The most significant part of the Chinese New Year is coming home to family.

During Spring Festival people in China do not use their time off to frequent vacation hot spots. They make a beeline home, where families await. It's not easy, in a country of more than 1.2 billion people, to get home when everyone else is trying to do the same. Traveling standby takes on a whole new meaning when you are on a 10-hour-or-longer train ride, literally standing in the aisle the whole way. It's not a comfortable trip, but people are smiling because they are anticipating their homecoming and the open arms that will greet them.

As Christians we are on our way to our heavenly home. Sometimes the road is difficult, but how fabulous our homecoming will be! All the heavenly parades of angels, the delectable feasts, and the glorious festivities will pale in comparison to the greeting we'll receive when at last we come home.

"The Lord himself will come down from heaven . . . and the dead in Christ will rise first. After that, we who are still alive and are left will be caught up together with them in the clouds to meet the Lord in the air" (1 Thess. 4:16, 17, NIV).

LAURA WEST KONG

ARE YOU A WORKER?

The harvest is plentiful but the workers are few.
Matt. 9:37, NIV.

Following the initial shock of seeing a White man for the first time, children of the mountain village of Tag Biao Biao on the Philippine island of Palawan soon warmed to Clifton Brooks. Not only was he a curiosity to look at, but his backpack contained fantastic wonders.

Not to be outdone, the children produced gadgets of their own. A crudely fashioned set of underwater goggles made of bits of inner tube, plastic, and pitch was proudly displayed. Next came a fishing spear gun carved from a jungle tree branch with a piece of rubber attached to hurl the spear. Then the children introduced Clif to their favorite playground—the river.

Skipping down the trail to the swimming hole, one of the children tripped on a tree root, tearing a large gash in his foot. The little fellow instinctively came hobbling back to Clif. They returned to the hut, where Clif retrieved a first-aid kit from that marvelous backpack. A few minutes later the wound was cleaned, disinfected, and dressed with a snow-white bandage. Then it was off to the water.

Diving, splashing, and fishing filled the afternoon. As Clif and the children made their way up the trail to the village, Clif stopped in astonishment. A large group of villagers with every imaginable malady awaited him. Completely overwhelmed, Clif tried to explain that he was an airplane pilot and mechanic, not a doctor.

"Jesus went through all the towns and villages, teaching . . . preaching . . . and healing every disease and sickness. When he saw the crowds, he had compassion on them, because they were harassed and helpless, like sheep without a shepherd. Then he said to his disciples, 'The harvest is plentiful but the workers are few. Ask the Lord of the harvest, therefore, to send out workers into his harvest field' " (Matt. 9:35-38, NIV).

Are you, like Clif and Jesus, struck by the need you see around you? "Lord, use us as Your workers today." Amen.

DON STARLIN

CLEARER VISION

By your words I can see where I'm going.
Ps. 119:105, Message.

Have you ever tried to play tennis with only one good eye? I once lost a single contact lens before a game, and I tried to play without it. I was dismayed at just how awful my depth perception was—I couldn't hit the ball to save my life (and driving home afterward was quite a hair-raising experience)!

Our understanding of the life God wants for us can be much like that tennis game—on the myopic side. Many times we can't see His purpose very clearly, and when trouble bounces our way, we can't focus on it well enough to send it flying back over the net. How can we hope to win the game without clearer vision?

Thankfully, God has given us two lenses through which to see clearly—His Word and the life of His Son, Jesus Christ. If we view our options through these lenses, we can correct our defective vision and learn to play the game of life with confidence.

The psalmist says, "By your words I can see where I'm going" (Ps. 119:105, Message).

Studying God's Word brings our flawed vision into focus and directs us to the missing lens: "Keep your eyes on Jesus, who both began and finished this race we're in. Study how he did it. Because he never lost sight of where he was headed—that exhilarating finish in and with God—he could put up with anything along the way: Cross, shame, whatever. And now he's there, in the place of honor, right alongside God" (Heb. 12:2, 3, Message).

"So let's keep focused on that goal, those of us who want everything God has for us. If any of you have something else in mind, something less than total commitment, God will clear your blurred vision—you'll see it yet! Now that we're on the right track, let's stay on it" (Phil. 3:15, 16, Message).

Make the time to dig into God's Word today, take Jesus as an example for living, and prepare to win the game!

LORELEI HERMAN CRESS

February 1

LOVE, LOVE, LOVE

Love comes from God, and when we love each other, it shows that we have been given new life. 1 John 4:7, CEV.

Popular songs and movies are about finding love, losing love, unrequited love, spurned love. Advertisements from soft drinks to resort vacations are about love. Romance novels are complete fantasy. The reality TV dating shows are staged, scripted, and ultimately unrealistic! (Never mind the Internet dating sites with misrepresentations and blatant lies.) Politicians of every party speak of love for country, but their actions often show disdain for their constituents while fawning over their contributors.

I knew a pastor, at the time a bachelor, whose license plate on his red sports car read "MY WIFE." (I wonder what his plate changed to when he married.) One person falls in and out of love as easily as changing a shirt, while another person loyally and doggedly perseveres when it seems there's no hope of returned affection.

For all the talk of love, is it love? What is love? It depends on whom or what you're talking about. Everyone wants fulfillment, happiness, appreciation, and a sense of belonging. In Abraham Maslow's hierarchy of needs, those qualities are listed in the "love" category, about halfway up the ladder from physiological needs (bottom) to self-actualization (top). The love that we strive to give and receive is at the top of the scale. The characteristics Maslow lists as self-actualized are mostly those of a fulfilled and godly human being, and we, with apologies to Maslow, might call them Christ-actualized!

The beloved disciple wrote in 1 John 4:7-11: "My dear friends, we must love each other. Love comes from God, and when we love each other, it shows that we have been given new life. We are now God's children, and we know him. God is love, and anyone who doesn't love others has never known him. God showed his love for us when he sent his only Son into the world to give us life. Real love isn't our love for God, but his love for us. God sent his Son to be the sacrifice by which our sins are forgiven. Dear friends, since God loved us this much, we must love each other" (CEV).

In word and deed. Amen.

Christy K. Robinson

INFLUENTIAL PEOPLE

And in the church God has appointed . . .
those able to help others. 1 Cor. 12:28, NIV.

People with whom we have relationships affect us profoundly, far more than celebrities, politicians, or world leaders do. Answer these questions, if you can: Name the five wealthiest people in the world. Name the most recent five Heisman Trophy winners. Name the lastest five winners of the Miss America contest. Name 10 people who have won the Nobel or Pulitzer Prize. Name the latest six Academy Award winners for best actor/actress. Name the past decade's worth of World Series winners.

Few of us remember the previous headliners. They are the best in their fields. But achievements are forgotten and awards tarnish. Accolades and certificates fade and get filed.

Here's another quiz. See how you do on this one: List teachers who aided your journey through school. Name three friends who have helped you through a difficult time. Name three people who have taught you something worthwhile. Think of a few people who have made you feel appreciated and special. Think of three people you enjoy spending time with. Name a half dozen heroes whose stories have inspired you.

Easier? The people who make a difference in your life are not the ones with the most credentials, the most money, or the most awards. They are the ones who care.

Are you a hero or an inspiration to someone else? You are if you complimented someone at work, wrote a supportive letter to the newspaper op-ed page, donated a pint to the local blood bank, rehearsed with a church vocalist, drove a teenager to a youth meeting, took your neighbor to the doctor, or cut a bouquet of roses for a friend for no reason at all. These are a few examples that answer the question: What would Jesus do?

One gift of the Holy Spirit is to be a helper and encourager (1 Cor. 12:28). It's listed along with apostles, teachers, administrators, and those gifted with language. And it directly precedes 1 Corinthians 13, about the greatest gift of God: love for others. It's all about love and relationship.

CHRISTY K. ROBINSON

THE INGREDIENTS OF LOVE

Taste and see that the Lord is good.
Ps. 34:8, NASB.

My friends tease me when I use cooking illustrations in sermons. Somehow they believe that I cannot cook. I make great vegetarian chicken cacciatore. Any dish worth savoring has at least four necessary ingredients. Like mouthwatering meals, agape love, God's deep, constant, unconditional regard for all (Rom. 12:9), has many ingredients. I've found the following four to be most important in the divine-human partnership.

Friendship love: When Paul said, "Be devoted to one another" (Verse 10, NIV), he searched for an effective word to communicate the passion and permanence of "devotion." Instead of using *antecho* (Matt. 6:24), he created the word *philostorgou* by combining two common terms: *philos,* meaning an extraordinary friend that is closer than a brother (John 15:14), and *storgou,* denoting a love that is like glue, holding things together no matter how far or how much they are stretched.

Brotherly love: *Philadelphia* (Rom. 12:10) shares the same root as *philos* but describes the tender affection in a filial relationship. It is the kind of love between siblings, but also that describes affections for family in Christ that causes one to look out for a member of a community bonded by the grace of God.

Passionate love: Paul did not use the term *eros* but referred to a close cousin when he said believers are to be "fervent in spirit, serving the Lord" (Verse 11, NASB). Fervent indicates earnestly, but it also describes that which is boiling over. It echoes the passion of eros, the love that burns hotter than humans can handle for any extended period of time.

Hospitality love: Paul called on Christians to contribute "to the needs of the saints, [by] practicing hospitality" (Verse 13, NASB). Again, he used two words *philos* (friendship love) and *xenos* (a stranger) to convey the gift of hospitality that is always needed in a community of committed disciples of Jesus Christ.

I would never offer you a pie recipe. I am sure you'd be too savvy to use it. However, I am confident that the above ingredients work best when expressing agape love. Just try it, then "taste and see that the Lord is good" (Ps. 34:8, NASB).

HYVETH B. WILLIAMS

ALL MY LOVES

Neither death nor life, neither angels nor demons, neither the present nor the future, nor any powers, neither height nor depth, nor anything else in all creation, will be able to separate us from the love of God that is in Christ Jesus our Lord.
Rom. 8:38, 39, NIV.

When Annika was 2½ years old she graduated from a baby crib to a twin bed. She enjoyed helping choose new sheets for the bed and delighted in jumping on this bouncy new addition to her room.

However, when nighttime came and darkness surrounded her, she longed for the comfort of something soft and cozy. Annika's solution was the "Loves," her name for her stuffed animal collection. Rather than choosing one or two Loves, she brought them all to bed and arranged them beside her. It became a nightly ritual to tuck the Loves in under the covers, where they preferred to sleep. Some Loves even like to stay under the covers during the day, Annika informed me one morning while making her bed.

As Annika grew bigger, the collection of Loves in her bed also grew. Soon as many as 15 to 20 Loves shared the bed with her each night and kept watch during the day. It was amazing there was any room left in the bed for Annika.

One evening when kissing her father good night, Annika noticed that he had no furry Loves. She ran back to her room and carefully selected a very special Love: her cuddly bunny, which plays a lullaby. She brought the rabbit to him and said, "Here's a Love for you, Daddy. Now when you miss me, you won't have to feel lonely anymore." Annika wanted to make sure her daddy had the Love to remind him that even though she was sleeping down the hall in her own room, she would always love him.

God wants to remind us of His unfailing love for us. Aren't you glad that nothing can separate us from God's love?

"For I am convinced that neither death nor life, neither angels nor demons, neither the present nor the future, nor any powers, neither height nor depth, nor anything else in all creation, will be able to separate us from the love of God that is in Christ Jesus our Lord" (Rom. 8:38, 39, NIV).

LAURA WEST KONG

GROWING LOVE

He has covered me with the robe of righteousness,
as a bridegroom decks himself with ornaments,
and as a bride adorns herself with her jewels. Isa. 61:10, NKJV.

"Tell me your story. How did you meet?" Each couple's story of meeting and falling in love is a mix of romance, humor, and divine intervention. In certain cultures you may hear, "My parents chose the person I married." In our Western culture we can hardly imagine not knowing our mate before we marry.

All through history, and certainly in many Bible stories, we find that marriages were arranged as political and commercial alliances where clans, tribes, and nations were forged. Hosea was directed by the Lord to marry the unfaithful Gomer, to learn firsthand about God's relationship with His people. Joseph was instructed to marry his fiancé, Mary, and cherish their Son, Jesus.

When Abraham was about 120 years old, he asked his steward of a half century, Eliezer, to find Isaac a wife in Mesopotamia, a woman with similar heritage and religious beliefs. Eliezer reluctantly accepted the huge responsibility. Abraham said, "The Lord God of heaven, which took me from my father's house, and from the land of my kindred . . . he shall send his angel before thee" (Gen. 24:7). What trust, what faith, and what confidence in God's leading!

Isaac's relationship with his father was noteworthy. At 40 years of age he submitted to his father's judgment on choosing a wife, and as a result he was given the beautiful, intelligent, kind, and virtuous Rebekah.

Parents in cultures that arrange marriages for their children want the best for their offspring. Many arranged marriages are successful and happy because love grows and matures once the relationship is sealed. God-fearing, experienced parents put forth much prayer, research, and effort in selecting a compatible partner for their child.

May we be open to God's gift of love. He has arranged a marriage for all of us. "I will greatly rejoice in the Lord, My soul shall be joyful in my God; for He has clothed me with the garments of salvation, He has covered me with the robe of righteousness, as a bridegroom decks himself with ornaments, and as a bride adorns herself with her jewels" (Isa. 61:10, NKJV).

PANSY CHAND

EGYPTIAN WEDDING PRELUDE

The bridegroom was a long time in coming,
and they all became drowsy and fell asleep.
Matt. 25:5, NIV.

The day before a wedding was to be held in our church in Heliopolis, Egypt, I was asked to play the organ. In a pinch I can plunk out a hymn. However, Wagner's "Bridal Chorus," Mendelssohn's "Wedding March," and other pieces are more of a challenge for me. The bride's uncle said that the wedding would begin at 7:00 p.m., but according to "Egyptian time," 7:30 p.m. or, at the latest, 8:00 p.m. would be more realistic.

I arrived at the church at 7:00 p.m. I had been too busy to practice, so I calculated that I had at least 30 minutes to rehearse. I ended up practicing for an hour, and at 8:00 p.m. I felt that I could stumble through the pieces. The church was now full; it was a hot day, and the amount of body heat generated overcame the air-conditioners, so the windows were opened. Like the Matthew 25 bridesmaids who were prepared with extra lamp oil, I'd brought clothespins to keep the music pages from blowing.

Children became restless and came to investigate what I was doing. They would pat me on the arm and say, "Miss, Miss," to get my attention. They wanted to practice their English or poke an organ key to hear its sound. I was having a hard enough time hitting the right notes, much less conversing in Arabic or English! Finally, at nearly 9:00 p.m., the pastor gave me a break by playing recorded music. It was then that I learned that the groom, who was bringing the wedding dress, was late in arriving and the hairdresser wouldn't style the bride's hair until she was dressed.

When we heard the women trilling, well after 9:00 p.m., we knew the bride had arrived. The candles were lit; I got back to the organ, and the wedding progressed. The bride was beautiful and the groom handsome. After this experience, I have a new appreciation for "the bridegroom was a long time in coming, and they all became drowsy and fell asleep. . . . Therefore keep watch, because you do not know the day or the hour" (Matt. 25:5-13, NIV).

Joyce Neergaard

HOW GOD'S LOVE TRANSFORMED MOSES

Now Moses was very humble—more humble than any other person on earth. Num. 12:3, NLT.

It can be tempting for Christians to criticize others whose customs or beliefs differ from their own, even those with whom they fellowship. This spirit of criticism has divided companies of worshipping believers since Cain became angry with Abel. Many new Christians, rejoicing in their newfound freedom, have joined with local groups of believers only to encounter many of the same problems common to human relationships.

Perhaps you're a new Christian, rejoicing in the freedom and assurance that come from a hand-in-hand walk with the Lord. Maybe, along the way, someone has slighted you or discouraged you by their words of criticism. Or maybe you're simply offended by their beliefs, which you feel are inconsistent with the Scriptures or with a saving relationship with the Lord. Imagine the frustration and anger Moses felt when, after spending 40 days in the presence of God, he descended the mountain to find the Israelites praying not to God but to a golden calf they had made in honor of an Egyptian god. These were the people for whom he had left Pharaoh's courts, and now they were an angry and dangerous mob best known for their complaints and criticism.

God, knowing Moses' mind, proposed that He destroy the Israelites and raise up a new nation through Moses (Ex. 32:9-14). It was a test for Moses, and a lesson for us. The answer, of course, revealed just how much Moses had grown since he had killed an Egyptian in anger. Now, after 40 quiet years in the wilderness and 40 days with God, Moses was filled with love and compassion (just like God Himself), and he offered to give up his own life and his own place in heaven if God would only spare them!

Israel's theology was definitely wrong. They were disobedient, ungrateful complainers. They didn't deserve compassion. But Moses' response reflects the patience and transforming love that was engraved in his heart, which was the result of spending time with the Lord.

ROBERT JOHNSTON

GOD'S TIMING: AMAZING!

There is a time for everything,
and a season for every activity under heaven.
Eccl. 3:1, NIV.

We learn from our mistakes and life experiences. I don't claim to be wise, but being the youngest of eight children does have advantages. As I watched my older siblings and their friends leave the nest, I saw with my own eyes that Christians who marry non-Christians set themselves up for conflict. Let's face it! Every marriage has its ups and downs. But this "being unequally yoked" problem was one that I wanted to avoid.

I was 16 and enjoying Christian high school, while looking for Mr. Wonderful. I dated a very popular young man, and we were talking about our future: college, careers, family. But it was apparent his plans did not leave much room for God.

During this time a La Sierra College quartet came to minister at an assembly. The second tenor sang as though the songs really meant something to him. I could tell by his countenance that he loved God. His name was Joedy Melashenko, and I began praying that night, "Lord, send someone into my life just like Joedy who will help me and encourage me in my walk with You." I prayed this prayer for two years.

Long after Steve and I had broken up, I was at a skating party with Tom, one of Joedy's friends. Joedy had recently broken up with his girlfriend. On several occasions during the past few months, Tom had asked me, "Do you know Joedy Melashenko? You ought to meet him. You have a lot in common!"

Joedy and I were introduced. In God's time (after two years of praying), we finally met. Two and one-half years later we were married. That was more than 35 years ago. I still see God's hand in our lives and our home. Are we immunized from troubles and challenges? Certainly not. But we know that God brought us together and has a plan for our lives—together—throughout eternity.

Isn't God's timing amazing? "There is a time for everything, and a season for every activity under heaven" (Eccl. 3:1, NIV). "In all your ways acknowledge Him, and he shall direct your paths" (Prov. 3:6, NKJV).

JUDY MELASHENKO

FEBRUARY 9

WILL YOU MARRY ME?

Your people will be my people and your God my God.
Ruth 1:16, NIV.

My dearest one:

When we married I had no idea who you were or for that matter who I was. And for some strange reason, that never seemed to matter. I have always known that you love and respect me. Without much outside coaching, except for our parents' models, we have been in unity together.

Providence put us together. In some ways we are opposite, but over the years it is obvious to me that we share all of the deepest convictions that make life worthwhile. I love the way you comfort me when I'm unreasonable and grumpy. I love the way you "mother hen" our daughters. My family is your family and your family is my family, quite like the oft-repeated sentiments of Ruth: "Your people will be my people and your God my God" (Ruth 1:16, NIV).

You patiently taught me how to listen by listening to me, and we have always been smooth when it comes to the management of money. Edna Maye, your warmth, charm, intellect, and clear Christian commitment have enriched me and my work more than anything else in life.

Even though I really didn't know what I was doing when I saw you, truly a gorgeous vision in wedding white coming toward me that August day, I now know how much I love you. Will you marry me?

WILLIAM LOVELESS

THINGS I NEVER EXPECTED

I hear my lover's voice. He comes running over the mountains, racing across the hills to me. . . My lover speaks to me.
S. of Sol. 2:8-10, TEV.

Dear love of my life,

Happy surprises have added to the "I do's."

Pressing my hand gently in place on your knee before maneuvering a driving function, you seem to say, "Don't go; stay here with me."

Your enthusiasm for shopping with me has destroyed all preconceptions about male indifference. Whether we're seeking a quart of milk, a gallon of paint, a dress for me, some shoes for you, or a new computer, you consistently initiate dual excursions—times for renewal and bonding.

After completing a doctorate, you said it was my turn. Later, when my research project didn't jell and I wanted to quit, you quietly responded, "You'll always be sorry you didn't finish. Now I'm taking you to the library to work on a new research design." You spurred me on. I had no idea we'd share so many conversations about what we had been reading or contented periods of quietness as we pursued reading and writing tasks.

Two people in love on their wedding day expect never to argue over money. Today, wiser and more in tune with "life," I'm surprised those expectations about no money hassles came true. Generous and prudent—you're an asset on any budget.

When we embarked on the unknown path of parenthood, you supplied strengths to achieve balance—more playful, more energetic, more emphatic. The girls knew where to turn to when they needed your specialties.

At home, it's a duet when we make the bed, when we entertain guests. Chalking up vast vacuuming hours, you also amaze me with your cheery whistling while mopping the floor or washing the dishes. It's the sound of my love; I cherish it.

I'm a woman in love, who joins the love song: "I hear my lover's voice. He comes running over the mountains, racing across the hills to me. . . . My lover speaks to me" (S. of Sol. 2:8-10, TEV).

EDNA MAYE LOVELESS

ALL GOD'S CHILDREN

*What marvelous love the Father has extended to us!
Just look at it—we're called children of God! 1 John 3:1, Message.*

Halfway through a 30-minute drive to the pediatrician's office, my 2-month-old daughter, Annika, began to fuss. Soothing words and favorite lullabies brought no comfort to her. Soon the fussing turned to crying, and the crying turned to wailing.

I couldn't stop the car. We were already being squeezed into the doctor's schedule for this last-minute appointment. "We're almost there, precious girl. Please don't cry!" I pleaded. It was no use. Before long we were both crying, my distress as deep as hers.

Finally, we arrived at the doctor's office, and as I held her close, our tears faded away in sweet relief.

I discovered that as a parent I share not only Annika's joy at mastering a new skill or her contentment from feeling safe and loved, but also her sadness and her frustrations.

It's the same way with God. We are His beloved children. God does not just watch us from a distance, literally or emotionally. He is right beside us every step of the way. God shares our happiness. He delights in our personal growth. And God feels our heartaches and disappointments. This is just one of the many facets of God's incredible love for all His children. When I share Annika's joys and sorrows each day, it reminds me of God's amazing love for us and the special place we hold in His heart.

"What marvelous love the Father has extended to us! Just look at it—we're called children of God!" (1 John 3:1, Message).

LAURA WEST KONG

WARM FUZZIES NEEDED

You will keep him in perfect peace, whose mind is stayed on You, because he trusts in You. Isa. 26:3, NKJV.

In an airline magazine I found a staggering statistic: "110 million singles in the U.S." More than a third of our population is single. This is a very large segment of our society. What are we doing to build relationships and to encourage people? Many of our churches do not have a "warm fuzzy" atmosphere to absorb these special ones.

A single mom and her teenage daughter, Joan and Julie, came forward at an invitation for prayer. Later we visited together. Joan opened her heart. They attended a small church where most of the people were much older. She said, "I was out of the church for a while and came back, but I don't seem to fit in. There doesn't seem to be a place for Julie and me."

My wife, Jackie, and I gave her hugs, prayed together, and claimed several promises, including 1 Peter 1:3, 4; Isaiah 41:10; and Isaiah 42:16. And there's that beautiful text in Isaiah 26:3 that says, "You will keep him in perfect peace, whose mind is stayed on You, because he trusts in You" (NKJV).

What a difference the next evening! Her face was aglow.

Our churches would do well to focus intentionally on single adults and promote a "warm fuzzy" environment. Being the heart and loving arms of Jesus to bring encouragement and hope to these often-neglected ones will bring rich dividends in healthy friendships and promote a supportive church family. Pray with them and listen to their needs. Let me challenge you to reach out and be an encourager. Build relationships by talking and doing things together. Pray with them, and incorporate them in the activities of the church. I can assure you that the dynamics of your church will change. It will strengthen faith and commitment all around.

Warm fuzzies—we all need them. It's not just singles and single parents; young and old alike need to know they are loved and that we care. The world will be a better place if we start giving more hugs than frowns, more encouragement and less criticism.

BILL TUCKER

LOOKING FOR MR. RIGHT

For I have chosen him, so that he will direct his children and his household after him to keep the way of the Lord by doing what is right and just, so that the Lord will bring about . . . what he has promised him. Gen. 18:19, NIV.

A friend was speaking from the front of the church hall during a business meeting. During her talk she said that she was looking for a husband and that any help would be appreciated. From the back came a droll bass voice, "Shouldn't you be looking for a single man?"

She and I talk often about men. Of course, we don't want someone else's husband! We're waiting on the Lord's choice. We want men with demonstrable skills in commitment and loyalty. But pickings are slim. Why is that?

Across America two thirds of church members (in any denomination) are women. The other third are youth or married men. Many don't attend church regularly. So there's not a large population of Christian single men. Wouldn't it be great to market our beliefs and lifestyle to single men in an evangelism campaign directed at men? Think how the tithe revenues would rise after their baptisms!

Many men, looking for playmates instead of the Proverbs 31 virtuous woman, bewail the lack of "datable" women (aged 20-39, athletic, slim, childless, and willing to compromise morals). "Man [particularly the male gender] looks at the outward appearance, but the Lord [and most women] looks at the heart" (1 Sam. 16:7, NIV).

The heart of Mr. Right submitted wholly (and holy) to the Lord Jesus—that man is incredibly desirable. The intelligent, righteous, and moral man who commits himself to the ministry of the church and the community is very attractive—oh, be still, my beating heart!

Mr. Right is described in Genesis 18:19: "For I have chosen him, so that he will direct his children and his household after him to keep the way of the Lord by doing what is right and just, so that the Lord will bring about . . . what he has promised him" (NIV).

There are godly single people of both genders. Perhaps our focus should be less on finding the One Perfect Specimen and more on bringing new people into our communities of faith and, by example and fellowship, developing their potential to be all that God has planned for them.

CHRISTY K. ROBINSON

VALENTINE'S DAY

I've called your name. You're mine.
Isa. 43:1, Message.

This month's devotional essays are about love. Family love, married love, love for God, love for humanity. There's even some romance seen through the eyes of couples married 35 and 55 years.

To learn about Valentine's Day origins, type "Valentine" into a search engine and wait exactly .44 seconds for 1.9 million references to pop up.

Today, in the middle of the month, let's do something that Hebrew literature did and put the crux of the poem, the pinnacle of thought, right in the middle of the composition. Hear from God's lips how He loves you:

"This is how much God loved the world: He gave his Son, his one and only Son. And this is why: so that no one need be destroyed; by believing in him, anyone can have a whole and lasting life" (John 3:16, Message).

"Don't be afraid, I've redeemed you. I've called your name. You're mine. When you're in over your head, I'll be there with you. When you're in rough waters, you will not go down. When you're between a rock and a hard place, it won't be a dead end—because I am God, your personal God, the Holy of Israel, your Savior. I paid a huge price for you. . . . That's how much I love you! I'd sell off the whole world to get you back, trade the creation just for you. So don't be afraid: I'm with you" (Isa. 43:1-5, Message).

"But God demonstrates his own love for us in this: While we were still sinners, Christ died for us" (Rom. 5:8, NIV).

" 'Is not Ephraim my dear son, the child in whom I delight? . . . I still remember him. Therefore my heart yearns for him; I have great compassion for him,' declares the Lord" (Jer. 31:20, NIV).

"But the people you redeemed, you led in merciful love; you guided them under your protection to your holy pasture" (Ex. 15:13, Message).

There are so many more verses on love. Look up "love" in your concordance, and read your valentine from your Savior. He can't wait to take you in His arms and whisper sweet words in your heart.

CHRISTY K. ROBINSON

VALENTINES EVERY DAY

Dear friends, since God so loved us, we also ought to love one another.
1 John 4:11, NIV.

Annika knocked on our neighbor's door. When her friends answered, she ceremoniously presented them both with valentine cards. The two brothers looked baffled at the sight of the sparkly pink and red hearts. After all, Valentine's Day was several months ago!

February 14 had captured Annika's imagination. She was delighted with the idea of a holiday dedicated to giving flowers, frilly cards, and of course chocolate to the ones you love. And having the fun of making your own cards, complete with ribbons, glitter, and lace, made it all the better. "I wish it could be Valentine's Day every day," Annika declared.

So we made it Valentine's Day every day in our home. Annika picked a bouquet of flowers for her grandma in March, made chocolate-dipped strawberries for her grandpa in June, and crafted a valentine card for her aunt Ilene in August. Annika and I even invented a Valentine's Day game in which we wrote love letters and cards to each other and delivered them across the room to each other's mailboxes.

What fun! Why not enjoy Valentine's Day every day? We don't need to wait until February 14 rolls around again to show our loved ones how much we care. Write a love note to your spouse, just because. Send flowers to your mother. Telephone your father. Give a box of chocolates to a good friend. Pen a personal psalm to God. Any time is the right time!

God didn't wait for Valentine's Day to show His love for us. "This is love: not that we loved God, but that he loved us and sent his Son as an atoning sacrifice for our sins. Dear friends, since God so loved us, we also ought to love one another. No one has ever seen God; but if we love one another, God lives in us and his love is made complete in us" (1 John 4:10-12, NIV).

How can we show the love of God to those around us today?

LAURA WEST KONG

TRUE LOVE

Trust steadily in God, hope unswervingly, love extravagantly. And the best of the three is love. 1 Cor. 13:13, Message.

When I was younger, I thought romance equaled love—epitomized by the image of a young, attractive couple who were completely infatuated with one another and were planning a happily-ever-after life together. As a young adult, I made many unwise decisions based upon that false idea of love, and by God's grace, I have since learned what love really is.

True love is not based upon feelings—it is a decision we make every day about how to treat others. The apostle Paul explains in 1 Corinthians 13: Love is patient—it doesn't give up when troubles appear. Love is kind—it is caring. Love does not envy—it is not jealous or suspicious. Love does not boast and is not proud—it doesn't show off or think itself superior. Love is not rude—it is considerate and respectful. Love is not self-seeking—it puts others first. Love is not easily angered—it doesn't fly off the handle. Love keeps no record of wrongs—it forgives and forgets. Love always protects, always trusts, always hopes, always perseveres. Love never fails.

Feelings are fragile and fleeting. Relationships ruled by emotions are like roller-coaster rides: they pick up speed quickly, but they're bumpy, full of ups and downs, and over before you know it. In contrast, relationships based on the kind of love Paul describes will last a lifetime.

This is the love that God has for us, the kind He wants us to experience—not just with a significant other, but with everyone, including Him.

Paul concludes: "We don't yet see things clearly. We're squinting in a fog, peering through a mist. But it won't be long before the weather clears and the sun shines bright! We'll see it all then, see it all as clearly as God sees us, knowing him directly just as he knows us! But for right now, until that completeness, we have three things to do to lead us toward that consummation: Trust steadily in God, hope unswervingly, love extravagantly. And the best of the three is love" (1 Cor. 13:12, 13, Message).

LORELEI HERMAN CRESS

MERRIMENT IN LOVE

A merry heart does good, like medicine. Prov. 17:22, NKJV.

My wife and I have made an observation. We have found that couples must enjoy one another. Having fun and enjoying common interests is vital in a relationship. Laughing together is therapeutic!

When our kids were at home, one of the ways Judy and I would laugh together was to read a humorous book before we went to bed. We had to stifle our laughter in our pillows so as not to wake up the kids. They would still hear us laughing and would bang on the wall. "Stop laughing so loud! We can't sleep!" Don't you wish more homes had this problem? Sadly, in many homes the kids can't sleep because of the fighting, shouting, and arguing they hear between their parents.

When short-short haircuts were the rage, I decided to get my hair cut shorter than usual. When I came home, Judy cracked up. It was not a good haircut. So I told her to fix it with her clippers. The only way to fix it was to do a "buzz," a military cut. When she finished, she looked at me and said, "Oh honey, you're not going to like this!" When I looked in the mirror, it was hideous, the ugliest haircut on the planet. We rolled on the floor together, laughing so hard that the tears flowed! How could I be mad at her? It was my idea. Every time we relive this experience, we have a good laugh.

When's the last time you had a good belly laugh with your mate? When's the last time you experienced happiness and joy? Liking your mate is as important as loving him or her. I like the psalmist's cheerful lyrics: "Delight yourself in the Lord [and the relationship He gave you] and he will give you the desires of your heart. Commit your way to the Lord; trust in him and he will do this: He will make your righteousness shine like the dawn, the justice of your cause like the noonday sun" (Ps. 37:4-6, NIV).

JOEDY MELASHENKO

A WHISTLE A DAY KEEPS THE BLUES AWAY

Before they call, I will answer. Isa. 65:24, NASB.

The week had been stressful. There were conflicts at work, mechanical difficulties with my car, and a sick cat to ferry to and from the vet. Every evening I collapsed into restless nights that seemed much longer than the days. The greatest distress came from the silence that greeted me each evening as I opened my door and entered my apartment. How I wished I had someone to come home to.

One morning as I dressed, I began to complain (whine) to the Lord. "Why does every other minister have a spouse? Why does my aunt keep telling me there's a stick in the forest for every hoe in the garden? What does that mean, anyway? And where's my stick?" By the time I grabbed my briefcase to rush to my car, I had worked myself into an angry frenzy.

I ran down the flight of steps two at a time, daring gravity so I could break a bone and stay home, for good. I was about to open the car door when I heard a sharp wolf whistle. I was appalled! Woe to the man who made that mistake. I swung around, ready to vent righteous invectives when the whistle came again. I looked up, and there he was: a bird, whistling at me.

I realized that God had heard my heartfelt cries for a soul friend. He had answered. Not in the way I expected, but much better! I smiled sweetly at the bird as all my despair melted away. Tucked in my heart from that moment and forever is the surprise of God. I remembered His promise: "It will also come to pass that before they call, I will answer; and while they are still speaking, I will hear" (Isa. 65:24, NASB).

God whistled at me, and it was good.

HYVETH B. WILLIAMS

TAINTED LADY

Her sins, which are many, are forgiven, for she loved much.
Luke 7:47, NKJV.

I spent an evening with a modern "woman at the well." She is as soiled, fallen, and, to casual eyes, unworthy as the Samaritan woman was. She has four failed marriages, four ex-husbands, and an assortment of children; undoubtedly, she is the focus of gossip and rejection.

But when a tired, thirsty Jesus stopped at the well in Samaria, He saw something else: a priceless human soul. He gave her His full attention. Her warm heart and sprouting faith gave Him the refreshment He needed. Her spontaneous enthusiasm and joy drew her whole village to the One who could supply living water. Jesus saw her potential and helped her connect with it. From that moment her life mattered and has continued to matter for two millennia.

My "tainted lady" radiates a degree of caring and sensitivity rarely encountered in today's world. When no one else thought of it, she included my ill and depressed son and me, a widow, at her Christmas dinner table. When my son died, she ministered to me with a depth of compassion and insight I had never before experienced.

We've prayed often together. She talks to God as her cherished Father with intimate, loving expressions that help me feel His presence beside me and His arms around me.

I am not surprised. My friend's closeness to her heavenly Father and her level of confidence and trust in Him have been refined over long years in the furnace fires of suffering and affliction. She is forgiven. She is reborn. She and Jesus walk together every day. That relationship shines on me, making me a better person.

I know why certain "tainted ladies" were special to Jesus. They understood love.

"I say to you, her sins, which are many, are forgiven, for she loved much. But to whom little is forgiven, the same loves little" (Luke 7:47, NKJV).

AILEEN LUDINGTON

SAYING GOODBYE

Therefore encourage each other with these words.
1 Thess. 4:18, NIV.

Eight months ago my aunt Ellie thought she had a bad case of flu. However, soon after she was admitted to the hospital, she was diagnosed with colon cancer and underwent surgery. It was so widespread that the doctors were unable to remove it all. When I went to visit her in the nursing home, she told me that she was 80 years old and had decided to let nature take its course. She was at peace with this decision.

Aunt Ellie was a wonderful part of my childhood. She had a quiet humor that would often catch us by surprise. Her keen wit and clever observations would make us laugh and cause a commotion that she would never own up to.

When I went to visit her recently in the nursing home, she was free of pain, but the warm glow of her personality and mind were gone. She could no longer recognize me. As I kissed her goodbye for the last time, tears streamed down my face, and my heart broke.

I believe that we will be reunited with our loved ones at the resurrection, but it takes time to adjust to losing someone dear to your heart—a vital part of your family.

It's comforting to remember those good times, the warm memories of her and her relationship with our family. I was not saying goodbye to the memories. Memories console us. Neither was I saying goodbye to the hope of reunion, for I have the assurance of the resurrection when we will all be reunited in Jesus' presence. However, I was saying goodbye to the relationship that was and can no longer be. In time, I know the pain of losing her will lessen, but the memories will always be a fresh and radiant reminder of who she was and the impact she had on my life.

"Brothers, we do not want you to be ignorant about those who fall asleep, or to grieve like the rest of men, who have no hope. We believe that Jesus died and rose again and so we believe that God will bring with Jesus those who have fallen asleep in him. . . . Therefore encourage each other with these words" (1 Thess. 4:13-18, NIV).

BARBARA MOEN

February 21

IN LOVE, IN LIKE

Commit to the Lord whatever you do, and your plans will succeed.
Prov. 16:3, NIV.

It's easy to throw around the word "love" these days: I love football! I love golf! I love sports! I love gardening!

The love between a husband and wife is totally different. That love has many dimensions. Let's face it: marriage has been getting some pretty bad press in recent years. Too many people say the words "for better or for worse" and "until death do us part" but, in actuality, their mind-set is "until divorce is convenient."

Judy and I have been married for more than 35 years. Never once have we had a ball-and-chain attitude, gritting our teeth and grinding through. We made a commitment. There is a depth and permanence from working together year after year, knowing we are in it for keeps.

We still love each other, but we really like each other, too. We like being together, laughing together, walking together, singing together, traveling together, dreaming dreams and making plans—always together. It has everything to do with our commitment to each other—through thick and thin!

"We wouldn't think of building a stone fireplace without stones, or of baking an apple pie without apples. Why, then, are so many people trying to build Christian homes without Christ?" said Charles Crawford.

Looking ahead? Judy and I are already making plans on how we are going to spend eternity together in the presence of Christ. Now, that's commitment!

"Commit to the Lord whatever you do, and your plans will succeed" (Prov. 16:3, NIV).

That was our plan more than 35 years ago, and I have to say, it's succeeding! When you look at anyone—spouse, sibling, child, parent, next-door neighbor, fellow church member, coworker—look through the Father's, the Creator's, eyes of love. Guess what: their warts and wrinkles disappear like magic, and you'll find facets of those people that are not only endearing, but downright likable. Commit yourself today to see others through God's eyes, and fall in like with them!

Joedy Melashenko

SEEING THROUGH GOD'S EYES

The Lord does not look at the things man looks at.
Man looks at the outward appearance, but the Lord looks at the heart.
1 Sam. 16:7, NIV.

How easily we make judgments about others! It startles me sometimes how quickly I can come to a conclusion about someone based on very limited information—the way they're dressed, the way they talk, where they work, what car they drive.

When my parents were divorced, many people in our church were quick to leap to conclusions about who was at fault and who deserved their pity—without knowing the whole story. I witnessed their judgmental attitudes and the additional feelings of guilt, frustration, betrayal, and failure they heaped upon my already-shattered family. I thought to myself, *If this is how our church treats those most in need of its comfort, then I don't want to be a member!*

My faith was severely tested during that time. Thank God for my parents, whose faith never wavered—even though it was they who were being unfairly judged! Instead of giving in to intimidation, they renewed their commitment and became more actively involved in serving their church. Instead of retreating from the fellowship of church members, they sought out and befriended those whom others had left behind. Instead of condemning those who condemned them, they humbly accepted responsibility for their actions and continued to seek a closer relationship with God. They became more accepting, more loving, more giving people. They were learning to see others through God's eyes.

God doesn't make judgments based on limited information—He is all-knowing. No matter what we wear, what we say, where we work, or what we drive; whether the world counts us a sinner or a saint, we are greatly cherished—He is all-loving. No matter how gargantuan our mistakes, if we claim His sacrifice we are absolved—He is all-saving.

In God's eyes we are equally valued. The bum down the street is just as precious to Him as the pastor of your church. The next time you make a snap judgment about someone, look again and try to see them through God's eyes.

"The Lord does not look at the things man looks at. Man looks at the outward appearance, but the Lord looks at the heart" (1 Sam. 16:7, NIV).

LORELEI HERMAN CRESS

February 23

DEEPLY, FROM THE HEART

Love one another deeply, from the heart.
1 Peter 1:22, NIV.

My brother Brian is 27 months younger than I. Naturally, being the firstborn child, I "supervised" him during our childhood. When we played school, I was the teacher. When we rode bikes, I led. When he was naughty, I threatened to tell Mom. (Until he kept inventory of my misbehaviors—then we negotiated!)

We were not allowed to hit, pinch, slap, kick, or otherwise fight. During the inevitable spats, we kept quiet, because when Mom found out, that was trouble. Our verbal disagreements might last all of three minutes and then be forgotten, but if Mom got into it, we'd sometimes be spanked and always lectured for 30 to 60 minutes on why we should love each other. (Brian would maneuver a place where he could roll his eyes or make faces, while I, the dutiful—although unrepentant—daughter had to maintain composure in hope of shortening the sermon.) Decades later I remember the gist of the lectures: if all others forsake you or if "anything happens" to your parents, your sibling is your best friend. You share more DNA with your sibling than with your parents.

After college and two years on my own, Brian and I shared a home for seven years. We learned really to like and love each other and enjoy our own company. We shared values, had the same taste in decorating, people, and food, and trusted each other with our deepest thoughts. Love has carried us through when other relationships have faltered or failed. (Hey, Mom was right!)

The brash, choleric fisherman-turned-shepherd apostle Peter learned about loyal, abiding love from Jesus, who told His disciples that He had elevated their status to friends and brothers. Peter wrote: "Now that you have purified yourselves by obeying the truth so that you have sincere love for your brothers, love one another deeply, from the heart" (1 Peter 1:22, NIV).

It's a great blessing to love your siblings—and your brothers and sisters in the faith. It won't just happen by proximity. You have to make it happen. But Abba Father is eager to reconcile and create bonds between His children. Ask Him now!

Christy K. Robinson

PAPA, I LOVES YOU THIS BIG!

I have loved you with an everlasting love;
Therefore I have drawn you with lovingkindness.
Jer. 31:3, NASB.

Judy and I are grandparents. Our grandson, Conner, is the joy of our lives. When he was 4, we took him to a pumpkin farm. What a fun time we had riding the hay wagon and little train, petting the animals, and playing on the old farm machinery. On the way home Conner said, "Papa and Nanna, I loves you this big!" and stretched his arms out as wide as he could. You know the warm glow that comes to Papa's and Nanna's hearts. It's beyond description!

Hearing words of love and adoration from children and grandchildren has no equal. It ranks way up there in the scheme of things. We wouldn't trade those moments for anything.

What about our heavenly Father? Don't you think He enjoys hearing words of love and appreciation from His earthly children? When's the last time you told Him, "Abba, I love You?" When's the last time you told Him how much you enjoy His companionship or you expressed your adoration to Him? Just as much as we love to hear words of love from our children, how much more the heavenly Father loves to hear the same expressions from His earthly children! He has already told us in countless ways how much He loves us.

Need some examples? A stunning sunset. The beauty of your vegetable garden. A child's laughter. A majestic mountain. A cool babbling brook. Need more? The ultimate example: Calvary!

"I have loved you with an everlasting love; therefore I have drawn you with lovingkindness" (Jer. 31:3, NASB).

I was working late one night, and I was tired, grumpy, and stressed! Judy put her arms around me and said, "Honey, I really appreciate you! I love you so much!" Wow, after nearly four decades of marriage, she still loves me—in spite of my many faults and failures. It was as if she poured warm honey into every nook and cranny of my soul.

God loves to hear the praises of His children. He loves to hear our expressions of love and gratitude lifted heavenward.

JOEDY MELASHENKO

GREYFRIARS BOBBY

Keep this desire in the hearts of your people forever, and keep their hearts loyal to you. 1 Chron. 29:18, NIV.

Josh Billings said, "A dog is the only thing on earth that will love you more than you love yourself." This next story illustrates that point.

When John Gray died in 1858, his faithful dog, Bobby, a Skye terrier, was among the mourners in Edinburgh, Scotland. The morning after John was buried, the caretaker found Bobby lying on top of his master's grave. Dogs weren't allowed in the church graveyard, so Bobby was driven out. The next morning he was back and was again chased away. The third morning was cold and wet when the caretaker again found Bobby shivering by the grave. This time the old man had pity and fed the dog. As word spread about Bobby's loyalty, friends built a shelter for him on the church grounds. The lord provost paid the dog's license fee, and Bobby was given a collar so that he wouldn't be taken away as a stray.

For 14 years Bobby refused to stray far from his master's grave. During bad weather his friends often tried to keep him indoors, but he wouldn't have it and would fuss and howl until he was allowed to return to his faithful service at the grave or go to the coffeehouse for a bone, where his master had eaten lunch daily, with Bobby chewing a bone at his feet.

Bobby's heart was with his master, even through storms and rough weather. He never missed a night away from his master's grave, and he remained loyal until his death in 1872. A statue of the little dog stands on a busy street in Edinburgh.

May we humans, sons and daughters of the God who is love, learn faithfulness and loyalty from the example of a little dog.

"I know, my God, that you test the heart and are pleased with integrity. All these things have I given willingly and with honest intent. And now I have seen with joy how willingly your people who are here have given to you. O Lord, God of our fathers Abraham, Isaac and Israel, keep this desire in the hearts of your people forever, and keep their hearts loyal to you" (1 Chron. 29:17, 18, NIV).

ROBERT JOHNSTON

BORN TO THE PURPLE

What you say about yourself means nothing in God's work.
It's what God says about you that makes the difference.
2 Cor. 10:18, Message.

I'm descended from the "greats": French, Spanish, Nordic, Scottish, and Flemish royalty; Charlemagne; the Saxon king Cerdic; Ireland's Brian Boru; Alfred the Great; Rhodri Mawr and several great princes of Wales; and the sovereigns of England from 1066 to 1377. Plus all the royal families they married into and not a few canonized saints!

Genealogy is fascinating because knowing my ancestors literally puts a face on dry, dusty history. Granddaddy King John, a "monster of iniquity," was forced by my other ancestors to accept the Magna Carta, an enormously influential document in democratic societies. Reverend Samuel Stone was a founder of Hartford, Connecticut, and his 1663 tombstone says that he was New England's "greatest jewel." Mary Barrett Dyer, a Quaker missionary whose monument faces the Boston Common, was hanged by Puritans for obeying the gospel commission.

With all those "great" genes in my blood, I should accept curtsies, or at least crook my finger when I drink tea. None of that matters, though.

"'If you want to claim credit, claim it for God.' What you say about yourself means nothing in God's work. It's what God says about you that makes the difference" (2 Cor. 10:17, 18, Message). God said that Abraham was His friend, that David was a man after God's own heart, and that John the Baptist was the greatest man ever born. God's loving accolades are a mantle of purple!

No matter whom we descended from—peasant, emperor, exemplary, or infamous—you and I start fresh with the Lord every day. What will He say of you in the judgment? That you were a church pianist, preached an excellent sermon, were honest on your tax forms, dealt fairly with your customers? Actually, He will say something like "Because you loved your neighbors wholeheartedly, visiting and clothing and feeding them, you have shown yourself to be like Me. Enter into joy!" (see Matt. 25:40).

CHRISTY K. ROBINSON

JESUS, WONDERFUL COUNSELOR

*And he will be called: Wonderful Counselor, Mighty God,
Everlasting Father, Prince of Peace.
Isa. 9:6, NLT.*

Jesus doesn't berate you if you are too fat or addicted to chocolate or Prozac.

He had only three years to complete His work, so He spent His time on what really mattered. What were His priorities? He set His priorities very early in His ministry and never varied till He said on the cross, "It is finished." His priority was to attract believers, people who trusted Him because He trusted them. He had a single-minded focus on creating disciples. The prophet Isaiah called Him wonderful Counselor, mighty God (Isa. 9:6), and described Him as having the spirit of wisdom and understanding (Isa. 11:2). That's the kind of counselor I want—one who is wise, understands everything, and takes everything into consideration.

Look at the record of Jesus' acceptance of people. He ate and fraternized with tax collectors and other lowlifes described in the New Testament (Matt. 9:10-12) and redeemed a fallen woman (John 8:1-11).

Please don't confuse His acceptance for approval. He instructed the woman to return to a redeemed life and sin no more. As a Wonderful Counselor, He had keen discernment. His dialogue with the woman at the well (John 4:21-25) is a classic story of respectful treatment of a person accompanied by keen discernment.

You can't surprise Him, but best of all, He desires to hear from you even as you read this. He is the living, loving, accepting, discerning, Wonderful Counselor.

WILLIAM LOVELESS

FOOLISH TALK

Fools care nothing for thoughtful discourse;
all they do is run off at the mouth.
Prov. 18:2, Message.

Dave Barry, a humor columnist, commented on a dog's acceptance of his master: "You can say any foolish thing to a dog, and the dog will give you a look that says, 'You're right! I never would've thought of that!' "

It's satisfying to get that look, isn't it? Who doesn't like having their humor or sage observations appreciated and admired, especially when your audience is smarter than a dog? I've offended people with what I thought was gentle teasing, and others by expressing my political views. There's a nonscriptural proverb my mother taught: never discuss religion, bodily functions, or politics in polite company. Or any other place, for that matter, if they aren't immediate family.

So what is one to talk about? What's left? If I discuss medieval history, people's eyes glaze over. Current events lead back to politics, a banned dinner subject. I could talk about my pets or my garden, but that's only good for a minute.

Perhaps the answer is not to talk so much as to listen. We need to listen to our neighbors' spoken words and notice their body language so that we can understand their motivations. Saying the right words at the right time—there are lots of Solomon's proverbs about that, and James 3 and Ephesians 4 and 5 also provide guidance in that area.

Religious talk has minefields, particularly when we confuse changeable standards and unchangeable principles, but I've noticed that when we speak of the love and endless grace of God, people's eyes light up. You and I can never hear it enough times: God loves me, He cares for everything about me, He's waiting for me to relax in His arms and let Him take care of me, He created me especially to be His treasure, He's prepared eternal life and joy for me.

"Really?" they seem to say, "You're right! I never would've thought of that!" That's not folly—that's hope and encouragement and building up. Paul wrote in Ephesians 4:29, "Say only what helps, each word a gift" (Message).

Your words—and your listening silence—will be love in another person's ear.

CHRISTY K. ROBINSON

March 1

SALVATION: DOING AND BEING

Rejoice and be glad, because great is your reward in heaven.
Matt. 5:12, NIV.

Moses asked to see God, but the Lord said that to see His face would mean death for Moses. So instead God described Himself to Moses in terms of character and BE-ing. He said, I AM, I WILL BE WHO I WILL BE, "*compassionate* and *gracious* God, *slow to anger, abounding in love* and *faithfulness,* maintaining *love* to thousands, and *forgiving* wickedness, rebellion and sin" (Ex. 34:6, 7, NIV).

Micah 6:8 says, "He has showed you, O man, what is good. And what does the Lord require of you? To act *justly* and to love *mercy* and to walk humbly with your God" (NIV).

Do you see some cognate words in these passages? Compassion, mercy, love, humility, grace, slowness to anger, forgiving, loving. Those attributes of Jesus are His greatest aspirations for us: to be like Him. Even the Ten Commandments are a description of who God is and what He does. He doesn't act or speak out of holy character (1-3), He rests securely after creating and working for our salvation (4), He honors the created by giving them rest and respect for human rights and a pleasant, peaceful lifestyle (4-10).

All those descriptions of God are ways of being found in Christ, not ways of doing our salvation. Only God can save us. Since the obsolescence of the Old Covenant laws and the inception of the New Covenant, the Holy Spirit writes His law and will on our hearts (Heb. 10:16).

When Jesus sat on the Galilean hillside and spoke the Beatitudes, He told us what would make us not just emotionally happy, but happy in every recess of our souls—and that is to emulate Him, to have Him in our hearts. He wanted to communicate the joy that comes from an intimate fellowship with God. When Christ inhabits us body, mind, and soul, we have a sense of the fellowship of the Father, Son, and Spirit.

Jesus said to be joyful—dance—celebrate—because His Beatitudes promise that we are and will be filled with the kingdom of God, comforted, inherit the earth, filled with righteousness, receive mercy, see God, called sons of God, and rewarded in heaven.

Christy K. Robinson

DO CHRISTIANS STEAL SHEEP?

Accept him whose faith is weak,
without passing judgment on disputable matters.
Rom. 14:1, NIV.

For more than 150 years my denomination has emphasized the distinct beliefs that set us apart, but we also celebrate the fellowship of the entire family of God regardless of culture or denominational affiliation. I love that!

I've been a church musician since I was 10 years old. I've been employed by Presbyterians, Adventists, United Methodists, Disciples of Christ, evangelicals, charismatics, and Baptists. A person can learn sound Bible teaching in all of those churches. People love the Lord and seek His will. I have worked closely with pastors who devote their personal resources without reservation. I'm not concerned with being spiritually "contaminated." Instead I thank the Lord for the fresh bread and the new perspectives He's given me because of our fellowship. I know God has used me to bless those congregations—they said so.

My friends were talking animatedly in our church parking lot. "Did you get the invitation to the [evangelical-nondenominational-charismatic] church? They're targeting our members!"

I responded, "How can they steal our sheep if our flock is happy and healthy? But if they've been wounded, neglected, criticized, spiritually starved, or disagree with our beliefs, aren't the wounded ones better off in another fellowship of believers than washing the car, watching sports, or shopping during church time? Trust that the Holy Spirit will lovingly lead His children into the kingdom by the road He chooses."

Romans 14 says, "Accept him whose faith is weak, without passing judgment on disputable matters. . . . So then, each of us will give an account of himself to God. Therefore let us stop passing judgment on one another. Instead, make up your mind not to put any stumbling block or obstacle in your brother's way" (verses 1, 12, 13, NIV).

The health of your flock is your responsibility. If each person acted with responsibility, honor, love, and mercy toward every other member, weak or strong in the faith, wouldn't we have the fellowship we long for? Let's resolve to give our faith family reasons to stay in fellowship, not reasons to leave. And let's make our sheepfold healthy and safe so that when sheep are straying from another fellowship, we're the haven they seek.

Christy K. Robinson

GET WISE

Wisdom is supreme; therefore get wisdom.
Though it cost all you have, get understanding. Prov. 4:7, NIV.

The Bible speaks often of wisdom and its value—it is credited with providing health, success, happiness, and long life. It's safe to assume that all of us, given the choice, would choose to be wise rather than foolish. But the unpleasant truth is that we are given the choice, and yet so often we choose folly over wisdom! How can we learn to discern the difference and choose wisely?

Scripture tells us that God is the only source of true wisdom. "True wisdom and real power belong to God; from him we learn how to live, and also what to live for" (Job 12:13, Message).

A nurtured relationship with our Creator affords us the opportunity to receive wisdom straight from the source and the best possible guidance on daily living. Solomon puts it this way: "Skilled living gets its start in the Fear-of-God; insight into life from knowing a Holy God" (Prov. 9:10, Message).

We often think we know what's best without consulting our Savior. Solomon warned us against this, saying: "Trust God from the bottom of your heart; don't try to figure out everything on your own. Listen for God's voice in everything you do, everywhere you go; he's the one who will keep you on track" (Prov. 3:5, 6, *Message*).

In Proverbs 3 Solomon gives us some wonderfully straightforward suggestions on how to live wisely: Let love and loyalty guide your behavior—you will win God's favor and everyone else's. Honor God with all you own by giving Him your best, and you will be rewarded with abundance. Don't sulk when God corrects you—He only disciplines those He loves. Don't walk away from someone who needs your help. Don't put off repaying a debt if it's within your power. Don't pick fights or bully others.

So get wise! Tune in to God every day and follow His advice—your life will be transformed, and you'll spread happiness wherever you go!

LORELEI HERMAN CRESS

A COLOR-LOVING CREATOR

See how the lilies of the field grow. They do not labor or spin.
Yet I tell you that not even Solomon in all his splendor was dressed like one of these.
Matt. 6:28, 29, NIV.

One spring the California poppies were out en masse, and my husband and I drove to Antelope Valley to view the golden panorama. There were millions of flowers, carpets of dense orange gold, as far as the eye could see. We walked among the blooms, taking pictures and rejoicing in their beauty. What a gift from our color-loving Creator—God!

We hiked to the ranger station to look at the photographs and paintings of other desert flowers. A narrated slide show immersed us in further beauty. Happy and satiated, we were heading for the door when we noticed a placard: "Although today we revel in the breathtaking beauty of the desert flowers, did you know that nature did not evolve them for human enjoyment? Their colors, textures, and designs came about through the evolutionary ages in order to attract insects and birds, which carry the pollen that enables the flowers to survive."

As we drove home, I reflected on the lengths people must take to bypass the concept of a loving Creator. To my (logical) mind, couldn't "nature" just as easily have evolved insects and birds that would be attracted to gray generic flowers?

It reminded me of a trip we'd made one summer into the mountains of Colorado. As our group four-wheeled around the highest peaks, we encountered one meadow after another blanketed with virtual rainbows of wildflowers. We counted 86 different kinds that afternoon alone.

Someone quoted the text: "See how the lilies of the field grow. They do not labor or spin. Yet I tell you that not even Solomon in all his splendor was dressed like one of these" (Matt. 6:28, 29, NIV).

Yes, I thought. The people who believe in the "evolutionary ages" have a problem. How can they explain the infinite varieties, shapes, and colors of flowers apart from a caring Creator? I'm glad I believe in the Master Artist.

AILEEN LUDINGTON

A SUNFLOWER IN THE ONION PATCH

The Lord your God goes with you;
he will never leave you nor forsake you. Deut. 31:6, NIV.

Have you ever been through times when everything that could possibly go wrong does? When there's not only rain but also hail the size of golf balls on your parade? When the dog (or computer) really did eat your homework? When your best-laid plans turn to dust?

I was suffering through such a time in my life. In my job search I was not offered the position I hoped for because I "looked too young." The fixing up of our fixer-upper home was not going according to my (perhaps too grand) plans. In addition, other uncountable minor annoyances added to my misery.

I stepped out into the backyard to survey the fence that had fallen down—again—in yet another high wind. On the way I passed by the little green onion patch in my kitchen garden. To my surprise, I glimpsed a flash of sunny yellow bobbing gently in the breeze. I looked again and discovered a single miniature sunflower among the onions. I had not planted sunflowers in the backyard, and I had not noticed the plant growing there before, but there it was, bright and cheery, in the middle of all those smelly onions.

God wants me to be that sunflower in the onion patch, to smile in spite of adversity, to have faith even when I can't see the way out. Immediately I began to feel better. The fallen-down fence, even my disappointments, seemed less significant in the light of my new calling. If God could cultivate a sunflower in the midst of onions, surely He could and would sustain me through all my problems.

Before the Israelites could cross the Jordan River and enter the Promised Land they had to face many fierce nations. But they didn't face them alone. God went before Israel and handed the nations over to them. Moses encouraged them: "Be strong and courageous. Do not be afraid or terrified because of them, for the Lord your God goes with you; he will never leave you nor forsake you" (Deut. 31:6, NIV).

We, too, have no reason to be afraid because that very same God goes with us and before us and will never forsake us.

LAURA WEST KONG

FRUIT COCKTAIL

There is a holy, God-planted, God-tended root.
If the primary root of the tree is holy, there's bound to be some holy fruit.
Rom. 11:16, Message.

When I was little, one of my favorite breakfasts was fruit cocktail, with its peaches, pears, and fake-cherry grapes.

Now, I have more varieties of fruit in my yard than I have fruit trees or vines. My cherry tree has five different grafts on a cherry rootstock. I have one nectarine and three peach varieties on one trunk, plum, pluot (hybrid of plum and apricot), two kinds of almonds, Asian pear, black and white mulberries, and don't get me started on citrus! They're called fruit cocktail trees. They're meant to be space savers, but the branches also pollinate each other for a better harvest.

People marvel at how many fruits I have, assuming I know how to graft trees. No, I buy them at the nursery! It's a science to marry an alien sprout to the trunk successfully.

Grafters often start with a hardy, pest- and disease-resistant rootstock and trunk. Your gorgeous roses look very different from the puny blooms of the suckers, because the desirable part has been grafted to the wild roots. Ever taste an ornamental orange? (Don't.) Their roots are better adapted to resist bugs and harsh weather than the tender, grafted stock of sweet oranges.

"There is a holy, God-planted, God-tended root. If the primary root of the tree is holy, there's bound to be some holy fruit. Some of the tree's branches were pruned and you wild olive shoots were grafted in. Yet the fact that you are now fed by that rich and holy root gives you no cause to crow over the pruned branches. Remember, you aren't feeding the root; the root is feeding you" (Rom. 11:16-18, Message).

God grafted wild shoots, the Gentile believers (that's us), into the cultivar of the Jewish faith. The result was a new fruit entirely: the Christian faith.

Regardless of which variety of fruit we develop as a result of God's miraculous graft, let's remember to take our nourishment from our strong and hardy, tested and true Root, the Lord Jesus Christ. He is providing moisture and nutrients and protecting our souls from illness and injury. Let's make His day. Let's blossom and bear fruit!

Christy K. Robinson

HEART SIGHT

Now we see but a poor reflection as in a mirror; then we shall see face to face. 1 Cor. 13:12, NIV.

I am fortunate to have a beach near my home in Bainbridge Island, Washington. Each spring we have the low tide of the year. It's fun to walk on the beach at these times because the bottom of the ocean is exposed. It's not uncommon to see giant sunburst starfish in bright-orange and pink, sea anemones that look like giant green olives with purple centers, and massive sand dollar colonies. Thousands of sand dollars, jumbled on top of each other and half buried in sand, stretch to the sea, looking like dark coins spilled out of the vast hold of a Spanish galleon.

These creatures are there all the time. They just aren't visible to my eyes. The low tides are just a peek at the vibrant, different kinds of life invisible to me.

The Bible is full of stories about the things we cannot see. Elisha, in 2 Kings 6, has a vision of angels and chariots of the Lord protecting him from the King of Syria's attack. We are cautioned: "Do not forget to entertain strangers, for by so doing some people have entertained angels without knowing it" (Heb. 13:2, NIV).

When we get to heaven it might feel something like "low tide" on my little canal. The Lord's abundant grace in our lives will be revealed in new ways. We'll understand more fully how much God loves us and provides for us, even in ways that we cannot see or comprehend.

We can have faith that what Paul wrote in 1 Corinthians 13 is true: "Now we see but a poor reflection as in a mirror; then we shall see face to face. Now I know in part; then I shall know fully, even as I am fully known" (1 Cor. 13:12, NIV).

Pamela McCann

SODIUM CHLORIDE OF THE EARTH

You are the salt of the earth. Matt. 5:13, NIV.

Salt has many uses, some of which are flavoring, thawing, abrasiveness, preservation, buoyancy, cleansing, corrosion, and medicinal. Salt was an essential part of the Old Testament sacrificial system.

I walked into the Dead Sea with flip-flops and lost my footing as they kept pushing to the surface against my will. You can't help floating in the strong salt brine. Don't splash, either, as the brine will sting your eyes and lips.

Many roadwork crews use salt on highways both for thawing the ice and providing traction, but that salt prevents or kills plant growth along the highways, and it corrodes vehicles. For thousands of years salt has been a preservative for food, including meats, fish, olives, and pickles. It provides the fizz in soda pop, speeds the process in the ice cream churn, and scrubs the grime off whatever it's applied to.

Our bodies need salt to prevent dehydration. When I worked in hot and windy Jordan on an archaeology dig, I was encouraged to eat more salt than usual. But too much salt will cause water retention, which is not good for blood pressure or injured areas. Some medications and sports drinks are compounded with salts to efficiently disperse in our tissues.

We mostly think of salt as a flavoring. It enhances the flavor of herbs, vegetables, nuts, meats, and especially meat substitutes. Imagine Chinese food without salty soy sauce. Some foods are unthinkable without salt. Tofu, gluten, popcorn, and potato chips would be tasteless without salt!

Jesus said in Matthew 5:13, "Let me tell you why you are here. You're here to be salt-seasoning that brings out the God-flavors of this earth. If you lose your saltiness, how will people taste godliness?" (Message).

Do you see the yin and yang here? There needs to be balance. Without you and me, the salt of the earth, restoring balance, people of the world know only bland and boring. I want to be in God's saltshaker!

CHRISTY K. ROBINSON

MOVING DAY

Let us not become weary in doing good, for at the proper time we will reap a harvest if we do not give up. Gal. 6:9, NIV.

Moving day was fast approaching, and 9-month-old Annika was in her glory. The living room floor was scattered with cardboard boxes and the contents of various cabinets and cupboards. Obscure household utensils and miscellaneous knick-knacks came out from their hiding places and awaited discovery by my junior archaeologist. Stacks of already-packed boxes beckoned my miniature mountain climber. Every corner of the house was filled with a veritable abundance of exciting treasure.

As Annika and I sat in the middle of all this, packing tape and marking pen in hand, I packed box after box in preparation for our moving day. I stacked neat piles of books into boxes and just as quickly as I put them in, Annika took them out one by one and stacked them up next to her. Then, one by one, she put them back into the box, stopping now and then to examine the pages of a particularly interesting volume. This scene was repeated over and over during the course of the next few weeks with our pots and pans, linens, music CDs, and more.

In her enthusiasm, Annika packed several items deep into unknown boxes. The true extent of her participation wasn't fully evident until we finally unpacked the boxes in our new home.

Our heavenly moving day is also fast approaching. The results of many of our preparations are not always immediately apparent. This should not dampen our enthusiasm. Even a small kindness can make a difference to a hurting heart or bring someone closer to Jesus, helping to prepare people in this world for the heavenly moving day.

"Let us not become weary in doing good, for at the proper time we will reap a harvest if we do not give up" (Gal. 6:9, NIV).

Laura West Kong

OBSTACLES

Those who look to him are radiant;
their faces are never covered with shame. Ps. 34:5, NIV.

My border collie, Evie, was abused in her first 18 months of life; then she was abandoned at a county kennel. Because of her pure breed, she was fostered for six months by a rescue organization, then advertised on the Internet, and that's where I found her. Paula, her foster mom, therapist, and trainer for six months, described the numerous attempts to lead Evie through the agility course obstacles. Evie did well on weaving, diving through a tunnel, and leaping through a hoop, but balked at the high and narrow walk. She refused the walk at first. However, each time after that she approached the course with increasing confidence and purpose, looking forward to praise and treats with each success.

Paula said, "I gave the command, and she bounded in! I called to her to 'walk it,' and she trotted up. I sat on the ground and called her into my arms, as my tears spilled onto her coat. Evie ran the rest of the course off-lead, willing and wagging. I don't know the last time I have been so touched and so proud of a dog."

We've all been in a place where we're unsure or scared to move, even with encouragement. Fears are not entirely irrational; oftentimes they stem from previous experiences and injuries. God leads us through dark tunnels and obstacles, but still we balk. We fear speaking in public, showing strong emotion, being alone, not having enough money, being noticed, not being noticed. All the while, God keeps leading us into strength and confidence.

Each time Evie came to the obstacle, it got easier. Although the course didn't change in difficulty, she trusted her trainer to stay with her, and she knew that there would be love and treats afterward. Do you remember the times the Lord brought you through a challenge and you emerged victorious? There was intimacy in God's arms as He embraced you.

Psalm 34:4, 5 says, "I sought the Lord, and he answered me; he delivered me from all my fears. Those who look to him are radiant; their faces are never covered with shame" (NIV).

May we take a lesson from the furry children of God and find no reason to shrink from God's adventures and challenges. Let's move boldly out there, taking the steps God has planned for us.

CHRISTY K. ROBINSON

MARCH 11

GROW UP!

He who began a good work in you will carry it on to completion.
Phil. 1:6, NIV.

As an avid gardener, I have been accused of admonishing my roses, "Grow up, eh?" I want to ask, "OK, what is it this time? Too much water? Too little water? Too much sun? Too little sun? Bugs? What kind of bugs?"

Planting roses is quite a process. It takes me hours to get the soil prepared. I have to consider the mature plant size for the location and what season it flowers.

After the plant is purchased and carefully planted in the garden, I give it my pep talk and, of course, a healthy dose of Miracle-Gro fertilizer. I know it will grow beautifully and add a little hope to my version of "Judy's Butchart Gardens."

But sometimes the leaves look a little wilted and a yellow edge appears, and the plant looks less than wonderful. I've been through this how many times? Do I just give up after negative results? Of course not! Why? Because I love gardening; it becomes a challenge! Plants have nearly died, but I keep working with them, nurturing and pruning, and tending, and yes, most have grown into beautiful plants that I treasure.

How would it be if we spent as much time, care, and devotion on our children's emotional and physical well-being as we spend on our gardens? Each child requires varying dosages of tenderness, love, and encouragement. Sometimes we do not see immediate results, and discouragement sets in. I saw a T-shirt with the message "Who are these children, and why do they keep calling me Mom?"

I am humbled by God and His astounding mercy and grace, His patience, willingness to forgive, and eagerness to have a meaningful relationship with me. He wants to help me "bloom where I'm planted." Can we do any less for our children?

I claim the promise in Philippians 1:6 for my children, grandchildren, and my family: "He who began a good work in you will carry it on to completion" (NIV).

So, get out God's Miracle-Gro of prayer, encouragement, and perseverance. Happy gardening! Watch your family grow in Jesus!

JUDY MELASHENKO

BAD SOIL?

There are varieties of ministries, and the same Lord.
1 Cor. 12:5, NASB.

When I was a child, the parable of the sower troubled me (Matt. 13:3-9). With hungry birds, impenetrable rocks, scorching sun, and choking thorns there seemed to be little chance for the Word of God to grow. What hope was there for those unfortunate people born with bad soil in their hearts?

Although I never received a suitable answer, I grew up happy and well adjusted. It wasn't until my husband and I bought our first home that I understood.

When I took my shovel to the bare ground, I discovered the soil was as hard as the sower's path, and rocky besides. The only way this land could sustain even a single petunia was if I replaced every last pebble and grain of sand with fresh soil.

The solution I found was not to discard the soil but to plant something that would grow well in rocky hard-packed soil. Thyme, an herb native to the rocky hills of the Mediterranean, thrives in poor soil. It actually has more flavor when grown among the rocks than in good soil.

Thyme was sprinkled on sacrificial lambs during biblical times. Tired soldiers in ancient Greece bathed in thyme water to renew their strength. Thyme was used as a strewing herb during the Middle Ages—it has antibacterial properties as well as a strong and pleasant scent. Thyme has been healing respiratory problems for centuries. Thymol, thyme's essential oil, is found in cough syrup, mouthwash, and cosmetics. And of course thyme's sparkly green flavor enhances just about any dish one might cook.

If I had thrown away the bad soil and replaced it with good, my husband and I would never have enjoyed thyme's unique benefits. In the same way, a person who appears different, one who at first glance might be categorized as bad soil, could be just right to enhance the church and bless the world in a special way.

"Now there are varieties of gifts, but the same Spirit. And there are varieties of ministries, and the same Lord. There are varieties of effects, but the same God who works all things in all persons. But to each one is given the manifestation of the Spirit for the common good" (1 Cor. 12:4-7, NASB).

LAURA WEST KONG

SUBURBAN SAFARI

Many, O Lord my God, are the wonders which You have done. . . .
If I would declare and speak of them, they would be too numerous to count.
Ps. 40:5, NASB.

On her backyard outings calico cat Abby hunts for lizards and grasshoppers. When she catches something, she brings it to me for inspection. Bugs get eaten; lizards released.

Late one night I awoke to a shrill twittering. When I turned on the light, I saw a tiny gray field mouse cowering by the baseboard with Abby ready to pounce. She'd caught him in the screen porch and brought him inside to show me. The mouse looked exactly like one of Abby's toy mousies, only this one had locomotion and a sound card!

Abby and I chased the mouse around and under furniture (with different purposes in mind). Somehow I managed to "herd" the mouse into the bathroom and stop up the space under the door. Abby wasn't happy.

The next morning, I decided I'd better catch that mouse and put him outside. So I pushed the shower curtain over the closed shower door, and sure enough, there was a tiny thud when the mouse dropped onto the fiberglass floor. I let myself into the shower, and sat on the ledge, contemplating how to catch the mouse without hurting it. I think the mouse hoped his gray fur would blend with the white shower tile.

I began to think about how I appear to God. God has a plan; He wants to rescue me and set me in safety, but all I can see is this moment, and this moment is frightening.

My thoughts came back to the mouse in my shower. I sacrificed a tissue box, and slowly moved toward him. "No! No!" he squeaked. I moved closer. I set the box down over the mouse; I tumbled him down to the bottom and clapped a glass saucer over the top. I walked to the corner of my backyard and set the box down in the bougainvillea flowers. The mouse huddled in his new comfort zone, so I tipped him out of the box into a deep pile of pink flowers. When I checked on him 10 minutes later, he'd escaped to a world of blossoms. I saw the mouse again recently. Abby had him treed. The mouse still lives, and the cat is still frustrated!

The Lord's thoughts toward us are of compassion and care for His children. We have nothing to fear from His rescue.

CHRISTY K. ROBINSON

LIGHTING THE DARKNESS

I am the light of the world. Whoever follows me will never walk in darkness, but will have the light of life.
John 8:12, NIV.

When I was a little girl, I was afraid of the dark. Strange noises at night would send shivers down my spine, and I sometimes imagined I could see strange shapes in the darkness waiting to pounce. Some nights I couldn't sleep without leaving a light on!

Darkness is scary for good reason. You can't see obstacles in your path or danger lurking around the corner, and it's very easy to get lost.

Our world seems very dark and threatening at times. We can't see the dangers ahead of us, and when we encounter an obstacle, we often don't know which way to turn.

Thankfully, God has given us light to guide us safely through the darkness. Walking in Christ's footsteps, we can be certain that we will never stumble or lose our way. Christ said, "I am the light of the world. Whoever follows me will never walk in darkness, but will have the light of life" (John 8:12, NIV).

Another source of light is His Word. The psalmist wrote, "Your word is a lamp to my feet and a light for my path" (Ps. 119:105, NIV). The Scriptures can shed light in the bleakest of circumstances and show us how to overcome life's pitfalls and remain on course. God not only provides us with light, but calls each of us to be a light to others in darkness.

"You are the light of the world. . . . Let your light shine before men, that they may see your good deeds and praise your Father in heaven" (Matt. 5:14-16, NIV).

So how about it? Will you stumble around in the darkness or be a shining light to others today?

"For you were once darkness, but now you are light in the Lord. Live as children of light" (Eph. 5:8, NIV).

Lorelei Herman Cress

THE ULTIMATE LIFE

I have come that they may have life,
and that they may have it more abundantly.
John 10:10, NKJV.

In today's fast-paced life people often feel so pressured and stressed, so full of pain and disappointment, and so hopeless that they become increasingly willing to gamble their health, and even their lives, on almost anything that promises relief, no matter how temporary. "Follow your feelings," they are urged. "If it feels good, do it. Hurry, life is passing you by."

For every skid-row bum there are scores of closet alcoholics. And for every street punk looking for a "hit" there are many "respectable" people numbing their pain with prescription pills.

But people are becoming increasingly disillusioned. Lasting joy doesn't come in snorts, and they can't shoot up peace of mind. Bottles and pills don't erase guilt, and well-being cannot be purchased with a prescription. Even many medical breakthroughs are only temporary patch-up jobs.

Health and fitness are not enough; neither is wealth, fame, good looks, or power. The ultimate life must include spiritual growth and development. We didn't arrive in this world, as some evolutionists claim, with only the minimal equipment needed for survival. We are born with a conscience to keep us on track, a full range of feelings and emotions to enrich our lives, and a brain that we can never use up or wear out.

In every human heart there are deep, inexplicable longings for something better, longings implanted by our Creator to lead us to the One who can fill our lives with meaning, now and for eternity.

That's why Jesus came. He tells us, "I have come that they [you] may have life, and that they [you] may have it more abundantly" (John 10:10, NKJV).

AILEEN LUDINGTON

BY BEHOLDING WE BECOME CHANGED

And we, who with unveiled faces all reflect the Lord's glory, are being transformed into his likeness with ever-increasing glory.
2 Cor. 3:18, NIV.

I am constantly amazed at the scientific and technological advances we see in medicine: surgical procedures, cancer treatments using proton beams, stem cell research. Imagine replacing damaged organs. Look at the wonders of laser eye surgery, or the security systems that use the unique "fingerprint" of the cornea for ID purposes. How can one not be convinced of Creation when examining the human body with all its intricate parts and how they work together!

We spend a lot of time and energy when it comes to global warming, the ozone layer, and the environment. Ironically, there seems to be a lot more concern about environmental pollution than there is about soul pollution. We spend billions of dollars each year trying to ascertain why certain segments of our society are in trouble. We study children who watch an endless parade of violence on television or in movies. We spend millions researching the effects of pornography. We debate the proper parenting skills needed and whether or not to spank a child.

After all the billions are spent and the research is done, we see with undeniable clarity that there is a link between violence, drug addiction, pornography, and crime, and that a constant diet of "garbage" from TV and the entertainment industry has contributed greatly to the decay of our society. Amazing discovery? I don't think so!

"And we, who with unveiled faces all reflect the Lord's glory, are being transformed into his likeness with ever-increasing glory, which comes from the Lord, who is the Spirit" (2 Cor. 3:18, NIV). We are changed by beholding. So be careful what you behold.

"Whatever is true, whatever is noble, whatever is right, whatever is pure, whatever is lovely, whatever is admirable—if anything is excellent or praiseworthy—think about such things" (Phil. 4:8, NIV).

God alone knows how we are made, how our brains are wired, and the effects of sin upon us. Instead of forming our morals and values on the shifting sands of theories and studies, a revisit to God's Word and His unchangeable truths needs to take center stage.

Let's behold God and let Him change us for the better!

JOEDY MELASHENKO

MARCH 17

ST. PATRICK'S DAY

There is but one Lord, Jesus Christ, through whom all things came and through whom we live. 1 Cor. 8:6, NIV.

Are you wearing your green clothes today? Do you exhibit your shamrocks and leprechauns? Does the title "Saint" put you in mind of more myth than historical fact?

In my travels through Ireland I heard legends about Patrick, many of which sounded like pure superstition. I learned about Patrick and his missionary influence on the country.

Patrick wasn't even Irish. He was born in southern England or Wales to a wealthy Christian family. Patricius, son of Calpornius, was born around A.D. 410. At age 15 he was abducted by Irish slavers. He existed in misery and terror for several years as a shepherd in northern Ireland, "praying [for deliverance] a hundred times a day and as many at night," he said. Then one night in a dream an angel told him to escape. After a 185-mile journey he boarded a ship (or was abducted by more raiding sailors) and came ashore in continental Europe or Wales; he and the sailors nearly starved. When Patrick prayed for food, God sent a herd of pigs into their path, which they slaughtered and devoured. The pagans were impressed by Patrick's intimacy and favor with so powerful a God, and they converted to Christianity.

After religious education and ordination in Europe, he returned to Ireland as a missionary and founded an evangelistic movement that lasted for centuries. Many miracles were attributed to him, and some might be true! As a young man, Patrick realized where his true power rested: not in a talisman or legend, tradition or affiliation, nationality or culture. His source of power was Christ Jesus.

From an elegant and eloquent prayer Patrick composed, these words still inspire and convict us today: "Christ with me, Christ before me, Christ behind me, Christ in me, Christ beneath me, Christ above me, Christ on my right, Christ on my left, Christ when I lie down, Christ when I sit down, Christ when I arise, Christ in the heart of every man who thinks of me, Christ in the mouth of everyone who speaks of me, Christ in every eye that sees me, Christ in every ear that hears me. I arise today through a mighty strength."

CHRISTY K. ROBINSON

BETTER THAN ROBERT REDFORD

Haven't you been listening? God doesn't come and go. God lasts.
Isa. 40:28, Message.

Nothing could be better than Robert Redford! But when a crust topped with chocolate pudding, pecans, cream cheese, and a coating of whipped cream rests momentarily on your tongue, you sigh, "Ah, this is delicious. Much better than Robert Redford!"

The popular dessert served at hundreds of church potlucks—with a bevy of "Better Than . . ." names—has, at least for a moment, brought joy to the taste buds. But as taste buds have a way of doing, soon your mouth waters for a buttery ear of corn or a fragrant slice of fresh-baked bread. The dessert that was touted as better than Robert Redford is soon forgotten as a longing for something better, something different. We're constantly looking for something to satisfy a momentary need.

When your day is going horribly, when you have a desperate need, nothing is better than Jesus! When your boss heralds, "You're fired!" or your wife screams, "I want a divorce!" Or your son announces, "I'm gay," or your doctor reveals, "You have multiple sclerosis," nothing, absolutely nothing, is better than reaching for Jesus!

When you feel panic tighten in your chest and tears of despair sting your eyes, Jesus is nearby. He understands your panic, and tears also fill His eyes. He longs to hold you close to Him and say, "Don't be afraid, I've redeemed you. I've called your name. You're mine. When you're in over your head, I'll be there with you. When you're in rough waters, you will not go down. When you're between a rock and a hard place, it won't be a dead end—because I am God, your personal God, the Holy of Israel, your Savior. I paid a huge price for you: all of Egypt, with rich Cush and Seba thrown in! *That's* how much you mean to me! *That's* how much I love you!" (Isa. 43:1-4, Message).

Jesus does much more than satisfy for a moment. When you need comfort, He's there, right by your side. Let Him wrap you in His love. Let Him share your burden. In fact, He will carry it for you!

MARILYN SENIER

March 19

A LIVING SACRIFICE

Therefore, I urge you, brothers, in view of God's mercy, to offer your bodies as living sacrifices, holy and pleasing to God—this is your spiritual act of worship. Rom. 12:1, NIV.

In the days of the Old Testament animals were routinely sacrificed to atone for sins and achieve reconciliation with God. Obviously, these are not the kind of sacrifices Paul is referring to. He urges us to present our bodies as living sacrifices. The adjective "living" is defined as "active, functioning, and vivid." We are to offer our active, vital selves to God.

The word "sacrifice" means "an act of offering to a deity of something precious" or "a surrender of something for the sake of something else." We, as offerings, are precious in God's sight and so valuable to Him that He was willing to sacrifice His only Son to save us. Knowing that He wants what is best for us, we surrender ourselves to His will, and in exchange, we receive a more fulfilling life on this earth and eternal life thereafter with Him.

This sacrifice is not demanded or required. Instead, Paul beseeches us "in view of God's mercy." Our offering should not be one of fear of judgment or damnation, but a voluntary, intelligent response to God's abundant mercy and love, as demonstrated through the life and death of His Son.

How can this offering of our imperfect selves be "holy and pleasing" to God? That's what's so wonderful! If we accept Christ's sacrifice for us, we are justified in God's sight and can present ourselves without blemish.

Paul refers to this intentional offering of ourselves to God as a "spiritual act of worship." Offering ourselves in this way is an active, not passive, expression of our gratitude and love. It means demonstrating His love to those in need and sharing the story of His salvation with those in despair.

This is not meant to be a onetime act, but a way of living. We recommit ourselves as an act of worship every day. So offer your whole, active, precious self to God today. This kind of worship could change the world!

Lorelei Herman Cress

HOLY GROUND

And you are living stones that God is building into his spiritual temple. What's more, you are his holy priests. Through the mediation of Jesus Christ, you offer spiritual sacrifices that please God. 1 Peter 2:5, NLT.

Northumberland, England, is covered with fields of red poppies, golden barley, and grazing sheep. What pretty country! My eyes take in hilltop farmsteads and Bamburgh Castle in the distance. Cumulus clouds scud by peacefully. I'm sitting on a grassy bank at the harbor. The tide is high, and Lindisfarne Island causeway submerged. Sheep graze in a paddock behind me. Three fishermen walk by and, in a Northumbrian accent, one says, "It was six feet long."

The guys chuckle, and another one responds, "Yeah, right, and 150 pounds for sure." Fish stories.

I left the scene and walked on to the priory. I paid admission to the museum and church ruins and began to explore the area. With a carpet of grass, a ceiling of sky, and glassless windows to the North Sea, the apse was a semicircle where the missionary St. Cuthbert, famous for teaching both discipleship and grace, had been buried in the seventh century. I sat in the chancel on a block of stone, enjoying fluffy clouds in a pure blue sky, birds fluttering between the arches of the crossing, and the sun spotlighting me from a gothic stone arch. A golden day.

This was where the high altar had been for 700 years, and then bare stone for another 600 years. People had offered prayers, celebrated Communion, and taught the Word of God here. In that quiet and holy place, I worshipped God and thanked Him for bringing me here and showing me such beauty. Unmistakably, I heard the Lord speak to my heart: "Offer yourself as a living sacrifice, holy and pleasing to God—this is your spiritual act of worship."

I could sense God smiling, but why did He remind me of Romans 12? Then I remembered that I sat on a place representative of sacrifice. Because of Jesus' sacrifice of Himself, we no longer offer an animal sacrifice to represent our penitence and salvation. Because of Jesus, the death penalty on me is commuted to life in His kingdom. What a blessing that we can offer ourselves as living sacrifices. And it doesn't have to be on an altar: it's our lives that He wants, not our deaths.

Thank You, Lord, for Your gentle and humorous teachings!

CHRISTY K. ROBINSON

MARCH 21

THE MARCH EQUINOX

Listen, Heavens, I have something to tell you. Attention, Earth, I've got a mouth full of words. My teaching, let it fall like a gentle rain, my words arrive like morning dew, like a sprinkling rain on new grass, like spring showers on the garden. For it's God's Name I'm preaching—respond to the greatness of our God!
Deut. 32:1-3, Message.

According to the calendar, today in the Northern Hemisphere is the first day of spring. Sometime yesterday or today, the sun stood over the equator and day and night were approximately equal in length around the world. If you live in a southern climate, it's been spring for weeks already, and your African daisies, irises, desert poppies, and ranunculuses are at optimum bloom. If you live in northern areas, as my grandparents did, today is a day of rejoicing that the snow and ice will soon recede.

Astronomers built monuments to mark this date: the Sphinx, Stonehenge, and innumerable temples. They held fertility rites and rejoiced that their crops would soon be producing fresh food. Jews mark Passover at the first full moon after the equinox, and Christians celebrate Easter on the first Sunday after Passover. It's no accident that sunrise ceremonies, rabbits, eggs, and the fertility goddess Ishtar/Ashtoreth ("Easter") are connected to the Christian celebration of Jesus' resurrection from the grave. But don't let avoiding the pagan rituals stop you from thanking and celebrating Jesus for His sacrifice and resurrection!

God put our earth on a schedule marked by the relational movements of sun, moon, planets, and stars. He set feasts and Sabbaths by the astronomical calendar. Sunlight influences our food crops, our health, and even our skin color. In the twenty-first century we are privileged to have not only the book of nature to teach us of God's love and care for us, but the Bible, which documents His redemptive works and character and the cumulative research and wisdom of His servants, ministers, and teachers. Rejoice in the newness of the season, and remember the Creator all the time.

"Look around you: Winter is over; the winter rains are over, gone! Spring flowers are in blossom all over. The whole world's a choir—and singing! Spring warblers are filling the forest with sweet arpeggios. Lilacs are exuberantly purple and perfumed, and cherry trees fragrant with blossoms" (S. of Sol. 2:11-13, Message).

CHRISTY K. ROBINSON

SAFELY HOME

How precious are your thoughts about me,
O God. They cannot be numbered! Ps. 139:17, NLT.

A friend once told me about her beloved cat, which escaped one day from the safety of her backyard. She tried to lure the cat close enough to catch it, but the cat kept its distance. It wanted to explore the neighborhood, unaware of the dangers—hungry coyotes, mean dogs, hurtling cars. My friend wished that she could explain to the cat why it was important to come home—that she had its best interests at heart.

Is that how God feels when we stray from His guidance? He knows the dangers we face and the consequences from our actions; we don't. He gave us His law with our best interests at heart, but we feel confined and want to explore outside His kingdom. How can we learn to hear His voice and return to the safety of His loving arms?

We can begin by studying His Word. Scriptural knowledge brings enlightenment.

"The unfolding of your words gives light; it gives understanding to the simple" (Ps. 119:130, NIV).

We can also learn to hear God speak by allowing time to listen to His Spirit.

"Listen for God's voice in everything you do, everywhere you go; he's the one who will keep you on track" (Prov. 3:6, Message).

Little by little, as we come to understand Him better, we will see His purpose more clearly until we arrive safely home.

"My son [child], if you accept my words and store up my commands within you, turning your ear to wisdom and applying your heart to understanding, and if you call out for insight and cry aloud for understanding, and if you look for it as for silver and search for it as for hidden treasure, then you will understand the fear of the Lord and find the knowledge of God. For the Lord gives wisdom, and from his mouth come knowledge and understanding" (Prov. 2:1-6, NIV).

LORELEI HERMAN CRESS

MARCH 23

GOD'S HEALING POWER

I, the Lord, am your healer. Ex. 15:26, NASB.

When I was 3 years old, tragedy struck while I was visiting a relative—a dog bit me. The right side of my face was mangled from mouth to ear. I was rushed to the hospital in unimaginable pain. As I grew older, I learned that what I had experienced was nothing short of a miracle. If the dog had bitten me a few centimeters deeper, the entire right side of my face would have been paralyzed. Our heavenly Father was there at my side.

When I was older, I married a man who wasn't a Christian. For a year and a half I tried to make our marriage work, but no matter what I did, it just got worse. I felt that I had made a mistake but was too ashamed to admit it to my family, who had advised me against marrying him. During that time I became pregnant. Although I was happy about the baby, I knew that this would mean the end of my relationship. Frightened, I prayed for guidance.

Shortly after, I had a dream: I was standing outside staring at the sky when two large airplanes and one smaller one flew overhead. As I watched, one of the large planes veered away and the remaining large plane and the small plane continued to fly together. Confused by this dream, I consulted with my father. He interpreted the dream to mean that my husband and I represented the large planes and my unborn child was the small plane. The large plane that veered away was my husband, and the two that flew together were my unborn baby and me. Not long after, that interpretation came to pass, and my child and I moved on. My heavenly Father showed me the way.

Our heavenly Father's love is evident throughout our lives. He will never desert us, and He will never stop loving us. He promised this in Deuteronomy 31:8: "The Lord himself goes before you and will be with you; he will never leave you nor forsake you. Do not be afraid; do not be discouraged" (NIV).

NORMA FLYNN

WINDOW OF HOPE

Having hope will give you courage.
You will be protected and will rest in safety. Job 11:18, NLT.

Divorce tears lives apart. Hearts are broken. Words are spoken that shouldn't be. Days seem hopeless. The lonely nights are full of unanswerable questions.

Elizabeth was in the process of getting a divorce. After living in financial security, suddenly she faced a multitude of questions. Where would she and her two daughters live? Could they afford food and gasoline? Would the girls be able to continue their Christian education? They felt very much alone.

Oh, but Jesus was still in their lives, leading and nudging in the right direction, opening the right doors and closing the wrong ones. The child support and alimony ceased after a few months, but Elizabeth found a second job. Schools arranged for loans and applied for grants. She found a repossessed mobile home and a private loan.

Walking through the mobile home for the first time, Elizabeth wondered about the fist-sized holes in the doors and what colors might be hidden under the layers of grime. Their previous homes had green lawns, tall trees, and flower-laden bushes. This small yard was sandy and weedy with a broken sprinkler system. The mobile home represented their lives—broken down, unwanted, damaged, and seemingly unfixable.

Elizabeth entered the back bedroom. A small window a few inches from the ceiling framed the perfect picture: a vibrant blue sky with a majestic mountain peak reaching for heaven. That picture gave Elizabeth hope. She realized they were not alone. God was very near, making His presence known and giving them a small window of hope. In our darkest hours, God is always willing to place His loving hand on our shoulders and gently guide us through. If we look upward, we will each find our window of hope.

"There is far more to your life than the food you put in your stomach, more to your outer appearance than the clothes you hang on your body. . . . Give your entire attention to what God is doing right now, and don't get worked up about what may or may not happen tomorrow. God will help you deal with whatever hard things come up when the time comes" (Matt. 6:25-34, Message).

This is one of God's most beautiful promises. Let it fill your day with hope!

MARILYN SENIER

ANTS AND SLUGS

Go to the ant, thou sluggard; consider her ways, and be wise.
Prov. 6:6.

Ewww. I hate slugs and snails. And I'm really sick of ants, too. I remember this verse when I'm watering my trees or cutting back morning glory vines. I memorized it in church school, probably as work-ethic indoctrination!

I grew up in Arizona, where slugs and snails were unheard of until we got bedding plants shipped from California growers. Of course, there were ants. But not in the plague proportions I see in California, where I live now. Ants drop on me from the trees, and they climb my ankles. They rarely bite, but I don't want insects on me!

After fighting ant invasions in the house, I employed an exterminator. But they don't "do" snails, so I spend about $50 a year on snail poisons (beer and salt are not the answer). The baits kill the arthropods, but those nasty things can sleep in the soil for up to five years, so wave after wave hatch out.

Solomon had a point, though, comparing critters to people. Slugs can't be bothered with industry: they are parasites that eat desirable plants and destroy seedlings. (They're also hideous, smelly, and leave slime trails.) And ants, though not known for their IQ, can move mountains by teaming (and teeming) together. When the hose water floods the tree well where they have one of their many colonies, they mobilize the army and carry the eggs and larvae to higher ground to prevent drowning and preserve their community. Their colonies aerate the soil, their workers pollinate my flowers and fruit, and they don't bite (much), so I tolerate the yard ants.

Proverbs 30:25 says that "ants—frail as they are, get plenty of food in for the winter" (Message). Solomon calls ants the wisest of the wise. He also mentions marmots, locusts, and lizards because they are small, vulnerable, leaderless, and sneaky. Ah, they have God-given strengths that make them the best little creatures they can be!

What are your weaknesses? Ask God how He can turn those weaknesses into strengths. He can turn it around. He loves to surprise us with blessings!

CHRISTY K. ROBINSON

GIVE ME THE MOON!

If God didn't hesitate to put everything on the line for us,
embracing our condition and exposing himself to the worst by sending his own Son,
is there anything else he wouldn't gladly and freely do for us?
Rom. 8:32, Message.

One-and-a-half-year-old Annika reached up into the evening sky. She stretched her little arms as high as they could possibly go. "Annika cannot touch moon," she stated with a frown. "Mama get it." The request was as matter-of-fact as if she had asked me to take a ball down from the closet shelf.

Of course, I could not simply pluck the moon out of the sky and present it to my daughter as a plaything, but there is Someone able to pour all the blessings of heaven on us.

"If God didn't hesitate to put everything on the line for us, embracing our condition and exposing himself to the worst by sending his own Son, is there anything else he wouldn't gladly and freely do for us?" (Rom. 8:32, Message).

God is willing to give, but do we ask? Luke 11:9-13 states it clearly: "Ask and you'll get; seek and you'll find; knock and the door will open. Don't bargain with God. Be direct. Ask for what you need. This is not a cat-and-mouse, hide-and-seek game we're in. If your little boy asks for a serving of fish, do you scare him with a live snake on his plate? If your little girl asks for an egg, do you trick her with a spider? As bad as you are, you wouldn't think of such a thing—you're at least decent to your own children. And don't you think the Father who conceived you in love will give the Holy Spirit when you ask him?" (Message).

What is it that you are asking God for today? Are you asking God for the moon or simply a beach ball? What is it that you need in your life more than anything else? Toys are fun, but what about things of eternal value?

Whatever we need, even something as amazing as the guidance, comfort, and power of the Holy Spirit, God will gladly give us. He doesn't play games. Don't settle for trinkets that are easily lost, broken, or stolen. Ask God for the moon!

LAURA WEST KONG

MY JOURNEY WITH GOD

Whoever drinks the water I give him will never thirst.
John 4:14, NIV.

"Stacey, God told me you have to go to Ghana!" was the outburst from our student missions director, Jodi Cahill.

I prayed about it that night and the next morning, and I was convicted to go. I had tried to go on mission trips before, but had never been successful in actually going. Before that day, my reasons revolved around helping people, not about me and God. This time was different. God made *me* His mission; I realized that God had arranged for me to go. He knew that if it was only about helping people for my emotional well-being I would've ended up feeling responsible to "save" all of them myself and I would've come back more discouraged than ever.

While in Ghana, I discovered that God makes what seems impossible possible. Preaching every day for three weeks and twice on Saturday was a lot of work—it was overwhelming. But a river of living water flowed into my dry, thirsty soul each time. By the second day I was overflowing. The Holy Spirit revived me and made me whole. My experience called for a lot of spiritual preparation, a lot of one-on-one time with God, and definitely some introspection.

I learned that God alone is the source of fulfillment. "For what is seen is temporary, but what is unseen is eternal" (2 Cor. 4:18, NIV). I tried for so long to find fulfillment on my own, but I couldn't. The things of this world, including human relationships, leave us yearning for more. Only Christ can quench one's thirst.

Take it from someone who was dying inside. Jesus said, "If you knew the gift of God and who it is that asks you for a drink, you would have asked him and he would have given you living water. . . . But whoever drinks the water I give him will never thirst" (John 4:10-14, NIV).

He's calling you to experience Him fully, whether it's through a mission trip, more of those one-on-one talks, or anything that is pressing on your heart. So what do you think? Are you thirsty? He is awaiting your response.

Stacey Gurgel

Stacey Gurgel, a La Sierra University student at the time, preached an evangelistic series in Ghana in September 2004. The Quiet Hour helped with her expenses.

A CHILD'S PERSPECTIVE

Jesus said, "Let the little children come to me, and do not hinder them, for the kingdom of heaven belongs to such as these."
Matt. 19:14, NIV.

It was Easter weekend, and the church was providing a dramatic performance of Jesus' life, death, and resurrection. We arrived late, so we were placed in the overflow room. Little did we know . . .

Because it was a theatrical performance, all the actors and actresses were dressed in apparel unique to the time Jesus was on the earth. As we walked in, my son and daughter were awestruck. They could "see" Jesus and His disciples. The moment changed me as a father. I heard my 2-year-old and 4-year-old children say (rather loudly), "Daddy, Jesus is here! Jesus is here!"

We watched the program, and as our children's imaginations were brought to life, we were actively involved in answering the questions they asked. The questions were those of a child, but they were riveting and deep. I saw their emotion as they watched Jesus beaten and hung on a cross—mistreated and murdered because of our sins.

Caleb, my 4-year-old, was troubled to the point of being in pain. He looked at me with yearning eyes, trying to make sense of what he was seeing.

And then, the moment when Jesus came from the tomb, Caleb looked up at me and smiled. His smile said it all—Jesus was alive, and Caleb was OK.

After the program, we were told that all the actors and actresses were in the changing rooms and were not available. My son and daughter had been hoping to see Jesus. They knew He was alive; they saw Him come out of the tomb, didn't they?

Suddenly, in the back of the sanctuary, we spotted the actor who had played Jesus. My son and daughter saw Him too, and they ran to get close. Of course, they were a little nervous when they were in His presence, but as Jesus picked up Caleb, I will never forget the look on my child's face. I get a tear in my eye when I think about the reality of this event in his life. Caleb was being held by his Savior, and he KNEW.

He now tells me of the dreams he has of heaven, and how "Jesus took him to Pluto." The kingdom now belongs to him.

Cordell J. Thomas

IN GOD WE TRUST—JOYFULLY

But let all those that put their trust in thee rejoice: let them ever shout for joy, because thou defendest them: let them also that love thy name be joyful in thee. Ps. 5:11.

Although times were very difficult in Holland during the occupation of the Nazi forces, my family and I committed our lives to the care of God.

There was never enough to eat in those days, but sometimes my father was able to get a little food by trading with the farmers. Thousands of people were hungry, and the day finally came when we had nothing to eat at all—not even enough to make a sandwich for my father to take on his daily search for food. That evening our family knelt and earnestly prayed for God's help. Afterward, my youngest sister announced that tomorrow we would have a big dinner!

That night a friend who was staying with us had a dream in which she saw the face of a childhood friend. The next morning she asked for some bags; then she left for the day. She walked without direction, but was impressed to go to some row houses in the nearby town. She went to the rear of the building, walked down a long hallway, and knocked on a door. She was astonished when her childhood friend, who had earlier that day been named as the regional food distribution coordinator, opened it! Her friend had received free food samples in preparation for special food drops by Allied planes over occupied Holland.

Yes, we had a big supper that night, with enough food for everyone! Our God was near us during those difficult times. There were many times throughout our years of ministry when we felt His special care.

Like many of my generation who lived through the war, we have been very careful with our finances. We never spend more than we earn, and we are faithful in our tithes and offerings. Although my wife, Esther, and I are retired now, we volunteer at the Quiet Hour whenever we can, and we have a trust and charitable gift annuity there. It's good to know that when we no longer need the income, our funds will be used to help others learn to trust fully in our Lord.

"But let all those that put their trust in thee rejoice: let them ever shout for joy, because thou defendest them: let them also that love thy name be joyful in thee" (Ps. 5:11, KJV).

Johannes Nikkels

THE LINE IS BUSY

Not everyone who says to Me, "Lord, Lord," shall enter the kingdom of heaven, but he who does the will of My Father.
Matt. 7:21, NKJV.

No one answered when I pounded on the door at 1531 Shrader in San Francisco. Did I write the address wrong? I wondered. A couple across the street offered to let me use their phone. I dialed—the line was busy. I waited—then dialed again—still busy. Twenty minutes later—busy!

I dialed the operator. "I've been trying for 20 minutes to get a call through. The line's always busy."

"Sir, I'll try for you," she offered. Seconds later she reported, "The line really is busy." She added, "Folks often talk for hours."

"Operator, I have an appointment and seem to be lost. Please clear the line so I can get the correct address." She agreed, but I noticed she was having trouble.

After 10 minutes of confusion on the lines, she chuckled. "Do you know why the line is busy? You are keeping it busy. The number you're calling is on the party line of the phone you are using."

She explained, "You must get off the line. Give me time to dial the number; then pick up the phone." I hung up. Seconds later I came back on the line, and my friend answered. I was where I was supposed to be. The problem: I'd failed to follow instructions to open the large door, walk through a hallway and out through a garden, go up a flight of stairs, and then knock on the door.

Jesus' instructions are easy to understand. He says, "If you love Me, keep My commandments" (John 14:15, NKJV). Many will be lost because they fail to truly love. I've wondered why my prayers don't seem to reach heaven. Then I realize that it's me—self, selfishness, sin—that keeps the line busy between me and heaven. The wise man had it right when he wrote, "One who turns away his ear from hearing the law, even his prayer shall be an abomination" (Prov. 28:9, NKJV).

Jesus says, "Not everyone who says to Me, 'Lord, Lord,' shall enter the kingdom of heaven, but he who does the will of My Father" (Matt. 7:21, NKJV).

WELLESLEY MUIR

THE HAPPY HORMONES

*God's Spirit makes us loving, happy, peaceful, patient,
kind, good, faithful, gentle, and self-controlled.
Gal. 5:22, 23, CEV.*

Feel-good drugs are almost irresistible. From cocaine to caffeine Americans are reaching more and more for something that can help ease the numbing stress and paralyzing pressures that make up so much of modern life. But evidence is mounting that these drugs are destructive, and scientists are discovering that a healthy body can make its own "feel-good" substances that are both protective and health-promoting.

Years ago, Dr. Hans Selye found that fear or anger could trigger a blast of adrenaline in the body. The extra adrenaline produced a surge of energy that enabled the person either to fight or to flee the source of danger.

Research later demonstrated that fear and anger can harm the body if continued over long periods of time. Other negative emotions such as grief, hatred, bitterness, and resentment, if prolonged, can also exhaust emergency mechanisms and weaken the body's defenses against disease.

Norman Cousins opened the door to the new field of psychoneuroimmunology when he was healed from a fatal, hopeless disease by using such positive emotions as joy, laughter, love, gratitude, and faith—along with sensible health practices. Since then scientists have isolated many of the substances these emotions produce in the brain. They are endorphins, morphine-like substances that produce wonderful feelings of well-being. They also promote healing and strengthen the immune system.

These ideas aren't new. The Bible warns us of the consequences of sexual immorality, impurity, debauchery, idolatry, witchcraft, jealousy, hatred, discord, fits of rage, selfish ambition, dissentions, factions, envy, drunkenness, orgies, and the like. We are pointed to better things: love, joy, peace, patience, kindness, goodness, faithfulness, gentleness, and self-control (Gal. 5:19-23, NIV).

Not only are God's "medicines" health-giving, but there is an eternal payoff!

AILEEN LUDINGTON

APRIL FOOL'S DAY

Become wise by walking with the wise;
hang out with fools and watch your life fall to pieces.
Prov. 13:20, Message.

April Fool's Day is a holiday of uncertain origin known for practical joking. Prior to the adoption of the Gregorian calendar in 1564, the date was observed as New Year's Day by various people groups, from Romans to Hindus. The holiday is related to the festival of the vernal equinox, which occurs on March 21 in the Northern Hemisphere

Pranks will be carried out today. Some radio deejay will be fired for perpetrating a hoax or calling out emergency services unnecessarily.

If God didn't love humor, would He have created the okapi (a giraffe/zebra-looking animal)? baboons? platypuses? parrots? It's good for the body and spirit to enjoy a joke, providing it's not at the expense of hurt feelings.

My choice for funniest Bible verse is this: "Now Moses was a very humble man, more humble than anyone else on the face of the earth" (Num. 12:3, NIV). Really? On the entire planet? Did Moses write that of himself, or did an editor insert that?

Paul mentored young Timothy, explaining how rough the Christian life can be because of hoaxes and deceptions. "Anyone who wants to live all out for Christ is in for a lot of trouble; there's no getting around it. Unscrupulous con men will continue to exploit the faith. They're as deceived as the people they lead astray. As long as they are out there, things can only get worse. But don't let it faze you. Stick with what you learned and believed, sure of the integrity of your teachers—why, you took in the sacred Scriptures with your mother's milk! There's nothing like the written Word of God for showing you the way to salvation through faith in Christ Jesus. Every part of Scripture is God-breathed and useful one way or another—showing us truth, exposing our rebellion, correcting our mistakes, training us to live God's way. Through the Word we are put together and shaped up for the tasks God has for us" (2 Tim. 3:12-17, Message).

So be wary of Satan's traps today. Be alert for the tricks of your friends and family. And before you step out the door, open your Bible and ingest some wisdom on Christian living, perhaps from Proverbs. Solomon had much to say about fools!

CHRISTY K. ROBINSON

WHY ME?

O Lord, God of our fathers Abraham, Isaac and Israel,
keep this desire in the hearts of your people forever, and keep their hearts loyal to you.
1 Chron. 29:18, NIV.

Easter is a celebration of Jesus' death and resurrection. Every year as the season draws near, I find myself reflecting on a friend's betrayal that has left a lifelong wound on my soul. It was a trusted person who took advantage of my openness and vulnerability, then added many lies to cover up his tracks. Like Judas, who sat and slowly ate the morsel dipped in bitter herbs that Jesus handed him to alert him that He knew what Judas was up to (John 13:26), my friend faked loyalty while stabbing me in the back. If you've ever had that experience, you know somewhat how Jesus must have felt when a trusted follower failed to be truthful and real.

In a song titled "Why?" Michael Card has brilliantly captured the anguish and agony of betrayal, especially in his words that only a friend can betray a friend, and only a friend can cause real pain. A stranger just doesn't have that power over us.

In the midst of some deep feelings of pain and hurt from that betrayal, I learned that even though God is not the source of it, He often uses the experience to test us. Since then, Easter has been transformed into a season that brings out several important life lessons. Betrayal brings out the quality of our personal relationship with Christ, rooted in splendor and intimately acquainted with the depth of His love. It can challenge us to seek and find the awesome presence of God and cause us to develop a passion for Christ never before encountered. It can propel us into a quest for wholeness that begins with a careful examination of our own life with Christ.

"O Lord, God of our fathers Abraham, Isaac and Israel, keep this desire in the hearts of your people forever, and keep their hearts loyal to you" (1 Chron. 29:18, NIV).

So next time you are confronted with the dastardly deeds of a traitor, instead of asking "Why me?" praise God and say, "Thanks for the lessons. They make me a better person in Christ!"

HYVETH B. WILLIAMS

THEY ARE MY PEOPLE

They will call on my name and I will answer them; I will say, "They are my people," and they will say, "The Lord is our God."
Zech. 13:9, NIV.

The house swayed slightly on its 10-foot posts. Muffled voices from the stairwell and a sudden light from another room filtered through the fog of sleep.

They're early this morning, I thought, groggily assuming a missionary pilot had stopped by to take us to the airport so we could continue preparing the plane for its flight to the United States.

From beneath the mosquito net I could see a dark form looking through my computer bag in the living room. "Where is the money? We don't want trouble!" came a growl from a bedroom down the hall. A shot of adrenaline eliminated the 4:00 a.m. haze. We were being robbed!

"Dear Jesus, we are Yours, and everything here is Yours! You are the only one who can protect us!" I silently prayed as a large man held a gun to my head while an accomplice picked through my personal belongings. "Turn over and put the pillow over your head," the intruder commanded. "Poor man's silencer," I mused, feeling the barrel through the pillow.

They were gone as suddenly as they had come. Taking inventory, our hearts sank. Cash, credit cards, pilot and mechanic licenses, aircraft registration numbers, cameras, watches, and, most devastatingly, the computer bag containing our satellite phone, aircraft documents, and several thousand dollars for the flight from South America—all gone.

As dawn approached, one of our team ventured out to determine how the bandits had scaled the wall. In the yard sat the computer bag—contents intact!

The Lord promises, "This third I will bring into the fire; I will refine them like silver and test them like gold. They will call on my name and I will answer them; I will say, 'They are my people,' and they will say, 'The Lord is our God' " (Zech. 13:9, NIV).

I imagine God dispatching a big angel saying, "That's enough!" just as the bandits escaped over the wall. The Lord said of my family and me, "These are My people!" and trust me, I am so very glad that He is my God!

Don Starlin

APRIL 4

TAINTED BLOOD, SAVING BLOOD

The blood of Jesus, his Son, purifies us from all sin. 1 John 1:7, NIV.

Olympic athletes have been disqualified or lost medals because of "tainted" blood from performance-enhancing drugs. They went from being heroes to personal and national disgraces. Tainted blood has killed entire herds of livestock. It has greatly affected human society by carrying epidemic disease. When diphtheria had killed thousands in France, Louis Pasteur experimented with 20 horses with diphtheria. Only one lived, and then they killed it and used its blood serum to save 297 babies who would otherwise have died.

There is a far more serious disease that infects every human being ever born—the disease of sin. Sin can only be cured with the blood of a lamb! You and I are born tainted.

Yet there is a remedy, and it is found in the blood of one perfect Lamb—a Lamb that overcame the deadly infection of sin. Hebrews 10:4 declares, "It is not possible that the blood of bulls and goats could take away sins" (NKJV). One chapter earlier Hebrews 9:14 says, "How much more shall the blood of Christ, who through the eternal Spirit offered Himself without spot to God, cleanse your conscience from dead works to serve the living God?" (NKJV).

Jesus Christ is the Lamb of God who takes away the sin of the world. Jesus never succumbed to the taint of evil. He died so that His pure blood could save us from sin. In accepting Him as Savior and Lord, we have the assurance of complete cleansing through His precious blood. Praise God!

First John 1:7, 9 says, "But if we walk in the light, as he is in the light, we have fellowship with one another, and the blood of Jesus, his Son, purifies us from all sin. . . . If we confess our sins, he is faithful and just to forgive us our sins and purify us from all unrighteousness" (NIV).

Rather than suffering the disgrace of the tainted blood of sinfulness, we can live in the assurance that Jesus' pure blood can cleanse us from all sin. We have only to accept it and let it wash the darkness from our hearts, lifting us into His glorious light.

BILL TUCKER

SURROUND SOUND

Yes, because God's your refuge, the High God your very own home, evil can't get close to you, harm can't get through the door.
Ps. 91:9, 10, Message.

While waiting for the clerk to get your $300 TV and $275 CD/DVD player from the warehouse, you wander by a cubicle. Inside are two luxurious black leather chairs facing a large screen. They look wonderfully comfy. The enormous television's sound, color, and resolution are perfect.

You slip into the vacant chair. Sighing a bit, you relax into its arms. You are in a different environment. The scenes on the screen seem to involve you, and the surround sound comes from every direction, maybe even from under your chair!

Leaving the cubicle, you remember your new 27-inch TV and CD/DVD player with surround sound. Will it sound like the one you just experienced? That remains to be seen. At home you read the manuals and lay out the cables and parts across the floor. Two hours later you are relaxing in the comfort of your own chair, watching elephants thunder across the Serengeti Plain. The elephants seem to roar past you, but you're safe in your family room. (The experience is perhaps not as intense as the $6,000-plus setup at the store, but you are content.)

Surround sound gives you the opportunity to feel as if you are part of the action without being in danger. However, you can't stay inside all the time, and your four walls won't protect you from everything. God is our protector in safe and dangerous circumstances. He surrounds us with eternal protection.

"That's right—he rescues you from hidden traps, shields you from deadly hazards. His huge outstretched arms protect you—under them you're perfectly safe; his arms fend off all harm. . . . 'If you'll hold on to me for dear life,' says God, 'I'll get you out of any trouble. I'll give you the best of care if you'll only get to know and trust me. Call me and I'll answer, be at your side in bad times; I'll rescue you, then throw you a party. I'll give you a long life, give you a long drink of salvation!' " (Ps. 91:3-16, Message).

Take a moment to read Psalm 91, and find peace in the knowledge that God and His angels will surround you with protection from the evil that inhabits this earth. Hold on to Him for dear life, and He will give you salvation.

Marilyn Senier

TASTE AND SEE

Oh, taste and see that the Lord is good; blessed is the man who trusts in Him! Ps. 34:8, NKJV.

Five-month-old Annika watched intently as the people brought forks and spoons up to their mouths. Her lips moved in unison with theirs as they chewed their food. I knew then that she was no longer content just being a spectator at mealtimes.

The next day Annika had her very own bowl of infant rice cereal at the dinner table. She gleefully clutched her little spoon and brought the "num-nums" up to her mouth. When the spoon was licked clean, she gave it right back to me for a refill. Joy shone in Annika's eyes as she shared her first meal at the table with family and friends.

During the next few months, Annika added a variety of fruits and vegetables to her repertoire. Mashed bananas, apricots, applesauce, strained green beans, carrots, potatoes—all were tackled with great eagerness. And when she was sick, she greeted medicine droppers full of strange-tasting liquids with mouth opened wide. Whatever was on the menu Annika accepted with enthusiasm.

God has a menu for each of our lives, a menu created for us to enjoy and to help us prosper and grow. We can embrace that menu with hearts wide open or turn our heads away in doubt.

I hope that as Annika grows older she will continue to enjoy meals of healthy and delicious food. Even more, I pray that she will delight in the menu that God has prepared for her life.

"Oh, taste and see that the Lord is good; blessed is the man who trusts in Him!" (Ps. 34:8, NKJV).

Laura West Kong

WHAT'S IN A NAME?

I've called your name. You're mine. Isa. 43:1, Message.

I like my name. My parents took care to give it meaning. My first name, Christy, means "anointed for royal service," and it refers of course to Christ and Christians. My middle name, Kay, means "rejoicing." They wanted me to live up to my name, "Christ-follower, rejoicing." We Occidentals think of names as decorative identity labels, but the ancient Hebrew culture considered names as substantive—prophecies. Abraham, Sarah, Isaac, Samson, Samuel, Jesus (Yeshua), John, and many others were named by God, and the Scripture writers were careful to note why they received their names and how they lived up to them. At coming-of-age ceremonies around the world children have been renamed with a view toward their personality, their future, or a worthy accomplishment.

When we pray "in Jesus' name," we're not adding magical code words that will get our prayer answered. Hopefully we don't use the phrase to close a prayer the way we'd use "sincerely" or "the end." Rather, we're saying that we are confident that the thing we have just prayed about is going to be answered because we and God are tuned to the same wavelength. When we baptize in the name of the Father, Son, and Holy Spirit, we lose our old, sinful identity and take on the name—character—of God.

A name, to some cultures, and certainly the culture of the Bible writers, equaled character. Character is who you are when nobody is looking. God was specific about the use of His name (character) in the Exodus 20 commandment.

To assign a name was a privilege and an act of intimacy, expressing ownership or commitment to the future of the named. Isaiah 49:15, 16 says, "I will not forget you! See, I have engraved you on the palms of my hands" (NIV). Those nail-scarred hands of Jesus were engraved for me.

"You will be called by a new name that the mouth of the Lord will bestow" (Isa. 62:2, NIV).

God will give us new names in His kingdom. What do you want yours to be? Are you living up to it?

Christy K. Robinson

FROM A FAR-OFF LAND

My purpose will stand, and I will do all that I please.
Isa. 46:10, NIV.

I went to preach because God called me. I can see that for every step of mine, the Lord, my leader, has matched it. Before I went to my assigned church, I asked God to give me one little room to spend time with people. When I arrived, the elder said to me, "This little room is for you." Before sermon, I spent time with persons (one after one) with spiritual or health problems. This was encouraging for me. When I shook hands with everybody at the end of meetings, they said to me, "Thank you so much!"

For our group from Romania was one blessing because we had good time. We prayed together, we visited some beautiful places. We decided to prepare a meal for hotel leaders, and spent a few hours with them. We sang for them, and told important things about life.

Before the evangelism meetings, I felt that I needed to spend more time with God. So I found a room and spent three hours in prayer (was like short time). I ask: "Lord, give me one big experience with You, for Your glory. I need more by You." In that day was begun my dream to do much more for my Lord. He prepared every person in the time, for this plan with me. I praise our Lord!

My motto is "spend time with God," and my favorite verse from Bible is Isaiah 46:10, 11: "I make known the end from the beginning, from ancient times, what is still to come. I say: My purpose will stand, and I will do all that I please. From the east I summon a bird of prey; from a far-off land, a man to fulfill my purpose. What I have said, that will I bring about; what I have planned, that will I do" (NIV).

Today and every day I will fulfill God's purpose.

IVAN ELA

Ivan Ela, a ministerial student at the Theological Institute of Bucharest, preached a Quiet Hour evangelism series in Madagascar. His Romanian idioms and rhythms remain in this devotional piece.

FAKING IT!

Where I go, you cannot follow Me now; but you will follow later.
John 13:36, NASB.

There's a television program on the BBC-America channel called *Faking It*. The producers take ordinary men and women—farmers, servers, the homeless, or unemployed—and train them to pose as a member of Parliament, a university professor, scientist, movie star, and any other profession they choose. The faker must work with authentic members of that profession for a week and convince them that they are for real. If they are not detected by the end of the week, they receive large sums of money.

Some of us Christians would do very well on that program without much preparation because we are already experts at faking! We live comfortably and incognito under a veneer of holiness. We counterfeit spirituality by acting as if we love one another. Some mature members of our faith remember a time they faked a closer walk with Christ than they really had. We are all adept at making others believe we love Jesus with heart, soul, mind, and body while pretending to keep His commandments.

During those times we look so pious and prayerful, not even the best FBI (faithful Bible investigator) or CIA (committed inspired associate) agents or the most spiritually discerning person can detect that we are faking it. There are passages in John 13 and 14 that expose pretentious practices and provide opportunity for us to determine whether or not we are in an authentic relationship with God.

Jesus told Peter, "Where I go, you cannot follow Me now; but you will follow later" (John 13:36, NASB). Essentially, Jesus was saying that as long as we continue to fake our fellowship with Jesus, we cannot face the challenges of the taking up of our cross and following Him. However, when we are truly converted, as Peter became after the resurrection, we will be able to face the tests and difficulties with courage and leave a lasting testimony of faith.

We can all fake it! Sometimes life experiences press us into playing that role, but as you come closer to Jesus during this Easter and Pentecost season, reflect on the sacrifice that Jesus made to free us from the sin of pretentiousness.

HYVETH B. WILLIAMS

RAGGEDY PUPPY

You see, at just the right time, when we were still powerless, Christ died for the ungodly. Rom. 5:6, NIV.

Our 4-year-old grandson, Conner, had a favorite stuffed toy. It was a little floppy-eared rag doll that went with him everywhere. We called him "Puppy." Puppy lost most of his hair and had most of his cotton fleece "loved off." All kinds of kisses and hugs got mixed up together with little Puppy. His joints are now loose. There are times he has had the stuffing knocked out of him. Puppy is not a particularly attractive rag doll. But was he ever loved by Conner!

Conner's parents were visiting some friends. On the way home, when they were 75 miles down the road, they realized that Puppy was not with them. There was no question as to their options: Turn the car around and head back to recover Puppy. (They are a devoted family!)

There are two truths about this story that matter deeply. All of us are like Puppy—broken, bent, flawed, wounded, and in need of repair. We are all rag dolls. Like a splash of ink in a glass of water, this raggedness permeates our whole being. Our words, our thoughts, our actions, are never entirely free of it.

But we are God's rag dolls. He knows all about our raggedness, and He loves us anyhow. Our raggedness is no longer the most important thing about us. We were not created ragged. Raggedness is not our identity. Raggedness is not your destiny, nor is it mine. We may be unlovely, but we are not unloved!

Paul put it this way: "You see, at just the right time, when we were still powerless, Christ died for the ungodly. Very rarely will anyone die for a righteous man, though for a good man someone might possibly dare to die. But God demonstrates his own love for us in this: While we were still sinners, Christ died for us" (Rom. 5:6-8, NIV).

There is a love that turns one's raggedness into priceless treasure. There is a love that fastens itself onto ragged little creatures, for reasons that no one could ever quite figure out, and makes them precious and valued beyond calculation. This is the love of God. This is the love with which God loves you and me.

Joedy and Judy Melashenko

SPREADING THE GOOD NEWS

Go into all the world and preach the good news to all creation.
Mark 16:15, NIV.

I, like most of you, have long been anticipating the windup of this old world and our Lord's imminent return. Born into the Adventist Christ-is-coming-soon faith and nurtured on Scripture and prophecy, I've been mentally tabulating the end-time events marching across the world scene. As I saw increasingly large areas of the world shut themselves off from freedom and from God, it made perfect sense. Probation was closing! Life as we knew it would soon be over!

But it didn't happen that way. God has much more in mind for this world than we have ever dreamed.

"Look a little higher," an angel urged a Christian author. I believe God is saying the same thing to us today. It's like we've been standing on a hill, looking around, convinced we are seeing the whole picture.

But God brings us up onto a mountaintop, giving us a panoramic view of a dramatically changing world. Closed doors are now opening faster than the media can report them. Communication's long fingers reach the most remote areas of our world. Major news events can now blanket our planet in an instant.

God is setting the stage on a far larger scale than we as humans could have imagined. And around the world, the hunger for hope and truth and the thirst for God are swelling into a mighty tidal wave. Hearts are open, and the message is going farther and faster than ever before. No longer do people doubt that Christ's parting words, "Go into all the world and preach the good news to all creation" (Mark 16:15, NIV), will be fulfilled—God's people will reach the farthest corners of the globe.

Are you helping? Or are you watching it all happen on TV?

Aileen Ludington

April 12

THE WARRIOR'S PURSUIT

Pray for those who persecute you. Matt. 5:44, NIV.

"If they are calling on their God against us, though they bear no arms, they still fight us by pursuing us with hostile prayers," declared Aethelfrith (who died in A.D. 616), referring to Celtic Christian monks.

I've heard of prayer warriors, but this beats all! Would the "hostile" prayers be for curses to be rained down on the bad guys? Or for the enemy's hard hearts to be softened and turned to the Lord, thus bringing compassion and mercy back to the pray-ers? Christ tells His followers to pray for those who persecute us, to forgive them, and to sacrifice our own comfort to assist them.

Who's the first person that comes to mind when you think of an enemy? Man or woman, let's call that person Aethelfrith for now. That enemy destroyed something or someone you loved, or stole what was rightfully yours. Aethelfrith has, perhaps, pursued and hounded you, invaded your boundaries, or usurped leadership. Aethelfrith does not share your values, nor has he any notion of asking your forgiveness or making restitution, much less reconciliation.

So what do you do about Aethelfrith? Ignore him and hope he goes away? Take up weapons? Retaliate by invading his territory? Submit passively to his patently un-Christian authority and terrorist tactics? Burn with resentment?

The answer comes from an event 1,400 years ago. The Celtic Christians of northwestern Britain and Wales had been burned out, raped, pillaged, terrorized, and invaded by the pagan Anglo-Saxon King Aethelfrith. By Aethelfrith's testimony, they pursued him with "hostile" prayers, calling on the Lord of hosts to fight for them. Aethelfrith was killed in battle shortly afterward, and his immediate successors converted to Christianity, founding York Minster, monasteries, and Christian education all over the north of England.

So what will the Lord of hosts do when you pursue your Aethelfrith with "hostile" prayer? Regardless of the outcome of the situation, Jesus has already won the war at the cross, and He is just and merciful. If you ally with Him, you share in His victory.

"Love your enemies. Let them bring out the best in you, not the worst. When someone gives you a hard time, respond with the energies of prayer, for then you are working out of your true selves, your God-created selves" (Matt. 5:44, 45, Message).

Christy K. Robinson

UP!

Unto thee, O Lord, do I lift up my soul. Ps. 25:1.

One of Annika's very first words was "up." She uses it in a variety of situations. Annika raises her arms and says "up" to play a game in which I lift her up into the air and down again as she grins from ear to ear. Upon reaching the ground, she immediately says "up," to be lifted up again. This continues until my arms wear out and we have to find a new activity. She says "up" while she's climbing the stairs, "up" while she lifts up the towel rack, and "up" when she wants to be picked up and carried around or held.

Annika never seems to tire of playing the "up" game, climbing the stairs, or finding new things to lift up, whether it be a suitcase handle or a light switch. And at the end of a long, busy day, there is no better place to be than up in Daddy's or Mommy's arms.

King David knew the value of keeping his focus up. He started his day focusing up: "My voice shalt thou hear in the morning, O Lord; in the morning will I direct my prayer unto thee, and will look up" (Ps. 5:3).

And he looked up to God for help and deliverance: "But I am poor and sorrowful: let thy salvation, O God, set me up on high" (Ps. 69:29).

"Up" is a focus that we all would do well to adopt. An "up" focus never tires of looking up to God. As well as starting the day by looking up to God, an "up" focus includes turning to God in both joy and sadness, and it includes ending the day looking up to God. And the best part is that God's arms never get worn out from lifting us up!

An "up" focus is not simply keeping your head in the spiritual clouds, ignoring those around you; it means always finding new ways to lift people up, to brighten their lives and to bring them closer to God.

Keep on looking up! Look up until Jesus comes again.

Laura West Kong

WHAT SHALL I DO?

Whoever desires, let him take the water of life freely.
Rev. 22:17, NKJV.

My friend Henry was a passenger on an old DC–3 that was flying over the mountains of Mexico, headed for a lovely tropical city. The plane descended over the runway. Seconds before touchdown the pilot applied full power and took off again.

The plane climbed, circled, and approached the airport a second time. Instead of bringing the plane in for a landing, the pilot revved the engines, taking off again. When this happened a third time, my friend and 39 other passengers were frantic. Why aren't we landing?

An announcement from the cockpit increased their worst fears. "All the hydraulic fluid has leaked out of the cylinders that operate our landing gear. The wheels won't come down!" Hydraulic fluid—oil!

A desperate pilot conversed with the control tower. "Our fuel supply is running low. We can't stay in the air much longer!"

The tower responded: "We don't want you to try a belly landing. You'll tear the plane up and possibly kill your passengers. We have a mechanic here. Listen to him and do exactly what he says."

"Go ahead!" the pilot shouted.

The mechanic's calm voice gave assurance. "This is not what we usually recommend, but it could save your life. Collect all the water you have on board. Drinking water, water from the bathroom, water anyone has in a thermos—pour it in the hydraulic cylinders."

The steward found volunteers to collect water while the pilot remained at the controls. They filled the empty cylinders with water. The plane came down over the runway. The pilot pushed the landing gear control. The wheels went down. Henry bowed his head, "Thank You, Lord, for using water to save our lives." Both engines died before the plane reached the terminal—all the fuel was gone.

Water! Water can save your life too. " 'Come!' And let him who thirsts come. Whoever desires, let him take the water of life freely" (Rev. 22:17, NKJV). Jesus is the water of life!

Wellesley Muir

DEADLINES, DEADLINES

I have been crucified with Christ and I no longer live, but Christ lives in me. Gal. 2:20, NIV.

Not only in the United States but in other countries as well we have reached the deadline for filing last year's income tax information with the government. Some stayed up for hours last night, and some will join the lengthy lines at the post office before midnight tonight to obtain the postal cancellation that keeps us from being fined or prosecuted. Some did those convoluted, mazelike forms weeks ago and can smile indulgently at procrastinators.

I've always figured my own tax forms, groaned through the depreciation schedule, and documented every line on the profit/loss statement. Sometimes I had to insert a fictional number (like an n in algebra) to get a preliminary number to put on another form, to finish that section in order to come up with the correct n and then fix the first form! What devious mind invented that? In the years that I've expected a refund of overpaid taxes, I've done the forms early. In the years I have to pay additionally, I'm the procrastinator—I just don't want to think about the "damages."

Have you ever thought of the end of the world like that? Have you searched the Scriptures to find exact historical markers so that you can live as you like until the very last sign is fulfilled, before you fearfully meet God's deadline for hellfire insurance? Or have you searched the Scriptures for signs that God wants your heart (faith) and hands (actions) right now, submitted wholly to Him?

Your debts were paid at the cross of Jesus. "Tetelestai!" cried Jesus as He died. "It is paid in full!" No need to procrastinate—accept salvation now, and accept it again and again. No need to fill out a form. Just say, "Lord, I am a sinner. I have offended You, and I am sorry. I accept Your gift of complete forgiveness and unconditional love, and ask You to be Master of everything I think and do, from this moment on."

"I have been crucified with Christ and I no longer live, but Christ lives in me. The life I live in the body, I live by faith in the Son of God, who loved me and gave himself for me" (Gal. 2:20, NIV).

Christy K. Robinson

April 16

SPRINGTIME IN HEAVEN

The fruit of the Spirit is love, joy, peace, patience, kindness, goodness, faithfulness, gentleness and self-control. Gal. 5:22, 23, NIV.

Happy April to you! By now you should be done with the agony of tax preparation and settled into a beautiful spring. My garden is blooming and fruiting, and I hope that your garden or potted-plant window is also responding to the sunshine and nutrients. I practically hop around the backyard for joy that my peach and almond trees are setting their green fruits and that the mulberries are putting on leaves and the beginnings of tiny berries. I nearly lose control when I see the microscopic buds that will become seedless grapes!

When I see the baby fruits growing on the trees and vines, I think of Galatians 5:22, 23: "The fruit of the Spirit is love, joy, peace, patience, kindness, goodness, faithfulness, gentleness and self-control" (NIV).

Is the Master Gardener also rejoicing over the fruits that His garden is producing? Is He pointing to you proudly and joyfully, and saying, "Today, My child, [insert your name here], sprouted the fruits of gentleness and peace"? Is He rejoicing over you with singing?

Rather than anthropomorphizing God, making Him into a human image, let's imagine that as we are His children and have inherited His characteristics by both birth and adoption, that we can project our emotions back to our Creator and Father. I really can envision God becoming excited over the growth of His children's godly characteristics.

We see the fruit of the Spirit in each other as we corporately and individually experience spiritual growth. And we're pretty excited about growth of another kind: growth of the family of God. Evangelism teams, supported by your contributions and God's grace, teach thousands of people around the world each year. Hundreds are baptized, but untold thousands have found the love of God so compelling that they've given their lives unreservedly to Jesus and allowed Him to change them, producing more flowers and fruits for the Gardener.

Take a walk in the Lord's garden. Let Him cultivate a garden of fruit in your spirit. It's springtime in heaven, too!

Christy K. Robinson

GOD'S INVISIBLE LOCKPICK

You will have complete and free access to God's kingdom, keys to open any and every door. Matt. 16:19, Message.

Larry, a truck driver for many years and a backslidden Christian, made his way one Friday to the Quiet Hour office. Normally the front door is locked on that day because of our four-day work schedule, but the door was (accidentally and providentially) unlocked. As he entered and said, "Anybody here?" our vice president was working there and heard his voice. She didn't know what this long-haired man's intentions might be, but he indicated that he had wanted to visit the Quiet Hour's headquarters because its ministry had made a profound impact on his life.

For more than an hour Marilyn and Larry discussed his renewed faith and conviction to come back to the Lord. She invited Larry to visit the Adventist church a few hundred yards away, where I am an associate pastor in addition to my duties at the Quiet Hour.

Over the next several days I studied the Bible and prayed with Larry. He had a strong desire to renew his commitment with Jesus and seal it with baptism. He enthusiastically told me about a few experiences in which he shared Christ's love with people whom God had placed in his way, giving them a word of encouragement and directing them to a relationship with Jesus. It was thrilling to hear this man bubbling over at his newfound treasure. Larry was experiencing that "first love" Jesus speaks of in Revelation 2. (Jesus goes on to say that for the one who reclaims that fresh love of God and embraces repentance, "To him who overcomes, I will give the right to eat from the tree of life, which is in the paradise of God" [Rev. 2:7, NIV].)

It was a high and holy day for Larry and his friends and family who came from all over southern California to witness his rebaptism. Larry's accidental big splash from the slippery steps didn't detract from the moment that Larry and I shared in the baptismal waters. As he rose to his new life in the Lord, his joy registered from ear to ear, and the congregation broke into spontaneous applause and praise to God for what they had witnessed.

Now, who unlocked that door?

BILL TUCKER

HOLOCAUST REMEMBRANCE

He anointed us, set his seal of ownership on us,
and put his Spirit in our hearts as a deposit, guaranteeing what is to come.
2 Cor. 1:21, 22, NIV.

Holocaust Remembrance is celebrated this month in thoughtful commemoration of a very dark period in human existence: the 1930s and 1940s saw the obliteration of more than 13 million people, 6 million of them European Jews.

We live in a frightening, blood-soaked, war-crazed world, even now, decades after the Holocaust. It's one thing to read the news of war and genocide in another hemisphere or era; it's another to realize that there's warfare all around us. Police officers and children are shot to death because of drug trafficking or domestic violence; pension funds are lost because of callous greed. Dare we say that we're living in a spiritual Holocaust now? The flames feel pretty hot, don't they?

In 2 Corinthians 1:20-22 God "anointed us, set his seal of ownership on us, and put his Spirit in our hearts as a deposit, guaranteeing what is to come" (NIV). The Holy Spirit guarantees our salvation and the protection of our souls. The seal of God is the Holy Spirit Himself!

At the Quiet Hour we pray every day for requests that come in about family problems, relief from pain and sickness, that people will get a job or victory over addictions, or that they will discover God's will for their lives. There are battles going on all the time. We don't have divine promises that we'll have miraculous deliverance from these temporal pains and struggles. *But Jesus has won the war.* He loves us so much that He voluntarily laid down His life for our salvation. He came to live in our skin, and paid the death penalty of sin so that we could have an infinity of forevers, living with Him. We live this life with hope of eternal salvation because Jesus rose from His tomb, triumphant and victorious over sin and its effects.

So while we soberly remember the Holocaust and vow that its evils should never be repeated, we must remember that we are living—right now—in the spiritual kingdom of God, as citizens. Our Savior has promised that one day soon He will return and personally wipe away our tears. We will spend eternity with Him in perfect peace and joy.

Christy K. Robinson

IN GOD'S IMAGE

Let us make human beings in our image, make them reflecting our nature. Gen. 1:26, Message.

It was time to give my kitchen an "extreme makeover." The walls needed fresh paint, the cupboards needed a new look, and a little wallpaper would add just the right touch. It would not be an easy task, but after watching a number of decorating and home improvement programs on television, I had a basic understanding of the tools, equipment, and supplies I would need. I wanted the finished product to be warm and inviting.

Taking down the cupboard doors and removing the hardware was not too difficult. But the process of washing and sanding to create the right surface for the new, fresh, sunflower-yellow paint was more challenging. During this process I asked God for the strength to complete the project and to be proud of my accomplishments.

Gradually I saw progress, and soon it was time for the beautiful yellow paint. After two coats had been applied, the discouragement began again. I criticized my painting ability. As much as I tried to create the picture-perfect paint job, I still saw flaws.

I replaced the hinges and new handles and then reinstalled the cupboard doors and replaced the drawers. After I cleaned up the paint splatters and the brushes and put away the supplies, I noticed that it was beginning to take on the appearance that I had envisioned—except for the flaws that I could see. Then I invited my family to see my handiwork.

Their only comments were "Wow, Mom! This is great!" I began to apologize for the flaws and imperfections, but they couldn't see them. They saw only the whole picture—a picture of warmth and love, a reflection of my making, my creativity.

Sometimes I need to have an "extreme makeover" of the spirit. Yet even that makeover will still have some flaws. But Christ, my Creator, sees only the whole picture, not the flaws. His view of me is a picture of warmth and love.

Genesis 1:26 tells us, "Then God said, 'Let us make man in our image, in our likeness'" (NIV). And when God finished, He said, "It is good."

Charlene Hilliard West

THE FALL OF GIANTS

Though he was tall as the cedars and strong as the oaks, I destroyed his fruit above and his roots below. Amos 2:9, NIV.

One of California's more celebrated natural attractions is Sequoia National Park. In some ways, these huge cypresses outshine even their cousins in the magnificent redwood forests. Visitors always gravitate to the General Sherman Tree. Standing 275 feet tall and measuring 30 feet in diameter, it is surrounded by a grove of only slightly less ancient sequoias. The forest rangers tend it and its nearby elderly companions as the venerable gentlemen that they are. Standing in the presence of the oldest living thing on earth, even the most flippant tourist must feel awe. Indeed, the general was 500 years old when Jesus was born.

Wearing a coat of bark as much as two feet thick, a giant sequoia is impervious to brush fires. Immune to disease, it grows, reproduces, and lives. This tree, however, has one fatal flaw. The prophet Amos describes the problem: "Though he was tall as the cedars and strong as the oaks, I destroyed his fruit above and his roots below" (Amos 2:9, NIV).

Unfortunately, while the general's roots spread out over an acre of land, they lie no more than five feet deep in the ground. For 2,500 years it has done a delicate balancing act. Too much wind or heavy snow in its top branches could easily bring it down.

Jesus' parable of the handsome-but-fruitless fig tree points to the discrepancy between what is seen and what lies within and below. Sad as it may be, looking at a diseased tree is not as heart-wrenching as witnessing the fall of a giant. Consider the pastor whose influential, spiritual ministry ends in scandal. The "ideal" parents who abuse their children. The generous businessman who turns out to be corrupt. The devoted elderly couple who turn up in divorce court. The esteemed doctor who's a drug addict. The trusted friend who gossips. We've all watched the giants fall, crashing to earth with their spreading roots ignominiously turned up to the sky. Death by toppling over is the way the giants go.

Outward appearances may be what they will. We survive only by our invisible—even homely—root system. Roots that reach down and tap into the deepest wells of Christ-filled resources.

Dorothy Minchin-Comm

FACE TO FACE

I lifted him, like a baby, to my cheek, . . . I bent down to feed him."
Hosea 11:4, Message.

A church member passed away after a long battle with lung cancer. We had been only passing acquaintances in our large congregation, but we appreciated each other's ministry. Pamela Slade signed for the hearing-impaired at my church. I often watched Pamela's interpretation during the sermon or vocal solos because her movement and expression added layers of meaning to the message. Abstract concepts became concrete.

When the subject was forgiveness, Pamela would rub a slate clean. When Jesus' name was mentioned, she touched her palms to remind us of His nail-scarred hands. When love needed expression, she clasped her hands to her shoulders in an embrace. Rejoicing was a silent clap of the hands in an arc over her head. When a vocalist sang "Face to Face," and Pamela signed the lyrics, I told her after the service how blessed I was.

"Face to face shall I behold Him, far beyond the starry sky; face to face in all His glory I shall see Him by and by!" Our Occidental culture thinks of face-to-face communication as head-on, with a proper and comfortable distance between participants. Pamela upended that thought forever. As she signed the song, she touched her flat palm to her cheek and then turned her palm toward heaven and God's cheek, 13 times in four stanzas. It was better than nose to nose and eye to eye. This was cheek to cheek. Full contact. Intimate. "Cheek to cheek! Oh, blissful moment! Cheek to cheek—to see and know; cheek to cheek with my Redeemer, Jesus Christ, who loves me so."

Psalm 69:16 says, "Now answer me, God, because you love me; let me see your great mercy full-face" (Message). And God says of His people, "I lifted him, like a baby, to my cheek, . . . I bent down to feed him" (Hosea 11:4, Message).

How tenderly God loves us. He doesn't face us down, so we can be struck dead by our own sinfulness in the light of His glory. Instead, because Jesus has opened the veil of the sanctuary, we are lifted like beloved infants and cuddled, cheek to cheek. That's our Abba!

Isn't it wonderful that in the resurrection, Pamela will see her Savior face to face, even cheek to cheek, in all His glory. And so will we all.

CHRISTY K. ROBINSON

THE GREAT SHEPHERD'S ASSISTANT

For we are His workmanship, created in Christ Jesus for good works, which God prepared beforehand that we should walk in them.
Eph. 2:10, NKJV.

My family loves dogs. My mom still gets misty-eyed when I fondly recall a dog we had almost 50 years ago. It's amazing what devoted little companions they became, and though they're all gone now, my memories of those canine friends remind me to cherish our time with our family and loved ones.

After our little dog died unexpectedly, a friend asked if we could watch her border collie while she visited friends in England. Anxious for some canine company, we happily agreed.

I had never been around a border collie before, so I was delighted to get to know her. Border collies are the most intelligent of all breeds and are valuable to shepherds for their concentration and herding skills. Rachel (her name means "ewe lamb") would put her ball between her front paws, rest her muzzle on it, and give me the unblinking, focused stare that meant she wanted (no, intended) to play. That ball was the center of Rachel's purpose, her calling in life, her entire reason for living! Throw it, and you would see an impressive display of athleticism as she quickly controlled the ball and maneuvered it back toward you. Rachel's supreme joy was to have two balls thrown at once, so she could herd them back to the thrower.

God created this beautiful dog and gave her such remarkable instincts as a gift. Rachel didn't have to work to learn that skill—no one had to teach her! It's natural to a border collie. If she lived on a sheep farm instead of in a suburban home, those bred-for instincts and learned behaviors would actually preserve the lives of her flock (instead of barking madly at the doorbell, or herding toys down the hall). But whatever her circumstances, she is energetically living her life as part of a greater design: using her God-given talent to her utmost.

God has a plan for our lives, too. As Christians we're part of a grand design. "For we are His workmanship, created in Christ Jesus for good works, which God prepared beforehand that we should walk in them" (Eph. 2:10, NKJV).

ROBERT JOHNSTON

WHEN BAD PEOPLE DO GOOD THINGS

There is none that doeth good, no, not one.
Rom. 3:12.

One of life's vexing questions is why so many bad things happen to good people. We all know godly folk who eat right and live right but die young of cancer. We know dear church members who give generously and live selflessly for others until the day they are senselessly cut down by a thug. It is heartbreaking when a family member is scammed and financially ruined. We feel numb when a drunk driver walks away—unhurt—from an accident in which he or she has wiped out a half dozen other lives.

Good people work hard, take precautions, plan ahead, make careful decisions, and pray daily for God's protection and guidance. Why do so many bad things happen to them? Another question: how can really bad people do good things?

One of the amazing stories of World War II is captured in the film *Schindler's List.* Oscar Schindler was no saint. A shrewd businessman who schmoozed shamelessly with politicians, he is not the one you would expect to save Jews from Nazi extermination. But he did.

Recently I've read three books commemorating the 400th anniversary of the King James Bible. For many English-speaking Christians this is the only Bible worth reading. And its sonorous, pithy phrases have certainly enriched our language and culture.

Some of the key translators were not nice men. All but one of the nearly 50 translators were ordained. Many were brilliant scholars, gifted preachers, and very devout, spending several hours each day in prayer. They could write lyrically. Generations have been blessed by their work. But some ferociously persecuted Puritans. Others killed Catholics. Yes, there were a few sweet-natured fellows among them, but some of the best translators were crafty, shrewd, corrupt, nasty, merciless, and cruel.

"There is none righteous, no, not one: There is none that understandeth, there is none that seeketh after God. They are all gone out of the way, they are together become unprofitable; there is none that doeth good, no, not one" (Rom. 3:10-12).

How can bad people do good things? I can say only this: the fact that God could use people like this gives me hope for my church. And for myself.

Kit Watts

April 24

SUNRISE IN THE SIERRAS

The path of the righteous is like the first gleam of dawn, shining ever brighter till the full light of day. Prov. 4:18, NIV.

It had been a short night's sleep in Hawthorne, Nevada, where I'd stopped on my way south from Walla Walla, Washington. I was traveling alone, driving a rental truck, moving my daughter's household to southern California, where she would begin new employment. I had a choice of two routes that would bring me to Bishop, California. I chose the route that would take me past Mono Lake to the west and then south along the eastern slope of the Sierra Nevadas.

Daylight was just beginning to creep over the eastern hills as I pulled the truck out onto the deserted highway and headed south. As I reached the summit at the border between Nevada and California, the sun was just peeking over the horizon behind me. Ahead lay a 22-mile stretch of unbending highway headed directly toward the snow-covered mountains. The rising sun had just begun to bathe the snow in a brilliant shade of pink, in sharp contrast with deep blue sky beyond. The next few minutes caused me to reflect on the daily magnificent scenes provided by our heavenly Father.

In my wonder at this spectacular view, I couldn't help breathing a prayer of thanksgiving for the artistry of our heavenly Father in the brief moments at dawn and dusk. So often we give these scenes a quick glance and go on our way, seldom pausing to appreciate Him who provides this beauty for our enjoyment. Every sunrise and sunset is different. What love our Father shares with us, enriching our lives each day.

C. Elwyn Platner

BACK TO THE BASICS

"Tell them your story—what the Master did, how he had mercy on you." The man went back and began to preach . . . about what Jesus had done for him. He was the talk of the town. Mark 5:19, 20, Message.

A group of 48 students and adults from Upper Columbia Academy in Washington headed to the jungles of Borneo to the Malaysian village of Mentu. They were to build a church, provide medical and dental care, conduct Vacation Bible Schools for the children, and assist Pastor Mark Cox in evangelistic meetings.

The team packed their electronic equipment, prepared their PowerPoint presentations, and readied their Vacation Bible School supplies. Upon arrival, the health professionals organized their clinics. The children's ministers prepared their songs and stories, anxious to tell children about Jesus. The builders surveyed their project and organized their supplies and tools. Pastor Mark Cox set up the computer and video equipment. The group knew that the meetings would be successful. They had planned for this moment—the first meeting, the first story, the first patient, the first brick.

Now all they needed was electricity to power their equipment. After trying two generators without any success, it was clear that the group needed to consider other options. Thinking that the visual aids were necessary in order to capture the attention of the audience, Pastor Cox began praying. Not knowing much about the people of Mentu, he asked Pastor Ganchai, the local pastor, to tell the team about the villagers and those who would be coming to the meetings. The people knew very little about Jesus. They had simple ways and told stories to their children.

It became clear to the team that Jesus' simple storytelling evangelism method would be best. Pastor Cox reflected, "God did not turn the lights on for our machines, but He did turn on the lights in the hearts and minds of many people, including my own."

This is what evangelism is all about. A smile is simple and it opens hearts. It is fundamental to evangelism. And when the electricity fails, the smile continues to shine and make a difference.

CHARLENE HILLIARD WEST

APRIL 26

IT'S ALL ABOUT TRUST

Your ears will hear a voice behind you, saying, "This is the way; walk in it." Isa. 30:21, NIV.

As I was driving to work one morning, thoughts of my morning worship lingered in my mind.

I had recently completed a degree in business management and was unsure what career to pursue. I petitioned the Lord to direct me and to let me know His plans for my work. Through my job at Loma Linda University I was acquainted with many of the departments. I became unusually excited by the prospect of working as an officer in the planned giving department. I tried to imagine myself in this career. It would involve traveling and visiting with people, explaining estate planning concepts and types of agreements. I felt that this strong impression was from the Lord. There were no female trust officers at the university at the time, though.

However, I refused to allow the enemy to discourage me. While still driving, I prayed, "Lord, if this is the career that You have planned for me and if You open the way, I will agree to serve You as a trust officer." Now, I would just wait—and trust God—to see what developed. Several months later I heard that the university had opened the trust position to women. My spirit soared as I prayed, "Thank You, Lord. This was an impression from You." My faith strengthened, and I continued to trust and wait that He would bring it to pass.

One day the university president stopped by my office and told me that they had decided to have a female trust officer and that my name had been recommended. He wanted to know how I felt about that sort of career. I was so excited that I could hardly respond in a calm manner. My heart beat furiously as I told him that I was interested and would be happy to serve if appointed. He had a difficult time convincing my supervisor, but after a few weeks my boss mentioned the prospect. When I shared the experience from my morning commute, he sighed deeply and said, "I was afraid it was something like that. I will recommend you for the position."

"Your ears will hear a voice behind you, saying, 'This is the way; walk in it'" (Isa. 30:21, NIV).

BARBARA MOEN

CULINARY DISASTER

Have salt in yourselves, and be at peace with one another.
Mark 9:50, NASB.

I enjoy cooking, but more important, I enjoy cooking with my family. Spending time in the kitchen, perusing recipe books, and creating wonderful meals together is quality time that builds memories.

One Sunday evening we had a cooking competition and tasted each other's food creations. When it came time for them to sample my culinary experiment, I was excited and confident (by experience) that they'd enjoy my dish. There was no way that their treats would be better than mine. After all, I was the homemaker, the wife, the mother; I did 99.9 percent of the daily meal preparation. So how could I be beat?

My sons each sampled my creation. Then my husband took a bite. In fact, his bite was one of confidence, since he had already survived 26 years of my cooking. But then I saw the looks on their faces. It was not what I had expected. I did not see eyes closed in bliss or expressions that said, "Mom, you're the best." Their looks told me that my food was a disaster. I tasted my Iron Chef entry. It was terrible! Something was wrong. Something was missing—something very important. I had forgotten to put in the salt.

My dish was not good for anything, or good enough to be served with the rest of the meal. We threw it out. (How embarrassing. Not even the dog was interested.)

Jesus told the crowd on the mountainside near Galilee, "You are the salt of the earth. But if the salt loses its saltiness, how can it be made salty again? It is no longer good for anything, except to be thrown out and trampled by men" (Matt. 5:13, NIV).

That evening my family and I were reminded of the importance of salt in food, and also in our lives. We want to be worthy of sharing with others how God has blessed us.

Charlene Hilliard West

April 28

IF I HAVE THE FAITH OF SPARROWS

Do not fear therefore; you are of more value than many sparrows.
Matt. 10:31, NKJV.

Most of last night I spent fretting about today's devotional deadline, not knowing what I would share with you. What I came up with was FAITH.

What is faith? There are many definitions. However, this is what it means to me: a firm belief in something for which there is no proof; complete trust.

There are days I don't know what's happening. I pray and take my worries to Jesus, asking for help. Sometimes it seems as if I am on my own; that is where FAITH comes in. As a Christian I have faith that God has not deserted me. He has a plan that I am not aware of, and He has already answered my prayer, although it's not always evident to me.

Because of the physical demands of the world, we need jobs and income to survive. Our lives become an endless parade of meetings, paperwork, and deadlines. But when we feel discouraged, God whispers words of encouragement every step of the way.

There is always a little voice that comforts me and tells me over and over, "Do I not provide for the sparrow?" When I hear that voice, I know I'm hearing the Holy Spirit.

The sparrows' main source of food comes not from the pieces of bread I throw to them but directly from God. He provides His wild creatures with water so they will not thirst. He provides them shelter so they will be protected. And He says that we are worth more than many sparrows to Him. "Do not fear therefore; you are of more value than many sparrows" (Matt. 10:31, NKJV).

The food He provides is the Word of God, and the shelter He provides is Jesus. All we have to do is ask for it.

We get caught up in our own problems and forget that we need to have complete trust in God. We must give thanks to Him for the many blessings that He bestows upon us even when we do not ask for them and have faith to face all that He has planned for us tomorrow. The sparrows don't fret—why should we?

Norma V. Flynn

SOWING GENEROUSLY

You will be made rich in every way so that you can be generous on every occasion. 2 Cor. 9:11, NIV.

Six long years of training, hard work, and fund-raising left us exhausted. Missionary pilot Clifton Brooks, mechanic Andy Klein, and I agonized over the skimpy aviation budget. Should we eliminate the tools/equipment line item to allow earlier shipment of the plane to the Philippines? That reduced the budget by $10,000; however, it would leave the team with no way to perform routine maintenance.

Realizing this was a God-sized problem and concerned that discouragement might mean the loss of the crew, I suggested we leave the challenge with God. After all, He had called us to assist frontier missionaries working to reach 100 language groups without a Christian presence in the Philippines.

We knelt and poured out our hearts in prayer. Only God had the solution.

My phone rang. The pastor asked, "Is it possible to reschedule your presentation?"

"Those are strange circumstances; I wonder if God's hand is in this," I mused as I put the phone down.

Several weeks later, while greeting members after the service, an elderly couple shared how they had fallen in love with the Philippines and that they sponsored a school on one of the 7,107 islands. They explained that they attended this church only once a year and were so thankful to meet us that day!

They slipped me an envelope containing ten $100 bills! Not enough to deliver the plane, but seeing God at work confirmed that He intended to finish what He had started. Monday morning, I called to thank the couple for their timely contribution. The gentleman exclaimed, "God is so good! I sold enough machinery yesterday to clear more than twice what we gave for missions!"

This experience verifies Paul's statement; "You will be made rich in every way so that you can be generous on every occasion. . . . This service that you perform is not only supplying the needs of God's people but is also overflowing in many expressions of thanks to God" (2 Cor. 9:11, 12, NIV).

DON STARLIN

GOD'S "TOOL TIME"

Lord, you establish peace for us; all that we have accomplished you have done for us. Isa. 26:12, NIV.

Calling to thank a donor for a timely gift, together we marveled at the circumstances that led to our meeting. He then enthusiastically shared how God had recently blessed his business.

Sensing our new relationship to be of providential orchestration, I ventured to relate the challenge we faced in sending a mission plane to the Philippines.

"Your business card indicates that you deal in tools. You wouldn't happen to have good used tools at discounted prices, would you?" I politely inquired.

"Don, I have three large buildings and 40-foot semitrailers full of tools. You bring your list, and I will give you whatever I have!"

Hardly believing my ears, I glanced at the calendar and asked, "How would Thursday work?"

"Fine," replied the gentleman. "We'll see you Thursday."

Clifton Brooks, Andy Klein, and I went to see the tool man. We spent the day examining his inventory and selecting what we needed for the project.

After one of the most exciting days of our lives, we left with a pickup truck and tandem axle trailer filled with tools and equipment worth more than $7,000—all donated! Ninety percent of the items on the tools/equipment list were in hand!

God blessed as work on the plane continued through the summer and into the fall. Fueling steps and handles, right side door modification, fabrication and installation of the interior were all accomplished using tools donated by God's tool man.

Several months later the plane was flown to California where it was disassembled for shipping to the Philippines. Today it is supporting missionaries and saving lives—generating more stories of the hand of Providence at work.

"Yes, Lord, walking in the way of your laws, we wait for you; your name and renown are the desire of our hearts. . . . Lord, you establish peace for us; all that we have accomplished you have done for us" (Isa. 26:8-12, NIV).

Don Starlin

EXPECTING

Do you count the months till they bear?
Do you know the time they give birth? Job 39:2, NIV.

I am not a patient person. If I'm going somewhere, I want to get there as fast as possible (and anyone who's slowing me down had better watch out). If I've heard of a book I'd like to read or a CD I'd like to listen to, I want to go to Barnes and Noble and get it now. I like having things planned out ahead of time—and knowing what's around the corner before I get there.

Considering this, you can imagine that being pregnant has pretty much turned my world upside down. In this situation, I have absolutely no control, and expectations are useless. I can't fast-forward the nine-month process. I have no say about when and how my baby arrives on the scene. I can't see who she looks like, and I have no idea what her personality will be. I can't even get her to kick on demand! I'm forced to wait, take care of myself (and her!), and hope for the best. But oh, how I long for the day when she'll be in my arms at last! That will more than make up for all the waiting and wondering!

I believe that Christ has that same sense of expectancy as He waits for us to be born again in Him. I can picture the excitement on His face when one of His precious children is drawn to Him for the first time—He's so eager to hold us in His arms! He can't wait to show us how much He loves us. But He can't make us love Him. So He looks for opportunities to demonstrate His loving care, and He waits, hoping for the best. His patience is infinite—He'll never give up on us. So don't make Him wait any longer—throw yourself into His arms today!

"But you, O God, are both tender and kind, not easily angered, immense in love, and you never, never quit" (Ps. 86:15, Message).

Lorelei Herman Cress

May 2

PROMISES FOR SOMEONE ELSE

Not one of these people, even though their lives of faith were exemplary, got their hands on what was promised. Heb. 11:39, Message.

Following is a prayer request from the Quiet Hour Web site: "I'm contemplating leaving the Lord. I read the Bible promises, but it seems they have been written for someone else, as they never seem to apply to me. I've pleaded for God to heal me, but even prayer doesn't help. Today I shall put away my Bible, as reading it is too painful for me."

Have you ever wondered, *Where is God, and why doesn't He care about me?* If so, you are in good company with Job, David, Solomon, all Jesus' disciples, and a host of others. Even Jesus cried out on the cross, "My God, my God, why have you forsaken me?"

When I was in a pit, I tried to climb out by reading Hebrews 11, the so-called faith chapter. It lists the named and unnamed godly heroes, both men and women, who persevered because they had faith that even though they couldn't see the goal, God had said it was there before them, and they kept on trying in His strength.

However, I was dismayed at the closing verses of the chapter because it said, "Not one of these people, even though their lives of faith were exemplary, got their hands on what was promised" (Heb. 11:39, Message).

But Bible writers didn't compose with chapter and verse divisions. Read on into chapter 12, verses 1-3: "Do you see what this means—all these pioneers who blazed the way, all these veterans cheering us on? It means we'd better get on with it. Strip down, start running—and never quit! . . . Keep your eyes on Jesus, who both began and finished this race we're in. Study how he did it. Because he never lost sight of where he was headed—that exhilarating finish in and with God—he could put up with anything along the way: Cross, shame, whatever. . . . When you find yourselves flagging in your faith, go over that story again, item by item, that long litany of hostility he plowed through. That will shoot adrenaline into your souls!" (Message).

It's not reaching the destination that's important in the big picture: it's the journey there! And the Holy Spirit is before you, behind you, and as close as your skin is to your flesh. He is with you, and He is the faithful one. Cling to Him. He will bring you through.

Christy K. Robinson

PROMISES FOR ME

He comes alongside us when we go through hard times.
2 Cor. 1:4, Message.

My mother was born with asthma, which developed into emphysema by age 10. At 22 she was given a year to live, but like King Hezekiah, she pleaded with God to let her live to raise her children to Christian maturity. By God's grace she lived to age 55. She was an artist, musician, gardener, poet, and genealogist. She even represented herself to an Internal Revenue commission and won her case.

But as the years passed, she pleaded with God to heal her or let her die, to ease her constant struggle for breath and strength. On her last night, I read Bible verses to her as I held her hand and watched the monitors record her declining heartbeat and respiration. Those hours were the most precious and intimate of my life, and I'm certain that the next voice she hears after mine will be Jesus' voice, saying, "Wake up, little girl!"

God's promises are for you, though we may not understand the specific or temporal application. Read 2 Corinthians 1:4, 5: "He comes alongside us when we go through hard times, and before you know it, he brings us alongside someone else who is going through hard times so that we can be there for that person just as God was there for us. We have plenty of hard times that come from following the Messiah, but no more so than the good times of his healing comfort—we get a full measure of that, too" (Message).

These verses clinch my faith in God's ultimate faithfulness and victory over present circumstances: "Whatever God has promised gets stamped with the Yes of Jesus. In him, this is what we preach and pray, the great Amen, God's Yes and our Yes together, gloriously evident. God affirms us, making us a sure thing in Christ, putting his Yes within us. By his Spirit he has stamped us with his eternal pledge—a sure beginning of what he is destined to complete" (2 Cor. 1:20-22, Message).

Read that again! God's promises are sure, pledged with Jesus' blood and guaranteed by the Holy Spirit. God has certified by Father, Son, and Holy Spirit (three witnesses) that His promises can be trusted and will be completed. Maybe not in my sight or lifetime (and there's the rub), but I trust that He has accomplished His purpose already, and I await the resolution.

Christy K. Robinson

WIRED FOR SPEED

Step out of the traffic! Take a long, loving look at me,
your High God, above politics, above everything.
Ps. 46:10, Message.

When Annika was very small, I would take her for walks in the stroller around our neighborhood and at the mall. She loved riding in the stroller and enjoyed the movement and the ever-changing scenery. Occasionally I would stop to chat with a neighbor or look at something in a store window. Almost immediately, Annika would make her displeasure known with a heart-wrenching cry that did not cease until we moved on once again.

A similar phenomenon often occurred while driving in our car. Annika slept peacefully as long as we maintained a cruising speed of at least 55 miles per hour. When it came time to slow down and exit the freeway, Annika would wake up with a jolt and begin a sorrowful wailing that could not be pacified until we reached our destination and rescued her from the car seat that imprisoned her. Annika appeared to be wired for speed—her contentment was directly connected to the velocity at which she traveled.

Now Annika is no longer a tiny baby, but an inquisitive toddler. A stop along a neighborhood walk is no longer cause for a meltdown but an opportunity to examine the pansies growing in a neighbor's front yard, to pick up an interesting leaf that has fallen on the ground, or to watch an ant crawling across the sidewalk. A pause at a shop window presents a never-ending supply of shiny new merchandise to inspect. Riding in the car, Annika can entertain herself with conversations and books for increasingly long journeys. Wired for speed no more, Annika is discovering the joys of life in the slow lane.

Psalm 46:10 states, "Be still, and know that I am God" (NIV). In the still and quiet times Annika sees things she hasn't noticed before, things that make her life richer. By slowing down, she gets to see the playful kitty pouncing in the grass and the delicate butterfly fluttering among the flowers.

In this fast-paced, technological world, we too need to slow down and be still. When we are still, God can reveal Himself and His abundant blessings to us.

Laura West Kong

A MATTER OF PRIORITIES

You shine like stars in the universe
as you hold out the word of life.
Phil. 2:15, 16, NIV.

Some years ago when I purchased a new car, I discovered a useful gadget that I hadn't known existed. The key ring came with a gizmo that allowed me to press a button and unlock the car door while several feet away. I'd never missed this particular "little wonder" before, but now this gadget is an integral part of my life. I find myself feeling irritated when I have to use a key to open the car door.

This experience made me think of a trip we'd made to a provincial city in Russia. As I became acquainted with our precious Christian people, I found myself feeling upset, even angry, that they were forced to live such deprived lives. In a superpower nation, with people in space, why couldn't they get a telephone? In a country with enough modern weapons to wipe out the world, why were they washing clothes in bathtubs and standing in long and sometimes useless lines for food?

But I could detect no resentment, no complaining on their part. What they'd never had was not a big item to them. What was a big item was their religious faith. Many had been persecuted for that faith; some family members had been killed, and nearly all were denied higher education.

Yet these people felt highly privileged. The disillusionment and despair of their atheistic countrymen did not touch them. While others chain-smoked through their days and drowned themselves in vodka by night, the church members were busily building a new church for their Lord.

I found myself greatly moved by their simple lives, their unshakable faith, their great joy in their Lord. I thought of the text, "That you may become . . . children of God without fault in a crooked and depraved generation, in which you shine like stars in the universe as you hold out the word of life" (Phil. 2:15, 16, NIV).

These people have their priorities straight!

Aileen Ludington

GRANNY CONQUERS POWERPOINT

There will be more rejoicing in heaven over one sinner who repents than over ninety-nine righteous persons who do not need to repent.
Luke 15:7, NIV.

I am retired after 33 years of nursing. I have a burning desire to spread the gospel to all, as Jesus told us. I went to Guyana as a Quiet Hour evangelism team member in October 2004.

I am not computer literate, but my daughter showed me how to use it. In a short period of time I learned how to operate PowerPoint for the illustrations and Bible texts. My son-in-law tangled up the computer cords, but I detangled them, and put them together like you wouldn't believe! So when the need arose and God whispered my name, I was more than ready. Isn't our God great?

The local elders helped me with the health message, and they did a great job with cultural adaptation and language translations. There were so many answered prayers, which grounded me even more in faith in my loving God. One young man said to me, "The message was excellent, but your health message has led me to make a choice tonight—to join your church and be baptized." That put me on a spiritual high! I wanted to stay on and preach more, touch more lives. Oh, what a feeling of joy!

I know why Jesus said, "There will be more rejoicing in heaven over one sinner who repents than over ninety-nine righteous persons who do not need to repent" (Luke 15:7, NIV). It was encouraging to see the people come for prayers for health or for problems at work and home.

I was amazed at the attendance. The kids and parents loved what they heard and came every night to the meetings. I thought because I was a woman preacher that they wouldn't like it, but in this "man's world" they wanted to do everything for me except preach. I didn't mind.

God used me for my benefit! I learned so much—things I didn't know before. This mission trip opened my eyes. My life has taken a 180-degree turn for the Lord. I want to do more for Him; I didn't want to come home from Guyana. I'd return in a heartbeat if money permits. I know from experience that God works for me, and I love working for Him.

SUE ATKINSON

THE FLEXIBILITY OF LOVE

That we might receive the adoption as sons. Gal. 4:5, NASB.

I sat with my 29-year-old son, Larry, in the home of one of our pastor friends. With us were Eva Mae, a sweet-faced little woman, and her daughter, a petite brunette with a happy laugh and a deep Southern drawl. For a few moments we all just stared at one another, scarcely able to breathe. My adopted son had just met his birth mother and his half sister for the first time.

"Does it bother you," I once asked Larry, "knowing that you have a connection with other unknown people out there?"

In his usual deliberate way he replied, "No. I hardly ever remember that I am adopted."

Therefore, we decided to meet his biological family together. Cries of doom arose all around us: "I've seen these meetings before, and they hardly ever turn out well." "What if Larry wants to live with them instead of you?" "My adopted daughter wants to meet her family, and I'm frantic." "How can you let him think of anyone else as mother?" "Don't you hate her?"

Instead, I had this fine, upright son to present to Eva Mae. I thanked her for the happiness he'd brought me. Weeping again, she said, "I never dreamed that this day could ever happen." We've been friends ever since. Twice Eva and members of her family even came out West to visit us.

She carried him for nine months, and then gave him away with a broken heart. Although she gave birth to him, he's mine in the way that comes only with rearing one sweet little boy from babyhood to manhood. I'm the one who comforted him through childhood illnesses. I'm the one who sent him off to school on the first day with his little blue lunch box, and then, later, flew halfway around the world to attend his high school graduation at Far Eastern Academy.

The apostle Paul rejoiced that God sent forth His Son so that "we might receive the adoption as sons" (Gal. 4:5, NASB). In so saying, he touched on the true meaning of adoption. True love, divine and human, makes room for everyone. That's a fact! The experience taught us all the essence of God Himself—His marvelously flexible and infinitely expandable love. Moreover, love can take risks because it knows that it's inexhaustible.

Dorothy Minchin-Comm

THE SUBSTANCE OF THINGS HOPED FOR

Now faith is the substance of things hoped for, the evidence of things not seen. Heb. 11:1.

When I was a little girl and adults asked me what I wanted to be when I grew up, the answer was always "A mommy!" A few months ago I found out that my childhood dream would finally come true. I was pregnant! When I heard the news, I was overjoyed. But even after blood tests and physical changes reconfirmed what I knew to be true, it still seemed hard to believe. A new life being generated inside me—what a strange and wonderful idea! But still, in my mind, an idea. I couldn't see or hear or touch the baby. It wasn't real to me yet—just a cherished dream.

Then came the day of the sonogram. I could see the baby moving, hear her little heart beating. I could watch her displeased reaction to the invasion of her space, and see her jiggle when I laughed with delight. Though I still can't feel her, I now know without a doubt that she's there. She's no longer a concept—she's a reality to me.

Our relationship with God can be very similar. We can't see or hear or touch Him, and sometimes it's hard to believe He's real, and not a figment of our imagination. But if we seek to know Him better through prayer and the study of His Word, we can catch glimpses of Him. Little by little, as we nurture the relationship, we see more evidence of the new life He's creating inside us, and our faith grows until He is no longer a dream, but a reality.

"Now faith is the substance of things hoped for, the evidence of things not seen" (Heb. 11:1).

Lorelei Herman Cress

ONCE UPON A TIME

Count yourselves dead to sin but alive to God in Christ Jesus.
Rom. 6:11, NIV.

As a little boy, once-upon-a-time stories intrigued me. My mom would sometimes start with this phrase to capture my attention. She would say, "Once upon a time, I told you to take out the garbage," or "once upon a time, be nice to your sister."

This lingo was fine, but as the years went by, this phrase became a little facetious to me. It was apparent that the once-upon-a-time beginning statements were not working. She started using such lines as, "When you were a little boy, I could get you to do things so much easier." I would reply, "When I was a little boy, you tricked me into actions that I really didn't want to do." This obviously hurt her. It made some difference, but not enough to change my directions.

My mom and I always have been close. Even though I have lived my own life, I have maintained a close relationship with her. She has put up with me, and I with her. However, something happened that changed everything about these little insights. Fatherhood entered the picture and my young son, Lucky Day, now loves to hear stories. One doesn't have to be a rocket scientist to guess what stories he likes to hear. He loves once-upon-a-time stories. Well, here I go again with the side of life that God, parents, and older folks know so well: we are creatures of heredity, environment, and most of all, growing up. We love to hear stories.

Once upon a time, "the Lord made the heavens and the earth, the sea, and all that is in them" (Ex. 20:11, NIV). Not only did God create the world, but He made a plan to save it from sin. "The death he died, he died to sin once for all; but the life he lives, he lives to God. In the same way, count yourselves dead to sin but alive to God in Christ Jesus" (Rom. 6:10, 11, NIV).

Once upon a time, Jesus died for us, so that we could be alive to God, forever.

Bob McGhee

LOVING THE LIONESS

"What is your mother? A lioness among lions! She lay down among the young lions and reared her cubs."
Eze. 19:2, NLT.

Honoring your father and mother is an injunction from earliest recorded history (Ex. 20:12). Thus, Mother's Day and Father's Day evolved, all full of hearts and flowers. We eulogize the love, sacrifice, and long-suffering of good mothers.

I would like to celebrate another very wonderful characteristic, loyalty. "What is your mother? A lioness among lions!" Ezekiel exclaimed. "She lay down among the young lions and reared her cubs." The prophet took another eight verses to describe the excellence of her strength.

My father and mother married just before the Great Depression ravaged America. As a perfectly contented child, I didn't realize that my schoolteacher parents were pitiably poor. My mother's name was Leona, a derivative of lion. She defended family solidarity. She was the scourge of the playground, often defending her younger sister. Yet, if she pledged her loyalty to a friend, nothing in the universe could destroy it.

All her life, Mom disciplined our family in thriftiness—even after the Great Depression passed. Not only did we clean our plates (for the sake of starving children in Africa), we had little opportunity to become materialists. All clothing was necessarily homemade. We received new pajamas constructed out of heavy flour sacks. The garments lasted forever; it felt like sleeping in a ship's sail.

My mother used the same pattern for Dad and me. Bored with fashion, I didn't try the pajamas on until they were almost finished. Then I became alarmed! Four-inch hems and a great bulk around the middle. The waistband up to my armpits and the crotch sagging below my knees. Arms at least six inches short of the ends of the sleeves. The grotesque sight startled even Dad. "Jumping gingers!" he exclaimed. "What is that?" What indeed!

Dear Mom! How often we laughed at her strict economies. Then we quickly regretted it, because our loyal mother never found these episodes humorous. The lioness simply must take care of her own. I'd still like to find a Mother's Day card featuring a very fierce lion. The metaphor works.

DOROTHY MINCHIN-COMM

THE "LOOK"

I look to you, heaven-dwelling God, look up to you for help.
Ps. 123:1, Message.

My family always took a summer vacation trip from Arizona to northern Minnesota, where my parents' families lived. We'd load the avocado-green Rambler station wagon and hit the road. We saw Yosemite, the Snake River, Mount Rushmore, Yellowstone, the Ozarks, and the Rockies—some of those aren't even on the way to Minnesota!

Once we arrived, there would be family reunion feasts and picnics, where the grown-ups would sit at the table for hours after the cousins had slithered under the table to play outside with the elderly horse. But not me. Although I tried to dodge her eyes, my mom gave me "the look," which, because she'd trained me ahead of time, meant to clear the table and wash the dishes. The relatives would say with admiration, "What a nice girl, so courteous, such manners, [etc.]." But I wasn't gracious on the inside: I was unwillingly scraping dishes and scrubbing the stuck-on pans. Thanks a lot, Mom! (Such a Cinderella.)

Surely your mother or father gave you the look, and without words you knew what was required of you or you'd face the consequences of disobedience.

But now, as grown-ups ourselves, we think of our heavenly Father, who loves us so much He can't take His eyes off of us. Those are eyes we don't mind meeting! With that in mind, we are inspired to look back at God in the way the psalmist describes: "I look to you, heaven-dwelling God, look up to you for help. Like servants, alert to their master's commands, like a maiden attending her lady, we're watching and waiting, holding our breath, awaiting your word of mercy" (Psalm 123:1, 2, Message).

We are looking at God with all our attention, ready to leap into action at His command to show mercy, compassion, and justice (Micah 6:8) to the rest of our human family. With only "the look" from heaven, we go to do His will with grace in our hearts.

Christy K. Robinson

May 12

IN A FAMILY WAY

You're blessed when you can show people how to cooperate instead of compete or fight. That's when you discover who you really are, and your place in God's family.
Matt. 5:9, Message.

Most of my school friends would have given me a vote of "no confidence" as a father. They'd have been right. I worried about unimportant details and was far too relaxed about other things.

If you haven't already experienced it, a woman becoming a first-time mom will undergo a transformation that is amazing. And you, Romeo, will not be the center of her life anymore. You will see a miracle take place that can only be a gift from God. If you think your girlfriend treated you well before you were married, and if you have been delighted with her love and tender care as her new husband, just wait until her first pregnancy. If you don't already have a clear picture of what's really important in life (I didn't), you will soon figure it out!

Watching Lillian go from girlfriend (four years) to wife (eight more years) to mom (20-plus years so far) has been one of God's most precious gifts. Her love and tender care for our children has never ceased to amaze me. Not a single detail slips by without her careful and loving consideration and unselfish love. It's pure and rich and overwhelming. Being a mom has taken over her life, and watching her love in action has changed mine.

Being the dad was mostly easy. I made sandwiches, washed sticky hands, fixed toys, taught them to read and count, and slept near our ill child. We wrestled, ran races, and played hide-and-seek. We felt surrounded by my wife's love and secure in everything we did. Her love, and her gift of a daughter and a son, changed me in ways I would never have imagined. My school friends would never have believed it!

"You're blessed when you can show people how to cooperate instead of compete or fight. That's when you discover who you really are, and your place in God's family" (Matt. 5:9, Message).

Robert Johnston

THE FATHER'S MATERNAL LOVE

As a mother comforts her child, so will I comfort you; and you will be comforted over Jerusalem. Isa. 66:13, NIV.

There are highly educated, deeply spiritual people of both genders who refer to God as "She" and "Mother," and although I find it somewhat distracting, it doesn't make them wrong and me right. God is infinitely more than we can imagine. More intelligent, more broad-minded, more loving, more compassionate, more forgiving, and more accepting. Just more. His ways are higher than my ways. With that in mind, and Genesis 1:27, which states that God created both male and female in His image, I submit that God is not confined to gender as we perceive it. God is Spirit. His appearance is defined by His character (Ex. 34:6, 7; 1 John 3:1; 1 John 4:8).

Not every human mother deserves the honors we are commanded to pay them (Ex. 20:12). Nor is every woman who yearns to be a mother able to bear children or raise a family. Parent/child relationships are only an ideal, pointing to the real Creator/creature relationship. God is powerful, protective, and farseeing. He wants the best present and future for us. Listen to God's parental words: "Can a mother forget the infant at her breast, walk away from the baby she bore? But even if mothers forget, I'd never forget you—never" (Isa. 49:15, Message).

"O Jerusalem, Jerusalem, . . . how often I have longed to gather your children together, as a hen gathers her chicks under her wings, but you were not willing" (Matt. 23:37, NIV).

"I will extend peace . . . ; you will nurse and be carried on her arm and dandled on her knees. As a mother comforts her child, so will I comfort you; and you will be comforted over Jerusalem" (Isa. 66:12, 13, NIV).

The grace-full tenderness that we have received so generously from God, the maternal Father, we must share by praying for those around us, and by reflecting (in God's image!) our Parent's compassion to troubled friends or coworkers. Then, to complete the circle, we return that love to God with heartfelt gratitude and joy.

CHRISTY K. ROBINSON

May 14

THE HUMILITY BLOCK

He is the Rock, his works are perfect, and all his ways are just. A faithful God who does no wrong, upright and just is he.
Deut. 32:4, NIV.

In my spare time I enjoy quilting. I love the rich colors and graphic patterns. A finished quilt can hang on the wall to be admired, or wrap around a loved one.

The blocks women pieced throughout history give us a window into their world. "Churn Dash" portrays the device used to churn cream into butter. "Grandmother's Flower Garden" reveals a relaxing moment.

Women expressed themselves through their quilting. Mathematically inclined women drafted intricate geometrical patterns. Before women could vote at the ballot box, many boldly communicated their political views through the quilts they stitched. The Amish, who refrained from wearing bright colors, displayed their love of color with daring color combinations. Some women included what was known as a "humility block." This was a block made with a deliberate mistake. It indicated that only God is perfect.

The concept of the humility block was initially hard for me to accept. I could never put all that hard work in and then deliberately mar an otherwise perfect work of art. As time went by, though, the humility block grew on me. I came to view it as charming. If one was good, why not four or five?

My embracing of the humility block, however, was not in the true spirit of the woman who initiated this custom. She used it as an acknowledgement of God's perfection. I had reduced it to nothing more than a fashion statement.

For her, the humility block was a constant witness of who God is. It was a reminder to her family who went to bed and woke up every morning under her quilts. When she went about her daily chores, she would see the quilts and remember who God is. Passersby would see a quilt hanging on the clothesline and would be reminded of who God is.

"I will proclaim the name of the Lord. Oh, praise the greatness of our God!" (Deut. 32:3, NIV).

Laura West Kong

IT'S NOT THE END

The Lord your God goes with you.
Deut. 31:6, NIV.

Have you ever noticed that Americans devote one day to mothers and an entire week honoring pickles?

The price that mothers have paid has been immeasurable. At 19 Marie was the example of what every mother tells her daughter not to become: a single teen mom. She saved every nickel she could. She scrounged to see what might have fallen to the floor. Sofa cracks and creases never produced what she needed.

Marie had had an impeccable scholastic record and been offered an Ivy League scholarship. During the carefree summer she exuded enthusiasm. But by fall registration she'd be in her second trimester. In what seemed like the blink of an eye she had gone from the top to the bottom. Fear. For the first time pure fear entered her life. It seemed to consume her. *What is the use?* she would ask herself. *Nobody cares now. I am an embarrassment,* she would think. *There is no way I can do this by myself* became her cry.

Walking from her apartment to the closest coin-operated laundry with dirty linens in her basket, she tripped and spilled her heavy load. She began to weep there on the sidewalk. She dropped to her knees. It seemed like the whole world passed her by. She felt a soft hand on her shoulder. "It's not the end," said a soft voice. Marie looked up to see the smiling face of an adorable little girl. "What did you say?" she asked.

"My mama always says when I cry, 'It'll be OK in the end, baby, and if it's not OK, it's not the end.' "

Marie realized that God hadn't left her, that He was as close as He always had been. No matter what she had given up, He had given more. He gave His life. Marie and her daughter live in the knowledge of God's sustaining love and His ultimate sacrifice. They live by the verse that says, "Be strong and courageous. Do not be afraid or terrified because of them, for the Lord your God goes with you; he will never leave you nor forsake you" (Deut. 31:6, NIV).

Stephen Robertson

GOD'S MOSAIC

God . . . gave His only begotten Son, that whoever believes in Him should not perish but have everlasting life.
John 3:16, NKJV.

Pick up almost any newspaper. Turn on the radio. Watch a TV newscast. The messages are distressingly familiar: wars, riots, famines, atrocities, disasters, shootings, corruption—an endless parade. And it isn't just the news. Today our scientists and ecologists are becoming even more frightening doom-mongers than the most eloquent hellfire revivalists. The pace of life, with its pressures, perversions, paralyzing pessimism, and stark panic, swirls about us, and it's difficult not to be caught up in the frantic frenzy.

But optimism, hope, and faith are not dead. They've just been lost by a bewildered, neglected generation born into a chaotic and violent world. Rather than infecting us with the restless anxiety of people about us, these awesome times can awaken us to a renewed understanding of, and appreciation for, our Christian faith and its relevance in coping with the present pandemonium.

God did not create this world and its people to let them end up suffocating into oblivion from their own follies and filth. God has a master plan—the plan of redemption—and within it is a meaningful place, an important role, for every willing human being.

What a destiny! What a time to be alive! What a challenge to share with the world the hope and joy we know, the honor we feel at being needed and involved in the finishing of God's plans for our world.

"God . . . gave His only begotten Son, that whoever believes in Him should not perish but have everlasting life" (John 3:16, NKJV).

One day God will pull back the curtain and show us the whole picture. We'll be able to see for ourselves how the differing parts and pieces of our lives fit together, creating a great and wondrous mosaic that will stretch into eternity.

Aileen Ludington

JUST AS I AM

He presented himself for this sacrificial death when we were far too weak and rebellious to do anything to get ourselves ready.
Rom. 5:6, Message.

I attended two Billy Graham crusades: one in Phoenix when I was 4 (I remember the bleachers, the tent, and the altar call) and his last Los Angeles crusade in 2004 at the Rose Bowl. As the choir and much of the crowd of 90,000 sang "Just as I Am," thousands of people filled the floor of the stadium, repenting and asking forgiveness for sin and committing their lives to Jesus.

Perhaps the theology behind that hymn's lyrics comes from the story of the wastrel son who was accepted and welcomed by his father, unclean and guilty though he was. The father covered the filthy son with his family mantle and put his own seal ring on his son's hand. It's as if we can hear the father saying, "I love you just as you are."

Of course both wanted restoration for the son, but the reunion was about relationship: parent and child, lost and found, surprise and grace, joy and unconditional love. The cleansing will come shortly: "How blessed are those who wash their robes! The Tree of Life is theirs for good, and they'll walk through the gates to the City" (Rev. 22:14, Message).

A popular movie had a memorable declaration: "I like you just as you are." There was forgiveness and acceptance—on both sides—as they realized that their at-odds relationship would progress to a new level. Don't we all hunger for those words? We're inspired to grow and change, but first we crave unconditional acceptance. We want to be loved and to be worthy of that love.

"Just as I am, Thou wilt receive, wilt welcome, pardon, cleanse, relieve; because Thy promise I believe, O Lamb of God, I come, I come."

The Lord's answer to that plea for acceptance is "Every person the Father gives me eventually comes running to me. And once that person is with me, I hold on and don't let go" (John 6:37, Message).

Yes, Lord, hold on tight—don't let me go!

Christy K. Robinson

GET OFF MY BACK

We are not trying to please men but God, who tests our hearts.
1 Thess. 2:4, NIV.

There is an ancient story about a father and his son who were walking along a road one day with their donkey. They met a man who told them how foolish they were to walk when they had a donkey that could be ridden. So the father and son hopped on the donkey.

They hadn't gone very far when another man criticized them for both riding on the back of the poor donkey. They were both too heavy for it, he contended, and were being inhumane. The boy got off and let his father ride.

A third traveler engaged them in conversation along the dusty road and accused the father of being inconsiderate because he made his son walk while he rode. So the two switched places, and the boy rode while the father walked.

As fate would have it, they met another stranger on the road who charged that the son was not being thoughtful of the father, who was so much older and deserved more respect. When last seen, they were both trudging down the trail carrying the donkey!

There is a moral to this little story. No matter how much you try, you can never please everyone. If you live your life trying to please everyone, you will be one very frustrated person. Everybody has their own tastes and preferences. No two people are alike.

As Christian musicians, we see this all the time. Some people like inspirational music or the old hymns, while others like a more contemporary sound; still others enjoy gospel or Southern gospel music as well as many other styles.

A song in the 1970s said, "You can't please everyone, so you gotta please yourself." Whom are you trying to please? If you listen to the crowd and try to dance to their tune, you will always be frustrated. If you are overly sensitive to the opinions and criticisms of others, you will end up carrying needless burdens of guilt and inadequacy. And if you try to please just yourself, you will be egocentric and selfish.

That's why we, as God's children, seek to please God, not other people. Paul wrote, "For to me to live is Christ" (Phil. 1:21).

Our accountability is to God. And we know that He loves us unconditionally!

JOEDY AND JUDY MELASHENKO

BEING A BLESSING TO OTHERS

Leave your country, your people and your father's household and go to the land I will show you.
Gen. 12:1, NIV.

Moving can be difficult, especially when there are unknowns ahead. But when we commit our lives to being a blessing to those around us, moving can be easier and might even become an adventure!

As my wife and I contemplated moving from Cyprus, in the Mediterranean, to Redlands, California, we wondered if we would be able to sell our apartment, our car, and our sailboat, which at one point had served as our home.

Karen and I spent one of our last Sabbaths in Cyprus hiking along the Mediterranean Sea and enjoying some quiet time before our move. As we sat on a bench overlooking the Mediterranean, we heard a car engine slowly turning over, but without enough speed to start. I wandered over to ask the driver if he needed some help. He said he needed a jump start and asked if I had jumper cables. I carry cables in our car, so I quickly jump-started his vehicle.

My new friend Pambos invited us to stop by his house for a visit before we headed home. During the conversation we discussed our upcoming move from Cyprus and the need to sell our apartment, car, and sailboat. Pambos mentioned that his brother was about to get married and might need an apartment and his sister would need a car when she returned from her studies. Another friend said he could put up a for sale notice for the sailboat at the yacht club.

Pambos and his brother came to see the apartment and the car, but they also wanted to see the boat. As we sat on board the boat, enjoying the cool evening breeze, he made an offer for the apartment, car, and boat!

In less than two weeks we finalized the required paperwork for the transfer of ownership of the sailboat, the car, and the apartment and the money was in our bank account.

We never know what will happen when we commit ourselves to being a blessing to those around us. Wherever and however God leads, following His voice can often be an adventure. God not only uses us to bless others—He also blesses us.

MICHAEL PORTER

May 20

JUST A LITTLE TALK

For all have sinned [missed the mark] and fall short of the glory of God.
Rom. 3:23, NASB.

My oldest son, Mark, is a serious archer whose goal is to make the United States Olympic archery team. This takes dedication and practice, as well as following the advice of his coach—his father.

A few Sundays ago Mark was practicing out on his archery range. Every so often I would glance outside to see how he was doing. Once, I could see that discouragement had set in, so I walked out and asked what the problem was.

"Where's Dad when I need him?" he asked me. "My arrows are too low, and every adjustment I make doesn't seem to help."

His father was out of town on business and would not be back for a week. This meant that Mark would have one week of training and practice alone. I then noticed Mark's cell phone lying on the nearby table next to some arrows and other archery supplies.

"Mark, why don't you just call your dad and talk about the problem?" I asked.

"Do you think that would help—that he would be able to understand the problem without seeing it?" Mark inquired.

"Try it," I replied, walking back to the house.

About an hour later Mark came in and put his equipment away. He told me that he learned a spiritual lesson. His father had already earned the title of U.S. National Champion. Thus his father had experienced all the problems and challenges an archer can encounter in becoming a champion, so it was not difficult for him to help. He was only a phone call away.

This is similar to our relationship with Jesus. He has already faced all the temptations and challenges. In our quest to become champion Christians, Jesus is only a prayer away and is waiting to help us.

When Mark made the commitment to become an archery champion, his father promised to be his coach and help him through all challenges. Jesus has promised to be there for us, even before we made the commitment to be a champion for Him.

"And, lo, I am with you alway, even unto the end of the world" (Matt. 28:20).

Charlene Hilliard West

OF CHEETOS AND SALVATION

He got us out of the mess we're in and restored us to where he always wanted us to be. And he did it by means of Jesus Christ. Rom. 3:24, Message.

I accepted the gift of salvation at age 27. I was raised in a Christian home and attended Christian schools where salvation by faith was taught, but we were simultaneously told in sixteenth-century English to "be perfect as God is perfect." (We didn't understand that the definition of perfection is completeness and maturity, not "without fault.") Perfection for humans is unattainable, so salvation must also be unattainable.

"What is the point in trying?" shrugged much of my generation.

I can perfectly observe my prescribed diet and exercise for 50 minutes daily but not lose a pound in three weeks. After all the hard work and no visible reward, there is severe temptation to binge on high-carb, high-fat, high-sodium Cheetos! (Eating Cheetos isn't sinful, but play along . . .)

Righteousness might be explained this way: God declares us to be in right relationship to Himself. He just speaks it, as at Creation, when He spoke everything into existence. He sees only His beloved and perfect (in behavior and attitude, as well as full and complete) Son, Jesus, whose greatest desire is to save me. Me! Caught orange-handed with Cheetos dust, with the evidence of sin all over me! God sees my Substitute, who stands protectively between me and the glory and perfection that could vaporize me. And, as at Creation, God speaks the word, "Good." And because Creator God says it is so—it can only be so!

"Since we've compiled this long and sorry record as sinners . . . and proved that we are utterly incapable of living the glorious lives God wills for us, God did it for us. Out of sheer generosity he put us in right standing with himself. A pure gift. He got us out of the mess we're in and restored us to where he always wanted us to be. And he did it by means of Jesus Christ" (Rom. 3:23, 24, Message).

The concept of salvation is profound and complex. And it's so simple that a little child gets it. All you have to do is call upon the name of Jesus. He wants to save you! He loves you and is yearning to walk with you. Let Him dust off the crumbs and look past your outward appearance to see the perfect creation that He intends you to be.

Christy K. Robinson

DICK AND LUCY'S HARROWBED

Jesus said, "I tell you the truth, if you have faith as small as a mustard seed, you can say to this mountain, 'Move from here to there' and it will move. Nothing will be impossible for you." Matt. 17:20, NIV.

"God will make a way, when there seems to be no way" are the lyrics to a song by Don Moen. Dick and Lucy, Quiet Hour Ministries supporters and lay evangelists, ministered in India and saw many needs they wanted to assist with. They committed to paying for some land to build a church and school, but they did not have the money at the time.

When they returned home to their tire shop in Monroe, Washington, Dick heard that someone wanted to buy a harrowbed truck, used for hauling hay. "I have one for sale," Dick said to his son. The truck's value was the amount they needed to honor the commitment for the land purchase in India.

On Monday Mike and Dave drove the harrowbed from Monroe to Bend, Oregon, where the truck's buyer lived. It was raining, but a harrowbed does not come equipped with windshield wipers, because no one collects hay in the rain! So after wiping rain repellant on the windshield, off they went. They decided to go over Snoqualmie Pass and down the back roads instead of busy Interstate 5.

Because it's not meant for long hauls, the harrowbed started heating up, and they had to refill the radiator over and over. They ran out of water, so the men used rainwater from the road—God's water, they called it. They didn't have a bit of trouble the rest of the way.

Dick and Lucy called their bank, but the harrowbed payment had not arrived, so they asked Mike and Dave to stay an extra day. The funds arrived the next morning. On their way home Mike and Dave stopped at several farm equipment suppliers and compared their prices. They felt blessed with the larger amount received from the harrowbed sale. A church and Christian school have been built in India because of the gift.

When you look through God's eyes, what needs will you see? Needs you can satisfy with your checkbook? Needs you can fulfill by being a loving arm of encouragement and comfort? Ask Jesus to show you what your task is today.

Christy K. Robinson, as told by Jackie Tucker

REMARKABLE SPIRIT

Two are better than one, because they have a good return for their work: If one falls down, his friend can help him up. But pity the man who falls and has no one to help him up! Eccl. 4:9, 10, NIV.

With the end in sight, Maranda pushes herself to a sprint and surpasses her worthy challengers. Before her is the destiny of a Special Olympics medal. Moments from victory Maranda hears a loud groan from the crowd. She peers back over her shoulder and discovers one of her opponents facedown on the track.

With all eyes on the fallen athlete, Maranda's 180-degree return journey goes unnoticed until she arrives at the fallen competitor. Maranda reaches down and says, "Take my hand, and let's finish the race together." United, both athletes begin again to a roaring crowd, cheering on the unexpected selfless act.

There is one in the audience who is not surprised at Maranda's nobility. Before coming to live with Kimberly, Maranda had been in 50 different foster homes in six years. Fifty times Maranda's hope for a loving and normal life were crushed. Maranda's mental disability is not obvious, but when a new family would take her home, they soon discovered that she didn't know how to brush her hair or teeth and take care of other basic things many teenagers do naturally.

Maranda was created with a remarkable spirit in order to endure such life-devastating challenges—to give hope to a world in despair.

Kimberly was determined to provide a stable and loving environment for Maranda. However, soon after the two began their lives as a family, Kimberly was diagnosed with liver cancer and given only months to live. Kimberly's extended family then put enormous pressure on her to give Maranda back.

"Those were dark and lonely times in my life," Kimberly said. But out of their brokenness, Kimberly and Maranda became whole. They discovered the only thing they had to give was themselves, and that is exactly what the other needed. Kimberly's cancer is now in remission, and she is working again. Maranda is extraordinary in competition. In life's race they joined hands with the other challengers and concluded the race together.

Todd Baker

DING-A-LING

The wolf will live with the lamb, the leopard will lie down with the goat, the calf and the lion and the yearling together; and a little child will lead them.
Isa. 11:6, NIV.

When we were given a Siamese kitten, my 8-year-old brother was given the privilege of naming the cat. Mom suggested that Siamese are given musical-sounding names; perhaps something that rhymed with ding-a-ling. "That's it!" my brother shouted, "His name will be Ding-a-Ling." And that was that. (Mom took the cat to the vet for the annual exam and shots. When the vet assistant called out, "Ding-a-Ling Robinson," Mom had to stand up in humiliation.) At home we called the cat Ding, except when introducing him to visitors—or the vet! Then it was "Ah-Ling."

Ding was protective of his family. He would calmly face down big dogs, who would always back off, looking everywhere but at the cat. You could almost hear them say, "Cat? What cat? I'm just dropping my tail, and moving off slowly, slowly . . . "

Some of my friends dislike, fear, and/or are allergic to cats, which is almost incomprehensible to me. I marvel at the beauty of the cat's graceful physique, the texture and colors of fur, and not least, their individual personalities.

You'll not find pet cats in the Bible of the Hebrews, although the Egyptians had cherished and worshipped domestic cats for thousands of years. In fact, the only felines mentioned in Scripture are leopards and lions, fearsome beasts (Isa. 11:6; Dan. 7:6; Rev. 13:2; Jer. 13:23, and others). The evil one is depicted as a lion seeking people to devour. But Jesus is symbolized as the Lion of Judah—regal, strong, and mighty.

In Jesus' kingdom, "The wolf will live with the lamb, the leopard will lie down with the goat, the calf and the lion and the yearling together; and a little child will lead them. The cow will feed with the bear, their young will lie down together, and the lion will eat straw like the ox. . . . They will neither harm nor destroy on all my holy mountain, for the earth will be full of the knowledge of the Lord" (Isa. 11:6-9, NIV).

To fill our world from Eden to the new earth with such delightful, mysterious, inspiring creatures as felines, shows me that our Creator loves us.

Christy K. Robinson

GYPSY

Greater love has no one than this, that he lay down his life for his friends. You are my friends if you do what I command.
John 15:13, 14, NIV.

When I was 5, my parents adopted a miniature poodle from the Humane Society shelter. We named her Gypsy. She was gunmetal gray, with soft, wavy hair—not curly like a poodle. Sometimes, her fur went all shaggy.

Although only about 25 pounds, Gypsy was a giant in spirit. She knew about 70 phrases and commands, which she learned with graham cracker treats. She came along on every vacation between Phoenix and northern Minnesota, where my grandparents lived. Gypsy would stick her head out the window, and her pink tongue would fly in the Rambler's slipstream. When we arrived at the lake cabin in Minnesota, Gypsy snuffled around the lakeshore while we frolicked in the water.

My teenage cousin Debbie had a similar hairstyle and coloring to my mom. When Debbie flew by the dock on water skis and released the towrope, Gypsy thought Debbie was Mom, and Mom seemed to be drowning. Gypsy, at full tilt, launched herself from the dock and paddled to Debbie to save her life. When Debbie turned around to swim back in, Gypsy discovered her mistake, gave up on the rescue, and headed back to shore, but her long fur dragged her down in the water. My dad ended up rescuing the struggling dog. Thirty years later we still laugh at the memory.

Another time, my family was playing on a hand-pulled monorail car, crossing the Verde River in Arizona. My younger brother shouted with laughter, and that was enough for the mighty poodle to launch from our elderly friend's care, diving into the swift river to save us. Again, Gypsy had to be rescued from her heroic mission.

God gave us domestic animals for love, companionship, to assist us in many ways, and to teach us lessons about our relationship with and obedience to our Master. The prophet Nathan used a pet ewe to teach David about his sin (2 Sam. 12). Many faithful animals love their masters more than their own lives, and their obedience is legendary.

Praise God for His wisdom and His gift of pets to brighten our lives and teach us about love, tenderness, obedience, and loyalty.

Christy K. Robinson

KEEP THE MAIN THING THE MAIN THING

As you did it to one of the least of these . . . you did it to Me.
Matt. 25:40, NKJV.

A friend of ours has a motto hanging on a banner across the back wall of his office. It says, "The main thing is that the main thing is the main thing!" So simple, yet so profound!

Every one of us has a "main thing" in our lives. John's job is the most important part of his life. Lisa's children are her life. Julie's boyfriend is all she lives for. Greg is a sex addict. Family, career, money, sex, power: for many people, these describe the "main things" in their lives.

It is important for us as Christians, to identify the "main thing" in our lives, as well. Most Christians would say without shame, "Oh, Jesus is the most important thing in my life." Praise God. These song lyrics are the motto of many: "May the world see Jesus in me!"

But that is not the way many people see Christians. Churches split because they cannot agree on the color of new carpeting, what should be served at potluck, what songs to sing in church, or . . . you get the picture. Warning! The devil will do everything in his power to get you to focus on stuff that has very little to do with people's salvation, and everything to do with our culture and tradition. Ouch!

Jesus made it very clear what the "main thing" is. Just before He ascended to heaven, He said to His followers, "Go into all the world and preach the good news. And make disciples of all nations" (Mark 16:15; Matt. 28:19, NIV). He wasn't concerned with the political landscape. He said, "Go!"

At the Quiet Hour we take that commission seriously. Hundreds of people each year join a Quiet Hour evangelism team and travel to a foreign country in response to this commission. When participants taste for themselves the joy of the Matthew 25:40 principle in action, "As you did it to one of the least of these . . . you did it to Me," it has a life-changing effect. It helps us to focus on the "main thing" in greater measure. There is no greater joy than being what Jesus has asked us all to be—salt and light in this world. Be honest with yourself: is "the main thing the main thing" in your life?

Joedy and Judy Melashenko

GOD'S POWER

It is God who arms me with strength and makes my way perfect.
Ps. 18:32, NIV.

Our family is an archery family. Each day my husband is either teaching a group of children the technical skills of archery, or he is coaching a future champion. But my husband and sons not only shoot for the enjoyment or for the gold medal—they also shoot to illustrate God's power in their lives.

Frequently we are asked to share our talents for church groups, school groups, or youth organizations. With bows and arrows we demonstrate God's love, the importance of making wise decisions, and focusing on Jesus—the Center Mark.

One Bible principle we demonstrate is God's power. When people are learning to shoot with a bow and arrow, they immediately understand that the bow is the source of power that sends the arrow flying to the target. Without the bow and taut string, the arrow is meaningless. It has no purpose. It has no power.

Our lives are like an arrow standing in a quiver—powerless. We need God, the bow, to give us the power to be a witness for Him—to hit the center of the target. We need to take aim at our world, our community, and our family and friends. We need to be single-minded and focused on the task the Archer has set before us.

The more experienced an archer becomes, the more weight he or she is able to draw back on the bow, causing the arrow to fly farther and more accurately. The same is true in our spiritual life. When we have a strong relationship with God, we are able to do more with the power that He bestows upon us. We are able to reach more people and make a bigger impact upon our world.

"He shot his arrows and scattered the enemies. . . . It is God who arms me with strength and makes my way perfect. He makes my feet like the feet of a deer; he enables me to stand on the heights. He trains my hands for battle; my arms can bend a bow of bronze" (Ps. 18:14-34, NIV).

Charlene Hilliard West

REMEMBERING MERCY

He reached down from on high and took hold of me;
he drew me out of deep waters.
Ps. 18:16, NIV.

We had hoped to vacation on Koh Phi Phi, an island resort just off of Phuket, Thailand, on December 26, 2004, the day the massive tsunami waves wiped out the beach resorts and killed most of the inhabitants and tourists on the sandbar there. Instead, we spent the morning safely in Bangkok. After sitting stunned before the CNN broadcast for 12 hours, our family began the reluctant chore of getting on with our lives and trying to make sense of a senseless tragedy.

On Christmas I'd written an e–mail to friends in America: "Hi, from Thailand. My son is getting married tomorrow [December 26]." We had reservations for Phi Phi on December 27, so when friends read the e-mail on the other side of the date line the first questions were "Where in Thailand? Is Darryl OK?"

I replied to their queries with "We're OK, as you probably already know. We've diverted to another island on the other side of the peninsula in the Gulf of Siam, a place called Koh Tao (Turtle Island). It's beautiful here, but we're still sad for the deaths from the earthquake. Approximately 200 people died at Phi Phi Island. But not us."

Nearly a quarter of a million people were destroyed in minutes; but my family and I were safe. I thanked God for His mercies in sparing us from an unthinkable disaster. Yet it made me wonder about the master plan for His children elsewhere. I must trust in His wisdom and not question His motives. And I turn to Psalm 18:7-19, where it seems that David had a similar experience!

"The earth trembled and quaked, and the foundations of the mountains shook; they trembled because he was angry. . . . The valleys of the sea were exposed and the foundations of the earth laid bare at your rebuke, O Lord, at the blast of breath from your nostrils. He reached down from on high and took hold of me; he drew me out of deep waters. . . . The Lord was my support. He brought me out into a spacious place; he rescued me because he delighted in me" (NIV).

Darryl Ludington

ALIEN SPECIES

They are not of the world, even as I am not of it.
John 17:16, NIV.

During the 1980s and 1990s, perhaps in the hysterical run-up to the millennium, there were films and TV shows about space aliens invading the planet, or earth versus the universe. Dinosaurs, monsters, and alien-human hybrids stalked the streets.

Beasties are not new. Prophets Daniel and Ezekiel, 2,700 years ago, published their visions of monsters and conglomerate beasts (eyes all over, winged mammals, chariots of fire, etc.). But those were highly contrasted to the run-of-the-mill humans.

But wait! We Christians are not the khaki-beige average-Joe people we'd like to be. We are the aliens on this planet, and it is God who made us so. As the hymn says: "This world is not my home, I'm just a-passin' through." When we face persecution for our godly principles, when we're ostracized for our moral stands, when being an agape lover is reprehensible to those who hate, we feel very keenly that we do not belong on this planet. Someone once said that just because you're paranoid doesn't mean people aren't out to get you!

Some of Jesus' last words about his favorite earthlings are recorded in John 17:14-18: "They didn't join the world's ways, just as I didn't join the world's ways. I'm not asking that you take them out of the world but that you guard them from the Evil One. They are no more defined by the world than I am defined by the world. Make them holy—consecrated—with the truth; your word is consecrating truth. In the same way that you gave me a mission in the world, I give them a mission in the world" (Message).

Jesus said that His mission of love would alienate His followers from worldly people, that we'd risk losing everything dear to be His disciples. But He also promised a home where Emmanuel would wipe away our tears and keep us alive and healthy and joyful in His presence forever. And while we're traveling this world that's not our home, we have His guarantee that the Holy Spirit is with us and within us, to keep us company, encourage, heal, comfort, teach, and guide. We're only aliens for a nanosecond of time; then we have eternity to be at home in God's bosom.

Christy K. Robinson

I LOVE AMERICA

My kingdom is not of this world. John 18:36, NASB.

I love America and have never ceased to be grateful for my country. But talk about America being a Christian nation, suggest that God is with us more than with other nations, and suggest that we should elect leaders who are Christians so they will enact Christian-based laws, and I become very uncomfortable.

As I read the Bible, I see that Jesus came among the Jewish people, but I don't see Him much interested in building a Jewish nation. He could have done so. He was a great speaker, a great leader. What He could have done as a king! Imagine if Jesus had led soldiers into battle: anyone who was wounded He could heal, anyone who was dead He could resurrect, if the soldiers were hungry He could make food for them. If anyone had the chance to do some nation building, it was Jesus.

And yet Jesus resisted any attempts to make His movement a political power. Jesus was not at all a nationalist. When Satan offered Him the kingdoms of the world, He wasn't tempted. He kept talking about the kingdom of heaven. He told the authorities, "My kingdom is not of this world. If My kingdom were of this world, then My servants would be fighting" (John 18:36, NASB).

When in the Garden of Gethsemane one of His disciples took up a sword and began to fight, you'll remember, Jesus stopped him. "My kingdom," He said, "is from another place."

No matter how you slice it, you're going to have a hard time making Jesus a nationalist. Revelation calls Jesus the "King of kings and Lord of Lords." There is no country to which Jesus is especially partisan, for He is the Lord of the citizens of all countries.

All of this is to say that in Scripture people are not measured by which side they're on, which nationality they're part of, or which army they're fighting for, but only and solely by the spiritual quality of their lives.

Loren Seibold

SWITCHED PRICE TAGS

As he thinks within himself, so he is. Prov. 23:7, NASB.

Go back with me to the days when every little American town had a general store (before the days of Wal-Mart and K-Mart and UPC scanners). It was a favorite gathering place for all of the local farmers to exchange gossip and the latest news.

One evening some teenagers entered one of these general stores. They hid out and waited until the store was closed. They didn't vandalize, or burglarize, or spray graffiti. They stayed long enough to do what they came to do, and then left.

What did they do? They went through the entire store and switched all the price tags. A man's $50 suit now had a price tag of $2.99, and the $2.99 lunch box and thermos now had the $50 price tag. Wrigley's chewing gum: $4.99; Webster's dictionary: 10 cents! Everything in the store had switched price tags. The next morning the employees came to work and conducted business as usual. Unbelievably, the store operated for four hours before someone realized that something was wrong! Some shoppers got the best deals of their lives, while others really got fleeced!

Look at our country today. Values and traditions that we hold dear are being peddled for pennies, yet the cheapest filth and pornography is sold for millions. The filth that comes through our television sets is unfit to watch! Someone has broken into the store and switched the price tags.

It is important for us to recognize a life-altering biblical principle that will help us keep our price tags in order. The Bible says, "As he [or she] thinks in his heart, so is he" (Prov. 23:7, NKJV). And, by beholding, we become changed (2 Cor. 3:18).

The devil wants more than anything for us to switch the price tags and to focus our attention on those things that are not heavenly. Jesus said, "Do not store up treasures for yourselves on earth, where moth and rust destroy. . . . But store up for yourselves treasures in heaven" (Matt. 6:19, 20, NIV).

God is in the business of helping us refocus our lives on those things that are eternal.

Joedy Melashenko

June 1

FAITHQUAKES STRIKE EVERYONE

For the Lord your God is a merciful God; he will not abandon or destroy you or forget the covenant with your forefathers, which he confirmed to them by oath. Deut. 4:31, NIV.

Tragedy is everywhere: accident, illness, betrayal, job loss, divorce, death. When trouble strikes so intimately, one wonders, "Why can't I feel God's arms around me? Why would He allow such agony to happen to me when I've been His child all along?" The earth seems to have shifted beneath your feet. Author and pastor Doug Herman calls this a faithquake, and he titled his book after this concept.

If you've ever experienced an earthquake, at which time you are utterly helpless to change or stop the earth's groaning and aftershocks, you'll understand a faithquake.

We are not the first committed Christians in history to have wandered in a spiritual desert looking for God. We can act and walk in faith based on previous experience but still not feel that God is near. It seems we are praying to the ceiling. This is common. Herman wrote that after his trauma and desert wandering he discovered that God had never been silent at all. During that time, church people embraced him, though he was uncomfortable about it. He said that in refusing their outstretched arms he missed knowing the outstretched arms of Jesus Himself. Jesus may be trying to love and comfort you through His church. But you must be willing to accept it through the voices and love of the people around you.

If you're in the throes of suffering right now, recovering from the last assault or preparing for the next missile from the enemy's arsenal, remember that God has you in His arms. In your desert journey, He does have a spring of living water for you. He is always nearby, ready to catch us if our baby steps falter but giving us space to walk and run to His fatherly arms.

"For the Lord your God is a merciful God; he will not abandon or destroy you or forget the covenant with your forefathers, which he confirmed to them by oath" (Deut. 4:31, NIV).

Accept God's love through His people. He will show Himself to you if you open your eyes.

Christy K. Robinson

THE POWER OF TOUCH

Again the one who looked like a man touched me and gave me strength.
Dan. 10:18, NIV.

A searing experience left my emotions raw, my heart heavy. "Dear God, I need You. I need Your peace, Your assurance, some reminder that You are with me . . . that You care. I know You do, but right now, I feel so alone . . ."

Just then, my husband, passing through the room, stopped to give me a pat on the head and a quick hug. Peace flowed through my body, and I knew I'd been touched and healed by God. I know it was my husband who physically touched me, but God knew my need.

While on earth Jesus touched children, lepers, those who were blind, those who were mute, and other outcasts of society. Christ welcomed Mary's touch of perfume and love when she anointed His feet. I can only imagine what Jesus' touch must have meant to those poor, ill, lonely people, some who'd not been touched in years.

Studies show that hands-on therapy helps surgical wounds heal faster, burns clear up significantly sooner, circulation and breathing improve postsurgically, and premature infants have enhanced growth rates. Massage therapy significantly reduces the level of stress hormones in the body.

I felt that I'd been emotionally healed in the same way that the chronically ill woman of Matthew 9:21, 22 was physically and emotionally restored when she simply touched the hem of Christ's robe. The Lord knew her need, and her faith healed her. In the same way, when I reached out to the Lord through my pleas and prayers, He touched me through my husband's loving hands.

More than ever before, I believe God uses the people in our lives to remind us of His grand and lasting love. Sometimes, just listening isn't enough. Now, when a friend comes to me in need of loving understanding, I add a touch of my hand or a loving hug. It's an affirmation that I care.

"Again the one who looked like a man touched me and gave me strength" (Dan. 10:18, NIV).

AILEEN LUDINGTON

LESSONS FROM A CHOCOLATE BAR

God, who began the good work within you, will continue his work until it is finally finished on the day when Christ Jesus returns.
Phil. 1:6, NLT.

We were on our way to camp meeting and had stopped the car beside the road. That's when we discovered soda bottles in the tall grass. My brothers and I gathered up the bottles and headed across the street to a little store where we collected the bottle deposit money and divided it among ourselves. With my share in hand, I headed for the candy aisle. I spotted the biggest Baby Ruth bar ever seen. I had to have it.

In the car, my brothers were already stuffing their mouths with licorice. I knew their candy would be gone within a few minutes. I decided to hide my candy and eat it when all theirs would be gone. The next day, I reached under the car seat and pulled out the paper bag with my giant-size Baby Ruth inside. My little brother looked at that huge candy bar and said, "Joedy, where did you get that?"

"I bought it yesterday with my own money, and you're not getting any!" I replied.

My other three brothers piped in as well. "Oh, give us just a little bite! You're not going to eat that huge candy bar all by yourself, are you?"

As a silent answer I tore open the candy wrapper, opened my mouth as big as I could, and took a huge bite. But it didn't taste right. I looked at the candy bar and began spitting Baby Ruth out the window at 60 mph. The candy bar was chock-full of white, wiggly maggots, some only half there! We look so good on the outside, but on the inside we are filled with worms—sin and corruption! Even church folk in their "Sunday best" are lustful, greedy, and dishonest on the inside.

David cried, "Create in me a clean heart, O God; and renew a right spirit within me" (Ps. 51:10). David knew where the ugliness lay in his life. He had it together on the outside, but on the inside? He had worms in his soul. God can take those ugly parts of your life and make them sweet and desirable.

My paraphrase of Philippians 1:6 reads: "He who knows where the 'worms' are in your character can make you as sweet as a bar of chocolate!" Like David, ask God to make you sweet through and through!

JOEDY MELASHENKO

ONLY A PRAYER AWAY

Before they call I will answer; while they are still speaking I will hear.
Isa. 65:24, NIV.

While preparing to say grace before supper one evening, 3-year-old Annika declared, "I'd better get up and go near the window and pray really loudly."

When I inquired why, Annika replied, "Heaven is so far away, I want to make sure God hears me."

"We don't need to scream for God to hear us, sweetie," I explained. "It's like talking on the telephone, except better. Even if we whisper, God still hears our prayers. And best of all, God's phone is never busy."

Satisfied that God could really hear her, Annika prayed right there at the table, and then we ate.

How we should pray so God hears us has been debated since biblical times. The 450 prophets of Baal shouted, danced, and slashed themselves with swords and spears until their blood flowed in a futile attempt to impress their god (1 Kings 18:26-29). Elijah knew such a display was pointless, because he knew the Lord. No screaming, cavorting, or self-mutilation was necessary for God to hear and answer his prayer (verses 36-38).

The Bible writers go out of their way to emphasize God's desire to listen and respond to our prayers. Isaiah 59:1 states, "Behold, the Lord's hand is not shortened at all, that it cannot save, nor His ear dull with deafness, that it cannot hear" (Amplified). In Mark 11:24 it says, "Therefore I tell you, whatever you ask for in prayer, believe that you have received it, and it will be yours" (NIV). Most amazing of all, Isaiah 65:24 tells us, "Before they call I will answer; while they are still speaking I will hear" (NIV). Imagine that—God is already working out answers to our prayers before we even ask.

Whether we whisper at our bedside or shout from a mountaintop, God is listening. He wants to hear what we have to say. Give God a call today. After all, His line is never busy.

LAURA WEST KONG

WHITER THAN SNOW

Wash me thoroughly from my iniquity, and cleanse me from my sin."
Ps. 51:2, NKJV.

In 1949 Quiet Hour founder, J. L. Tucker, not only conducted three live radio broadcasts daily, but also pastored Oakland, California's, large Grand Avenue church and hosted evangelistic lectures in Oakland's 3,000-seat civic auditorium.

Another young minister and I received letters saying, "We want you to experience successful evangelism in a large city. In order to save money, we've arranged with J. L. Tucker for you to stay in the Grand Avenue church. You will need to take your own bedding."

We arrived in the early afternoon and went straight to Pastor Tucker's office. The busy pastor jumped up from his desk and gave us a welcome handshake. "So you're the young ministers from Central California. It's a privilege to have you join us." After giving us keys to the church, he said, "I'll show you where you will stay."

Walking down the hall, he stopped in front of the men's restroom and had us check it out. Next he led us up a narrow stairway to the third floor of the belfry. Pastor Tucker said, "We are going to give you men a private room. It's a nice bright room with two cots, and no one will bother you up here."

"Pastor Tucker," I asked, "where do we take baths?"

"We have the perfect place," he said with a twinkle in his eye, and he led us to the church baptistry. After showing us how to turn on the hot and cold water, he warned, "Whatever you do, don't let any church members catch you taking baths in here. It's a sacred place, and they may not understand." He added, "God's in the cleaning business—I think it's appropriate for young ministers to wash their bodies before they go out visiting people and inviting them to 'arise and be baptized, and wash away your sins' [Acts 22:16, NKJV]."

God wants us to live clean lives and have pure minds. The blood of Jesus cleanses from all sin. Before the meetings in Oakland finished, more than 300 people chose to be baptized. I determined to pray every day from then on, "Wash me thoroughly from my iniquity, and cleanse me from my sin" (Ps. 51:2, NKJV).

God promises to make us whiter than snow.

WELLESLEY MUIR

THIRSTY?

Whoever finds his life will lose it, and whoever loses his life for my sake will find it.
Matt. 10:39, NIV.

Many years ago a weary traveler hiked for miles across a desert with the sun beating down on him. It was hot! His water supply was gone, and he knew if he did not find water soon to quench his thirst, he would surely die and become food for the vultures.

He looked everywhere to find greenery—an oasis, or a spring of water. He saw absolutely nothing. Then, in the distance, he spotted an old cabin. Opening the creaky-hinged door, he discovered a rusty pump. He frantically pumped the handle to draw water, knowing he would live to see another day. He pumped hard, but the only thing that came out was dust and cobwebs.

Then he noticed a rusty coffee can nailed to the wall of the cabin with a yellowed note rolled up inside. The note said: "This pump is all right as of June 1932. But, partner, the washer dries out and the pump needs to be primed! Out the back door of the cabin I buried a jar of water and corked 'er up. There's enough water in the jar to prime the pump, but not if you drink some first! You gotta pour about a quarter of the water into the pump and let 'er soak for a minute or two to wet the leather washer. Then pour the rest medium fast, and pump hard! You'll get water! Have faith! This well ain't never run dry. When you get all watered up, I want ye to fill that bottle back up the way you found it and put it back under the rock for the next stranger who comes this way." The letter was signed, "Desert Pete."

Would you have the faith and courage to believe Desert Pete's note and pour that jar of water down a hole, knowing it was your only hope for life?

Jesus said, "Whoever finds his life will lose it, and whoever loses his life for my sake will find it" (Matt. 10:39, NIV). If you live your life selfishly, you will surely die. But if you give yourself away (lose your life) for the sake of the gospel, you will surely live. Your thirst for happiness and fulfillment will be quenched.

Desert Pete wrote prophetically when he said, "This well ain't never run dry"! Likewise, God has a well that "ain't never run dry"! God's faithfulness and promises are true. He has never failed those who trust in Him!

JOEDY AND JUDY MELASHENKO

June 7

INVEST IN THE FUTURE

The Spirit of the Lord will come upon you in power.
1 Sam. 10:6, NIV.

Investiture. The word conjures up the image of children receiving honor badges for craft projects or wilderness skills. Or perhaps it brings memories of being "invested" with campaign ribbons or medals after a military conflict. In some cultures, investiture means the enthronement of a bishop or royal person.

Investing, to most people, means money spent in order to gain a financial return, or to commit oneself to a cause or purpose. But there are some other definitions for investing. One is "to endow with authority or power." That implies that you have authority or power to share. Do you? Oh, yes! In Luke 9:1 and 10:19 Jesus gave His 12 disciples, and the larger group of 72 disciples and missionaries, power and authority over evil spirits, illness, and dangerous situations. When you were baptized, you were anointed with this dynamic power that can be exercised in the name of Jesus Christ. He has commissioned His followers to go into all the world and share His power, lighting candles and bonfires with His message of atonement and peace.

Another meaning for investing is to besiege or surround with troops, to envelop and cover completely. That is what our Quiet Hour evangelism teams are doing! They are troops sent in by Christ our Commander, to win souls away from the enemy. Around the world, teams of pastors and believers have already begun giving Bible studies and testifying of Jesus' saving power. They're working even now, as you read this devotional. Pray that the Lord will lead them to hearts that need Him, to lives that need salvation from sin. Pray that angels will protect the missionaries from danger. And that we, who live comfortable lives in a free country, will find the compassion and strength to do what God encourages, empowers, and enables us to do.

"The Spirit of the Lord will come upon you in power, and you will prophesy with them; and you will be changed into a different person. Once these signs are fulfilled, do whatever your hand finds to do, for God is with you" (1 Sam. 10:6, 7, NIV).

Christy K. Robinson

INVEST IN A CAUSE

Now all glory to God, who is able, through his mighty power at work within us, to accomplish infinitely more than we might ask or think. Eph. 3:20, NLT.

I'm invested in a cause: sponsoring two girls through a Christian agency. One is a Ugandan orphan; the other is Indonesian. My monthly donation is the equivalent of a man's monthly income—that is, if he could find a factory or farm job. I'm not wealthy. I have to work like everyone else, and I welcome freelance jobs to afford little luxuries from time to time. But I believe in—am invested in—the future of these little girls: their Christian education and spiritual development, vocational training, medical attention, and food. I am blessed and repaid by the Lord! He has taught me to value my return on investment.

We who financially support the Quiet Hour have seen tangible returns: thousands upon thousands of lives changed, people baptized, Christian orphanages built, eyeglasses distributed by the thousands, mission planes funded. Throughout the year we send teams around the world, evangelizing. Some of us can't participate because of work commitments, physical impairments, or age. Some don't have the dollars for airfare and other expenses to go on a trip of this nature. But we can go along in spirit.

Definitions of investiture include enthronement or the conferral of power. Will you join this great adventure and be part of enthroning princesses and princes of the Most High God? Will you help spread the life-changing power of the gospel?

God will provide an amazing return on your investment. He has invested Himself in us. In fact, He "is able to do immeasurably more than all we ask or imagine, according to his power that is at work within us" (NIV). God doesn't need our tithes and offerings, although of course His ministries do! We need to give our offerings. He wants us to enjoy the fulfillment of investing in something bigger than ourselves. And He is pleased to give us the kingdom no matter how much or how little we give.

Pray about what God will have you do. Perhaps it's praying faithfully and fervently. Perhaps it's sending a sacrificial gift. Or perhaps it's being a team member or the helpful person who will raise funds or inspire other people to join a mission team.

CHRISTY K. ROBINSON

DON'T TALK—ACT!

Dear children, let us not love with words or tongue but with actions and in truth. 1 John 3:18, NIV.

Several years ago my husband and I traveled to St. Petersburg, Russia, to assist with some evangelistic meetings. Going into a provincial city in Russia felt like going backward in a time machine. Everything slowed way down. Life was much like I remember it as a child.

While we did not experience hunger or serious personal discomfort, we were deeply affected by what the people in this superpower nation have endured. Imagine spending your life standing in long lines for anything worth getting, and then often not getting it; putting up with erratic electricity and water supplies, or none at all; never having a telephone, a washing machine, a car, or even a decent iron; and accepting the most menial jobs in order to have the Sabbath day for worship and fellowship.

Our exposure to such raw human needs created a paradigm shift in our values. We see with new eyes. Our little mobile home looks like a lavish, luxurious palace. Our second car has become an indulgence. Our bulging closets and drawers remind us that we have an adequate wardrobe for years to come. Even our granddaughters are deciding that instead of asking for yet another new doll, they'd like to send one to a Russian child.

Don't talk—act! John says, "Dear children, let us not love with words or tongue but with actions and in truth" (1 John 3:18, NIV), and he is right on. We've always given generously to church, helped the missionaries, and tended the needy at Thanksgiving and Christmas. But there's a special light in our eyes and a new spring in our step these days as we happily search for ways to save a little more here, a little extra there.

This day-to-day involvement with human need brings God's love to life in a vivid and personal way. And that warm glow in our hearts, as we think of the joy and blessings our little "extra gifts" might provide, must be a glow straight from heaven.

AILEEN LUDINGTON

THE LORD PROVIDES

The Lord Will Provide.
Gen. 22:14, NIV.

God stopped Abraham's arm and credited him with righteousness because Abraham had already sacrificed the son of promise in his heart. He trusted, and the Lord came through. "So Abraham called that place [probably the Temple Mount] The Lord Will Provide" (Gen. 22:14, NIV).

The Quiet Hour staff perform multiple tasks and work extra hours to accomplish not just their jobs, but their calling. Even in the best of years, they are cognizant of stewardship. But many financial supporters live on incomes tied to the financial markets. If income declines, so do the offerings sent to causes, ministries, and charities. But the Lord provides. Remember, He created our world from a void to all its fullness!

An 88-year-old widow sent $200 in spite of setbacks. Another enclosed $100 and wrote of the things she's doing without. A 92-year-old sent $40 she received at Christmas. When the Lord provided, she gave it back to Him! "God's always taken care of me," she said. "I've never been in want."

Like the widow with her mites at the Temple, they gave from the abundance of their hearts. What can God do with a mite? Change the world, that's what! It wasn't the dollar amount: it was the sacrifice of all she had. That's the place where God begins to do mighty miracles.

A 32-year-old teacher is one of the Quiet Hour's most faithful supporters. She says, "I like contributing to projects that are immediately happening and that I can see are changing lives. I can hear about immediate results from the contributions."

A 47-year-old man began his full-time college education to become a physical therapist and use his health training on mission trips for the Quiet Hour. And how will he overcome the obstacles of finance and time management? The Lord will provide!

Many of us have made similar decisions, knowing what these sacrifices mean: to step out of the boat into the stormy waters and walk with Jesus. We know that God has been faithful in the little things, and we trust that He is faithful in the big things. He will provide!

CHRISTY K. ROBINSON

JUNE 11

WANT TO SEE SOME MIRACLES?

Now about spiritual gifts, brothers, I do not want you to be ignorant. . . .
There are different kinds of gifts, but the same Spirit.
There are different kinds of service, but the same Lord. 1 Cor. 12:1-5, NIV.

Service is an essential element of the Christian faith. If you say you're a Christian, but you have no way to do anything for anyone, you've missed the boat.

A lot of religions expect members to give of themselves, but Christianity says that God not only asks you to serve, but gives you some ability to do it. The phrase "spiritual gifts" means that God has gifted you with the ability to do something He needs to have done. It may be something as simple as setting up chairs. It may require as much preparation as public speaking. There are even tasks for those who can't walk—for no disability can prevent you from praying for someone else. There's a task for everyone, and when you do that task, your work is enhanced by God's power.

We often complain that we don't see enough miracles nowadays, but here is one place I have seen miracles. I have known folks who thought they had no talents to give God's church, but when they try, God gives them the ability to do it.

When I decided to be a minister, some people thought it wasn't a good choice. I was so shy I wouldn't go up in front. I had long bushy hair and liked the Rolling Stones. Not good predictors for success as a pastor! My first sermon was absolutely painful—to prepare, preach, and listen to—and all of six minutes long. There's not a week that I preach a sermon that I don't feel in my heart that I'm the same person I was back then, and I'm always surprised when it touches someone. That's why, when someone says "Good sermon, pastor," and I say "Thank you," I'm often saying to myself, "I've no idea how that could have been a good sermon except that God made it good."

Want to see some miracles? Open your heart to the Holy Spirit. He probably has a long honey-do list for you, but He's supplying all the tools.

LOREN SEIBOLD

BUILDING WITH PEBBLES

When you gather for worship, each one of you be prepared with something that will be useful for all: Sing a hymn, teach a lesson, tell a story, lead a prayer, provide an insight. 1 Cor. 14:26, Message.

It has always interested me how many people want to receive the gifts of the church, without trying to figure out if they have anything to give back. Now, there are parts of the body that you could do without, but not that many of them. Your appendix. Your wisdom teeth. Even though you can get along without them, it hurts to lose them. You can get along without a toe or two, but if you lose a limb or one of your senses, you can't do all the things you could with all of your parts. Most parts of the body just can't be dispensed with, and so if you check out of working the whole, you leave the rest unfulfilled as well.

The practical upshot of this is that God does something to churches to make them work—as long as we're not too stubborn to kick in and do our part.

There's an old Aesop's fable about a crow who had not had anything to drink in a long time. He happened to find a pitcher that had a little water in the bottom of it. The old crow reached his beak into the pitcher to get a drink, but his beak wouldn't quite touch the water. So he started picking up pebbles from the ground one at a time and dropping them into the pitcher. And as more and more pebbles accumulated in the bottom of the pitcher the water rose in it until finally the old crow was able to drink all that he desired.

That's a parable of the way God has chosen to work out His plan in our world. Each of us is responsible to drop in our own little pebble—teaching a class, serving on a committee, providing transportation for someone, visiting someone.

"So here's what I want you to do. When you gather for worship, each one of you be prepared with something that will be useful for all: Sing a hymn, teach a lesson, tell a story, lead a prayer, provide an insight" (1 Cor. 14:26, Message).

Utilizing the gifts that are ours to serve in the ways we can may not seem all that important on their own, but as the pebbles accumulate in the bottom of the jug and the water rises, God builds His kingdom.

LOREN SEIBOLD

JUNE 13

THE TWO BIKES

Train a child in the way he should go,
and when he is old he will not turn from it. Prov. 22:6, NIV.

Lance had made up his mind. After a week of intense searching, he'd settled on a bright-red Yamaha Enduro dirt bike. He had gone to the bank and withdrawn the exact amount of money he needed from his savings account. Now I watched him from across the room as he made the purchase. Every muscle in his 13-year-old body was tense with excitement, anticipation, and pride, as he counted out the money, so diligently earned, and watched the sale being written up. Then, with shining eyes, he approached his motorcycle, the salesman following with final instructions.

"Watching that son of yours has warmed my heart," another salesman commented to me. "You know, last week a father and son came in here. The boy was about 15. They picked out a beautiful bike, one of our most expensive. As the father was paying for it, the son walked over to look at some accessories. 'You must feel really thankful for a dad who will buy you such a nice bike,'" I said to him.

"'Why should I?' the boy retorted, glancing scornfully at his father, who was writing a check. 'He's loaded. He won't know the difference.'"

My mind jumped to some familiar words: "Train a child in the way he should go, and when he is old he will not turn from it" (Prov. 22:6, NIV).

Lord, my young son has been quite a witness today. Thank You for teaching me that careful attention and training in childhood will pay off in later years. Thirteen is not very old, but already I'm beginning to enjoy the rewards.

AILEEN LUDINGTON

THE FAITH MATTRESS

I will lie down and sleep in peace, for you alone, O Lord, make me dwell in safety. Ps. 4:8, NIV.

"My back hurts. I must have slept on it funny," my husband, Ivan, remarked one morning.

"Well, Dad, it must be that old-fashioned mattress," Annika answered. "You need a new mattress," she concluded, proud that she had solved his problem so promptly. She then went on to extol the benefits of modern mattress technology.

A good mattress, while comfortable, is not really what is required for a sound night's sleep. King David wrote the third psalm while fleeing from his son Absalom. "I lie down and sleep; I wake again, because the Lord sustains me. I will not fear the tens of thousands drawn up against me on every side" (Ps. 3:5, 6, NIV).

There are no soft beds to snooze on out in the deserts east of Jordan. And how could you possibly relax when your own son is hunting you down, plotting to take your crown and murder you? Things did not look good for David. In Psalm 3:2 King David himself admitted, "Many are saying of me, 'God will not deliver him.'" To that, he replied, "But you are a shield around me, O Lord" (verse 3, NIV).

David's faith in God's protection allowed him to sleep despite the fact that he was far from the comforts of home, surrounded by enemies, and heartbroken over Absalom's rebellion. He did not toss and turn, worrying about what tomorrow would bring. He woke up refreshed because, in faith, he turned over his troubles to God.

That is the real secret to a good night's sleep—complete confidence in the God who holds us in the palm of His hand. "I will lie down and sleep in peace, for you alone, O Lord, make me dwell in safety," David declared in Psalm 4:8 (NIV).

When we feel secure in God, we can rest well in spite of physical discomfort or the concerns of the day. If we do not fully trust God, even the most luxurious bed will not bring us relaxation. A new mattress makes the back feel marvelous, but faith in God brings comfort to the soul.

LAURA WEST KONG

June 15

FOI EST TOUT

My soul finds rest in God alone; my salvation comes from him.
He alone is my rock and my salvation; he is my fortress, I will never be shaken.
Ps. 62:1, 2, NIV.

My surname, Robinson, is a very common English name. Its derivation is "son of Robin," Robin being a diminutive of Robert, which means "famous brilliance." The family motto for Robinson is *foi est tout,* or "faith is everything." Well, it is, if you put your faith (belief and actions) in the Lord of hosts.

Foi est tout. When I had just moved away from everything familiar and found myself without enough money to scrape by, the Lord solved the problem, and my debtor paid up, alleviating my poverty. Later, when I had no job, I promised God that I would, by honoring our partnership, continue to give the same offerings every two weeks as if I had a regular paycheck, until God found me a job or I ran out of money. I got the job seven months later, but I never ran out of money. I paid my mortgage and bills on time, received a serendipitous scholarship to accomplish a long-held goal, and had enough left at the first paycheck to cover my bills as usual. It was like the widow whose flour and oil never ceased during a famine (1 Kings 17). By my figures, my emergency fund should have run dry in two months. How did the money last for seven months, with a cushion left over? Only by God's grace.

Foi est tout, but only if your faith is in El Shaddai, the Almighty Protector and Nourisher. People will let you down no matter how hard they try to keep faith with you.

King David the songwriter knew that *foi est tout.* "God, the one and only—I'll wait as long as he says. Everything I need comes from him, so why not? He's solid rock under my feet, breathing room for my soul, an impregnable castle: I'm set for life" (Ps. 62:1, 2, Message).

Whatever your needs, the Holy Spirit, the *parakletos,* "the One who is called alongside," is with you. He's as close to you as your skin is to your flesh. Right now, ask Him to increase your faith. Be greedy for that faith that comes from God! I'll gladly lend my ancient family motto to you: *foi est tout.* Faith—in God—is everything.

Christy K. Robinson

DAD FIXES THE DAY

He trusts in the Lord; let the Lord rescue him. Let him deliver him, since he delights in him. Ps. 22:8, NIV.

My dad was the fix-it man around the neighborhood. If it broke, he could fix it. He repaired appliances. He could build a house from the ground up. He fixed toys and bicycles. He restored broken relationships and mended broken hearts. It was comforting to know that whatever could go wrong would soon be made right.

One special June our family was prepared for a Father's Day picnic at the beach. The lunch was made; the car was packed; and we were ready to go. Then the phone rang. There was a pipe broken in the neighbor's yard. Dad had to fix it. It was his job. (He was the maintenance man at the boarding school where we lived on campus.) Soon he was sitting on the backhoe tractor in the neighbor's yard digging a ditch so he could make the necessary repairs.

My brother and I were angry because "they" had taken our picnic away. We knew once the pipe was fixed it would be too late to go on our picnic. We sat by the tractor and watched our dad create a ditch with the bucket from the tractor he was operating. Throwing rocks into the hole, we sat and complained about our disappointing day.

Suddenly my dad invited us to sit on the tractor with him. He helped us climb up onto the tractor, and sitting on his knees, we helped him "dig" the hole, uncovering the broken pipe. Shortly my mom arrived with the picnic basket in her hands. Soon our family was sitting together in the large front bucket of the tractor, enjoying potato salad, hot dogs, chips, and chocolate cake. We were still having a family picnic—only in the bucket of the tractor. Dad had fixed the day!

My dad represented the Lord to us that Father's Day. He did the work that needed to be done; he helped a neighbor in need; he put his own needs last; he honored the needs of his own family; and when the work was completed (with our "help"), he rested and enjoyed fellowship with his family.

"He trusts in the Lord; let the Lord rescue him. Let him deliver him, since he delights in him" (Ps. 22:8, NIV).

CHARLENE HILLIARD WEST

BIG WORK LIKE DADDY

For the works that the Father has given me to accomplish, the very works that I am doing, bear witness about me. John 5:36, ESV.

In equatorial Singapore one wakes up with the tired feeling that the day's already far spent, even at sunrise. On the morning of my seventh birthday, however, I had both youth and high spirits on my side. I bounced out onto the big screened verandah. At the far right end of the porch stood the folding batik screen that Mum had made to give Dad some privacy at his desk. Bookshelves lined the screen inside, as well as the two outer walls. His desk stood against the fourth wall. This, my father's most characteristic habitat, is where I loved to hang out and watch him at his typewriter. Vaguely, I hoped for the day when I would "do big work like Daddy."

This birthday morning, however, the verandah looked different. Then I spotted it! At the opposite end of the verandah stood a dear little blond desk, with a matching chair that turned out to be just the right size for my 7-year-old frame. A card on top read: "Happy Birthday, Dottie." A black tray held a rainbow display of pencils, all trimmed to needle-sharp points. The first drawer contained a fat pink eraser, scissors, a red ruler, and a green penholder, plus a dozen new nibs and a squat bottle of Quink ink. Also blotting paper to take care of the blunders I'd make. A pyramid of fresh, clean paper occupied the second drawer. All for me alone! I could do anything I wanted in the paper world, right there at my own desk!

To work "like Daddy," my own adored daddy, took on real meaning. Today that precious little desk blends in smoothly with the executive-size one I use now. Indeed, with the Singapore sunrise on that October day, I felt my feet set upon the path of my life.

Jesus told the skeptical Hebrew academics around Him: "For the works that the Father has given me to accomplish, the very works that I am doing, bear witness about me" (John 5:36, ESV).

First, He evoked the strong parental bond implicit in our aspiring to "do big work like Daddy." Second, God invites us to watch Him work. Then He dispenses grace for us to succeed. In other words, He gives us a desk to match His, along with some blotting paper!

DOROTHY MINCHIN-COMM

RIVERS OF SWEETNESS

This is my beloved Son, in whom I am well pleased.
Matt. 3:17.

Looking back at my life, certain images remain etched in my mind and are triggered by the slightest event. Holidays and special occasions come most readily to the forefront of my thoughts. Of all these days, one Father's Day stands out as the most memorable of all. My dad always made breakfast with the greatest amount of sugar possible—French toast, waffles, and pancakes with brown sugar, syrup, and honey, as well as a whole pantry of other delectable items that were on the menu.

Mom always leaned heavily on the more healthy-type breakfast style. Her meal preference included the nutritious route of oatmeal, cornmeal, bran, wheat, or nuts. Well, it would not take much study to understand which one I fancied and chose for my dream wake-up calls.

On this particular Father's Day I thought that I would make my dad a breakfast for champions. It would be one that he would savor. He'd be proud of me for honoring him as my father. I set forth with zeal and vigor to produce eggs over easy and French toast with sprinkled white powdered sugar. I prepared carefully, the way I had seen him do so many times. Bottom line: I made the biggest mess ever seen in my mom's kitchen. "Over easy" ended up being essentially raw eggs. Burnt French toast and pancakes were covered in syrup at astronomical high tide combined with storm surge.

My dad smiled and looked down at me and said, "Well done, my son," before he sat down and tucked into the holiday breakfast. Happily I thought how much my dad appreciated me and loved me. It is my heart and my best intentions that are seen by my "Father which art in heaven."

As a father myself, my sons' efforts to please me now remind me that perfection is as far away as the moon. Our heavenly Father's grace-filled words to His own Son still ring true as a bell to all fathers on this day everywhere, "This is my beloved Son, in whom I am well pleased" (Matt. 3:17).

Bob McGhee

June 19

FATHER'S DAY GIFTS

For he received honor and glory from God the Father when the voice came to him from the Majestic Glory, saying, "This is my Son, whom I love; with him I am well pleased." 2 Peter 1:17, NIV.

I have been trying to figure out what to get my dad for Father's Day. It is not easy to find a gift that tells him how special he is to me—how much I appreciate his love, his advice, his strength, and his example. How much I admire him and love him.

I, too, am a father. My son could struggle with the same questions. I could tell him the answer. I could tell him what would be the best, most precious gift. Better than all of the ties, socks, wallets, or the other gifts he has given me.

My son has called me many times for many things. As he was growing up, he would call for permission to go to a friend's house to play or for a ride home from work. He would call about homework, school rules, advice, money, and comfort. He calls for help. I am always glad to hear from him and am always glad to help.

The calls that bring the deepest joy are the ones where he says, "I haven't heard from you in a while, and I just wanted to talk." We ask each other how things are going. We laugh, reminisce, and share. Those calls are priceless. One call can fill my heart with joy for days.

I cherish him so much that a relationship with him is the best gift he could give me—keeping me a part of his life, as he is a part of mine. The same is true of my heavenly Father. He cherishes me so much that a relationship with Him is the best gift I can give Him. He wants a relationship. He wants me to keep Him a part of my life, as I am a part of His. While He enjoys me asking Him for things, what brings Him the deepest joy is when I call and say, "I just wanted to talk with You."

Now I have a better idea what to give my father for Father's Day. I'll find something to give him to honor him on his day. However, I am going to try to give him the gift most precious all year long. The same gift I want to give to my heavenly Father.

Randy Bates

SAFE IN THE FATHER'S ARMS

*In His arm He will gather the lambs and carry them in His bosom;
He will gently lead the nursing ewes. Isa. 40:11, NASB.*

Annika was one of those mixed-up newborns who, like a jet-lagged world traveler, slept during the day and stayed up all night. Visitors in the hospital remarked what a good, peaceful baby she was. When everybody went home for the night, Annika was well rested and ready for action—that is to say, baby action—cuddling, rocking, nursing, and diaper changing. Sleeping was not on her nocturnal agenda.

When Annika was 2 days old, we brought her home from the hospital. She snoozed through her very first car ride and arrival home. That evening she awoke for the night's activity. Between feedings, crying, and snuggling, neither Annika nor I got even a catnap. In the morning my husband, Ivan, came upstairs to the nursery and found us both still awake. He gently cradled Annika in his arms, lay down on a blanket on the floor, held her on his chest and tenderly stroked her head. Safe in her father's arms, Annika immediately drifted off into sweet slumber, and then I also was able to get some much-needed rest.

A father's arms give shelter from the storms of life, strength in times of weakness, safety in the midst of danger, and guidance in times of uncertainty. A father's arms provide for the physical needs of his child. A father's arms are the place where a child can always find love and acceptance.

Moses described God to the children of Israel as a loving father: "You saw how the Lord your God carried you, as a father carries his son" (Deut. 1:31, NIV). King David sang of God as "a father to the fatherless" (Ps. 68:5, NIV). The prophet Isaiah called Jesus our Everlasting Father (Isa. 9:6, NIV). Jesus instructed His disciples to pray to God as Father: "This, then, is how you should pray: 'Our Father in heaven, hallowed be your name'" (Matt. 6:9, NIV).

My experience with my father and watching Annika with hers helps me understand God better. But whether or not we are blessed with a loving earthly father, God's arms are open to us all. What a wonderful place to be—safe in your Father's arms!

LAURA WEST KONG

June 21

THE VEIL IS OPEN

Having boldness to enter the Holiest by the blood of Jesus,
by a new and living way which He consecrated for us, through the veil, that is, His flesh.
Heb. 10:19, 20, NKJV.

Today is the longest daylight of the year in the Northern Hemisphere. (But I once spent December 21 in Queenstown, New Zealand, with sunlight from 5:00 a.m. to 10:00 p.m.)

For thousands of years, this date has been observed by devotees of pagan gods, and bonfires were lit and vigils held during the short hours of darkness. Ancient peoples built their pyramids, stone circles, palaces, road alignments, shrines, and temples based on their solar observations on this day in particular.

At solar festivals (solstices, equinoxes, and the six-week intervals between—February 1, May 1, August 1, and November 1), the eve of solar holidays was seen as a time when the veil (something that conceals, separates, or screens like a curtain) between this world and the otherworld (of spirits, gods, fairies, and the dead) was very weak and powerful otherworld figures could cross through.

Christians are so blessed to live in peace and freedom from fear. We don't have to appease vengeful gods by burning sage, pouring out libations, or making blood sacrifices. We need not fear haunting or demon possession because Christ protects us with His veil.

Hebrews 10:19-24 says: "Therefore, brethren, having boldness to enter the Holiest by the blood of Jesus, by a new and living way which He consecrated for us, through the veil, that is, His flesh, and having a High Priest over the house of God, let us draw near with a true heart in full assurance of faith, having our hearts sprinkled from an evil conscience and our bodies washed with pure water. Let us hold fast the confession of our hope without wavering, for He who promised is faithful. And let us consider one another in order to stir up love and good works" (NKJV).

That's an encouraging, satisfying, peacemaking message from God. He is all-powerful, and we are His children, so let us go forth in His name, in His strength, and in His heart of grace. (And let's stir up love and good works while we're out there!)

Christy K. Robinson

THE PURPOSE OF A MOSQUITO

The blood of Jesus, his Son, purifies us from all sin. 1 John 1:7, NIV.

The good Lord didn't create anything without a purpose, but mosquitoes come close. Maybe they're only for our instruction. My parents are from northern Minnesota, where the mosquito is the state bird. It's not on the official seal, but this is accepted fact by some people! When our family vacationed in Minnesota each summer, we were fresh meat to those tiny terrorists. We were polka-dotted with calamine lotion by the end of our visit.

My dad tells the joke that two mosquitoes were flitting through the evening. They look down, see a man, and the first mosquito says, "Shall we eat him here or take him back home to the swamp?" The second mosquito whines, "No, we'd better eat him here. If we take him back to the swamp, the big mosquitoes will get him."

I'm sure that on the Creation day when flying and creeping things were formed by God's word, the mosquito's purpose was not to suck blood, cause itchy welts, or carry malaria and West Nile virus. Perhaps it was as beautiful as a butterfly or iridescent as a dragonfly, and its acrobatics or aquatic dance was simply meant to entertain. Maybe it was for pollination or to be food for frogs, birds, and fish.

But when sin entered our world, all creatures were transformed and became subject to death. Some became predators. It's interesting that those that depend on blood seem the most hated creatures to us today—for instance, leeches and vampire bats.

When we're stung by irritations or feel that we've been bled by circumstances, let's remember that only the blood of Jesus heals us and washes away sin's guilt.

"But if we walk in the light, as he is in the light, we have fellowship with one another, and the blood of Jesus, his Son, purifies us from all [every] sin" (1 John 1:7, NIV).

CHRISTY K. ROBINSON

LOVE YOUR BROTHER

Now may the God of patience and comfort grant you to be like-minded toward one another. Rom. 15:5, NKJV.

Since 1937 archery has been a part of the West family in many ways. My children's great-grandfather West began the business by making and selling archery equipment. He then coached his son and grandson to become state, national, and world champions. The love for archery is an intrinsic part of our family. But in addition to teaching archery, we use it to teach others about Christ and how we can use our talents for Him.

During one gospel archery program, my sons unintentionally demonstrated their love and respect for each other. By shooting arrows at balloons pinned to the target, Mark and Aaron were demonstrating a biblical principle of teamwork. However, Aaron, in his first shot at his three balloons, missed, and his arrow landed at a point between all three balloons. Of course, we were stunned! Now what do you do or say during a program to recapture the biblical principle that they were trying to illustrate?

Mark calmly picked up his bow, aimed at the three balloons, and shot his arrow. It landed neatly and precisely next to Aaron's arrow. The principle of teamwork had been demonstrated to the audience. But to his family, especially his brother, he had demonstrated brotherly love and respect. Mark did not want his brother to have feelings of failure, so he changed the "bull's-eye" to make his brother look good.

Many times we go through life thinking about our own needs and what will make us look good. But when Jesus was on earth, His whole ministry was to create a small team of people that would turn their eyes away from themselves and onto others. Jesus considered no service too small and no sacrifice too great when it came to showing God's glory. By following His example, everything we do or say should also point to God's glory.

"Now may the God of patience and comfort grant you to be like-minded toward one another, according to Christ Jesus, that you may with one mind and one mouth glorify the God and Father of our Lord Jesus Christ. Therefore receive one another, just as Christ also received us, to the glory of God" (Rom. 15:5-7, NKJV).

CHARLENE HILLIARD WEST

MANY JAMS

The land produced vegetation: plants bearing seed according to their kinds and trees bearing fruit with seed in it according to their kinds. And God saw that it was good. Gen. 1:12, NIV.

My baker's rack is groaning under the weight of bottled fruit and jams. The freezer is also full. Each year I peel and pit, squash or dice the ripe fruit from my backyard. I have a tree trunk with one nectarine and three peach grafts; several varieties of apple on another tree, seedless and Concord grapes, cherries, strawberries, feijoa, mulberries, almonds, avocados, tomatoes, peppers, and herbs. God blesses me bountifully. Some years I have so many peaches that I give away bags and bags of them!

Every evening in late June, most of my time is spent on peaches, preserving them in light syrup or making them into thick jams. A few get sliced and frozen for nonfat smoothies. Excess juice freezes for party punch.

I heard once that "forbidden fruits create many jams."

Most jam recipes call for more sugar than fruit. Four cups of berries or peaches need five cups of sugar, plus pectin, to thicken and jell. All those nutritious mulberries, perfectly provided by God for our delight and nourishment (come on, He could have just given us tasteless fiber and left it at that!), He declared "good." Now when God says it's good, it's good!

I don't want to know the extra calories I add to God's perfect, juicy fruit when I make sweet jam. I've made something into a forbidden fruit—to my diet—by adding a foreign substance. (I have recently learned to make delicious low-sugar jams.)

When you're tempted to sample the proverbial forbidden fruit, remember that it may seem sweet or exotic at the moment, but it's a deception. It's sure to make you ill or fat. Pluck from the tree of life, and find nourishment in "every word that proceeds from the mouth of God."

Christy K. Robinson

June 25

RED LIGHT, GREEN LIGHT

He causes his sun to rise on the evil and the good,
and sends rain on the righteous and the unrighteous. Matt. 5:45, NIV.

One of my pet peeves is tardiness. I dislike being late, and I have low tolerance for others who are late. Each morning at the Quiet Hour the staff has worship together. Recently, it was my turn to lead out in worship. I had left home with plenty of time, but a stalled car blocked lanes near my boys' school, and I was going to be late.

After I negotiated my car around the stalled vehicle, I accelerated, hoping to make it to the office in time to fulfill my worship commitment. The street that I was driving on had a number of traffic signals, so I prayed that God would give me all green lights—no red ones. Green lights would get me there in time. However, every other light was red. Apparently, opposing-traffic drivers were praying for green lights, too!

My father taught me about answered prayers back when I was a child. I had prayed for sunshine so we could spend the day with my grandparents at Mount Rushmore. Father had evening worship with me and heard my prayer. He remarked that the farmers in the area were praying for rain to water their crops. How would God answer both prayers?

The next morning I looked outside and saw clouds. It wasn't raining hard, though. We went to Mount Rushmore, and the farmers had moisture for their crops. God can answer yes and no at the same time and still answer prayers. "He causes his sun to rise on the evil and the good, and sends rain on the righteous and the unrighteous" (Matt. 5:45, NIV).

God gives us lessons that will help us become better people. If the lights before us are always green, what would we learn? We need red lights to measure our pace, or even stop us, and keep our eyes focused on God.

Maybe God meant for me to be late this time. My tardiness was not a disaster. As I arrived, my friend was playing the hymn and my coworkers were singing. I used my speaking time to tell this story, and I was urged to use this illustration for this devotional book. So God is glorified after all. Amen!

Charlene Hilliard West

ENCOUNTER WITH AN ANGEL

And surely I am with you always, to the very end of the age."
Matt. 28:20, NIV.

We finished our concert at a church in Hollister, California. Many young people had received Jesus as Savior, and we were experiencing a strong spiritual lift. My friend Louis and his family saddled up, and my wife and children, plus all the band's instruments, were loaded into my station wagon to head to Los Angeles in a two-car caravan. On Highway 5 Louis's headlights flickered and died. My headlights provided just enough light for him to stop safely.

We decided I would lead and he would follow close behind so my headlights would guide us both. My own alternator belt had "busted" back at the church, and I was running on battery only. Worse, we soon entered fog so thick that we had to slow to 30 miles per hour. We'd been creeping along for 20 minutes when I saw the red lights of a highway patrol car. Oh, great—now I would get a traffic ticket too!

The officer came to my window, and nervously I explained our predicament. He listened and said, "The way you're going can get you into an accident. There are six gas stations between here and Los Angeles that have battery chargers in service. Your battery will last only about 60 to 90 minutes before you'll need to recharge. Stop at each one, recharge, and get home safely. Meanwhile, let me lead you out of the fog. There will be no more fog the rest of the way."

We followed the officer for about 10 minutes. Suddenly the fog lifted, and we were in the clear. I was relieved to see Louis still behind me. When I looked forward again, the patrol car was gone! There wasn't a place where that car could have U-turned or parked. It just wasn't there.

But our experience was not complete. We found six gas stations, recharged at each one, and got home safely. There was no more fog in the 300 miles left that night. My heart still races when I recall how God's angel protected us. "And surely I am with you always, to the very end of the age" (Matt. 28:20, NIV).

FRED HERNANDEZ

ARE YOU JESUS?

I tell you the truth, whatever you did for one of the least of these brothers of mine, you did for me. Matt. 25:40, NIV.

Eric, a young man with long hair and full beard and dressed in military fatigues, rode his Harley-Davidson motorcycle through the city on his way to a local hangout to find some action. He looked older than his 18 years. He was proud of his tough image. It was his style. It was no surprise to many of his friends when he was arrested for shoplifting. Since he was a first-time offender, the judge sentenced him to community service time instead of jail.

Eric chose the local "Loaves and Fishes" soup kitchen. Many homeless people frequented this shelter. Eric peeled potatoes, served hot food, and mopped floors. The place really depressed him. The sights, sounds, and smells—gross! It was a place for the poor, lonely, broken, bruised, battered, and afraid—people who reminded him of himself.

But Eric began to talk with the people and make friends. They weren't all drunken bums. Many were people caught in a poverty trap. There were Vietnam veterans, abused women with their children, an older woman who lost her home after her husband died. The stories broke his heart. He didn't feel so tough after a while. In fact, he began to enjoy how he felt when he served others. He had fun sitting on the floor putting puzzles together and playing checkers with some of the kids.

One evening while he was wiping tables after supper, he felt a tug on his camouflage pants. A young girl looked up to him. "Mister," whispered the child, "are you Jesus?"

The question startled him. "Huh?" he asked, confused.

"You must be Jesus," she insisted. "Mommy told me that Jesus loves poor people like us."

Jesus said 2,000 years ago, and says today: "I tell you the truth, whatever you did for one of the least of these brothers of mine, you did for me" (Matt. 25:40, NIV).

That is one of the most important reasons we are here on this earth. When we discover the joy of service, it can be a life-altering experience. Our prayer: "May the world see Jesus in me!"

JOEDY AND JUDY MELASHENKO

JESUS' FEET—PART 1

For the Lord himself will come down from heaven, with a loud command, with the voice of the archangel and with the trumpet call of God.
1 Thess. 4:16, NIV.

Someone posed the following question on the Quiet Hour's Web site: "When Jesus comes again will He touch the earth?" Perhaps this individual wondered if a charismatic human could be Jesus, back on earth for a secret rapture. Perhaps she's thinking of Jesus' prophecy in Matthew 24:5 that there will false messiahs. Maybe she wanted to start an argument for which she's convinced of the answer already. Does the answer matter?

The Bible doesn't say that Jesus' feet won't touch the earth or that whether His feet touch soil is a test of His identity as God, but it says we will rise to meet Him in the air.

Paul wrote in 1 Thessalonians 4:15-18: "According to the Lord's own word, we tell you that we who are still alive, who are left till the coming of the Lord, will certainly not precede those who have fallen asleep. For the Lord himself will come down from heaven, with a loud command, with the voice of the archangel and with the trumpet call of God, and the dead in Christ will rise first. After that, we who are still alive and are left will be caught up together with them in the clouds to meet the Lord in the air. And so we will be with the Lord forever. Therefore encourage each other with these words" (NIV).

The bigger questions are: When every eye sees the heavens parted and clouds of glory coming in the east, will we recognize Jesus by His loving character? Will we recognize the voice of our Shepherd? Will we lack fear at His awesome presence? Will we be the ones who joyfully greet our Master? Or will we be the ones who call for the mountains to fall on us?

Let us resolve to join enthusiastically, joyfully in the great chorus: "Amen. Come, Lord Jesus." And when you're rising to meet Him in the air, don't look down!

CHRISTY K. ROBINSON

JESUS' FEET—PART 2

You did not put oil on my head, but she has poured perfume on my feet.
Luke 7:46, NIV.

One of the most beautiful stories in the Bible is the one of the woman who anointed Jesus' feet with perfume, tears, and kisses. Bible commentaries suggest that she had been a prostitute. She may have risked stoning to come out in public to see Jesus. The dinner host, Simon the righteous church leader, had insulted Jesus by omitting the kiss of greeting and the washing of His feet. The other guests observed the insult, but the woman acted. Her love and outrage made her forget the hostile, contempt-filled crowd as she crept to Jesus' feet.

She kissed His travel-worn, dusty feet. She offered her love in tears and kisses, to cover the insults Jesus had received. She unveiled her hair and let it fall over His feet as a towel. This was a physically intimate gesture that outraged the company.

Her extremely expensive perfume may have been used in her prostitution business. In her love, the woman gave the value of a year's income, and with it, her heart, as she poured the perfume on Jesus' feet. The scent filled the room, ascending with her prayer of devoted love. Jesus turned toward the woman, but addressed Simon, his host. A woman of ill repute, she was honored by Jesus forever in God's Word.

"Do you see this woman? I came into your house. You did not give me any water for my feet, but she wet my feet with her tears and wiped them with her hair. You did not give me a kiss, but this woman, from the time I entered, has not stopped kissing my feet. You did not put oil on my head, but she has poured perfume on my feet. Therefore, I tell you, her many sins have been forgiven—for she loved much" (Luke 7:44-47, NIV).

Worship is not always something you feel during hymns or prayer, although those are means of entering God's presence. You can anoint Him with the perfume of kindness and mercy toward God's children. Imagine sending a bolt of light and joy back to God! He'll tell you the same thing He told this loving woman: "Go in peace, your sins are forgiven, for you loved much."

Christy K. Robinson

JESUS' FEET—PART 3

God is there, ready to help; I'm fearless no matter what.
Who or what can get to me?
Heb. 13:6, Message.

Over the years, my pastors have often preached on Luke 10:38-42, Jesus visiting the home of Martha and Mary of Bethany. Their subjects were on prioritizing spiritual matters over physical needs, managing stress, determining if you were a Mary or a Martha, and other sermon topics. I like to think about the relationship Jesus had with this family.

In a culture in which women were property, Martha surprisingly owned the home. Her siblings, Lazarus and Mary, and Uncle Simon depended on Martha for their home. She must have been quite the "Proverbs 31" woman! Between Martha's family and servants, Jesus, at least 12 male and an unknown number of female disciples, and the obligatory community invitees, Martha must have managed food, hygiene, and lodging for more than 30 people anytime Jesus came by! And she wouldn't have opened her home to Him unless the love and honor were heartfelt.

Perhaps when Mary had anointed Jesus' head and washed His travel-weary feet before the meal, she got lost in His message or His adventure stories of recent travels and abandoned her basin and cloth to sit at Jesus' feet. She could look up into His eyes, drink in the animation of His face and hands, and feel herself enveloped in warmth, unconditional acceptance, and the completion of everything missing in her life. Why would you remember to prepare supper when the Bread of Life and the Living Water were satisfying every need? So when Martha asked for help, Jesus reminded her that being in close proximity to Him was the treasure.

That's where we want to be—at Jesus' feet. When it comes to career or house and garden, it's OK to be a Martha. But remember that though home or livelihood may be taken away, our relationship with Jesus cannot. He freely gives us the gift of His love and salvation, and He will never withhold His love. Be relaxed and content with what you have—a friendship with Jesus.

"Since God assured us, 'I'll never let you down, never walk off and leave you,' we can boldly quote, God is there, ready to help; I'm fearless no matter what. Who or what can get to me?" (Heb. 13:5, 6, Message).

Christy K. Robinson

July 1

CITIZENSHIP

The kingdom of God is within you. Luke 17:21, NIV.

Jan and Dorothy, nurses, have dual Canadian-American citizenship. Antoinette, from the Azores Islands, is a resident alien in America. Steve, a New Zealander, was adopted by Arizona's Pima Indian tribe before moving back down under. Cordell is "Jamerican," a Jamaican-born, naturalized American. Lance, from Australia, recently was sworn into American citizenship. Ana Maria, from Ecuador, is a health educator in a jail system. One of her sons is in pastoral training. Darwin, from Missouri, sat in a Niagara Falls Canadian-side restaurant, looking at the American shore. "Across that river lies freedom," he declared melodramatically. The server was not amused.

My friends are from all over the world. And the best friends of all don't even belong to this world! We are aliens. We're not green and tentacled, but we don't fit in with most other earthlings. We belong to the kingdom of heaven.

The kingdom of heaven is not a pie-in-the-sky futuristic kingdom that we'll see shortly after Jesus' second coming. It's now, and it's been here since we accepted salvation or "got saved." We may choke on smog, see cigarette butts and homeless people in the gutter, and hear of oppression everywhere on the globe, but we Christians are, at this moment, living in the kingdom. It's both current reality and future promise.

We who live in democratized countries don't usually understand the distinction between a reign and a realm. The reign is a time and place of government rule. But the realm is the territory or sphere of influence. And because the kingdom of heaven is in our hearts and our monarch is Jesus, He is our King now as well as after His advent.

"Once, having been asked by the Pharisees when the kingdom of God would come, Jesus replied, 'The kingdom of God does not come with your careful observation, nor will people say, "Here it is," or "There it is," because the kingdom of God is within [among] you'" (Luke 17:20, 21, NIV).

Christy K. Robinson

LIFTING THE BURDEN FOR OTHERS

The righteous will go into eternal life. Matt. 25:46, NLT.

Recently I entertained 90-year-old Alice Smith as a house guest. She was being honored as a nursing professor of great gifts. I worried about her negotiating the stairs to my second-floor guest room. I needn't have worried. She walks two miles a day.

At the event designed to honor her Alice demurred to talk about her extraordinary academic experiences, reciting instead a hilariously funny poem she and her colleagues had created years ago while working in obstetrics. Only in private, when questioned, did she return to the topic of her tenure as chair of nursing at a suburban Washington, D.C., college. It was the time of civil unrest in the late 1960s. The college students were tutoring children in the inner city of Washington, D.C. Their mothers were on welfare.

Alice's pastor said to her, "Alice, these city kids have parents on welfare. How about teaching them to be nurses' aides? You know what nurses' aides need to know!"

Alice went home to pray about it. "Lord, you know I don't have any burden for people on welfare," she began. "And," she reported later, "the Lord said to me, 'I'll give you the burden.'"

So into the inner city went Alice Smith, the consummate professional. She collected a corps of nursing instructors. No one was charged. No one got paid. Alice was a great teacher. Every ghetto mother in the program received credentials. Some went on to become registered nurses.

Encountering her in the hospital later, an ample-sized ghetto mother would embrace Alice, size two. "My children are so proud of me!" she'd say. "Now I have a real job."

Alice's story adds a line to the words of Jesus addressing the faithful of all nations in the last day: "When I was hungry, you gave me food; when thirsty, you gave me drink; when I was a stranger you took me into your home, when naked you clothed me; when I was ill you came to my help, when in prison you visited me" (Matt. 25:35, 36, NEB).

Imagine Jesus' words to Alice: When I had no job, you taught me. You led me on the path to sustenance and dignity.

EDNA MAYE LOVELESS

JULY 3

AS YOU WILL

Yet not as I will, but as you will. Matt. 26:39, NIV.

Now and then, like everyone, I find myself in the examining room with a physician. I like to be an informed consumer of medical care, for I am increasingly aware, the older I get, that physicians are not omniscient, no matter if some think they are. A few years ago, I had to have a simple operation. I hate operations—being put to sleep, someone cutting into my body. I like to be in control. Yet this is one area where I had to be out of control. I had to trust my physician to react to whatever he found when he cut me open. Not only did he know more about that operation than I did, he had a view of my insides that I couldn't have. He was awake while I was drugged out. So beforehand, I asked questions. I tried to make a good decision. But in the end, I had to say, "Do what you think is best when you get in there."

There is hardly anything more important that you can say in your prayer than this: "Lord, You know what I want. I've told You what I think the solution to this would be. I've told You what I need. But whatever I want, when all is said and done, I want You to do what You know is best."

There is no truly mature prayer that does not contain this thought. I have heard many prayers prayed for some specific thing that a person wants. I myself have prayed many of those prayers. In fact, most of our prayers are lists of requests. I have even heard people demand answers of God, demand that He fix some part of their lives, or demand that He work a miracle for them. Name it and claim it, but demanding was not in Jesus' prayer vocabulary. Jesus asked for what He wanted. But in the very next line after He made His request to God, He said, "Still, Father, I trust You to do what You know is best."

LOREN SEIBOLD

PATRIOTISM

But the man who looks intently into the perfect law that gives freedom, and continues to do this, not forgetting what he has heard, but doing it— he will be blessed in what he does. James 1:25, NIV.

Independence Day is always a fun holiday. It lacks the pressures of Thanksgiving or Christmas; there's no need to use the day for chores or a dental appointment. On the plus side you get the day off and there are fireworks, picnics, swimming parties, parades, news stories about heroes, and sales. At church this week we sing "America the Beautiful" and "Faith of Our Fathers." Flags and bunting are everywhere. We dress in national colors.

My favorite Independence Days were ones spent in Washington, D.C., with the symphony orchestra playing and the shells bursting over the Washington Monument; and at Lake Powell, Arizona, where we swam and boated, watched a parade, met Navajo code talkers, and saw fireworks from a sandstone mesa. I once spent July 4 at the British Museum in London, where I wore my colors and was wished well by a tour guide!

Patriotism means supporting our government and armed forces, waving the flag, cheering for our country in sports, and having the "correct" political beliefs. Are we true patriots for doing these acts, or are there other ways of expressing love and honor for our country?

What about obeying the laws, including speed limits and zoning ordinances? Do we hire and pay people under the table to avoid taxes? Do we lie on tax forms? Do we study the voter information and the news reports and vote for issues, moral principles, and qualified people, or do we vote a party ticket? (Do we vote at all?) People offered their lives for these liberties we sometimes discount and for the lifestyle we believe is our right.

"But the man who looks intently into the perfect law that gives freedom, and continues to do this, not forgetting what he has heard, but doing it—he will be blessed in what he does" (James 1:25, NIV).

It's been said that you are your true self when no one is looking. Are you a patriot? Are you a doer or a talker? Wave your flag with pride, but follow it up with a life worthy of a citizen of the kingdom of God.

CHRISTY K. ROBINSON

SAVED BY A BOUQUET OF FLOWERS AND HIS SWEETHEART'S LOVE

For God so loved the world, that he gave his only begotten Son, that whosoever believeth in him should not perish, but have everlasting life.
John 3:16.

The great evangelist Billy Sunday loved to tell the story of a judge in Jacksonville, Florida, who was engaged to be married to a young woman. Sadly, one day they had a serious quarrel and broke up. The judge, just a few days later, became desperately ill. He was taken to the hospital, where he lingered between life and death.

His former fiancée had time to do some deep thinking. She realized that she was still deeply in love with him. So she went to a florist and bought a beautiful bouquet of flowers. Then she asked the doctor if he would take the flowers in and present them to the judge. The doctor happily agreed to do so. There he found the young judge in fitful sleep. It was clear that his life was ebbing away. He laid the flowers on the judge's chest and stood by and waited. In a few moments the judge became aware of the flowers on his chest. He opened his eyes and saw the flowers, then looked up into the face of the doctor. With a weak voice he uttered, "Thank you for the flowers, doctor."

The doctor responded, "They are not from me. On this little card you will see the name of the one who sent them." With trembling hands the young man held the card up and read it. It said "With all my love" and was signed by his former sweetheart. The judge asked, "Doctor, did you beg her to do that, or did she do it of her own free will?"

The doctor assured him that she had done it of her own free will. A miraculous change began to come over that young man. He began to improve immediately. In fact, just nine days later there was, in the hospital annex, a beautiful, quiet wedding service, as that judge and his sweetheart pledged their love to each other for the rest of their lives. He was saved by a bouquet of flowers and his sweetheart's love.

Praise God, nearly 2,000 years ago He sent the "fairest flower of heaven and earth," His own Son, to this earth for us, and along with it, He sent a message of His love. "For God so loved the world, that he gave his only begotten Son, that whosoever believeth in him should not perish, but have everlasting life."

HERMAN BAUMAN

PROMPT AND PERSONALIZED MIRACLES

For the pagans run after all these things,
and your heavenly Father knows that you need them.
Matt. 6:32, NIV.

There are, it seems to me, four differences between how the young deal with their desires and how mature people should.

The first is proximity. Children want what they want here and now. Maturity ought to teach us that what is best for us comes to us neither directly nor quickly. In fact, potential can be as precious as having the desired object in hand.

The second is identity. Children want for themselves. Each child is the center of his or her own world. As we grow, we should learn to look through the eyes of others. We see that happiness doesn't come only from getting what we want, but from making the greatest number of people happy.

A third difference has to do with understanding what it is that we need. Children are convinced that what they need is that specific toy or treat or to stay up late or to play with particular friends. Adults see that sometimes, when they've received what they've most wanted, it hasn't made them happy.

A fourth difference is that children see life as a matter of cause and effect. Children are sensitive to reward and punishment, which is why Santa is making a list and checking it twice. Maturity brings (or should bring) the understanding that sometimes we get both misfortunes and blessings we don't deserve, and sometimes we don't get consequences that we probably do deserve.

So it is with maturing in faith. When we first come to know the Lord, what may draw us in is a lively belief in the Lord's prompt, personalized response. We come to Him to get specific prayers answered. I need thus and so, and I will pray about it, and the Lord will give it to me.

Consequently, most of the miracles that people experience are for the purpose of drawing to God those who are young in faith. But as we mature in the faith, we begin to realize that not all prayers are answered, because God doesn't want them to be. He knows best who needs His blessing, and when, and of what kind. So a mature believer knows that we don't always get what we deserve, at least in the short term, either the good or the bad.

LOREN SEIBOLD

THE GOD WHO SENDS RAIN

Certainly God has heard me;
He has attended to the voice of my prayer. Ps. 66:19, NKJV.

The Meitei people, who live in the hills of northern India, are still largely unreached with the gospel. Ranjit Singh and his wife worked for several days to plant 2,500 cabbage plants in their garden. But as they worked, they noticed that some of the cabbage plants were beginning to wither. The ground was dry, and there was no sign of rain. Without rain there would be no harvest, and the family would face a difficult year.

The Singhs had lost faith in the gods they had called upon throughout their lives, but they did not know where to turn for help. Which of Hinduism's 300,000 gods would answer their prayer for rain to make their cabbages grow?

Then Mr. Singh recalled hearing someone say that the God of the Christians was all-powerful. He talked it over with his wife, and they decided to pray to this unseen God for rain. "If the God of the Christians hears our prayer and answers, then we will know that He is the true God," Mr. Singh told his wife. For the first time in their lives, the couple poured out their hearts to God for help.

That night it rained. The next day, the couple stood in amazement when they realized that the rain had fallen only on their cabbage patch and nowhere else in the village.

"Certainly God has heard me; He has attended to the voice of my prayer" (Ps. 66:19, NKJV).

Mr. Singh did not hesitate; he set out to learn how he could become a follower of this powerful God who had answered their prayer. But his wife hesitated.

Mr. Singh found a Protestant pastor and asked him how he could become a Christian. The pastor baptized him that day, and Mr. Singh went home happy. But he did not know what it meant to live as a Christian. What should a follower of God be doing? How should he worship? What did God expect of him?

Some time later Mr. Singh met an Adventist pastor and asked him, "What does it mean to be a Christian?" Through a series of Bible studies the pastor showed the couple what it meant to follow Christ. Both Mr. and Mrs. Singh were baptized.

Jim and Jean Zachary

UNDER HIS WINGS

The Lord God, who inspires his prophets,
has sent his angel to tell his servants what will happen soon. Rev. 22:6, NLT.

Over five months of intense activity the plane had been disassembled and prepped. Engine, wings, tail, landing gear, interior, instrument panel—everything. Paint stripping, cleaning, repairs, and modifications followed. The team was near exhaustion.

Aircraft reconstruction is painstaking work, usually executed by a few skilled craftsmen. This project had the unique distinction of including kids—lots of them. Nearly every weekend, dozens of energetic young people became part of the first youth-sponsored missionary aviation project in history.

Relying on the hospitality of a local facility for workspace had its challenges. Each time the space needs of the host changed, production ceased and hundreds of pieces needed to be moved. The seventh stoppage came two weeks before a gathering of 26,000 youth, at which final assembly was to be completed. The highly publicized event featured a white dove in flight—representing the Holy Spirit and peace—in its logo.

In discouragement I analyzed the work remaining—impossible. I walked into the hangar intending to break the news and give everyone some much-needed rest. One of our crew quietly pointed to the steel beam above the airplane parts. In stunned silence, my gaze fell on a beautiful living white dove. "Where did that come from?" I finally managed to ask.

"Nobody knows," replied one of our mechanics.

"If God cares enough about this project to send a dove to encourage us, then we need to keep working!" Daily, over the next two weeks, the dove flew from the hangar, but always returned to its watch over the rebuilding area. Four hundred sixty-five kids worked on the airplane. Assembled and dedicated for mission service at the event, it was flown back to the facility for finishing. The dove was gone.

"Have I not commanded you? Be strong and courageous. . . . Do not be discouraged, for the Lord your God will be with you wherever you go" (Joshua 1:9, NIV).

When, even through obedience, we find ourselves in difficulty, stop, look, and listen. He is Emmanuel: God with us.

DON STARLIN

JULY 9

GOD'S PECULIAR TREASURES

Ye shall be a peculiar treasure unto me above all people.
Ex. 19:5.

Comedienne Rita Rudner said, "I wonder if other dogs think poodles are members of a weird religious cult." Poodles are mostly shaved, but they have hairy pom-poms on their ankles and tail. We were told our family dog was pure poodle, but she had only wavy, not curly, hair. So we groomed her as a very cute schnauzer.

You've probably observed religious practitioners of many denominations who dress distinctively. Mennonite women wear a bonnet signifying their prayer life, and Jewish men wear the yarmulke cap. Devout LDS (Mormon) families wear special undergarments, and their outer clothes are always modest. In some charismatic faiths, the women don't wear slacks, only dresses, and their hair is never cut. Some communities believe in plain dress, with no buttons or bright color allowed. In some fundamental churches, men's neckties are required, but women's necklaces are disallowed. And the difference would be . . . ?

Four hundred years ago the King James Version of the Bible was translated from Latin, Greek, and Hebrew sources. One Jamesian word, "peculiar," has been used as a reason for godly people to set themselves apart from the worldly. (Today *peculiar* means strange, weird, eccentric, or odd.) "But ye are a chosen generation, a royal priesthood, an holy nation, a peculiar people; that ye should shew forth the praises of him who hath called you out of darkness into his marvellous light" (1 Peter 2:9), and "Now therefore, if ye will obey my voice indeed, and keep my covenant, then ye shall be a peculiar treasure unto me above all people: for all the earth is mine" (Ex. 19:5).

The Lord called us His chosen, holy, obedient treasures! Seventeenth-century peculiar meant special and sanctified, and set apart for holy purpose, not the twenty-first-century meaning, odd and bizarre. Not dowdy and unattractive. Like living sculptures of precious metal, we are God's treasures, His jewelry, if you will. As handiwork, the poema of the Creator (Eph. 2:10), our bodies and our spirits should shine, sparkle, glow, and reflect the Lord's glory as Moses did on Mount Sinai. Knowing that we are the special, holy treasures of God gives us reason to "shew forth the praises of him who hath called you out of darkness into his marvellous light!"

CHRISTY K. ROBINSON

ARE YOU REALLY READY?

Be careful, or your hearts will be weighed down . . .
and that day will close on you unexpectedly like a trap. Luke 21:34, NIV.

In 1990 a medical student warned me of the impending passage of Sunday laws by the U.S. Congress. He felt that this would usher in a time of religious persecution, and every sign pointed to this occurring before the end of the year. He cautioned me to cease renovating our church and hasten to teach our church members survival techniques that would help them flee Boston's doomed inner city for the mountains of New England.

Many share these beliefs. Some have built underground shelters; others have fled from urban jungles to a rural hideaway. Still others hoard canned food as they calculate events that they claim are unfolding in our nation and world.

Since then, we've had a terrorist attack on America—September 11, 2001. We are involved in wars that are consuming lives in the military, as well as innocent "collateral" lives. The 2004 tsunami disaster left hundreds of thousands dead and millions homeless. Yet, there is still no passage of a Sunday law.

There are two qualities in people who look for end-time tribulation with fear in their hearts. (Some people are looking for the time of trouble. I'm looking for Jesus' second advent. Big difference!) The former are not rooted in Scripture and zealously rely on prophecies of doom. Where the Word of God is neglected, there's a fanatical self-preservation that leads to miscalculation of events forecast by Jesus in Matthew 24 and Luke 21.

Fleeing to a remote mountain or cave is silly. Photosensitive equipment can measure people's presence even 24 hours after they've left a location. Sonar and radar penetrate soil and rocks, as we saw in Afghanistan, and satellites record a dog crossing the street hundreds of miles below. Where can we run? Where can we hide? We really don't know the day or the hour (1 Thess. 5:2, 3), because life will be progressing as usual (Matt. 24:37).

So are you really ready? Daily we must make Christ our personal Savior. If I make this decision today, I can answer unequivocally, "Yes! By His grace, I am really ready."

HYVETH B. WILLIAMS

THE CHANGED HEART

I will give them a heart to know me, that I am the Lord.
Jer. 24:7, NIV.

"My husband hates the Bible!" the woman wept. "He was angry when he found me reading it. He threw it against the wall; then he tore it up. Finally, he tried to burn it. This is all that I have of my Bible." She held up a few torn pages. "Then yesterday he struck my 5-year-old daughter on her head. I don't know what to do."

Mrs. Dauphney listened carefully as the woman poured out her misery to her. Then she said, "God loves you. And He does answer prayers. May I pray with you now?" Afterward, Mrs. Dauphney told her friend about some seminars being held nearby to help families find happiness.

Just then the woman's husband came home. Out of work, he was angry and desperate. He told her how a friend had offered to help him secure drugs he could sell to earn money. Again Mrs. Dauphney listened; then she said quietly, "God loves you and your family. He wants a better life for you. God is faithful, and His promises in the Bible are true."

The man asked, "Can you help me get a Spanish Bible?"

Mrs. Dauphney tried not to show her surprise and joy. "Yes, I can get a Bible for you," she smiled.

The following day Mrs. Dauphney brought the man a Bible and stayed to study with the couple. She invited them to attend an evangelistic series, and to her joy, they both agreed to come. The couple took turns attending the meetings while one of them remained in their unfinished home to guard the family's meager possessions.

Each morning Mrs. Dauphney joined the two pastors and 34 church members to give progress reports, plan their daily visitation, and pray for the nearly 500 people interested in the Bible. Through their efforts more than 1,000 people came to the evangelistic meetings each night.

As she shared how God changed the heart of an angry husband, her eyes filled with tears of joy. He and his wife are studying for baptism. God used the talents of a simple woman filled with love to win a family to Himself. He can use you, too, if you are willing to let Him.

JIM AND JEAN ZACHARY

THE GIFT OF A SMILE

He puts a smile on my face. He's my God.
Ps. 42:5, Message.

"Wear a smile and have friends; wear a scowl and have wrinkles. What do we live for if not to make the world less difficult for each other?" George Eliot said.

My 3-month-old daughter, Emmeline, loves to smile. She smiles at every face she sees—whether it's young or old, pimply or hairy, smooth or wrinkled. When she recently met her great-grandmother, I was afraid she'd react fearfully to that dear, deeply wrinkled face, but she simply beamed! I believe that this response comes from the knowledge that she is loved; the security of that love gives her the ability to respond with love and trust to everyone she meets.

A smile is a simple thing, but it can make a big difference in someone's day. It can make anger or resentment disappear, dissolve tension, show someone you care, or inspire laughter. One smile can turn an enemy into a friend, a despairing person into a hopeful one, or a frustrated person into a cheerful one. And it doesn't only work on others—wearing a smile can change your own outlook as well.

Mother Teresa once said, "Every time you smile at someone, it is an action of love, a gift to that person, a beautiful thing." Isn't that a lovely thought? Every day provides us with many opportunities to give away this precious and inexpensive gift, yet how often we neglect to!

We have a heavenly Parent who loves us more than we can fathom—enough to sacrifice His only Son so that we can spend eternity with Him. What better reason could we have to radiate His boundless love to others than with a smile?

Today, think of His love for you, and let the joy of that knowledge well up in your heart until it bursts out all over your face—smile!

"Why are you down in the dumps, dear soul? Why are you crying the blues? Fix my eyes on God—soon I'll be praising again. He puts a smile on my face. He's my God" (Ps. 42:5, Message).

Lorelei Herman Cress

July 13

GET A LIFE

[He has given us a spirit] of power and of love and of calm and well-balanced mind and discipline and self-control. 2 Tim. 1:7, Amplified.

"A solitary person, completely alone—no children, no family, no friends—yet working obsessively late into the night, compulsively greedy for more and more, never bothering to ask, 'Why am I working like a dog, never having any fun? And who cares?' More smoke. A bad business" (Eccl. 4:8, Message).

"My time is short—what's left of my life races off too fast for me to even glimpse the good" (Job 9:25, Message).

Hey, I resemble those remarks! I was searching an online concordance on another theme when I found these verses, and they pierced my soul. OK, not enough to leave the office and go home and play with the dog, but enough to make me rethink balancing my life.

My mother used to say that I needed balance when I was working 60-hour weeks and leading the singles ministry for my state and being a church musician on Saturdays and Sundays. (But I thought Mom was jealous of my time.) My boss told me to find balance. My doctor said that being tired and stressed was preventing weight loss. I'm not so unbalanced that they ganged up on me: these are comments I've heard over many years. (And I haven't learned yet?)

A partial defense is that I earned my Christian high school and university tuition, paid for my own second-rate car, and found employment without the advantage of being the relative or crony of someone "important." I relish solo vacations. I made my own family-of-choice at work and church. Work is fun, and it's good fellowship, so I often steal from leisure time to work at home. I love working at church. As a single woman with a mortgage, it's terribly difficult to say NO to work—or to a request from the pastor, who thinks that 1 Corinthians 7:34 means that singles have oodles of time for church projects!

But a weekly rest with God and making a daily "quiet hour" to commune with Him tends to level the teeter-totter of my life. If someone says, "Get a life," I can say, "Thank you, but would you like some of my excess?"

Christy K. Robinson

THE GIFT OF REST

Learn the unforced rhythms of grace.
Matt. 11:29, Message.

Have you ever observed people around you in the bank, the grocery store, a doctor's office, mall, or the Department of Motor Vehicles? How many of them seem carefree and happy? How many appear tired, frustrated, worried, impatient, or downright angry? How often during the week do you feel relaxed and worry-free? Do you often wish that you could take a break from the hustle and bustle and just "be"?

When He created us, our heavenly Father knew that we would need time to recharge our batteries, so He ordained a day of rest for us as a gift—the Sabbath.

I grew up in a household with many rules about what could or couldn't be done on the Sabbath. Because of this, my brothers and I learned to dread the Sabbath as a day when nothing enjoyable was allowed. We couldn't wait for the sun to set so that we could begin having fun again!

As an adult, I've learned that the Sabbath isn't about what you can and can't do—it's about reconnecting with ourselves, our family and friends, and most important, our Creator. He gave us this gift of time to get away from the stress of daily life and focus on what is most important—our relationship with Him. Quality time to spend with our family and friends. Time to meet with others who share our beliefs and support us in our walk with Him. Time to rejoice in the beauty of His creation. Time to thank and praise Him for the blessings of life and love. Time to remember how to truly live.

God created the Sabbath as a joyful day of praise and thanksgiving and fellowship. A day we can look forward to all week and wish could last forever. A gift for our enjoyment and for the refreshment of our souls. A foretaste of heaven.

Jesus says, "Are you tired? Worn out? Burned out on religion? Come to me. Get away with me and you'll recover your life. I'll show you how to take a real rest. Walk with me and work with me—watch how I do it. Learn the unforced rhythms of grace. I won't lay anything heavy or ill-fitting on you. Keep company with me and you'll learn to live freely and lightly" (Matt. 11:28-30, Message).

LORELEI HERMAN CRESS

July 15

GRACEFUL TONGUES

We all stumble in many ways. If anyone is never at fault in what he says, he is a perfect man, able to keep his whole body in check. James 3:2, NIV.

Wouldn't it be nice if we really could be perfect? How many times have we all said things we wished we had not said! James insists if we could just tame our tongues, we could be perfect! He goes on to compare the tongue to a horse's bridle, a ship's rudder, and a tiny spark. In each case, something relatively small and seemingly insignificant is shown to be much more important than it may have seemed.

It can be a challenge getting the bridle into the mouth of a large horse, especially if he has other ideas, but once the bridle is in place, the large horse can be controlled and directed.

While at sea, I went to my cabin to get some sleep, leaving my crew in charge. When I came back on watch, I was confused that we had traveled some 21 miles, but our position showed we had progressed only nine miles. A quick look at the plotter showed a zigzag course. The crew had not properly used the rudder to steer the boat. Something so small makes a big difference.

When I was a young boy, it was my job to load up the burn barrels and haul them to the dump at one corner of our farm. What I did not realize one Friday afternoon was that there were still some live embers in the bottom of one of the barrels. Around 3:00 the next morning a passing motorist knocked on our farmhouse door to alert us to a large fire burning in the dump area. The fire continued to burn and smolder for many months, all because of tiny sparks.

James counsels us to carefully choose our words. What comes from the mouth reveals who we really are. But we could also note that what we say can have an effect on what we become. The things we spend time thinking about are often expressed, further strengthening that thinking. Many people process thoughts through "out loud" expression or by talking through their ideas. Others ponder things silently. In any event James urges us to ensure that we put into our minds only things that will allow our tongues to give praises to our Lord.

Michael Porter

ONE THOUSAND GALLONS A MINUTE

Like newborn babies, crave pure spiritual milk,
so that by it you may grow up in your salvation,
now that you have tasted that the Lord is good. 1 Peter 2:2, 3, NIV.

The summer field trip to the city fire station is a much-anticipated highlight for the children of Loma Linda, California. First, the firefighters show off the shiny red fire engines. Boys and girls alike gaze in wonder as one by one the truck's many compartments are opened to reveal marvelous lifesaving tools of all shapes and sizes. Hidden inside was everything from medical equipment for treating injuries to sledgehammers, axes, and the "jaws of life," giant hydraulic cutters that can tear off a car door in seconds to free trapped accident victims.

Next came the protective gear, from the top of the helmet down to the steel-toed reinforced boots. When fully suited up, not an inch of skin was left unprotected. The whole ensemble weighed more than many of the kids present.

At the front of the truck, the children lined up to sit in the engineer's seat. My daughter, Annika, climbed steps that reached up to her waist. She had to stretch her arms out wide to grasp the gigantic steering wheel.

Outside, the children examined the different hoses used to put out fires. The largest attacks fires with a gush of 1,000 gallons of water per minute. Then each got to practice putting out a "fire" on a board painted with a house and hinged wooden flames in a window that fall over when hit with the stream of water. Water flew everywhere as the children struggled to aim the nozzle in the right direction.

Inspired by the excitement of the afternoon, some kids expressed the wish to someday become a firefighter. Although it will be many years before any of those children are able to fill the firefighters' boots, cut away crumpled car doors, maneuver a fire engine through crowded city streets, or wield the mighty water cannon, with the right training they can grow up to reach their goal.

We as Christians, with the right preparation, can also grow in Christ to do great things!

LAURA WEST KONG

AYN MOUSA, THE SPRING OF MOSES

You . . . have refreshed the hearts of the saints.
Philemon 7, NIV.

Several years ago, Candace, Audrey, and I, amateur archaeologists, took a weekend off from excavating near Amman, Jordan, and visited the ancient city of Petra, where building facades and interiors are carved from the red sandstone of a dry desert canyon. Boys pointed to their donkeys and asked, "Taxi, madame?" Audrey and Candace hiked to the top, while I walked downhill in the morning, saving the uphill return journey, in the July afternoon heat, for a camel taxi.

Near Petra, we saw the tan, barren, rolling hills where Moses and the Israelite multitude spent 40 years camping, grazing their flocks, collecting manna, living, and dying. From an air-conditioned car we saw the black goat hair Bedouin tents and laundry drying on rope lines, as they've done for thousands of years.

After being on our dig for only a few weeks, we were thrilled to have hot showers, toilets, and bug-free beds in our hotel. We slipped out to the pool for a night swim—what bliss. On our return journey we found a sign that read "Ayn Mousa, the Spring of Moses." For several thousand years, predating Muslim times, this has been thought to be the place where Moses struck the rock for water, though God had told him to speak to it. Water gushed from the rock nevertheless, and the Israelites were saved yet again by God's grace (Num. 20:7-12).

Ayn Mousa is a block building with a paved floor. It backs up to the base of a cliff; a boulder juts from the floor, and a stream of cool, fresh water pours from the base. (We drank some; it was sweet.) That water supplies the town around Petra, including our hotel and its pool. When we asked our supervising archaeologists if this was truly the Spring of Moses, they said probably not, but it could be the place.

I hope it is the same place, with its miraculous water flowing steadily for 3,200 years. I like the idea that at the hotel pool we were swimming in God's grace, being cooled, refreshed, and exhilarated after our exertions.

"Your love has given me great joy and encouragement, because you . . . have refreshed the hearts of the saints" (Philemon 7, NIV).

CHRISTY K. ROBINSON

FAITH AND CONVICTION

I believe that you are the Christ, the Son of God, who was to come into the world. John 11:27, NIV.

"When Martha heard that Jesus was coming, she went out to meet him, but Mary stayed at home. 'Lord,' Martha said to Jesus, 'if you had been here, my brother would not have died. But I know that even now God will give you whatever you ask.' Jesus said to her, 'Your brother will rise again.' Martha answered, 'I know he will rise again in the resurrection at the last day.' Jesus said to her, 'I am the resurrection and the life. He who believes in me will live, even though he dies; and whoever lives and believes in me will never die. Do you believe this?' 'Yes, Lord,' she told him, 'I believe that you are the Christ, the Son of God, who was to come into the world' " (John 11:20-27, NIV).

Martha has gotten a bad rap in some circles. And as a woman with "Martha" tendencies, I've had a lot of guilt about my inclination to be task-oriented. So when I recently read this story, I was very encouraged to see there was more to Martha than what we normally think. Martha had great faith in Jesus. She believed that her brother Lazarus would not have died if Jesus had come when she called Him; she also believed in the resurrection. And most important, along with Peter, she proclaimed her faith that Jesus was the Christ, the Son of God—a remarkable proclamation in her situation.

It seems that Martha is a good example for us after all. Like many of the Bible's characters, she is flawed. She could let the tasks get in the way of the moment, and she might have missed some important things, being so caught up. But at the same time, she had a strong and certain faith in her Lord—a conviction about who He was and what He could do.

Next time when we read Jesus' words "Martha, Martha" in Luke 10, perhaps what we'll hear is the tones of a loving Christ who saw her for all she was, rather than the way we sometimes read them today—as a scolding. Jesus sees us for all that we are, just like Martha, and He loves us completely. When He calls us away from our task-intensive lives into fellowship with Him, it isn't a scolding. It's to fellowship with a loving Friend who longs for our company.

PAMELA MCCANN

JULY 19

HAIR ON MY SHIRT

We are justified freely by his grace through the redemption that came by Christ Jesus." Rom. 3:24, NIV.

I'm a cat lover—so much so that we have five of them at home, all of which are indoor cats. One of the joys of having feline friends is that we get to enjoy the very thing that makes them so cuddly: their hair. The guard hairs and undercoat fibers appear everywhere: bedspreads, furniture, floors, and especially on the seats of the dining room chairs. The cats love those chairs. It seems they spend most of their time sleeping there.

It has become a daily ritual, right after breakfast, for my wife and me to use a lint roller to remove the cat hair from our clothes before going to the office. Every morning we stand and slowly rotate under a light to catch every hair we can see, and just when it appears we are finished, we catch a glimpse of another few we missed, and expressions such as "Honey, honey, there are some more here on my back!" can be heard occasionally.

We walk out of the house into the garage, sit down in our car, put on our seat belts, and just when I'm ready to turn the ignition key, I look down to my trousers, and what do I see? More cat hair! Didn't we go over those areas three times already? Where did they come from? Do the tiny hairs actually follow you, like a cat stalking its mouse toys? (Yes, on dry, windy, static-cling days, they do!) Keeping cat-hair-free is a losing battle.

It is equally futile to try to remove every trace of our sinful nature by our own effort, "for all have sinned and fall short of the glory of God" (Rom. 3:23, NIV). Just when we think we have that sinful nature under control, it rears its head to show us how fruitless our efforts are.

Only then do we find that we are "justified freely by his grace through the redemption that came by Christ Jesus" (verse 24, NIV).

By God's grace we can put on the perfect robe of righteousness, washed to perfection by our Savior.

FRED HERNANDEZ

A MISSIONARY IN A BAR

The righteous cry, and the Lord hears and delivers them out of all their troubles. Ps. 34:17, NASB.

One summer I sold large sets of Christian books to families in an effort to earn money to pay for my university tuition. I was driving my white Toyota Camry over the backwoods roads of Michigan when a friend, who also sold books, called my cell phone. She said, "Hey, have you heard? There's a tornado watch!"

I eyed the ominously darkening sky in front of me. It grew blacker and greener by the minute. The trees swayed. I decided that I should drive back toward the home where I was staying.

By the time I returned to the main highway, rain was falling in torrents, and just as I thought it couldn't get worse, it turned to hail! I pulled into a church parking lot and prayed for safety. The hail subsided, and I continued down the road.

I turned on National Public Radio just as the regular programming was interrupted by a monotone beep. It was the emergency alert system. I turned up the radio. A tornado had been sighted on the very highway I was traveling between the village I'd just left and the next town. That's very close by, I realized! The emergency alert advised those driving in that vicinity to pull off and take shelter immediately.

I searched for the next building along the country highway, which happened to be a bar. Feeling quite self-conscious, I jumped out of the car and dashed to the door, praying that the Lord would protect me even if I took shelter in a bar! As it turned out, I wasn't the only one out of place in there. A few children (obviously too young to be in a bar) were also hiding inside with their parents. After a half hour of nervous silent praying and listening to the meteorologist on the bar's TV, we refugees dispersed.

On my drive home, I praised the Lord for His angels' protection in averting the danger! God truly does hear the prayers of His people when they cry to Him in their distress.

JOELLE MCNULTY

THE WHOOP-DEE

Our citizenship is in heaven.
And we eagerly await a Savior from there, the Lord Jesus Christ.
Phil. 3:20, NIV.

Annika's Aunt Ilene, aka Ku-Ku (a Chinese word for aunt), is a graduate student in physical therapy. As any college student knows, classes, labs, and impromptu study sessions mean that schedules vary from day to day. Therefore, Annika never knows the date or time that Ku-Ku will be home. Sometimes Ku-Ku is there when Annika visits her grandparents, and sometimes she is not.

Whenever Annika hears the garage door opener at her grandparents' house, she knows that Ilene has come home. Annika immediately stops whatever she is doing and excitedly announces, "I hear the whoop-dee! Ku-Ku is here!" (Whoop-dee is the name Annika gave to the sound of the garage door opener when she was just learning to speak.) Then Annika dances around excitedly as she hurries to the back door to greet her aunt.

Annika always hopes and watches for Ku-Ku's arrival. Because of the close relationship they share, she is overjoyed at the sound of the whoop-dee. There are special games that Annika plays only with Ku-Ku. Time spent with Ku-Ku is a much-anticipated event and makes the remainder of her day a happier one.

We also are waiting for the arrival of Someone special. Like Annika, we don't know the day, and we don't know the hour, but if we know Jesus, we look forward to His return with joy. "Our citizenship is in heaven. And we eagerly await a Savior from there, the Lord Jesus Christ, who, by the power that enables him to bring everything under his control, will transform our lowly bodies so that they will be like his glorious body" (Phil. 3:20, 21, NIV).

"For the Lord himself will come down from heaven, with a loud command, with the voice of the archangel and with the trumpet call of God. . . . And so we will be with the Lord forever" (1 Thess. 4:16, 17, NIV).

When we finally hear that whoop-dee, we too can rejoice and dance excitedly like Annika, because Jesus' return is not just for the afternoon, but for eternity.

Laura West Kong

A HUMMINGBIRD'S HEART

A miserable heart means a miserable life;
a cheerful heart fills the day with song.
Prov. 15:15, Message.

Hummingbird hearts beat 1,260 to 1,400 times per minute. Their wings beat 55 to 75 times per second, creating the famous humming noise. They live an average of three years. Some migrate thousands of miles in a single season, following the blooming plants. They need to eat (flower nectar and tiny insects) about every 10 minutes to maintain their metabolism. They can't walk or hop, but they can hover. Their two-inch-wide nests are made of plant down, spiderwebs, and stray bits of fluff.

"My" green-and-tan hummingbirds love blue sage and lavender spikes, ripe black mulberries, and pink orchid trees. They're boldly curious little beasts, hovering close and checking me out as I water the plants or read in my garden nook. They perch in the trees, do aerobatics, and buzz the dog's head. When they scold my cats for just existing, their chirps can be heard many meters away. The tiny ones peer in the kitchen window as I'm preparing a meal. When the young hummer is temporarily abandoned in the orchid tree, she chitters for her parents for 10 minutes before she's hungry enough to seek and sip her own nectar (which was why she was "abandoned" in the first place).

Like many other species, the hummingbird is not mentioned in the Bible, which is admittedly not a scientific nature handbook. They are native to the Americas, not to the Bible lands. Would it be a stretch to liken our desire for a relationship with the Lord to a hummingbird's heart? Is your heart beating for the Lord? "Love the Lord your God with all your heart and with all your soul and with all your strength" (Deut. 6:5, NIV).

Perhaps this hum is an example of having a song in your heart! "A miserable heart means a miserable life; a cheerful heart fills the day with song" (Prov. 15:15, Message).

Christy K. Robinson

HOLDING ON TO HOPE

As surely as the sun rises, he will appear;
he will come to us like the winter rains, like the spring rains that water the earth.
Hosea 6:3, NIV.

I love to read adventure stories: they can be so full of suspense, and it's thrilling when the story resolves and the good guys win. Recently I was rereading J.R.R. Tolkien's *Lord of the Rings* trilogy with my husband. While I had read the stories several times, he was hearing them for the first time. The experience for him was very different than it was for me. Because I had read the stories before, I knew how they ended. I could enjoy the suspense with a confidence that things would turn out OK. He didn't know. In a way he was experiencing the book through the eyes of the characters—the uncertainty, the doubt, the possibility of death and destruction.

When we look at the stories in the Bible, we know how they end. They don't really carry the same amount of uncertainty that they did for the people described in them. When Abram was told by God to go to a new country, he didn't know what to expect or what would come of it. When Moses went to talk to Pharaoh, he didn't know exactly where he would be leading the Hebrews or how. When Jesus died on that cross and was buried, the disciples surely had such hopeless feelings.

And as I look at my life today, I don't know what tomorrow holds. Things can look dark, beyond hope, and uncertain. At the end of time, and only then, will we know exactly how our story turns out. While we're living it, we're just like those people in the Bible, waiting for the ending. Fortunately, we have the same God—the faithful One who never changes.

Hosea 6:3 says, "Let us acknowledge the Lord; let us press on to acknowledge him. As surely as the sun rises, he will appear; he will come to us like the winter rains, like the spring rains that water the earth" (NIV).

PAMELA MCCANN

THE TWO BABIES

Yet will I rejoice in the Lord, I will be joyful in God my Savior." Hab. 3:18, NIV.

There was a knock at the door of my chaplain's office. A young couple introduced themselves.

"We have just come to speak with you and get a final opinion," the husband said.

"We want to make sure we are not doing anything wrong," continued his wife. She had recently given birth, but tests indicated that their baby had no brain function, and they were going to turn the life support off that afternoon. After talking it over, they declined further help and requested use of the chapel for prayer as they prepared to say goodbye to their baby.

This couple had hardly left when there was another knock at the door. Composing myself, I found another young couple, but these parents had their baby in their arms. They were as radiant and proud as any parents I have seen. "We are so thankful that God has given us a beautiful healthy baby," the dad said. "We want to dedicate her to God. Would you pray with us in the chapel?"

This second couple had no concept of how difficult it was for me to concentrate, knowing that at the moment we were offering prayers of thanks and dedication to God for this child, there was another couple turning off the machines that maintained the last vestiges of life for their child. Much of the sense of futility we experience comes because we hang on to the questions raised, rather than utilize the insight gained in facing that which we do not want to be true.

The prophet Habakkuk, who was very forthright with his questions to God, said, "The righteous will live by his faith" (Hab. 2:4, NIV). Faith permeates almost every aspect of life. The prophet concludes his oracle by stating: "Though the fig tree does not bud and there are no grapes on the vines, though the olive crop fails and the fields produce no food . . . yet will I rejoice in the Lord, I will be joyful in God my Savior" (Hab. 3:17, 18, NIV).

While we have little or no control over events, faith gives us the ability to scramble over the landscape of life and continue our unique mission to provide help and support to whomever we meet under whatever circumstances.

K. LANCE TYLER

APOPLEXY OR APOCALYPSE?

He who began a good work in you
will carry it on to completion until the day of Christ Jesus."
Phil. 1:6, NIV.

While staffing our Quiet Hour exhibit at a fair, I attended the Steve Green vocal concert. A thousand fans enjoyed the repertoire of this musical minister. Earlier, he had autographed my copy of his CD and had visited our exhibit.

At the concert I glanced at the open laptop computer of the man next to me. Instead of enjoying the program, he was typing a Bible study on Revelation, and he was having trouble with the spelling of "apocalyptic." He attempted several versions, but kept getting the spell-checker's red underline. Finally he accepted an alternate spelling the program offered: he clicked "apoplectic," and it was automatically inserted.

I was becoming apoplectic myself, stifling my giggles during the music. Apologizing for my visual eavesdropping, I whispered to the writer that perhaps the word he wanted was for end-time major events, not for cerebral hemorrhage.

After the concert, I opened my Bible to the text Mr. Green had written in his autograph. It was "He who began a good work in you will carry it on to completion until the day of Christ Jesus" (Phil. 1:6, NIV).

I've been writing stories and articles since elementary school. At age 14 I sold my first article to a newspaper, and in university I studied writing and print communications, which has been my career. My skills are by no means "complete," but God is not finished with me yet. Nearly all my writing and editing is for Christian publications and institutions.

One Quiet Hour subscriber wrote that the apostle Paul should have listed Christian writers with evangelists and teachers. Paul was a gifted writer. When there was no word to describe a concept, he invented one. He was colorful, intellectual, logical, and, above all, directed by the Holy Spirit. God did some of His best work in Paul!

What are your gifts? Have you asked God to bring you the experiences and insight to develop your gifts to full potential? Will you allow Him to carry you to completion in Christ Jesus? How will you use your gifts today to expand the borders of His kingdom?

CHRISTY K. ROBINSON

NOTHING BETWEEN

We also rejoice in God through our Lord Jesus Christ, through whom we have now received reconciliation.
Rom. 5:11, NIV.

I remember a father whose son had been alienated from the family for many years. Finally, after a long time the son came home. He wasn't a son one would normally have been very proud of. He had too-greasy hair, tattoos and piercings, was uncouth, and smelled like the substances he drank and smoked. That father, though, was so glad to have him home that every time he looked at him you could just see the pride. He magnified all his son's good points and minimized his bad points. The mere fact that his son was now talking to him made him a new creation in the dad's eyes. It was a marvelous example of grace in action. Reconciliation had happened. As far as the dad was concerned, there was nothing between his child and himself.

Perhaps you remember this old hymn: "Nothing between my soul and the Savior, naught of this world's delusive dream. . . . Nothing preventing the least of His favor; keep the way clear! Let nothing between."

The hymn writer understood that it isn't God that puts up the obstacles between us and Him. Usually, we throw those in there. That father could (and, I suspect, will) love that son forever, no matter what he does. The son now has a marvelous chance to change—a place to live, a supportive family.

What he does with that is up to him. In the end, some of it is the choice of the son about whether he'll "get it"—whether or not his dad's love will open doors to a better life for him. And in the end, that's the only motivation that counts for us, too.

LOREN SEIBOLD

July 27

A COMPELLING LOVE

For Christ's love compels us,
because we are convinced that one died for all, and therefore all died.
2 Cor. 5:14, NIV.

Theologians have often debated the metaphysical meaning of the atonement. There have been theological wars over this in the Christian church. I've never really spent much time looking into it because, for me, this text gives me the simple meaning of the atonement: Christ's love compels us. Christ died to convince me that He loves me so much that He wants me to love Him back.

God seems to be saying, "You folks go about your work and your play down there, your sinning and warring and all that stuff you do, seemingly unaware of My desire that you have something better—a better life here and in the next life. What can I do to convince you?

"Well, how about this: I'll present Myself for martyrdom to help you see just how much I love you. This is the one thing even you people, as out of tune with the spiritual universe as you seem to be, won't be able to miss."

Jesus died on the cross to say, "This is how much I love you." Now, doesn't that make you want to be more loving too? Christ died to convince me that He loves me so much that He wants me to love Him back.

We should spend part of every day contemplating Christ on the cross. Not in a macabre sense (as I think some Christians do), but to remind ourselves of the reason for the suffering. "He did this because He loves me."

Doesn't that make you want to respond in turn? I hope so. And how should you respond? Simply: "And he died for all, that those who live should no longer live for themselves but for him who died for them and was raised again" (2 Cor. 5:15, NIV). No longer live for yourself!

"Living for Jesus, a life that is true, striving to please Him in all that I do, yielding allegiance, glad-hearted and free, this is the pathway of blessing for me."

Loren Seibold

WORDS MAY BE ALL YOU HAVE

Walk with me and work with me—watch how I do it.
Learn the unforced rhythms of grace. I won't lay anything heavy or ill-fitting on you.
Matt. 11:29, Message.

You witness an accident and find the victim bleeding, moaning, and writhing in pain. Most of us would frantically try to determine what we should do. (In emergencies, this means calling 911, and then possibly applying first aid.) Doing something in an emergency or crisis is often essential, but that's only one aspect of how to help an injured person.

In our haste to find the right thing to do, few of us think, *What can I say?* Indeed, why should we think that words could have any effect? But studies have demonstrated that every word, every thought, even every intention can cause a measurable physical reaction.

There's another way of approaching that accident. Make the phone call. Then calm yourself and pray. Introduce yourself, determine whether first aid must be administered, and then say: "I've called 911, and help is on the way. I can see that your leg needs attention. Why don't you scan the rest of your body to see that everything else is all right. The ambulance is on its way. Try to relax and think of someplace else that you'd rather be right now. You can allow your mind to go to that place, and you can begin to feel comfortable right now."

Trauma is an assault on the mind as well as the body. The right words can help calm a person in the throes of a panic attack or soothe the chronically ill. The right words can physiologically and emotionally alter the outcome of serious situations and can ease the dark night of the soul, both in the present and in the future.

We may be intimidated by our lack of resources or paralyzed by fear or by our feelings of incompetence, but in an emergency situation we need to focus on the injured person. We need to speak in a calm, reassuring manner and simply stay with them so they don't feel alone.

Your willingness will enable you to connect with people in a profound way. It is then that you move from first aid to rescuing the person with the power that involves the unforced rhythms of grace.

"Walk with me and work with me—watch how I do it. Learn the unforced rhythms of grace. I won't lay anything heavy or ill-fitting on you" (Matt. 11:29, Message).

BARBARA MOEN

POWER TO BELIEVE

Worship the Lord with gladness; come before him with joyful songs.
Ps. 100:2, NIV.

Alec Nasichovich grew up in a Muslim family in southern Russia. As a teenager, Alec became involved with some youth who introduced him to drugs, Eastern religions, astrology, and extrasensory perception. Fascinated by these new ideas, he began communicating with spirits, hoping to find success and happiness. But all he found was trouble with the police and threats from Mafia thugs.

One day Alec was talking with some friends when one of them threw out a challenge: "Satan is stronger than God!"

"I do not know God," Alec replied, "but He must be stronger than Satan." Alec's words planted a seed in the heart of his friend that sent him searching for God. Imagine Alec's surprise when he learned that his friend had become a Christian! Alec saw the changes in his friend's life and wondered, "Is God really that powerful?"

Alec and his friend heard about some evangelistic meetings and decided to attend. Soon Alec too was convinced that the Bible was God's Holy Book. The two attended every meeting, studying and learning. Alec accepted Jesus as his Lord. His heart overflowed with God's love, and he yearned to share it with others. He wrote a song in which he poured out his love for God and expressed the joy he had found. He sang it at a meeting. "Alec," the pastor's wife said, "you could do so much for God through your singing!"

Alec began to write poems, describing the joy he found in Jesus. As he strummed his guitar, melodies came into his mind. Eagerly he put his poems to music and sang them whenever he had a chance. Alec has become a singing evangelist, and many have told him, "I found Christ through your music."

Alec has found his spiritual gift. "I want to be a musical missionary for God," he says. Just before evangelistic meetings open in a city, Alec presents a sacred concert and gives his testimony of how Jesus saved him. Then he invites the people to the meetings.

Throughout Russia thousands are hearing the message of God's love and redemption in these last days. Pray for these new believers and for those who lead them.

Jim and Jean Zachary

TOO MANY PACOS

The world and its desires pass away,
but the man who does the will of God lives forever. 1 John 2:17, NIV.

A touching story by Ernest Hemingway tells of a great quarrel between a father and his teenage son. Their relationship shatters and the son leaves home. The father soon regrets the episode and goes in search of his son. But the city of Madrid is so large, so confusing—the father hasn't a clue where to look. He decides to put an ad in the paper. "Dear Paco, meet me at 10:00 a.m. tomorrow in front of the newspaper office. All is forgiven. I love you. Dad."

The next morning the father finds hundreds of Pacos in front of the newspaper office, searching, hoping.

Our world is full of hurting, heartbroken people—people who've been mistreated, neglected, alienated, victimized; people who are angry, resentful, bitter, lonely, depressed, fearful, and guilt-ridden; people consumed by hatred and self-pity.

But these same people long for love, acceptance, compassion, and forgiveness. The spiritual hunger of people in our world is reflected in the skyrocketing sales of books on religion, spirituality, and inspiration. As one writer put it, in the human heart there are longings for material things that are unattainable. But God implants a longing for the eternal things.

John, the beloved disciple, put it this way: "Do not love the world or anything in the world. . . . For everything in the world—the cravings of sinful man, the lust of his eyes and the boasting of what he has and does—comes not from the Father but from the world. The world and its desires pass away, but the man who does the will of God lives forever" (1 John 2:15-17, NIV).

AILEEN LUDINGTON

July 31

YOU ARE SPECIAL

To those sanctified in Christ Jesus and called to be holy, together with all those everywhere who call on the name of our Lord Jesus Christ—their Lord and ours. 1 Cor. 1:2, NIV.

When my children were small, I taught them a song that included these words: "I am a possibility . . . I am a great big bundle of potentiality."

That song conveys a very important message for all of us. Each of us is truly a one-of-a-kind masterpiece in the making. God has uniquely created each of us. He has brought people and events into our lives that have shaped us for a very special life and ministry. The process will continue.

"What is that in your hand?" In Exodus 4:2 God asked Moses this question when Moses was struggling to accept God's will for his life. All of us, at some time, need to answer this question. What has God placed within me and around me to prepare me to be and to do what He wants for my life and ministry?

As we begin examining our personal estate (everything in our hands), we remember how God has led us. We see His fingerprints of guidance not only for our present but for our future. This includes our home, body, natural talents, spiritual gifts, upbringing, intellectual capacity, and spiritual background. Other items could be our vocational background, financial resources, failures and successes, dreams and visions, family, trials, special people in our lives, special opportunities, open and closed doors, and more.

As we see the depth, enormity, and uniqueness of our estate, we will see how very special we are. None of us is alike. Our creative God has been at work in us for a long time, and He continues His work today.

We should discover and celebrate our own uniqueness. Today God is grooming us for tomorrow.

God's will for you is found in a thorough understanding of His estate that He gave to you—the things He has placed in your hand. Even as God spoke to the people of Israel in Isaiah 43:1, He speaks to us: I have created you; I have formed you; "I have redeemed you; I have summoned you by name; you are mine" (NIV).

Joedy Melashenko

THE CUP OF SALVATION

My Father, if it is possible, may this cup be taken from me.
Matt. 26:39, NIV.

Perhaps you've wondered, as I have, the source of the metaphor "let this cup pass from me." Think of an ancient cup as a vessel with a handle, like a dipper, that a host would dip into the wine or food and then pour out onto a person's dish. The food served you could be good, or not so good. A guest would get good food; a prisoner, perhaps, would get spoiled food.

The Old Testament pictures God as the divine host of the world, and for His people He would dip up and serve either blessings or punishments. In the twenty-third psalm, for example, "my cup runneth over" as God pours out blessings to His sheep. Psalm 116 says that God pours out the cup of salvation. On the other hand, when Israel and Samaria sinned, God poured out for them what He called the cup of ruin and desolation (Eze. 23:33). God didn't make any excuses; He didn't blame it on Satan; He said very simply that He Himself was dipping up and serving to them a helping of punishment.

And that's what Jesus believed about His death, too. He believed that this was the fate that God had served Him, for God's own purposes. And frankly, He didn't want it. He wished He could take that cup of suffering and death that God had served Him and hand it back to God and say, "I don't want any of that, thank You. Pass it along to someone else."

I find it rather encouraging, in an odd way, that even Jesus did not welcome suffering. He knew, if anyone should have, that God had a purpose and that He was doing God's will. He knew that all things in God's will work together in the end. Still, like the rest of us, He got discouraged when in the immediate future it appeared that His whole world was falling apart. Even Jesus, a part of God's immediate family, even God Himself, got discouraged. So I'm encouraged because I know that Jesus doesn't condemn me for getting discouraged or depressed—He knows how it feels.

LOREN SEIBOLD

August 2

NATIONAL ICE-CREAM SANDWICH DAY

God's kingdom isn't a matter of what you put in your stomach.
Rom. 14:17, Message.

That's what the calendar says: National-Ice Cream Sandwich Day.

Today, because it's so hot and sticky outside, I'd love to stand at the grocery store with my head in a cooler, in the ice-cream section. Y'all can go for the ice-cream sandwiches if I can have a Klondike bar with Heath topping.

This is wishful thinking. I've been on diets all my life. My life has pretty much settled into vegetables: soups, fresh, steamed, salads, baked, boiled, any way but fried. And the medically supervised diet (oops—lifestyle program) has kept me otherwise healthy. So if I do stand at the frozen-foods cooler, it will be the spinach/broccoli/peas section.

I came home from church the other day, and my dog, who had been fed a fulfilling breakfast, had nosed her way into the pantry, pulled out the foil packet of cat treats, and gobbled them all up.

Why, when I'm a true believer in health, do I still have the desire for fattening stuff? When my dog has a full tummy, she steals or begs for more.

Perhaps it's because we're lacking other things in our lives: a romantic relationship, time with family members, fulfillment in a career, or enrollment in a dog agility class. My doctor would say that instead of a Klondike, I should crunch vegetables. ("Do you know how many truckloads of carrots equal one Klondike?") My dog's veterinarian would say, "Sure, join that exercise class!" My pastor would say that the carnal nature is at war with the divine nature God has given me.

The apostle Paul would say that it doesn't matter what you eat and drink. "God's kingdom isn't a matter of what you put in your stomach, for goodness' sake. It's what God does with your life as he sets it right, puts it together, and completes it with joy. Your task is to single-mindedly serve Christ" (Rom. 14:17, 18, Message).

I'll go with that last one. And because it's for God's glory, please pass the broccoli and hold the delicious cheese sauce.

Christy K. Robinson

HOW MUCH ARE YOU WORTH?

Don't be afraid; you are worth more than many sparrows.
Matt. 10:31, NIV.

The story is told of a speaker who started off his seminar by holding up a $20 bill. In the room of 200 people he asked, "Who would like this $20 bill?" Hands started going up.

"I'm going to give this $20 bill to one of you, but first let me do this." He proceeded to crumple the bill into a small wad.

"Now who wants it?" The hands went up again.

"Well," he replied, "what if I do this?" he unfolded the crumbled bill and dropped it on the ground and started to grind it into the floor with his shoe. He picked it up, now all crumbled and dirty.

"Anybody want it now?" All the hands still went up.

"My friends," he said, "You have all learned a valuable lesson. No matter what I did to the money, you still wanted it, because it has not decreased in value. It is still worth $20."

Many times in our lives we are dropped, crumpled, and ground into the dirt by the decisions we make and the circumstances that come our way. We feel as though we are worthless. But no matter what has happened or what will happen, we never lose our value in God's eyes. Dirty or clean, crumpled or creased, we are still priceless to Him.

Jesus said, "Are not two sparrows sold for a penny? Yet not one of them will fall to the ground apart from the will of your Father. And even the very hairs of your head are all numbered. So don't be afraid; you are worth more than many sparrows" (Matt. 10:29-31, NIV).

The worth of our lives comes not from what we do or who we are, but from whom we belong to!

"How great is the love the Father has lavished on us, that we should be called children of God! And that is what we are!" (1 John 3:1, NIV).

AILEEN LUDINGTON

August 4

PREPARE TO VOTE!

I have decided to make a covenant with the God of Israel and turn history around.
2 Chron. 29:10, Message.

It's about three months before Election Day in the United States. Are you registered to vote? Every citizen of legal age should be.

Voting is more than your privilege; it's your duty. If you don't vote, you shouldn't criticize policies, laws, or officeholders. Your vote could remove corruption, immorality, or ineptitude from office. It can place wise, visionary, and righteous people in authority—people who are responsible for forming laws and policies that will affect us for years to come.

Our founders fought and died for our rights, including the right to representative government. Even in modern times there have been martyrs for civil rights for all people.

Some voters know why they're of one political party or the other, and some just inherit their party the way they inherit their religion. I inherited my parents' party, but never voted the entire ticket, preferring to vote for people and issues. At the last state primary I filled out a new voter registration form. In the future I can more easily vote my conscience.

When the voter pamphlet arrives in the mail, spend an hour studying the candidates' platforms. Read the pros and cons of initiatives and propositions. One candidate statement was highly entertaining: he wanted to be state controller (the man who pays the bills) so he could get his admittedly illegal pet ferrets legitimized in the state. He didn't say a word about his fiscal experience or fitness for the job. Obviously, this man would not be my choice for any office, especially animal control. It does show that the pamphlet need not be boring and that there are some people who must not be elected!

King Hezekiah spoke to his people about worship, but this applies to modern government, as well: "I have decided to make a covenant with the God of Israel and turn history around so that God will no longer be angry with us. Children, don't drag your feet in this! God has chosen you to take your place before him to serve in conducting and leading worship—this is your life work; make sure you do it and do it well" (2 Chron. 29:10, 11, Message).

Christy K. Robinson

A NEW HEART

I will give you a new heart and put a new spirit within you;
I will take the heart of stone out of your flesh and give you a heart of flesh.
Eze. 36:26, NKJV.

Nikki was a little curly-haired puppy that we allowed to stay with us on a temporary basis one summer. He was cute and playful, but we soon realized that there were some deficiencies in his character. I joked about returning him to the breeder for a refund or exchanging him for a "good" dog. But my wife already loved him and wouldn't seriously consider my suggestion, so our temporary dog stayed on for 17 years.

Nikki was far from perfect: he was disobedient, would sneak away from the house at night, was short-tempered, stole food and toys from other dogs, had an arrest record, was charged in a paternity suit, fought big dogs and lost, displayed open contempt for cats, was chased by skunks twice and got sprayed both times, and would not learn from his mistakes. It was useless to talk to him about reforming his character.

I hurt Nikki once. He disobeyed me, and I reacted in anger. My excuse? I was stressed out and just plain tired. His excuse? He wanted to go for a walk. The way I treated him said a lot more about me than it did about him. He never trusted me again. It breaks my heart, but it was an important lesson for me to learn before I became a father. I owe much to that dear old dog.

Nikki never lived up to our hopes for him. We kept him only because my wife loved him and forgave him and gave him many "second" chances. He needed the one thing we were unable to give him: a changed heart. Me too, eh?

"I will give you a new heart and put a new spirit within you; I will take the heart of stone out of your flesh and give you a heart of flesh" (Eze. 36:26, NKJV).

ROBERT JOHNSTON

August 6

IN GOD'S STRENGTH

Watch and pray so that you will not fall into temptation.
Matt. 26:41, NIV.

That's one of the things prayer can do for us: keep us from falling into temptation. In the hours that followed this interlude in the Garden of Gethsemane Jesus' words were borne out far too clearly. With Peter, in particular, we see him tempted to deny Jesus, and we see him fall to that temptation. That isn't something Peter probably would have known to pray to prevent; he didn't know he'd face that particular set of people who would accuse him of being one of Jesus' entourage and threaten him with Jesus' fate. But had Peter prayed, as Jesus did, for God's will to be done within him, I doubt very much that we'd have recorded the story of Peter's three betrayals by the time the rooster crowed twice.

It is disappointing, but in a way encouraging, too. Jesus explained it this way: The spirit is willing, but the body is weak. Indeed, it is—very weak. I know it of me, and you know it of yourself. Thank goodness that the salvation of the world didn't depend on Peter, James, and John, on their actions, on their ability to stay awake, or on the eloquence of their prayers! Jesus could have been much comforted by the prayers of His friends. Fortunately, the plan of salvation didn't rest upon the prayers of human beings; it rested upon the sovereign actions of a sovereign God, working through His Son, Jesus. And where they were unfaithful, weak, thoughtless, and selfish, Jesus was not, and is not.

And so with us. Our salvation doesn't depend on our own strength. It depends upon what God has done on our behalf. We can accept it or reject it. We don't have to take it. But I pray that God's will be done in my life, and it is pretty clear to me what that will is. No matter how things turn out on this earth, God's will is to take me to heaven. He wants us to be with Him forever (John 14:3). Let's follow His will for our lives today and for eternity.

Loren Seibold

WALKING IN CHRIST'S FOOTSTEPS

And a highway shall be there, and a way; and it shall be called the Holy Way. . . . The redeemed shall walk on it. Isa. 35:8, 9, Amplified.

The summer after I graduated from Christian high school I had the privilege of touring the Holy Land. It was amazing to see, with my own eyes, places I'd read about and pictured in my mind since childhood! We walked through Herod's desert fortress, Masada, floated in the salt-saturated water of the Dead Sea, and rinsed off in the refreshing waterfalls of En Gedi, where David hid from Saul. We saw the ancient ruins of Jericho, waded through Hezekiah's Tunnel, and were wowed by the architectural magnificence of the Roman amphitheater and aqueduct at Caesarea.

But the most wonderful memories I have are of walking where Jesus walked: we sailed across the Sea of Galilee to the Mount of the Beatitudes where He multiplied the loaves and fishes; we stood on the Mount of Olives overlooking Jerusalem where He began His triumphal entry; we saw the Pool of Bethesda where He healed the crippled man; and we visited the Jordan River where He was baptized and the Garden of Gethsemane where He prayed, "Not my will, but yours be done" (Luke 22:42). We walked the Via Dolorosa and visited the Garden Tomb. The experience renewed my faith and refreshed my spirit.

Though not all of us can travel to the Holy Land, we can all walk in Christ's footsteps. His life is a guidebook for us—a roadmap to the most fulfilling life here on earth. If we invite Him into our hearts, He can guide us on His paths to a life filled with grace.

He asks: "Are you tired? Worn out? Burned out on religion? Come to me. Get away with me and you'll recover your life. I'll show you how to take a real rest. Walk with me and work with me—watch how I do it. Learn the unforced rhythms of grace. I won't lay anything heavy or ill-fitting on you. Keep company with me and you'll learn to live freely and lightly" (Matt. 11:28-30, Message).

What a wonderful invitation! Will you walk with Him today?

Lorelei Herman Cress

LAUNDROMAT LIFE

How good and pleasant it is when brothers live together in unity!
Ps. 133:1, NIV.

Life feels rich and beautiful. It is breathtaking. Sometimes it is so easy to miss the poetry of life. It comes through disguised, flowing through and over us like water and wind.

The place where I rent a room doesn't have laundry facilities. The other day I had to do laundry. I hate the laundromat. It is filled with people who look indigent and need a shower. It is humid, and on bad days diapers in the trash pollute the airspace—a less than desirable place to spend your time. Reluctantly I arrive at the laundromat and start my three loads in three different washers. I have a book and iPod with earphones on to establish my disinterest in mixing with others. The book is good and the music loud.

After a while, I begin to people–watch. There is an old, gray Asian couple, a few young adults like me, and some young mothers with kids abusing the laundry carts. Then I spot a woman training her daughters how to do laundry. The girls are captivated by the wisdom of their tutor. I look back at the Asian couple, who are stealing a quick kiss, thinking no one is looking. A mother admonishes her child not to horse around with the laundry cart. And here in this moment I am broadsided by the poetry of life. Life is unfolding itself like a beautiful cloth napkin. I see these people I'd wanted to keep at a distance as holding some piece of my puzzle. I begin to see them as they are: beautiful, unique, and needy creatures. What an amazing opportunity to experience life. What a beautiful place to see God's poetry in action. We are one—all of us.

The laundromat is a microcosm of life at large. It breaks those who would be unbroken, who are too good to acknowledge their own needs. It broke me. Missing the poetry of life is easy. It doesn't always present itself wrapped in a cute little package imploring your attention. It finds you when you least expect it. I am grateful for my laundromat life.

"How good and pleasant it is when brothers live together in unity!" (Ps. 133:1, NIV).

Stephen Robertson

BELONGING AND INHERITANCE

The boundary lines have fallen for me in pleasant places;
surely I have a delightful inheritance.
Ps. 16:6, NIV.

It's always fascinated me that many of our laws come directly from the Bible. Moses, the law writer, was in many ways a scribe for God, and we have a tradition of law and justice that comes from God Himself. I was recently talking with a friend who had used the Bible as part of his thesis for his law degree. He told me that he was very interested in a particular portion of Scripture in the Old Testament and made it the focus of his thesis. The passage is Ezekiel 47:22: "You are to allot it as an inheritance for yourselves and for the aliens who have settled among you and who have children. You are to consider them as native-born Israelites; along with you they are to be allotted an inheritance among the tribes of Israel" (NIV).

He told me that Jewish law was the only law, and may still be, that provided a sense of "inheritance" for aliens, people who were not Jewish but lived in the community. As the Lord is telling the people how they are to divide the land of promise, He includes aliens with the tribes. And I was thinking how interesting it is that God seems, in His heart, to have always provided a way for the alien—those of us who aren't Jewish by heritage—to participate in the generous inheritance He has promised: life everlasting.

"I pray also that the eyes of your heart may be enlightened in order that you may know the hope to which he has called you, the riches of his glorious inheritance in the saints" (Eph. 1:18, NIV).

"The boundary lines have fallen for me in pleasant places; surely I have a delightful inheritance" (Ps. 16:6, NIV).

Pamela McCann

AUGUST 10

MERLIN AND THE COWS

If you believe, you will receive whatever you ask for in prayer.
Matt. 21:22, NIV.

Merlin Beerman had just reread the booklet *Prayer Power,* by J. L. Tucker, founder of the Quiet Hour. Merlin says he spent an hour and a half on his knees in prayer that morning.

After his devotions Merlin decided to go jogging. As he was running along, he noticed that his neighbor's cows had escaped their field enclosure.

Merlin and his neighbor lived in rural northwest Arkansas near the Missouri and Oklahoma state lines. The cows were headed for a major highway. Merlin did his best to chase the cows back into the pasture, but they were stupidly scattering in all directions except the right one. If the cattle wandered onto the freeway, not only would they be run down, but motorists and truckers could be killed or seriously injured in the collisions.

Merlin began to pray, "God, please make these cows turn around. Don't let anyone be killed." Within seconds the cattle did a peaceful about-face and returned to their pasture, safely behind the fence.

What did those cattle see that Merlin didn't? Perhaps the same angel assigned to Balaam's donkey (Num. 22) stood on the interstate highway with flashing sword!

What if Merlin had gone jogging hours before the cattle escaped? What if he hadn't taken responsibility to chase them home? What if he'd tried to budge a cow on his own power? Instead, he relied on God's power, and the day was saved for the neighbor, the cows, and the freeway travelers. You don't know what God and His angels are doing for you right now, but thank them now and ask for their continued protection.

"I tell you the truth, if you have faith and do not doubt . . . you can say to this mountain, 'Go, throw yourself into the sea,' and it will be done. If you believe, you will receive whatever you ask for in prayer" (Matt. 21:21, 22, NIV).

JACKIE TUCKER AND CHRISTY K. ROBINSON

PERSEIDS METEOR SHOWER

Men and women who have lived wisely and well will shine brilliantly,
like the cloudless, star-strewn night skies.
Dan. 12:3, Message.

Mom and I would climb the ladder, take a blanket up to the still-hot roof, and watch the Perseids meteor shower in the northeastern sky while we talked softly and laughed. The brightest meteors fell after midnight. My dad and brother, early to bed, missed it all. When Phoenix, Arizona, was a small city in clear desert air, we could see the Milky Way. Phoenix is a megalopolis now, and city lights have overcome the starry host.

Laurentius was a Christian deacon martyred by the Romans in A.D. 258. They roasted him on an iron stove, from which he reportedly (and improbably) cried out, "I am already roasted on one side and, if thou wouldst have me well cooked, it is time to turn me on the other." The saint's death was remembered on his feast day, August 10, and the shooting stars of the Perseids meteor shower also became known as the fiery Tears of St. Lawrence.

The meteors we see are only the size of a grain of sand, with a few reaching the size of a pea or marble. They are the "exhaust" trail of the Swift-Tuttle Comet, which circles our sun every 130 years. Earth passes through this grainy trail every year at this time, and the grains fall through our atmosphere at 37 miles per second, flaming with heat friction.

The Lord was not obligated to create anything, much less such fascinating beauty. But He has His reputation to keep up. The beauty was not lost on the ancients, either.

"Look at the night skies: Who do you think made all this? Who marches this army of stars out each night, counts them off, calls each by name—so magnificent! so powerful!—and never overlooks a single one? (Isa. 40:26, Message).

"Has anyone ever seen anything like this—dawn-fresh, moon-lovely, sun-radiant, ravishing as the night sky with its galaxies of stars?" (S. of Sol. 6:10, Message).

As Daniel suggests, may we live according to God's plan so that we will shine like the stars forever. "Men and women who have lived wisely and well will shine brilliantly, like the cloudless, star-strewn night skies. And those who put others on the right path to life will glow like stars forever" (Dan. 12:3, Message).

Christy K. Robinson

August 12

THE SEAM RIPPER

Therefore, if anyone is in Christ,
he is a new creation; the old has gone, the new has come!
2 Cor. 5:17, NIV.

The seam ripper is a modest but effective little tool. It can rip out errant seams, cut open buttonholes, and precisely guide tiny pieces of fabric under the sewing machine needle. It has a sharp point to cut wayward stitches and a smooth end to protect your project from tearing. When I first began quilting, I had no teacher, so I learned by trial and error. Some days I spent more time sewing in reverse with my seam ripper than forward with the machine! Now, though I am experienced, I still keep my seam ripper nearby. It helps hold my fabric in the right place, keeping my fingers clear of a sharp and dangerous needle. In addition, I do a lot of experimenting. Not all experiments turn out right the first time, so I need to remove many stitches.

I have learned to be careful not to misplace my seam ripper. Using other objects in its place is hazardous to fingers and projects.

When I find a mistake, it is tempting to ignore it in hopes that the problem will simply go away. Stopping immediately and fixing the error with my seam ripper can save me untold trouble later. Overlooking mistakes does not pay. It can take 10 hours to undo what took only 10 minutes to stitch on a fast machine.

In my life, although I have gained years of experience, I still need Jesus beside me, just like the seam ripper in my studio. Jesus is the only one who can rip out my sin and make me new again. Ten sins or ten thousand, Jesus has the ability, the desire, and the patience to remove each one. We can live our lives confidently, knowing that Jesus is right beside us, not only forgiving our sins, but also guiding us. We don't have to ignore problems or make futile attempts to correct our lives on our own. That is a part of the old life; now we have the new. Colossians 3:10 tells us, "[You] have put on the new self, which is being renewed in knowledge in the image of its Creator" (NIV).

"Therefore, if anyone is in Christ, he is a new creation; the old has gone, the new has come!" (2 Cor. 5:17, NIV).

Laura West Kong

CRITICAL THINKING

Don't pick on people, jump on their failures, criticize their faults—
unless, of course, you want the same treatment.
Luke 6:37, Message.

Criticism isn't always a bad thing. The first dictionary definition under "criticize" is "to consider the merits and demerits of and judge accordingly." In our daily lives we are constantly called upon to make choices, and this kind of critical thinking is necessary in order to live wisely. However, there is another definition that we encounter far more frequently: "to find fault with." It is this kind of criticism that creates discord and suffering among us.

A friend was recently the target of some anonymous, mean-spirited criticism at work. The nameless critic wasn't aware of the circumstances involved in the behavior they were criticizing. They didn't evaluate fairly; they found fault—and rather than lovingly confronting, they anonymously attacked.

She could have just dismissed this criticism, but her better judgment forced her to examine it for a basis in fact. Upon reflection, she concluded that there was legitimacy in one of the behaviors criticized, and she determined to do her best to improve in that area. The rest of the criticism, clearly meant only to wound, she left in God's hands.

Although we can do our best to live a perfect life, we cannot hope to always impress others as we would wish. We are flawed people living in a flawed world, and things in our lives don't always work out as planned. What can we do to avoid being victims of this kind of criticism?

Absolutely nothing. We cannot control others' behavior—only our own. It is our job to follow Christ's example in the way we live our lives and, with His help, avoid being critical of others. Jesus gives this advice: "Don't pick on people, jump on their failures, criticize their faults—unless, of course, you want the same treatment. Don't condemn those who are down; that hardness can boomerang. Be easy on people; you'll find life a lot easier. Give away your life; you'll find life given back, but not merely given back—given back with bonus and blessing. Giving, not getting, is the way. Generosity begets generosity" (Luke 6:37, 38, Message).

Lorelei Herman Cress

August 14

BLESSED ARE THE PRUNED

Happy the clean in heart—because they shall see God.
Matt. 5:8, YLT.

You won't find this beatitude in your English-language New Testament. But the original Greek word for "pure" (of heart) is katharos, from which we get "cathartic." It means cleansed by fire, and it can mean "pruned."

Pruning a tree can not only keep it in a manageable and attractive shape, and direct the tree's energy to producing flowers, fruit, or new foliage, but it can save the tree's life. Yesterday morning, I backwashed the spa, and the water ran out into the grass and into the low-lying tree wells. I thought this a responsible use of water in an arid climate! But two hours later, a freak thunderstorm, with 90 minutes of lightning, gusty winds, and about a tenth-inch of rain, blew through the valley. When I looked out the window, my 5-year-old bauhinia orchid tree had bent over to the ground. This tree had large white orchids blooming on its long, flexible branches, and earlier this summer, it had become top-heavy with growth. With the combination of soggy soil beneath and windy downdrafts, my tree was doomed.

After the storm, with the August sun steaming up the place, I took the long-handled pruner and cut off two thirds of the tree branches, lightening the load for the trunk. Relieved of weight, the trunk began to stand a bit higher. With great effort, and much swatting of gnats, I drove a metal stake into the ground, and a neighbor pulled the heavy tree toward the stake so I could brace it with ties. My tree, although much altered in volume, is growing straight again. While we were bracing the tree, a pair of hummingbirds came boldly to drink the nectar of the remaining blossoms. Life goes on!

"Happy the clean in heart—because they shall see God" (Matt. 5:8, YLT).

That beautiful tree, in its pruned, cathartic state, will remind me that in persecution or adversity the Lord can still make a blessing from the enemy's curse. And rather than bending toward the earth in defeat, the Gardener is pruning and strengthening us so we can reach toward the heavens and there see God.

Christy K. Robinson

ONE ALL-IMPORTANT DOCTRINE

Believe on the Lord Jesus Christ, and thou shalt be saved.
Acts 16:31.

One of America's great preachers lay on his deathbed. His dear ones were all gathered around. One of the sons leaned close and said, "Dad, what doctrines are really important to you now?" The old man of God roused a bit, opened his eyes, and responded, "When I started in the ministry I had 100 doctrines that I felt were absolutely crucial. By the time I had reached 30 years of age that number was reduced to 50 significant doctrines. Reaching my fiftieth birthday, I had reduced that number to 10 truly vital doctrines. But now, as I stand at the valley of the shadow of death, there is only one doctrine that is important to me." His son urged him to name that one all-important doctrine. With lips quivering, but with the strength of his conviction, he responded, "Now, the only doctrine that matters to me is that I am a great sinner but that Jesus Christ is an awesome, all-sufficient Savior."

That, friend, is the most important doctrine in the world today. Knowing Jesus is the only way anyone will leave this world with the assurance that he will live again in that better world God is preparing for us.

Paul made it very clear in Ephesians 2: "For by grace are ye saved through faith; and that not of yourselves: it is the gift of God; Not of works, lest any man should boast" (verses 8 and 9).

We are saved simply by accepting, by faith, Jesus as our Savior. Paul gave a very succinct statement in Acts 16:31: "Believe on the Lord Jesus Christ, and thou shalt be saved."

In 2 Corinthians 5:17 Paul wrote, "Therefore if any man be in Christ, he is a new creature: old things are passed away; behold, all things are become new."

What a beautiful assurance: one who accepts Christ as Savior passes from being a lost sinner to being a new creature; he or she is saved by God's grace and, incidentally, called a saint.

Paul tells us how this becomes a reality. "For he hath made him to be sin for us, who knew no sin; that we might be made the righteousness of God in him" (2 Cor. 5:21).

Herman Bauman

WHAT MUST I DO TO BE SAVED?

Those who heard this asked, "Who then can be saved?"
Luke 18:26, NIV.

Is there any question more important than that? I think not.

What a truth: God caused Christ, who was perfect and knew no sin, to become sin for us (2 Cor. 5:21). He took our filthy sins upon Himself and died to pay the price for them. Then, in exchange, He gave us His perfect righteousness. We are accounted as righteous before God, just as righteous as Christ is! Jesus was treated in the way we deserve, so we may be treated as the Creator and Redeemer deserves. Praise God for this marvelous provision.

There is absolutely nothing we can do to earn our salvation or to make ourselves acceptable to God. When we fall in love with Jesus, we will find joy in doing those things that honor and please Him. As Jesus admonishes in Matthew 22:37-40, "Thou shalt love the Lord thy God with all thy heart, and with all thy soul, and with all thy mind. This is the first and great commandment. And the second is like unto it, Thou shalt love thy neighbour as thyself. On these two commandments hang all the law and the prophets." Jesus adds later, "If ye love me, keep my commandments" (John 14:15).

The first four commandments tell us how to love God, and the last six tell us what it means to love our neighbor. Thus, the Christian willingly and happily observes the Ten Commandments with the strength God gives him. The godly person should be the best citizen and the most loving person in the community.

Christians show love for Jesus in the way we relate to God's will. However, the obedience to God's will plays no part in redemption. Salvation is absolutely free. Obedience is simply a response of love.

Paul sums it up in Galatians 2:16: "Knowing that a man is not justified by the works of the law, but by the faith of Jesus Christ, even we have believed in Jesus Christ, that we might be justified by the faith of Christ, and not by the works of the law: for by the works of the law shall no flesh be justified."

Yes, we are saved by grace, praise God. And because I am saved by grace, and born again into His family, I demonstrate my love by living in a way that would make Him proud of me.

HERMAN BAUMAN

MAKING FRIENDS FOR CHRIST

In all your ways acknowledge Him, and He shall direct your paths.
Prov. 3:6, NKJV.

Tanya is the 26-year-old wife of a Russian pastor living in Archangelsk, a major city in northern Siberia. While Tanya enjoys her Christian friends, she eagerly seeks out friendships with non-Christian women. And in the past few years she has won 10 of her friends to Christ.

Recently, she received a telephone call from a friend who lives in the city where Tanya and her husband served before moving to Archangelsk. Her friend called to thank her for sharing the joy of knowing Jesus and to tell her that she had just been baptized.

As Tanya shared this good news with others, she added, "I praise the Lord that 10 of my friends are now friends with Jesus also." When asked how she finds her new friends and wins so many to Christ, Tanya answered, "They are my neighbors. I just enjoy visiting them and sharing my life with them. I do not preach, but as we become acquainted they ask me what it is that makes me so happy."

Tanya gave an example of her friendship ministry. Recently she was preparing a meal for some visiting church leaders and asked Natali, her neighbor, to help her. As the two women worked together preparing the meal, Natali began asking Tanya questions. "Who are these people from Moscow and Washington, D.C., who have come to our city? Why are they here?" Tanya used this opportunity to tell Natali about her church and its mission. The foods she chose to prepare for the guests and the absence of liquor led to a discussion of biblical health principles.

As the women's friendship grew and Natali saw more of Tanya's way of life, she was impressed by the peace and joy this family enjoyed. Sometime later, Tanya learned that Natali had convinced her husband to stop smoking and drinking. Without realizing it, Natali and her family already are beginning to experience the positive results of the Christian lifestyle.

Tanya says, "The Lord is working. It won't be long before an opportunity will come to discuss our beliefs." This time Tanya may win more than a friend for Christ; she may win her friend's husband, too.

J. H. AND JEAN ZACHARY

OUTDOOR COMMUNION

Then Jesus went with his disciples to a place called Gethsemane, and he said to them, "Sit here while I go over there and pray." Matt. 26:36, NIV.

Probably because of illustrations I'd seen, I had always pictured Gethsemane as a sort of park. There were, however, no public parks in ancient Jerusalem. The word "Gethsemane" has the unromantic meaning of "oil vat," which simply means that this was someone's olive orchard in the country. It was a place that at night they could go and be alone.

When I was growing up on a North Dakota farm, one of my favorite things was to go walking in the country at night. It is something that, as a city dweller now, I miss. Out in a dark field, far from any but the most distant lights, with only the moon and stars above you, the sounds and smells of the night around you, it was a marvelous place to feel the presence of God. Many times I thought to myself the words of Psalm 19:1-3: "The heavens declare the glory of God; and the firmament sheweth his handiwork. Day unto day uttereth speech, and night unto night sheweth knowledge. There is no speech nor language, where their voice is not heard."

If you've never had the experience of being able to contemplate God at night by gazing up into the heavens, away from streetlights and headlights, I hope someday you will. God seems especially close under an open sky. Fortunately, we don't have to have this type of experience to talk to God—we can pray anyplace that we happen to be at the moment, and I'm glad for that. Even though Jesus once recommended praying in a closet (which simply means in private—there was no such thing as a clothes closet in those days), in this case He chose to pray in the open air, where He could look up at the skies and really sense the presence of His Father.

After Jesus ascended to heaven, He sent the Holy Spirit to be with us. Just as you breathe in the fresh air surrounding you as you enjoy the night sky, breathe in God's Spirit and be filled with Him!

LOREN SEIBOLD

MY WAYS ARE NOT YOUR WAYS

"For my thoughts are not your thoughts,
neither are your ways my ways," declares the Lord.
Isa. 55:8, NIV.

I attended an author lecture at the University of Washington, near my home. The author, Ronald C. White, Jr., has researched and written extensively about President Abraham Lincoln. Mr. White's book, *The Eloquent President,* was the subject of this discussion.

What struck me about his presentation was that we are used to thinking of President Lincoln, one of our greatest American presidents, as a hero. But during his lifetime Lincoln was beset by trials at every turn. He didn't even know if he was going to be president as he traveled to his first inauguration because the electoral college had not ratified the election yet—the head of that college was a Confederate sympathizer.

In his research Mr. White was focused on things that would help us understand Lincoln's thoughts—to replace awe with understanding. Evidently Lincoln was quite a journal keeper, but not in the conventional ways we think of. He had a habit of writing thoughts on slips of paper and sticking them in places where he could pull them out and reflect on them. This particular slip of paper ended up in his stovepipe hat. It is a reflection about the war. He had doubts about whether either side was right during the war, and he came to the conclusion in one of his private writings that "it is quite possible that God's purpose is something different from the purpose of either party—and yet the human instrumentalities, working just as they do, are of the best adaptation to effect His purpose." In other words, he thought perhaps God's purpose was something different than anyone thought.

Lincoln was open to the notion that God doesn't work according to our own limited understanding. How easy it would have been for Lincoln to write off the people in the South. Many of his contemporaries had. But he had a sense that God was at work, even when Lincoln didn't understand exactly what would come of it.

It's important to remember that God doesn't always work in ways that I understand or even see. I need to have a perspective like President Lincoln's and leave room for the unknown—for God to work beyond what I can see or understand, even in the toughest situations.

Pamela McCann

BLUE-COLLAR SABBATICAL

Treat others as you would like them to treat you.
Luke 6:31, NEB.

My friends who are specialists in world religions tell me that every religious group teaches a principle similar to the golden rule: "Treat others as you would like them to treat you" (Luke 6:31, NEB). Human behavior specialists call this idea the achievement of reciprocity of an alternative point of view. Native Americans called it walking in another's moccasins.

Unwittingly embarking on a golden rule process, President Jack Coleman of Haverford College pursued "blue-collar sabbaticals" as a ditch digger, garbage collector, and short-order cook—all to further his professional interests as a labor economist. He asked, "Can I make it out there without my name and connections? What do people talk about on the job? What are their satisfactions?" One of his answers (meager satisfaction) came when, in his 50s, he was picking up some particularly sloppy garbage at a motel. An elderly woman watching him asked, "Will you ever amount to anything?"

He also explored another venue, living as a homeless person for 10 days in New York City during the winter. He mastered the art of selecting the best cardboard to shelter himself from the rain. He ran from fellow homeless people when they disturbed his sleep. He scavenged to put money in his pockets. Later he asked, "What does it feel like to be a prisoner with no control over your life?" In prison Coleman posed as an inmate. His questions: Are there other ways of controlling crime? How can we develop programs to deal with victims and their families rather than offering them the mere pleasure of seeing the criminal punished?

All of his pretending was initiated, he said, for academic reasons. But in taking the role of another person Coleman found himself being drawn in sympathy, which he hadn't known before, for the plight of street people and prison inmates. His subsequent research into alternative treatments for warehoused inmates brought involvement in a council on prison justice and support for a halfway house in a nearby city. He and his unlikely associates were blessed because he chose to walk in their shoes, thereby aligning himself with the golden rule.

Our Creator and Savior chose to take a "blue-collar sabbatical" and walk in our moccasins. Because He did, our destiny is changed—for eternity!

EDNA MAYE LOVELESS

BUILT UPON THE ROCK

What may be known about God is plain to them, because God has made it plain to them. Rom. 1:19, NIV.

After receiving my university degree in another state, I moved back to my family's church. My comments during the Bible study were the "correct" answers I'd learned in 16 years of Christian school. But the young adult teacher, Steve, saw the world, the Bible, and God very differently. I was frustrated that my memorized answers were shot down with a staccato "No," but the simple answers offered by those less educated but more spiritually mature than I were accepted with "Yes! That's it exactly!"

Instead of accepting every teaching at face value or having it run through the "acceptability filter," Steve persisted in making us look for the gospel in every Bible verse we studied. In time, the Holy Spirit spoke to my heart, and I found His gracious salvation. Praise God for Steve's role in that time of my life—and in all my study since!

California is famous for its landslides and unstable soil, particularly during the rainy season. Buildings buckle and wash away, because they're founded upon sandy soil, not anchored on solid rock. In Matthew 7:24-27 Jesus spoke of the wise and foolish builders, investing in the places where they kept their temporal treasures. He said that whoever puts *His words* into practice is like the wise one who built upon the solid rock.

Jesus' story is not about building codes, architecture, or geology—it's about the primacy of *His words.* "When Jesus had finished saying these things, the crowds were amazed at his teaching, because he taught as one who had authority, and not as their teachers of the law" (Matt. 7:28, 29, NIV).

The religious leaders of that time quoted from commentaries, doctrinal theories, and various schools of thought. They let others think for them. But Jesus, the very Word of God, quoted Scripture and spoke with divine authority. The lesson is that we seek first the words of Jesus and how they apply to our lives. Security and salvation are not built on the sandy interpretation or commentary of fallible humans but upon the solid, clear words of Jesus Christ. That's all anyone needs.

CHRISTY K. ROBINSON

August 22

GOD'S RESOLVE

But God demonstrates his own love for us in this:
While we were still sinners, Christ died for us. Rom. 5:8, NIV.

There are two legitimate topics for religion. (This is to some extent true of most religions, but it is clearly true for Christianity.) One is God's actions, and the other is our actions. What God has done, and continues to do, and what we have done and ought to do. Now, here is what you must understand: God always does His thing before we do ours! God always does what He does even if we never get around to doing ours.

Salvation has already been secured. The necessary steps have been taken. This is preventative grace: grace that goes before us and makes sure everything is in readiness just in case we need it, which we surely will.

Spiritual transformation can't be completed unless we pitch in. You can give a couple bums a $100 bill, and they may even promise to improve their lives with it, but you can't guarantee they will. You've still given the gift, even if they spend it on booze. You've provided something for them. But they've got to receive it in the spirit in which it was given for it to make a difference to them.

I'll say it again: God's part is not dependent upon us doing our part. God did His part and will keep doing it. The resolutions that matter in our lives, the resolutions that can transform our lives, aren't the resolutions that we make. They're the resolutions God made. Before we asked for it, before we needed it, God had a plan. Even though some people will never realize that they need it, Paul says in 2 Corinthians 5:19, "God was reconciling the world to himself in Christ, not counting men's sins against them" (NIV).

This is the heart of Christian soteriology (the study of salvation). No matter how you feel about God, no matter if you turn your back on God, God has opened the door to you. Reconciling means to resolve a problem. Put things to rights. Reunite the alienated parties. So from God's point of view, in the words of the old hymn, there's nothing between my soul and the Savior.

Loren Seibold

POTS OF GOD

I consider everything a loss compared to the surpassing greatness of knowing Christ Jesus my Lord. Phil. 3:8, NIV.

The tag on a pot of mint I purchased at my local garden center reads "vigorous perennial." This is horticultural code for "wildly invasive plant that will take over your entire yard if given half a chance." Thus, experienced gardeners are cautious with mint and do not plant it straight into the ground, but rather in a pot sunk in the soil. This keeps mint's invasive root system in check, preventing it from usurping the whole garden.

I, however, let my mint grow unrestrainedly, enjoying and sharing a bountiful harvest of mint. Underground runners spread the mint and its cool, refreshing fragrance throughout my garden.

There are many uses for this prolific family of herbs. Peppermint has the greatest concentration of essential oil and is the best mint for medicinal purposes. It can alleviate nausea and indigestion as well as soothe headaches, sore throats, and tired feet. Spearmint is mild and used to flavor candy and gum, as well as savory dishes. Chocolate mint is a wonderful dessert mint. Mediterranean, Southeast Asian, and Middle Eastern cuisine wouldn't be as enticing without mint's distinctive flavor. Pennyroyal is a natural insect repellent. You can rub it on your skin to keep away mosquitoes, flies, gnats, fleas, and ticks.

If I restrict my mints to a pot, I restrict the bountiful flow of blessings I can receive from them. The religious leaders in Jesus' day tried to restrict God's blessings in not only their lives but also in the people's. Jesus warned them, "Woe to you, teachers of the law and Pharisees, you hypocrites! You shut the kingdom of heaven in men's faces. You yourselves do not enter, nor will you let those enter who are trying to" (Matt. 23:13, NIV).

God is a god of overflowing abundance. His grace and blessings cannot be confined to a pot, a limited portion of the garden that is our lives. The apostle Paul wrote, "I consider everything a loss compared to the surpassing greatness of knowing Christ Jesus my Lord, for whose sake I have lost all things. I consider them rubbish, that I may gain Christ" (Phil. 3:8, NIV).

May God's abundant grace and blessings fill our lives.

LAURA WEST KONG

AVOCADO CHRISTIANS

By this shall all men know that ye are my disciples,
if ye have love one to another."
John 13:35.

When I was in the fifth grade, we lived in Massachusetts, where I attended a church school in the church basement. There were about 40 students in the entire school. One of my classmates, "Jill," was the most uncoordinated, socially challenged, and homely girl on the planet. She was always chosen last for any game. Anything associated with Jill had the "cootie syndrome" attached to it. You did not want to touch it, be associated with it, or like it in any way. When Jill opened her lunch pail, we all groaned at her "gross sandwich" made of oxidized avocados. I had never tasted an avocado in my life. The year before, we had moved from Saskatchewan, Canada, where avocados were unknown. Based on the fact that Jill liked avocados, there was no way I would ever be remotely tempted to even try one. In my mind, they were gross.

Fast forward six years. We had moved to California. One of my eleventh-grade female classmates had a crush on me, and vice versa. One evening we went out to dinner, and she ordered guacamole dip, made from, of all things, avocado! No way was I going to eat that! "At least try it," she coaxed, so I relented, cringed, and bit in. It was delicious! I ordered another. Since then, avocados have become one of my favorites.

Doesn't that say a lot about human nature and the Christian life? So many in this world are guilty of judging the Christian life by some prior unpleasant experience and associate all Christians with the blackened avocado label. The Bible says, "Oh, taste and see that the Lord is good" (Ps. 34:8, NKJV). Sadly, many have not genuinely tasted the Christian life. Their attitude is based solely on those miserable Christians they have encountered.

Genuine Christianity can be summarized in a few words: "By this shall all men know that ye are my disciples, if ye have love one to another" (John 13:35).

Joedy Melashenko

HOW GOD CHANGED ME

The Spirit helps us in our weakness.
Rom. 8:26, NIV.

Evangelism is much more than teaching and preaching and telling others how to change. I found this out when I went on a Quiet Hour evangelism trip to San Salvador in March 2005. My experience taught me to watch and pray more, to think more clearly before I act or speak, to shut my mouth when I think I know it all, and to look to God and pray when there is difficulty. I realized that I don't know all the answers and I can't solve all problems.

Before the mission trip, I was trying to fix my own problems. But I have learned that I must not be a fixer. Instead, I must place my total dependence on God. I must go to Him with my problems and wait patiently on Him for my help. God works when we get out of the way. God is mightier and more powerful than I ever could have imagined.

And so, after conducting clinics and teaching people health and biblical truths, I witnessed more than 1,000 people baptized, which will result in more than 200 new congregations. The mission trip taught me to "wait patiently" on God, to "watch and pray," to "look to Him for help." He is the "health of our countenance," the "Author and Finisher of our faith," and the "Prince of Peace" in the midst of our troublesome storms.

Mission trips are not for the fainthearted, but they are for those who trust wholly in God; who press on in the face of difficulties; who not only want to teach lessons to others but who are willing to learn big, painful, and important lessons themselves.

Praise God that He is in charge of the work and that through small missions He is preparing us for bigger and better missions until that biggest one—going home with Him and sharing these experiences of His grace with each other and with unfallen beings.

PHYLLIS VALLIERES

PERFECT PEACE

In that day this song will be sung: . . . You will keep in perfect peace him whose mind is steadfast, because he trusts in you.
Isa. 26:1-3, NIV.

Returning from the International Association of Missionary Aviation annual conference in east Texas, we made a stop in Collegedale, Tennessee, to drop off a passenger and take on fuel for the final leg to Berrien Springs, Michigan.

Flight service station weather reports indicated perfect timing. A line of spring thunderstorms had just moved to the east of our northbound course. Another batch was brewing to the west, but trailed several hours behind the first. Radar showed a wide corridor of clear air along our flight path. This was great news because our radios had been removed for a new stack to be installed before launching a mission to the Philippines. Our communication capability was limited to a handheld radio. It was a no-instrument flight.

We climbed into the starry sky. I checked in with Chattanooga approach and navigated while Clifton Brooks flew the plane. Between communications with controllers we chatted peacefully about missions and the privilege of serving God.

Just north of Indianapolis a bright flash reflected off the windshield. I turned to look out the rear window. No more than a couple of miles behind us, two large cumulus clouds, illuminated by flashes of lightning, towered into the night sky. "I've got the airplane; turn around and look at that!" I exclaimed.

"Wow, we were just there!" Clif countered. The weather continued clear ahead, closing behind us as we flew north.

While life and flying don't always turn out this way, a sense of peace attends those surrendered to the Father's will. Jesus stayed awake communing with the Father while those around Him slept. This allowed Him to sleep while those around Him were terrified.

"A real love for others will chase those worries away. The thought of being punished is what makes us afraid. It shows that we have not really learned to love" (1 John 4:18, CEV).

Perfect peace awaits you. Fear not; surrender to Him today.

DON STARLIN

DARKNESS AND UNCERTAINTY

Let him who walks in the dark, who has no light,
trust in the name of the Lord and rely on his God.
Isa. 50:10, NIV.

Two doctors from our church have just returned from a short-term mission trip to Africa. They were sharing their experiences, and they told us about hiking up Tanzania's Mount Kilimanjaro with their sons shortly before leaving Africa. The volcanic mountain is 19,340 feet in altitude, includes several climate zones and types of terrain from rain forest through alpine, and takes several days to conquer.

They said that the hike began at midnight. The pitch-black African darkness all around them made it impossible to see any path. They had flashlights that showed just a few feet in front of them, and they followed the light their guide provided ahead. As the dawn broke, they could see more of their surroundings. A sheer edge on the side of the path was now revealed in the light; however, it had not been even a consideration when they were simply walking in the dark with limited visibility.

Not only were they unaware of the danger, but they also were unaware of how far they had come. As the dawn broke, they realized their several hours' early start meant that much of the climb was now behind them. Their guide was wise to choose to start the hike at such an odd hour.

Their story reminded me of other stories I have heard about near misses or disasters avoided through providence and God's protection. Sometimes it's good that we can only see one step ahead—you never know how far you've come in the dark until the dawn breaks.

"If you are walking in darkness, without a ray of light, trust in the Lord and rely on your God" (Isa. 50:10, NLT).

PAMELA MCCANN

August 28

NO BIBLES

Thy word hath quickened me.
Ps. 119:50.

Living in the twenty-first century, we have the benefit of written Scripture in our modern vernacular and thousands of years of commentators. But to people who had no Bible and only inherited stories, the audible words of God, the clouds of glory, and supernatural wonders were awesome! (Even in this age of special effects and computer-generated imagery, we are still struck by the power of an earthquake, hurricane, or flash flood.)

Noah and Abraham acted on God's audible command. Job trusted without comfort of Scripture. Moses led millions before he wrote the Pentateuch. David's and Solomon's subjects didn't have Scripture (only Moses' books), because most of the psalms, wisdom, prophecy, and historical chronicles were compiled and edited during the exile to Babylon and Assyria and thereafter. It's easy for us to say, "Those stiff-necked people should have studied their Bibles and known better than to disobey God." Their Scriptures were hand-copied on sheepskin or metal scrolls and were expensive and in short supply.

Do we treasure our Bibles? We do. We have several versions on the shelf, our favorite at our bedside, and one in the car to take to church or just have on hand when needed. We have www.BibleGateway.com bookmarked on the computer. There's no shortage of the Word of God—now.

But " 'the days are coming,' declares the Sovereign Lord, 'when I will send a famine through the land—not a famine of food or a thirst for water, but a famine of hearing the words of the Lord. Men will stagger from sea to sea and wander from north to east, searching for the word of the Lord, but they will not find it' " (Amos 8:11, 12, NIV).

There is life-giving bread, satisfying water, and a healing touch, though. "This is my comfort in my affliction: for thy word hath quickened me" (Ps. 119:50).

Quickened means "conceived" or "brought to life," and we can all use that. God's Word produces eternal life in all of us. So set down this book right now and open your Bible. You need to fill your life with eternal life!

Christy K. Robinson

JESUS' LIQUID BANDAGE

If we confess our sins, He is faithful and just to forgive us our sins and to cleanse us from all unrighteousness.
1 John 1:9, NKJV.

Recently I was working in my garden, a four- by six-foot space in the backyard. Normally I plant a few tomatoes and cucumbers. After getting home from a short-term mission trip I had a few moments to get my hands in the dirt. It felt good. I pulled up the old stalks of dried tomato vines and arranged the wire cages.

As I speared the earth with the tomato cages, the spiked ends were sharp and one went into my hand—a puncture wound. After I yelled in pain I thought, "Lord, You had this done to Your hands and feet, and You had thorns in Your brow." Blood appeared, and I ran water on it and then let hydrogen peroxide drip on it. After a while the pain subsided, and I applied a "liquid bandage" solution to close the wound.

I forgot about it until a few days later when I noticed a little redness. At a Quiet Hour weekend retreat a doctor noticed my hand and said that I had an infection and needed immediate treatment, or it could poison my blood and I could possibly lose my hand.

He got my attention. Soon I was downing the proper antibiotics on a regular basis. Two days later my hand shrank to its normal size, and I had a stronger grip than before. A few days after that, my hand was healed. I thanked the Lord for His providence and for a doctor who noticed at the critical time what I needed most. I could have ignored the symptoms, and I would have suffered serious consequences, but I chose to follow the counsel of a wise physician.

In the spiritual realm we have the power of choice, but we too often make wrong choices and suffer the effects of our actions. However, there is a Great Physician who has our best interest at heart and wants us to enjoy a better quality of life. His diagnosis encourages us all to come to Him just as we are with our sinfulness. His own antidote for sin is His blood that was shed on Calvary. We are healed, cleansed from the infection of sin, by His blood, His "liquid bandage."

BILL TUCKER

August 30

LIKE A PRECIOUS BOWL

Parents are the pride of their children.
Prov. 17:6, NLT.

My mother is very special to me, as I'm sure yours is to you. She was very talented in many ways. She baked the best homemade bread. The dresses she made for me were crafted with fine details and special features. She taught me how to can peaches, apricots, and tomatoes. The pictures hanging on the walls in our home were her paintings of beautiful seascapes and rushing rivers. And it was her soothing hands that made me feel better when I was sick. She taught me to love God.

But today my mother is not baking bread or sewing dresses. Neither is she painting pictures or canning fruits and vegetables. After several health episodes she now sits in a chair viewing the outdoors through a window or listens to the conversations around her. But her face still shines with love and compassion.

Recently I was visiting a friend and admiring the bowl on her mantel. It appeared to have a special place in my friend's home and to be very precious to her. She said that the bowl was very old and had been in the family for many years. It had held flowers from her grandmother's garden. At one time it was a candy bowl for her father's favorite chocolates. When the bowl was given to her, she kept loose change in it. And occasionally it was used to serve food for a special holiday meal. It was now "retired" to the mantel, but the shine was still there.

It reminded me of my mother. She was so giving, so encouraging, and so forgiving. She did so much for me. Now she is "retired," but her glow is still there. She is very precious to me and will always have an honored place in my life.

"And thine age shall be clearer than the noonday; thou shalt shine forth, thou shalt be as the morning. And thou shalt be secure, because there is hope; yea, thou shalt dig about thee, and thou shalt take thy rest in safety" (Job 11:17, 18).

Charlene Hilliard West

NOT GOD'S ONLY OPTION

For if you remain silent at this time,
relief and deliverance . . . will arise from another place.
Esther 4:14, NIV.

"If not you, God will use someone else." That's kind of a startling statement, isn't it? I came across it recently when I was doing some work for a women's organization I led. We had decided that "for such a time as this," taken from the story of Esther, would be a good touchstone for us as Christian women professionals. So as I was preparing for a meeting, I reread Esther 4:12-14: "When Esther's words were reported to Mordecai, he sent back this answer: 'Do not think that because you are in the king's house you alone of all the Jews will escape. For if you remain silent at this time, relief and deliverance for the Jews will arise from another place, but you and your father's family will perish. And who knows but that you have come to royal position for such a time as this?' " (NIV).

Wow, I was hit hard with that statement! This was not about special selection—this was a story about invitation. Esther was being invited to be a part of God's work and to use what God had given her for His purposes, but at the same time she was being reminded that she was not God's only option. I like to think about the things God has brought into my life as my work, but this passage helped me to see it differently. It's His work, and I can have a role in it if I say yes to His invitation. For our little organization we decided we couldn't separate the last part of the verse from the first—we needed to take in the invitation and the promise together. It changed our whole meeting and our focus.

Sometimes we need to be reminded that God will have His way with or without our help. But how much better for us if we say yes to Him and become an instrument in His hand, an essential element of His plan, just as Esther did!

PAMELA MCCANN

SEPTEMBER 1

SURRENDER

For whoever wants to save his life will lose it,
but whoever loses his life for me and for the gospel will save it.
Mark 8:35, NIV.

Poet Christina Rossetti wrote: "What can I give Him, poor as I am? If I were a shepherd, I would bring a lamb; if I were a Wise Man, I would do my part; yet what can I give Him? Give my heart."

What God wants more than anything else is you. All of you.

I personally believe that those who give of themselves to God will not have to give up anything. I believe that those who give their time to God will have enough time for themselves. Those who give their means to God will have enough for themselves. Yet I would never want you to give money or time or talents or anything else to God for that motive. The purpose of returning to God is not to get anything but to give everything. Jesus said this: "Whoever tries to keep his life will lose it" (Luke 17:33, NIV).

Here's Oswald Chambers' commentary on the topic: "Our motive for surrender should not be for any personal gain at all. We have become so self-centered that we go to God only for something from Him, and not for God Himself."

If you surrender, whatever you surrender, you give it initially without any thought of receiving. I've heard people call for offerings in such a way as to suggest that if you give $100 to the church, God is going to give you $500 extra for yourself. Frankly, God may, and He may not. But you see, if that's the motive you use to give, then you're not really practicing the principle of cheerfully returning all you've received, but you're really, in a twisted sort of way, being a taker from God. You give only to try to get for yourself.

However, I want to assure you that if God asks you to come to Him and give Him your all, He's not going to leave you with nothing. If you give without thought of taking, then and only then does the rest of that passage come true: "For whoever wants to save his life will lose it, but whoever loses his life for me and for the gospel will save it" (Mark 8:35, NIV).

LOREN SEIBOLD

LEST WE FORGET

But others were tortured, refusing to turn from God in order to be set free. They placed their hope in a better life after the resurrection.
Heb. 11:35, NLT.

As I travel from country to country, I have been touched by the conditions in which many of our fellow Christians live and work. I sat in a church filled with worshippers, but no church workers were present because they had been imprisoned for their faith. The Bibles the members so reverently held had been smuggled into the country.

In another town I visited a little house on the edge of a city. Each week church members secretly entered the house to worship; they sang in whispers to prevent detection. Then one day police officers raided the house and arrested the pastor. He remains in prison.

Another time I met an elderly man sitting by himself in church. When he had refused to send his children to school on the Sabbath, the authorities took and sent them to a Communist boarding school. Today, the children are atheists. Only God knows the depth of this man's sorrow.

I know of a Christian pastor's home that was bombed by a radical religious group. Yet, he continues to preach the gospel.

One time a teenager came to an evangelistic meeting, her face and arms covered with bruises. Her father had beaten her to discourage her from accepting Jesus. Today the young woman rejoices in the Lord in spite of persecution.

In another country I stepped into a pastor's one-room apartment. A bare light bulb hung in the center of the room. The pastor knelt on the floor beside his bed, preparing a Bible study. I prayed that, for his safety, the police had not seen me enter the apartment. It would have been far too dangerous to visit the secret house church.

Unsung heroes live and work in many dark and dangerous places around the world. They are determined to serve God at any cost.

"Therefore whoever confesses Me before men, him I will also confess before My Father who is in heaven" (Matt. 10:32, NKJV).

J. H. ZACHARY

RESTLESS BUT AT REST

I have told you these things, so that in me you may have peace.
In this world you will have trouble. But take heart! I have overcome the world.
John 16:33, NIV.

My brother Jim has a beagle named Ringo. Like most dogs (or cats), Ringo has a somewhat inflated sense of his place in the house. He thinks that he runs it. And he thinks of the people in the house as his "pack." Ringo gets very stressed when the pack is not together. He runs from room to room, checking to see where people are and trying to get them in the same place.

On a recent visit to our home, Ringo also demonstrated his idea that our home was indeed now his and we were added to the pack as long as he was here. He was not at rest until we were all together in the same room.

Another time, when Jim and his girlfriend Laurie took Ringo cross-country skiing with them, he ran alongside between the two of them, barking when they got separated. He would only be quiet once he had succeeded in getting them back on the same trail and close together.

These instances got me to thinking about Ringo and his sense of responsibility and control and how sometimes I'm just like him. I think that when I get all the pieces in place I can relax. I'm stressed when I feel as though things aren't where they should be in my life, and sometimes I feel as if I have to bark or cause a ruckus to get them back together.

Well, the funny thing is, Ringo really had nothing to do with the fact that we finally got together around the fire or that Jim and Laurie finally ended up on the same ski trail. Just as we don't have control of the pieces of our lives, all our barking and ruckus-making doesn't change things or accomplish what we desire. Someone else is actually in control of all that. Ringo reminded me that I need to do what I can and trust the Master.

PAMELA MCCANN

I'M BIGGER!

I've named you friends because I've let you in on everything I've heard from the Father."
John 15:15, Message.

Preschoolers Annika and Matthew walked out the door of Chuck E. Cheese's Pizza and down the sidewalk. Wanting the fun to continue, Annika stepped up onto the curb and announced proudly, "I'm bigger." Not to be outdone, Matthew went back up the sloping sidewalk just past Annika and stood next to her, proclaiming, "I'm bigger."

Matthew and Annika continued their friendly competition until they reached the top and ran out of curb to stand on. Their eyes quickly darted around, searching for a higher pedestal. Before either one could start climbing the walls I declared them both the biggest. They seemed to accept this pronouncement, and we continued toward the parking lot, where we said goodbye to Matthew and his mother. On the way to our car Annika found her pedestal, a raised concrete block in the grass. She stood on it triumphantly and called out to Matthew, "I'm bigger!"

For a preschooler always looking up at the world, being "bigger" is worth bragging about. Many of us also have achievements we are proud of, and rightly so. But whether I can claim to be the best or someone else has stolen that title away does not change God's regard for me. "What you say about yourself means nothing in God's work. It's what God says about you that makes the difference" (2 Cor. 10:18, Message).

And what God says about us, His people, tops any boast we could make or any earthly accolade we could receive.

Jesus told His disciples (and us!), "I'm no longer calling you servants because servants don't understand what their master is thinking and planning. No, I've named you friends because I've let you in on everything I've heard from the Father" (John 15:15, Message).

God also says, "I am God, your personal God, the Holy of Israel, your Savior. I paid a huge price for you. . . . That's how much you mean to me! That's how much I love you! I'd sell off the whole world to get you back, trade the creation just for you" (Isa. 43:3, 4, Message).

LAURA WEST KONG

THE "RESTART" GENERATION

We too may live a new life.
Rom. 6:4, NIV.

One of the most accomplished marketing minds in the world was talking to us at a seminar a number of years ago. He spoke of the different ways that people experience life and how technology is changing us. He said that the kids growing up with Nintendo are learning how to push the "restart" button as a way to solve problems. I've thought about that a lot: we are living in a culture that seems very good at "restarting." Don't like your marriage? "Restart." Not ready for a child right now? "Restart." School getting to be a drag? "Restart."

Restart is a powerful button. It wipes out the past like it never existed. After hitting restart, you can start over, clean. The truth is, in life, "restart" is actually much harder than pushing a button. The past is rarely entirely wiped out. We are left with the consequences of the choices we have made, and lives are affected in those choices. Wrongs can be so hard to make right. When things get so tangled that the way to make it right can't be found, we often feel as if we have to try the "restart" button.

Sin is like that. Humans are so hopeless; we are caught in sin with no way out. Fortunately, God gave us a "restart" when He sent Jesus to die for us. It's not something we could do for ourselves, as Paul reminds us throughout his letters in the New Testament. I'm so grateful that God provided a way for us to restart and experience a forgiveness that wipes out our past sins. Aren't you?

"We were therefore buried with him through baptism into death in order that, just as Christ was raised from the dead through the glory of the Father, we too may live a new life" (Rom. 6:4, NIV).

PAMELA MCCANN

THE DAY AFTER LABOR DAY

As long as the earth endures, seedtime and harvest, cold and heat, summer and winter, day and night will never cease.
Gen. 8:22, NIV.

I'll admit: I missed you. OK, maybe not the first day, but by the second . . . or was it the third? I'm glad to be back after my vacation. Aren't vacations wonderful? Have you enjoyed this Labor Day weekend? Are you glad to be back to work today?

God knows it is good to be back at work. He said so. In Ecclesiastes 3 it says, "There is a time for everything, and a season for every activity under heaven" (verse 1, NIV). It contrasts birth and death, planting and harvest, killing and healing, destroying and building, weeping and laughing.

Maybe for you, right now it is not so great to be back at work. You have been working hard for a long time with no break. There are tasks here demanding your time and effort, there are children or a spouse at home demanding your time and thought. God guarantees rest. Did you know that?

In Genesis 8:22 God says, "As long as the earth endures, seedtime and harvest, cold and heat, summer and winter, day and night will never cease" (NIV).

Did you catch it? Right at the end, it says day and night will not cease. Day and night, work and rest. No matter where you are, ready to work or ready to rest, God will give you what you need.

I love the phrase in the hymn "Day by Day" that says, "He whose heart is kind beyond all measure gives unto each day what He deems best. Lovingly, its part of pain and pleasure, mingling toil with peace and rest."

God promises the cycle will continue. Seedtime and harvest, cold and heat, summer and winter, day and night. It will not be all work. It will not be all rest. But it will be what He deems best.

RANDY BATES

SINGIN' IN THE RAIN

Let Wilderness turn cartwheels, Animals, come dance.
Ps. 96:12, Message.

There's a General Electric "green" commercial playing on TV, and I drop everything to watch the commercial when I hear its theme, "Singin' in the Rain," in the background. Not only does it have a light, carefree melody and orchestration, there's the happy tappity-tappity tap dancing of—not Gene Kelly—a baby elephant frolicking in the puddles of a rain forest. The carefree, splashy choreography is amazingly like the 1952 movie. A macaw and chimp watch the tap dancing pachyderm with amazement and a little envy.

And I know just how they feel. I wish I could dance. Not only did I grow up in a Christian environment that discouraged social dancing, but I had a disabling accident at age 23 that required extensive physical therapy even to walk again. Certain sports are impossible. I'm grateful to be able to walk several miles without a cane, brace, or a limp. But when I walk, I must constantly look at the path or sidewalk before me to avoid tripping. I rarely look at distant scenery unless I stop for breath. Compensating for my paralyzed muscles, I must look sharp for level changes, rocks, acorns or pine cones, cracks in the cement, and many other tiny hazards that could send me painfully sprawling. So, to see an elephant joyfully tap dancing in the forest makes me smile, and I join the little guy, if only in my spirit.

When Emmanuel comes to rescue us from this world of infirmity, we'll be glorified and we shall be changed, inside and out, in an instant (1 Cor. 15:51).

"Get out the message—God Rules! He put the world on a firm foundation; he treats everyone fair and square. Let's hear it from Sky, with Earth joining in, and a huge round of applause from Sea. Let Wilderness turn cartwheels, Animals, come dance, put every tree of the forest in the choir—An extravaganza before God as he comes, as he comes to set everything right on earth, set everything right, treat everyone fair" (Ps. 96:10-13, Message).

"What a glorious feeling, I'm happy again!" Tappity, tappity, tappity, tappity, tappity, tappity . . .

CHRISTY K. ROBINSON

THE GOSPEL OF THE KINGDOM

This gospel of the kingdom shall be preached in the whole world as a testimony to all the nations, and then the end will come.
Matt. 24:14, NASB.

"This gospel" refers to the Lord's previous remark, "But the one who endures to the end, [he/she] will be saved." Later in this same discourse, Jesus described the Son of Man coming in the clouds with power and glory and sending forth His angels to "gather His elect," who are the members of His kingdom. At the end Jesus gathers to Himself those who are His. This is the future dimension of salvation—to be gathered with the other saved persons to Jesus at His second coming.

An angel spoke to Joseph concerning Mary: "She will bear a Son; and you shall call His name Jesus, for He will save His people from their sins" (Matt. 1:21, NASB). Jesus' very name embraces the idea of salvation. Jesus in the Hebrew language is "Yashua," or "Joshua." As Joshua brought the Israelites into the Promised Land after bondage and the Exodus, so Jesus, our Deliverer, redeems us to our heavenly destination.

How does Jesus save us? As they celebrated the Passover, Jesus passed the cup, saying, "Drink from it, all of you; for this is My blood of the covenant, which is poured out for many for forgiveness of sins" (Matt. 26:27, 28, NASB). Through the shedding of His blood we are saved as we accept this substitutionary sacrifice through sheer faith. He took our place; bore our guilt, shame, and sin; and in exchange, clothes us with His righteousness.

What does the expression, "the gospel of the kingdom" mean? Gospel means "good news," and kingdom means "rule" or "reign." The "gospel of the kingdom" refers to God's reign through the Messiah King, Jesus Christ. Believers become citizens of the kingdom described in Matthew 5:1-12.

Those who rejoice in this salvation are motivated to endure to the end. They stand up to Satan's temptations, and they share the gospel of the kingdom with the unsaved. Once this vital message is proclaimed worldwide, then the end will come. Jesus has a plan for your life and a work for you to do. His kingdom is safe, secure, permanent, and eternal!

LARRY CHRISTOFFEL

RECIPROCITY

How can I repay the Lord for all his goodness to me?
Ps. 116:12, NIV.

There is a feeling of profound gratitude in the heart of the psalmist. He recognizes that by the very nature of things, simply by being born on this earth and existing, he is a receiver of blessings. And he credits all of those blessings back to God. Even where people have been the intermediaries of those blessings, God is the ultimate source of them.

So he gives God the credit and asks, "Is there any way that I can repay the Lord for all this?" Of course, the answer is probably not. Thank goodness God doesn't ask for repayment! Take salvation, for instance. Remember what Paul said: "For by grace are ye saved through faith; and that not of yourselves: it is the gift of God" (Eph. 2:8).

So can you ever repay the Lord for the gift of salvation? If you could, you couldn't have salvation, because it can only come as a gift. So the answer to the psalmist's question is no, you can't completely repay the Lord. But you can show your appreciation by joining God in bringing blessings to others.

This theology of blessing is salted all through the Bible. This idea of receiving and giving is the whole substance of Jesus' prayer for His disciples in John 17:7: "Everything you have given me comes from you" (NIV).

James said, "Every good and perfect gift is from above, coming down from the Father of the heavenly lights" (James 1:17, NIV).

Paul exclaimed, "Thanks be to God for his indescribable gift!" (2 Cor. 9:15, NIV).

Though you can never repay the Lord for salvation or His other blessings, nonetheless, it is that yearning to repay the Lord that marks the difference between a taker and a returner. The taker says, "I've received a few good things; what more do I have coming?" The returner says, "I've received so much; what can I give back?"

LOREN SEIBOLD

MOVE FROM HERE TO THERE

If you have faith the size of a mustard seed, you will say to this mountain, "Move from here to there," and it will move; and nothing will be impossible to you.
Matt. 17:20, NASB.

As my Christian high school classmates and I looked around the tiny church in a Romanian mountain village, we wondered how God would solve two logistical predicaments.

We were already several days into sharing the gospel at evangelistic meetings, and we were running out of chairs to seat visitors. In this village, according to the locals, we could not purchase any chairs. Second, the only other room in the church, which was located in the small balcony, was too crowded with almost 50 energetic kids attending our children's meeting. After praying earnestly for a solution, one of our school sponsors, Rob, and the translator went to visit the mayor of the village. Meanwhile, we students distributed advertising flyers for the meetings and prayed.

The mayor was in a meeting, so Rob and the translator had to wait. Suddenly the town hall's door burst open, and a man entered. He seemed inebriated, but the translator talked to him and told him our problem. He said, "Oh, go talk to my wife. She's the director of the school next to your church, and she'll let you borrow all the chairs you need."

Rob and the translator went to the director of the school, a gracious, cordial woman. As a bonus, she taught English and could converse directly with him! After chatting awhile, Rob asked to borrow chairs. She immediately obliged. "Of course! How many do you need?" She sent the chairs to the church at once.

But Rob kept smiling and praying. He decided to ask one more favor. He explained the dilemma with our children's room, and asked if we could use one of the school's rooms for our children's program. She told him yes! When Rob returned to tell us, we were delighted to hear that both of our prayer requests were answered!

God loves to answer our seemingly impossible requests. We should look at difficult situations in life as an opportunity to grow our "mustard seed" of faith.

Joelle McNulty

THE WAR OF THE BEES

You will not have to fight this battle.
Take up your positions; stand firm and see the deliverance the Lord will give you.
2 Chron. 20:17, NIV.

Enemies were determined to destroy Laiagam, a village located in the eastern highlands of Papua New Guinea. For several weeks warfare disturbed the entire community. Houses were burned to the ground. Several persons had been killed on both sides. Not only were spears and bows and arrows used, a few villagers owned guns. The guns brought new terror to solving tribal differences. To inflict as much hurt as possible, tribal warriors cut down trees, destroyed crops, and slaughtered animals. The war raged for almost one month.

A Christian church was located in Laiagam. Their situation was very dangerous. The two warring tribes were located on either side of Laiagam. During battles, weapons landed in Laiagam. Arrows with firebrands attached had destroyed several homes. The church stood amid the carnage.

The little group of believers decided the best course would be to leave for a safer location. They made this decision in their beloved church. They believed that this would be the last time that they would see it standing.

However, Alo, a young member, decided to remain. Shortly after the others left, he observed an advancing war party headed for the church with lighted torches. In minutes the church would burn to the ground.

Alo fell to his knees. He earnestly prayed for help from God. "Lord, help me do what I can to save this church." He picked up a piece of plastic pipe with a funnel attached to one end. This homemade "trumpet" was used to call worshippers to the church. He gave the trumpet a loud blast and again asked God for help. The mob advanced to a few meters from the church. The sky seemed to darken. A huge swarm of bees declared their own war against the attackers. Weapons dropped. The mob frantically swatted bees and ran wildly through the village ruins.

The church was saved. Alo's prayer had made the difference. What a praise meeting followed when the congregation returned. "We know that God has saved our church. God sent His angels to direct the bees against our enemies."

JIM AND JEAN ZACHARY

SUCCESS: GOD'S BUSINESS

They are the ones the Lord has sent to go throughout the earth.
Zech. 1:10, NIV.

Oleg and I arose from our knees. The future rested with God. We knew He had answered our prayers, but how He had would continue to be revealed over many years, even to the present. Several days after the prayer, tears moistened his eyes as Oleg shared God's confirmation of His plan for the aviation ministry. His testimony has fortified us over the years as storms of discouragement have repeatedly beaten upon us.

"After prayer that night I went home," recounted Oleg. "I went to bed and dreamed a vivid dream, like nothing I've experienced before. I saw AWA [Adventist World Aviation] personnel gathered at an airfield with young missionary aviators in training. Strangely, some were mounted on the most majestic, beautiful, powerful horses I've ever seen. The horses sounded eager, like well-tuned throaty engines, ready to run. They were of various colors: red, white, and brown.

"I awoke, and puzzling over the dream, I could not go back to sleep. Not wanting to disturb my wife, I went to another room and picked up my Bible. It fell open to Zechariah. Chapter one, verse eight leaped off the page!

"During the night I had a vision—and there before me was a man riding a red horse! He was standing among the myrtle trees in a ravine. Behind him were red, brown and white horses. I asked, 'What are these, my Lord?' The angel who was talking with me answered, 'I will show you what they are'" (Zech. 1:8, 9, NIV).

Oleg was on the edge of his seat. "Yes, what do these mean?" he wondered, heart pounding.

"Then the man standing among the myrtle trees explained, 'They are the ones the Lord has sent to go throughout the earth'" (verse 10).

When tempted to give up, throw in the towel, and call it quits because the task seems impossible, remember to hold on to your faith and move forward. Success is God's business. Obedience is ours.

DON STARLIN

THE LORD IS GOOD

I will rejoice in the Lord, I will be joyful in God my Savior.
Hab. 3:18, NIV.

Coming out of church one afternoon, I met an old friend who had lost his wife a few years before. "Come meet my new bride," he beamed, introducing me to the smiling woman at his side.

"I'm so glad for both of you," I said as I greeted them.

"Yes, God is good, God is good," he murmured.

How easily those words roll off our tongue when things are going our way! I couldn't help thinking about his state of mind while he'd sat at the bedside of his dying wife. I'm sure he would not have said, or even let himself think, "God, You aren't very good to me," but perhaps, "Why God, why? I don't understand."

A mother told me the story of praying and relinquishing her critically injured and apparently dying son to the Lord as the rescue helicopter whisked him off to the hospital. Her trust in God was rewarded, and today that son is a minister.

Yes, praise the Lord. Yet such stories worry me. As a physician, I also deal with people who pray—but children die anyway and cancer victims are not delivered from their disease or their pain.

Are these people short on faith? Is their trust somehow flawed? Have they failed to enlist enough people to "storm the gates of heaven" with them? That seems to be the subtle implication behind so many of the success stories and answered-prayer stories we hear.

Yet buried in a tiny Old Testament book we find these startling words: "Though the fig tree does not bud and there are no grapes on the vines, though the olive crop fails and the fields produce no food, though there are no sheep in the pen and no cattle in the stalls, yet I will rejoice in the Lord, I will be joyful in God my Savior" (Hab. 3:17, 18, NIV).

Think about this: What if God had answered Jesus' prayer, "Father, let this cup pass from me," by saying yes?

AILEEN LUDINGTON

THE LORD'S SONG

By the rivers of Babylon we sat and wept when we remembered Zion. There on the poplars we hung our harps, for there our captors asked us for songs, our tormentors demanded songs of joy; they said, "Sing us one of the songs of Zion!" How can we sing the songs of the Lord while in a foreign land? Ps. 137:1-4, NIV.

After several months a peace agreement was signed and hundreds of thousands of elated Kosovo refugees made plans to return to whatever was left of their homes. Suddenly people were free! It was expected that they would await organized transport and make their way home when things were safe. But instead, thousands and thousands of people arranged their own transportation and headed north. They were heading home at last!

Their outlook had changed as they packed up their belongings and began the long journey home. Before, people had looked dejected and hopeless, but now they were going home! It was a party atmosphere—even though many knew they were returning to destroyed homes. They were going home!

With the surge of people heading home, it was suggested that each family should be given a month's supply of food and supplies as they crossed the border heading back to Kosovo. Adventist Development and Relief Agency (ADRA) was tasked with managing the distribution. A drive-through lane was set up where people would receive a month's ration of food and other supplies as they headed north. Dozens of trucks filled with supplies backed up to both sides of the lane. At the peak of the distribution, cars, buses, trucks, and tractors with farm trailers would merely drive slowly by the supply trucks and receive their food, plastic sheeting, hygiene kits, cooking sets, and other items. On average, during the five weeks of operating the drive-through lane, it was estimated that each six seconds a refugee received their one-month ration. The people were going home at last; what a day that was!

We know that God is on His throne and that He yearns to come and put an end to all the troubles here in this old sick world. How can we sing the songs of the Lord in this strange land? Maybe it's not easy, but this is what we're about! Singing the songs of the Lord! We sing the songs with all our hearts—that's how! Jesus is coming quickly, and it is our joy to share this wonderful news!

MICHAEL PORTER

SEPTEMBER 15

THE BAND-AID SOLUTION

[God] comforts us in all our troubles, so that we can comfort those in any trouble with the comfort we ourselves have received from God.
2 Cor. 1:4, NIV.

"That's just a Band-Aid solution. It's like putting a Band-Aid on a broken arm." Although much maligned, the humble Band-Aid is tops in my household. In our medicine cabinet, we always have at least four or five different boxes of them. They help keep wounds clean and provide an environment conducive to healing. There are Band-Aids with cartoon characters, rainbows, and happy faces printed on them. Some Band-Aids are shaped like hearts, and others glow in the dark. I keep a little stash of Band-Aids in my purse for injuries that might occur while away from home.

It is true that a broken arm requires much more than a Band-Aid, but that doesn't mean we should throw all our Band-Aids away. Although it is simple and small, a Band-Aid is often just the right solution for a variety of wounds, real and imaginary.

My daughter, Annika, loves Band-Aids. There's nothing better for a scraped knee than a kiss and a princess Band-Aid. Band-Aids are good for imaginary as well as real cuts. Even if I cannot see the owie she is presenting to me, a Band-Aid still makes things OK. When Annika is playing in the yard with her friends and one of them falls down and needs a Band-Aid, it is not long before all of them also report various injuries that also call for a Band-Aid.

You don't need a medical degree to apply a Band-Aid, and you don't need a theology degree to reach out to someone who is hurting. Every day we encounter people who are suffering from numerous wounds, seen and unseen. Jesus did not belittle the simple gesture of kindness. He taught, "If anyone gives even a cup of cold water to one of these little ones because he is my disciple, I tell you the truth, he will certainly not lose his reward" (Matt. 10:42, NIV).

Each one of us has the responsibility, as well as the ability, to bring comfort and healing to others. "[God] comforts us in all our troubles, so that we can comfort those in any trouble with the comfort we ourselves have received from God" (2 Cor. 1:4, NIV).

LAURA WEST KONG

BEING GOOD

Find out what pleases the Lord.
Eph. 5:10, NIV.

One of my dad's ancestors was Hywel Dda ("the good"), a tenth-century Welsh king. Hywel's "good" appellation did not come from his holiness, although he was a Christian, because statesmen of the era had to be ruthless. Rather, he compiled and combined the Celtic *brehon* law with Christian laws and customs. Hywel's laws, which stood for 600 years, were noted for their fairness, and especially for the emphasis placed on restoration over punishment.

Growing up in a Christian home and enrolled in Christian schools from first grade through university, I had many advantages. I became a church pianist and organist at age 10. I knew my Bible proof texts and obeyed my parents, pastors, and teachers. One might conclude that I was "good" because I didn't do "bad" things. The danger was that I might've been convinced that whatever decision I made was good because I was good. Not so! The very thought that I'm "good" is corrupt!

If we refrain from immoral, unethical, unlawful things, and we support the downtrodden or work for the church, we must, by default, be good people, right? The Bible says that no one is good or without sin (Rom. 3:10). We can only claim the goodness and righteousness of Jesus shining through us. Without Christ's nature, we are the people who say, "Lord, we did these things in Your name," but Jesus answers, "I never knew you. Away from me, you evildoers!" (Matt. 7:23, NIV).

How do you enter an intimate relationship with God? First, get rid of your pride in being "good." Earnestly ask God to show you where He wants you to fit into His will. Ask Him to forgive and fill you with His righteousness, declaring you acceptable because of His sacrifice. And in that humble, healed attitude, you can take baby steps and then lengthen your stride as you run after His leading. Every experience, positive and negative, can build your faith and trust if Jesus is always in view!

"For you were once darkness, but now you are light in the Lord. Live as children of light (for the fruit of the light consists in all goodness, righteousness and truth) and find out what pleases the Lord" (Eph. 5:8-10, NIV).

CHRISTY K. ROBINSON

SEPTEMBER 17

CHRIST'S REAL PASSION

Whenever we are in need, we should come bravely before the throne of our merciful God. There we will be treated with undeserved kindness, and we will find help.
Heb. 4:16, CEV.

A media event that caused a lot of interest was, surprisingly, a 2004 film called *The Passion of the Christ.* It is surprising because usually most of the media's attention isn't religious, much less Christian. When religion becomes entertainment, it becomes no more permanent than entertainment.

Some people reported that the film had a positive spiritual effect on them. I won't criticize anything that shines a good light on Christianity—rare enough nowadays—but I'll tell you why I shied away from seeing the movie: it seemed disproportionate to me. Jesus' beating and flogging is barely mentioned in Scripture; however, it was one of the many focuses of the movie. If it bothers you at all when people take some small part of the Bible and amplify it until it becomes their whole message, then it should bother you that the movie amplified the beating and flogging of Jesus and turned it into the whole message.

The Gospel writers mention the beating only in passing, because they want us to be moved not by the raw emotions—after all, lots of people besides Jesus were beaten and flogged, and it was always gut-wrenching—but by the meaning. You see, the meaning of all of this is not suffering, but love. We don't believe that it was Jesus' suffering that saved us, but His love for us. The suffering was part of what He was willing to endure to show His love. "God loved the people of this world so much that he gave his only Son, so that everyone who has faith in him will have eternal life and never really die" (John 3:16, CEV).

It isn't the suffering that saves me; it is His love that saves me. And that love was shown throughout His life—not just in how He died, but in how He lived. I don't think a portrayal that focuses just on the suffering of Jesus tells the story in a balanced way.

So while it is true that Jesus suffered, let's not focus on what others did to Him. Let's focus on what Jesus is doing for us now. Jesus is not suffering for our sins now. The cross is empty. Jesus is alive. He is in heaven, and He continues to reach out to us and hear our prayers.

LOREN SEIBOLD

A GOLDFISH STORY

Is not this man a burning stick snatched from the fire?
Zech. 3:2, NIV.

Four-year-old Annika wriggled with excitement. She was going to the Loma Linda Fair to win goldfish at a carnival game. Annika paid her dollar and received three balls to toss into an inflatable pool. For each ball thrown into a floating bowl, she would receive one fish. For a ball in a small floating cup, she could get two fish. The first ball bounced short of the pool. The second flew way beyond. All concentration, Annika tossed her final ball right into one of the floating cups and collected two coupons for free goldfish at a local pet store. Mission accomplished, she settled down to enjoy the rest of the fair.

At the pet store we were directed to the back of the shop to a counter with a sign marked "delicatessen." There, along with crickets, mice, and brine shrimp, one could purchase small goldfish, 12 for a dollar, possibly for feeding pet sharks. The employee chased down one orange and one black. Annika promptly named them Alexandra and Elina.

At the checkout counter Annika wanted rainbow pebbles and plastic plants. I inquired what it would take to keep these free goldfish alive. Thirty dollars poorer, we left the pet store to set up Alexandra and Elina's aquatic paradise in a plastic urn with hot-pink pedestal—a great deal of trouble and expense for 17 cents' worth of fish snatched from the shark's mouth.

Chosen by God, we too have been snatched from the shark's mouth. "The Lord said to Satan, 'The Lord rebuke you, Satan! The Lord, who has chosen Jerusalem, rebuke you! Is not this man a burning stick snatched from the fire?' Now Joshua was dressed in filthy clothes as he stood before the angel. The angel said to those who were standing before him, 'Take off his filthy clothes.' Then he said to Joshua, 'See, I have taken away your sin, and I will put rich garments on you.' Then I said, 'Put a clean turban on his head.' So they put a clean turban on his head and clothed him, while the angel of the Lord stood by" (Zech. 3:2-5, NIV).

Just as Annika delighted in outfitting her goldfish in style, God delights in clothing us in rich garments of righteousness.

LAURA WEST KONG

WAIT FIVE MINUTES AND IT'LL CHANGE

You bless all of those who trust you, Lord,
and refuse to worship idols or follow false gods.
Ps. 40:4, CEV.

Life in the Southwest has its advantages when it comes to the cool season. We have gorgeous winters with clear, crisp air and brief storms, and nearby are mountains with snowy mantles to remind us how, just a few miles from that snow, we are able to wear flip-flops for gardening, even in winter. The downside is that we get windy blasts after each storm, which blow desert dust over the cities, knock down palm fronds, uproot large trees, and blow big vehicles off the highways.

In general, the weather is predictable. All summer long it's hot, rainless, and smoggy in California; and in Arizona there are monsoon thunderstorms rolling off the piney mountains and down across the sun-blasted desert. All winter, there are long periods of perfect weather punctuated by welcome rains.

My friends in Oregon and Georgia, though, say that if you don't like the weather there, wait five minutes and it'll change. In their pop-up downpours, there's almost no oxygen because the water is falling so densely!

Life on earth is always changing. All lives, flora and fauna, are made to change from conception until death, and even then, we push up daisies! Change is inevitable, but many of us find change frightening because we can't see the future and plan for it or take control of a situation. We are helpless to change the weather, our stature, or the future (Matt. 6:34).

Perhaps God forbade our consultation with astrologers, mediums, or the occult because our *not* knowing the future places us, like trusting, innocent children, in God's hands where we belong. "Blessed is the man who makes the Lord his trust, who does not look to the proud, to those who turn aside to false gods" (Ps. 40:4, NIV).

He who is unchangeable and holds our destiny is preparing a home for us where we can forget all the stress and hassle of changing. Our joy and peace, our fuller knowledge of God's grace and character, and our love for each other will increase through the ages of eternity.

Christy K. Robinson

EXPECTANCY

They are like trees planted along the riverbank, bearing fruit each season.
Their leaves never wither, and they prosper in all they do.
Ps. 1:3, NLT.

Near our Washington home is a nature preserve with 150 acres of extravagant gardens. My husband and I make it a point to visit the gardens regularly, to walk and talk and see what's next: the glory of springtime when trees burst into bloom; the golden autumn with leaves drifting like rain in the fall breeze; the winter when the bare branches of the trees and bushes are lightly covered in frost or snow.

What has struck me as we've gone on this little journey is that each season has a life of its own. And it's as if each season is building toward the next. There's a kind of expectation about what's coming. There isn't a "dead" season, as I used to think that winter was. It's as if each one brings its own hope—in and of itself there is something to look forward to in each turn of the seasons. We have learned that seeing the garden isn't a simple stroll once a year at the peak blooming season. Seeing this garden is a yearlong experience.

Our own lives are like that garden. How many times do we feel as if we're going through something awful, only to see later how God put that season in our lives to lead to the next? If we knew what was coming, would we look differently at the season or the struggle we're facing?

If I stopped thinking of some times as dark "wilderness experiences" and looked for something positive in each season, what might my life be like? If I stopped looking at the negative side of the situation and started asking God to help me see what good could come of this season, might I be more in tune with what God is doing in my life and through it? It can be hard to see beyond the pain or disappointment we feel, but we know that God has promised to never forsake or abandon us in the low places. We can confidently live in the expectancy not only of the next better season in our lives, but of what God will do with this season.

"And we know that in all things God works for the good of those who love him, who have been called according to his purpose" (Rom. 8:28, NIV).

PAMELA MCCANN

SEPTEMBER 21

CLOUDS IN THE EAST

For in the wilderness shall waters break out, and streams in the desert. And the parched ground shall become a pool, and the thirsty land springs of water. *Isa. 35:6, 7.*

One late-summer day in Phoenix, Arizona (where it gets very hot), I'd taken my mother to the air-conditioned mall. I left her and the purchases in her wheelchair inside the cool building, took out my sunglasses and car keys, and inhaled a deep draft of chilled air before charging through the blast furnace to my parking space. But a monsoon storm and its cool downdraft had swept in from the east while we'd been shopping, and the temperature had dropped 30 degrees. I loaded Mom in the car and thought about another monsoon thunderstorm that had broken a seven-month drought. As the torrents of rain had fallen, cars had stopped on a busy road, and people were dancing for joy, reveling in the refreshing drops.

Unfortunately, summer seems to drag on and on in the Southwest. On the East Coast the leaves are turning colors, and people are winterizing the garden for spring. Department stores have nothing but sweaters and knit caps for sale. But here I want the hot, smoggy, endless summer to be finished! It's still 140 degrees in my car when I leave for lunch, and my lawn looks like stubble. At my job I'm working on multiple, overlapping deadlines for major projects that must be accomplished well before Christmas.

It's dry and dusty, and everything is hot to the touch. We need the cool refreshing rain to fall from heaven. The same can be said of our time on earth. It seems like we've been waiting forever for Jesus to come, and many signs seem to point to His imminent return, but where's that miraculous cloud in the east? (Most storms, riding the jet stream and prevailing winds, come from the west.) "Where is He?" we demand impatiently.

The answer is that He's with us always (Matt. 28:20), and nothing can separate us from the love of God (Rom. 8:39). Until He comes He protects us from sunburn and heat stroke by His pillar of cloud. When we are stressed, we need to rest in Him by casting our troubles at His feet.

"The promise of 'arrival' and 'rest' is still there for God's people. God himself is at rest. And at the end of the journey we'll surely rest with God. So let's keep at it and eventually arrive at the place of rest" (Heb. 4:9-11, Message).

CHRISTY K. ROBINSON

EMERGENCY

Peace I leave with you, My peace I give to you; not as the world gives do I give to you. Let not your heart be troubled, neither let it be afraid.
John 14:27, NKJV.

"Nine-one-one—what is your emergency?"

"Hurry, we need help! My sister choked herself and isn't breathing!"

"Remain calm; I'm sending an ambulance right now."

"OK! Thank you . . . Please hurry!"

"Amanda! Call your dad! Get him home now!"

"I've tried! He's not answering his cell phone!"

I could write pages describing the following seven days. It all began with my middle daughter choking, being rushed to the emergency room, and being placed into a coma while her body and mind were put back together by God's amazing grace. However, I want to examine God's grace in greater proportions as displayed through smaller events.

My oldest daughter, Amanda, is 15, and she is generally quiet and introverted. She wants simple rules and instructions. She had never seen an emergency situation before. She was told to call 911 and then me. When calling my cell, I couldn't be reached. I was at church and had put my silenced phone with my jacket.

Here's where it gets good. Amanda had enough insight at that incredible moment to call the church. If you've ever called a church during a service, nobody answers! But someone was in the office at that moment, and they knew exactly where I was. A few seconds later I was rushing home.

My involvement wasn't crucial. I didn't save my daughter's life or get her to the hospital. But nothing about this event is trivial. God helped Amanda to stay calm and focused enough to call the church, and He placed someone in the office to answer her call and find me. But even better than that, He mobilized His army of believers to pray. My church service is broadcast on the Internet, and at that moment more than 7,000 people began to pray when I announced that there was an emergency in my family. That is where God's grace really shone that day, in a seemingly insignificant couple of phone calls. That is where I found God's grace and peace.

TIM EVANS

SEPTEMBER 23

LEAVING MESSAGES

For the word of God is living and active. Sharper than any double-edged sword, it penetrates even to dividing soul and spirit, joints and marrow; it judges the thoughts and attitudes of the heart. Heb. 4:12, NIV.

I have an aversion to the telephone. Don't ask me why—I'm not even sure where it started. But it's there, and most of all, I really hate to hear the voice mail attendant cheerfully tell me that I have new messages. At one time I had no less than five voice mailboxes between my home, my work, and my other obligations, resulting in literally hundreds of new messages each week. The weight of it seemed literally overwhelming to me.

I felt guilty for missing the call, obligated to find answers I may not know, and dread at the idea that someone might not be happy about something and I cannot resolve it. All this went through my head before I even heard the first message. True, some of the messages were hard to hear, but not all the messages were terrible. In fact, most of them weren't, and sometimes they were a real blessing, like my little nephews and niece singing "Happy Birthday" or a friend calling to say hi. I would've missed out on some blessings if I hadn't overcome my fear and listened to those messages!

I think that a lot of people look at the Bible that way. They see it as a big book full of messages from God. Have you ever heard someone say, "Oh, the Bible is just full of rules I can't hope to follow" or "I can't make sense of all that the Bible says, so why try?" or "The Bible is an old book, it isn't relevant for me today." Actually, the Bible is God's message to us, but many of us are intimidated by it. True, it says some hard things, but it has wonderful promises as well. And unlike any other message we might receive, it's full of life. We miss so much when we aren't in communion with God through His Word every day! I'm going to start picking up my messages more regularly—how about you?

PAMELA MCCANN

WHEN LIFE BEGINS TO FAIL

*Trust in the Lord with all thine heart;
and lean not unto thine own understanding. Prov. 3:5.*

Why does the Tower of Pisa lean? The tower, which was constructed in 1173, is built on unsuitable ground for such a heavy and tall building; only about six feet above sea level, its foundation is on a bed of sand and clay. The so-called Leaning Tower of Pisa in Italy is actually the bell tower of the Cathedral of Pisa. Shaped like a cylinder, the tower is made of white marble and has eight arcades one over the other. The center of the tower is hollow, and there is a spiral staircase by which one can climb to the top of the tower.

The tower slowly but steadily continues to lean more each year. Today its deviation from the vertical is more than 14 feet. In spite of many efforts to stop the leaning, nothing has yet worked. Experts say that the tower cannot be straightened without it toppling over in the opposite direction. It's anyone's guess as to how long the tower will remain standing.

Life is like a building. Our life needs an adequate foundation. Jesus spoke of the foolish man who built his house on the sand, and when the storms came, his house collapsed. Jesus spoke, too, of the wise man who built his house upon the rock, and when the tempest blew, his house remained safe and sound. Jesus made it clear that the true rock on which to build is His own teaching. Other teachings are like sand and do not provide a sufficient foundation for life (Matt. 7:24-29).

We need not wonder, then, when a life begins to lean over precariously. The chances are that it has been built upon sand. How is the foundation of your own life?

"Trust in the Lord with all your heart; do not depend on your own understanding. Seek his will in all you do, and he will show you which path to take" (Prov. 3:5, 6, NLT).

LLOYD A. DAYES

SEPTEMBER 25

WHAT ARE YOU WEARING?

Go ye into all the world, and preach the gospel to every creature.
Mark 16:15.

Picture a well-used overstuffed easy chair. The chair's owner enters the room with a bag of cookies in one hand and a glass of milk in the other, a fuzzy robe wrapped around him, soft slippers on his feet, and a tired face. Return to the room in 30 minutes and you'd hear him snoring.

Imagine another setting. Thousands of people are sitting in a huge stadium. The sky is blue, the air is cool, and the crowd is hushed. Gently flapping in the breeze is the familiar flag of the Olympic Games. In aerodynamic attire the women athletes crouch at the line with their feet in the starting blocks and their hands supporting their forward-leaning bodies. They are waiting for the start signal. A world record could be set in the next 30 seconds.

In these two settings, who is prepared to GO? It would be easy to find out. Just walk up behind them and yell, "GO!" Mr. Easy Chair would probably be wearing his milk and cookies while Ms. Sprinter would be halfway to the finish line.

On the wall in the Quiet Hour lobby is a text that begins with "Go." The full text says, "Go ye into all the world and preach the gospel to every creature" (Mark 16:15). In this case, the finish line is more than a trophy; it is the full restoration of the relationship between God and humanity. We have a mission.

But the first step is for us to choose to run in the race. If I showed up at the Olympics and asked to run the 100-meter dash, how do you think I would do? Choosing is not enough. I must be ready to run, which means whole-life training. I must be rested and healthy. I must understand the basic gospel that God is love. I must continually listen for God's voice calling me to share His love. And I must be listening for the command to GO. This is not something I do alone. God promises to be with me always. "And be sure of this: I am with you always, even to the end of the age" (Matt. 28:20, NLT).

Have you chosen to run in the race? Have you committed to training? When God says "GO!" will you be wearing cookies and milk, or will you be halfway to the finish line?

RANDY BATES

YOU CAN TRUST GOD

If you trust me, you are trusting not only me, but also God who sent me.
John 12:44, NLT.

One of the hardest things for Christians to learn is total dependence on God. Although there are many instances in the Bible when the faith of God's children was tested, some tests were brought on as a direct result of following God's leading.

After Jesus was baptized, God publicly proclaimed His love and pleasure in His Son as the Holy Spirit descended upon Jesus. But when you read the account without paragraph breaks, you will note that the very next verse states, "The Spirit immediately drove him out into the wilderness" (Mark 1:12, RSV). Immediately after such public affirmation came a severe test of Jesus' faith!

Long before, the children of Israel had also witnessed a clear and convincing display of God's power and protection through the plagues and their deliverance from slavery in Egypt. It seems amazing to us that after working powerfully to save their lives God would lead them into such peril, trapped between the Red Sea, the mountains, and the most powerful army on earth (Ex. 14). The whole thing was commanded and permitted by God!

What gives? Can the Lord lead us even in the depths of our trials when we see no way of escape? Is this the same God who promised never to forsake us? Are we missing something of real significance—of even greater importance than our own comfort and safety?

Here's a friendly challenge: Can you find a chapter in the book of Hebrews that mentions the trials of God's saints? Can you name a book in the Old Testament that deals with unfair suffering? Do you recall a psalm that assures us of God's protection in times of danger? Do you remember a verse in Revelation in which Jesus says He is with us always, even to the end of the world? Pick up your Bible and reread those famous, familiar, and beloved chapters. You can trust God—people all through history have done so. Think about the times that you have seen His leading in your own life, and remember that He is faithful.

ROBERT JOHNSTON

SEEING GOD

If you seek God, your God, you'll be able to find him if you're serious, looking for him with your whole heart and soul.
Deuteronomy 4:29, Message.

Victor Hugo set about writing his masterpiece, *Les Miserables,* in 1845. In 1862 it was published, nearly 20 years in the making. No wonder it's so long! Recently our pastor used an illustration from the book and encouraged us to read it unabridged. It took me six months to complete, but I'm so glad I did!

It is a story about faith, grace, and redemption. In it we meet a priest named Monseigneur Bienvenu, who is the catalyst in the story. He is a dedicated Christian who loves God and has the gift of mercy. He is loved by the people in his little village and known for his gentle spirit and good works. His relationship to God is predominant in our understanding of him. He is well known for his act of grace to the convict Jean Valjean, who is the centerpiece of the story, but if you miss the relationship of Father Bienvenu with God, you miss the whole story.

I was struck by this passage as I skimmed through the book again. Father Bienvenu is meditating in the evening, looking up at the sky full of bright constellations: "He [Father Bienvenu] contemplated the grandeur, and the presence of God; the eternity of the future, that strange mystery; the eternity of the past, a stranger mystery; all the infinities hidden deep in every direction; and, without trying to comprehend the incomprehensible, he saw it. He did not study God; he was dazzled by Him."

I'm glad Victor Hugo reminded us that when you ponder God, it's nearly impossible to be anything but dazzled by Him. It's more than seeing with our eyes or mind, it involves seeking Him with our hearts. That's a reminder I need!

"If you seek God, your God, you'll be able to find him if you're serious, looking for him with your whole heart and soul" (Deut. 4:29, Message).

PAMELA MCCANN

THE KEY TO PEACE

Bear with each other and forgive whatever grievances you may have against one another. Forgive as the Lord forgave you.
Col. 3:13, NIV.

"Stacy," a wealthy and well-educated but depressed woman, sought counsel. She suffered from recurrent headaches, ulcers, and obesity—especially obesity. "I'm bloated with fat," as she put it. "He did it to me," Stacy sobbed. Her husband, a respected politician, had had an affair. The affair had occurred several years before, yet the woman remained obsessed with her bitterness and anger. "I hate him for it, and I hate the woman even more. See what she's done to me? She's ruined my life."

A painful memory is a mental wound, and it must be allowed to heal. Stacy had to stop picking at the scab. She began to realize that she needed to move away from her "poor me/pity me" attitude and begin to tackle her problems and learn to solve them.

"The moment I started to hate that woman," she reflected, "I began to be her slave. All those years she had a tyrannical grasp on my mind and body. No more! I now know that I can learn something positive from this situation. That woman will not steal my joy for even one more day of my life."

Stacy finally realized how wrong it was to mortgage her present by clinging to her past. The words of Paul in Philippians 3 encouraged and inspired her: "But one thing I do: Forgetting what is behind and straining toward what is ahead, I press on toward the goal to win the prize for which God has called me heavenward" (verses 13, 14, NIV). Paul knew that the present was what mattered, and he lived the present with zeal.

Stacy decided to let go of that scrapbook of painful memories. She chose the healing option, to forgive and forget. She finally buried the past and found peace at last.

It's been said that our attitude toward the past is far more important than the past itself. Attitude involves choice. What do we do about the injustice and hurt in life? Do we let them make us bitter? Or do we choose to let the difficulties in life make us better?

AILEEN LUDINGTON

LIKE STARS IN THE UNIVERSE

Become blameless and pure, children of God without fault in a crooked and depraved generation, in which you shine like stars in the universe as you hold out the word of life. Phil. 2:15, 16, NIV.

Margaret, the granddaughter of King Edmund Ironside of England and King Stephen of Hungary, was born in 1047. She read scriptures in Latin in preparation for a religious vocation. Her brother, Edgar the Ætheling, and father, Edward the Ætheling, were English nobility. The Norman invasion in late 1066 disrupted the royal succession, and Margaret's family fled to Scotland. There she married the king of Scotland, Malcolm III Canmore, in 1070.

Her spiritual beauty was legendary. "Whatever pleased her, [the king] loved for love of her," historians reported. "She induced him to carry out her pious wishes. For he, perceiving that Christ dwelt in the heart of his queen, was always ready to follow her advice." Malcolm gave royal authority to his wife, by which she forever changed the social and spiritual life of Scotland.

The *Anglo-Saxon Chronicle* wrote of Queen Margaret: "The Creator knew beforehand what he would have made of her. For she was to increase God's praise in the land and direct the king from the erring path and bend him to a better way and his people with him. . . . And her customs pleased him and he thanked God who had by his power given him such a consort; . . . he was very prudent and turned himself to God."

Scotland had been Christianized to some extent six centuries before by Irish missionaries. Margaret revitalized the church by winning the hearts of the wild (sometimes pagan) clan chiefs, and their subjects followed. Her charity at the "first hour of the day" was famous: she waited tables among the orphans and poorest people of Edinburgh—but it was never for show. She redeemed English slaves held by Scots and founded and patronized traveler hostels and churches. Margaret was the mother of eight children and several royal lines in Europe. She died on November 16, 1093, and was canonized in 1250. Margaret's influence shines, starlike, a thousand years later. The hymn tune for "O Love That Wilt Not Let Me Go" is titled "St. Margaret."

Does our work and influence reflect the light of the Lord's countenance? Will people remark that we have been with Jesus?

Christy K. Robinson

PERSPECTIVE FROM THE BIKE SEAT

Small is the gate and narrow the road that leads to life, and only a few find it.
Matt. 7:14, NIV.

My road bike weighs approximately 18 pounds, is blue, silver, and white, and wants to fly. Unlike my mountain bike, which is solid and built for tough terrain with knobby tires for traction and shocks to cushion the ride and improve control, my road bike has skinny, rock-hard tires to reduce friction, a lightweight, aerodynamic frame to reduce drag, and no shocks. A road bike is built for speed.

One afternoon I called Steve and said, "Let's ride!" Steve has been riding road bikes for much longer than I have, so I asked him where we should go.

He said, "Let's go to Riverside." I thought that seemed like a very long way, but we headed out. As we rode, he took the lead. At one point I was in front, and I took a corner too fast. There was sand, a big curb, and a telephone pole in front of me. I missed the pole, but not the curb. I took flight and rolled—reminding me to let him lead.

Steve provided directions: "We are taking a right" or "These railroad tracks are really rough" or "Clear!" as he led through an intersection. He also provided companionship. We talked when I could catch my breath.

There is another Friend who never leaves our side, who coaches us through the ride, who is there for us when we tumble, and who provides a good example. One of the things Jesus modeled was a strong sense of perspective. He did not let His earthly situation dilute His heavenly perspective.

On my bike ride it would have been easy to focus on what I saw and felt. I didn't know the route, I couldn't keep up, and I was tired and winded most of the time. I wondered, *What would it look like if I looked at it with heavenly perspective?*

"I'm writing out clear directions to Wisdom Way, I'm drawing a map to Righteous Road. I don't want you ending up in blind alleys, or wasting time making wrong turns. Hold tight to good advice; don't relax your grip. Guard it well—your life is at stake! Don't take Wicked Bypass; don't so much as set foot on that road. Stay clear of it; give it a wide berth. Make a detour and be on your way" (Prov. 4:11-15, Message).

RANDY BATES

SET IN CONCRETE

I'll remove the stone heart from your body
and replace it with a heart that's God-willed, not self-willed.
Eze. 36:26, Message.

I'm sure you've heard individuals make a plan but allow for wiggle room by saying, "Yes, but it's not set in concrete." Do you remember finding fresh, damp concrete with no one around? It was the perfect opportunity as a kid to write your name or scratch "Skooter + Pookie," hoping to make an eternal mark.

It's been said, "Some minds are like concrete, thoroughly mixed up and permanently set." We all know those people. (Not ourselves, of course. And don't cast your eyes about the room just now!)

Concrete sidewalk and driveway sections can trip you when the inexorable tree roots heave them upward. All around seismically active southern California we see cracks, raised or sunken sidewalks, crumbled places where trucks crushed a curb, freeway barriers broken from impact, old bridges being replaced, concrete-lined rivers with sections washed out . . . the list is endless. Concrete is not permanent. It erodes, breaks, even tumbles down flood channels.

The problem is that the only way to change concrete is to destroy it. We read in Exodus 7:13 that Pharaoh's heart (mind) was hard and repelled the lessons of God. Solomon had low regard for the concreted mind when he said in Proverbs 27:22, "Though you grind a fool [one who is morally deficient] in a mortar, grinding him like grain with a pestle, you will not remove his folly from him" (NIV). Earlier in the chapter Solomon writes, "Stone is heavy and sand a burden, but provocation by a fool is heavier than both" (verse 3, NIV).

So what's the plan? Although it's important to stand solidly on moral ground and to build your foundation on the Rock, remember to balance those worthy goals with a soft heart on which the Lord can write His law of love. Surely Paul was remembering Ezekiel 36:26 when he wrote: "You show that you are a letter from Christ, the result of our ministry, written not with ink but with the Spirit of the living God, not on tablets of stone but on tablets of human hearts" (2 Cor. 3:3, NIV).

Would you rather be set in your ways or a living love letter from Christ?

Christy K. Robinson

GOD'S WAY

This is the way; walk in it.
Isa. 30:21, NIV.

"I'm going to call AWA [Adventist World Aviation] to a greater role in missionary aviation training," came the growing, undeniable, overwhelming conviction.

"But Lord, you know how strapped we already are with overseas mission projects," I argued. "Besides, we don't have the tools, equipment, personnel, airplanes, facilities, or the finances to acquire them."

As we prayed over the issue, God began to reveal His plan. An airline mechanic suggested it was time to start an aircraft maintenance shop in which young people could gain real-world experience prior to overseas deployment. A former missionary pilot/mechanic turned FAA inspector suggested we look for an airport within a geographic box defined by northwest Arkansas, southwest Missouri, eastern Kansas, and Oklahoma. God was becoming geographically specific. Unsolicited copies of *General Aviation News* began arriving at my home.

A visiting missionary picked up one of the periodicals and moments later called my attention to a classified ad. He read aloud, "'The Blackwell-Tonkawa Airport Authority is looking for someone to set up a fixed base operation (FBO) on their airport.'"

Blackwell is in north-central Oklahoma, 60 miles south of Wichita on I-35—in the box the FAA inspector was talking about. I called.

One of the airport authority trustees answered the phone. "There are two proposals already on the table, but I'll take the idea to the board. If there is any interest, we'll get back to you."

Several weeks later the phone rang. The chair of the Blackwell-Tonkawa Airport Authority identified himself and announced, "Last night we voted to extend an invitation for you to come see us."

As we flew to Blackwell, a sense of wonder enveloped me. I recalled the words "Whether you turn to the right or to the left, your ears will hear a voice behind you, saying, 'This is the way; walk in it'" (Isa. 30:21, NIV).

Don Starlin

GOD'S PLAN

"For I know the plans I have for you," declares the Lord.
Jer. 29:11, NIV.

Five of us converged at Blackwell, Oklahoma, from various parts of the country to consider what God's plan might be, relative to missionary aviation training. We sensed He was at work, but we weren't quite sure how we fit into His design.

Three days of Bible study, prayer, and seeking God's will produced a rough draft of a program to prepare missionary aviators for the unique demands of the twenty-first century. On the third evening airport authority representatives joined us: "You fellows have been working all weekend, and we'd like to hear your proposal."

We laid out the overall vision for a maintenance facility that would serve the public and provide opportunities for aspiring missionary aviators to gain experience through a mechanic apprenticeship program. The strategy also included ideas for flight and cross-cultural missionary training.

The airport authority representatives listened and then responded. "We like your ideas and would like you to pursue the plan at our airport. If you provide services to the community, we'll provide an 80' x 80' hangar, rent and utilities paid. You can also use the three-bedroom, two-bathroom doublewide trailer on site. We'd like you to manage the airport, cut the grass, perform minor maintenance, and take commissions on fuel sales and T-hangar rent. How soon could you start?"

God has a plan. Let's seek Him with all of our hearts today and align them with His good and perfect will. He desires to prosper us for His honor and glory.

DON STARLIN

AT THE END OF RESOURCES, BELIEVE

Then they believed his promises and sang his praise.
Ps. 106:12, NIV.

"Your offer is very generous, but we don't have the tools, airplanes, personnel, or cash to begin. Give us five weeks to do some networking. At that time we'll either submit a letter of intent or advise you to continue your search for a fixed base operator," we replied to the Blackwell, Oklahoma, airport authority representatives.

Five weeks passed. Phone calls and e-mails flew across the country. AWA's board of directors endorsed the concept to move ahead in faith. "We've prayed for 10 years that God would provide a place to call home," the board responded.

An hour before the scheduled meeting I faxed a letter of intent to the Blackwell-Tonkawa Airport Authority.

The next morning the chair called. "The airport authority accepted your letter of intent. I have authorization to negotiate a contract."

Stalling for time, I reasoned that we both had businesses to run, and with Christmas, a wedding anniversary, and New Year's around the corner, it would be best to negotiate after the first of the year.

Everyone was looking to me for answers to problems for which I had no solutions. The airport authority expected performance. AWA's board expected leadership from its CEO. Others involved in the project were asking questions I didn't have answers to. I had nothing in my possession to accomplish the task, nor did I have a clue how it was going to come together.

When man comes to the end of his wisdom, resources, and strength, it is only then that it is safe for God to step in. Like Martha at Lazarus' tomb, Jesus waits for us to confess, "I believe that you are the Christ, the Son of God, who was to come into the world." And Jesus responds, "Did I not tell you that if you believed, you would see the glory of God?" (John 11:27, 40, NIV).

Believe in Him today! See His glory!

DON STARLIN

OCTOBER 5

STUDY THE SCRIPTURES

These are the Scriptures that testify about me. John 5:39, NIV.

"Lord, I'm at a total loss. I can't see where You are leading. The airport authority is going to call. I can't honestly negotiate a contract we can't perform." Continuing my study of Mark, I turned to chapter 10. The last story in the chapter caught my attention.

"Jesus, Son of David, have mercy on me!" called blind Bartimaeus. (Mark 10:47, NIV).

Wow, that's me, I thought.

" 'What do you want me to do for you?' " Jesus asked him.

"The blind man said 'Rabbi, I want to see' " (verse 51, NIV).

Oh, Lord, so do I, I prayed.

" 'Go,' " said Jesus, " 'your faith has healed you' " (verse 52, NIV).

Thank You, Lord, but I still can't see what You're doing, I confessed.

Keep reading, came the reply.

"Go to the village ahead of you, and just as you enter it, you will find a colt tied there. . . . Untie it and bring it here. If anyone asks you, 'Why are you doing this?' tell him, 'The Lord needs it' " (Mark 11:2, 3, NIV).

It hit me like a ton of bricks: that is what happened when we went to Blackwell. We shared with the airport authority the Lord's need for a facility at which to train missionary aviators, and they offered us their donkey!

"When they brought the colt to Jesus and threw their cloaks over it, he sat on it" (verse 7, NIV). *So that is what You want us to do, Lord; put what little we have into developing a fixed base operation, and You'll ride it. But then what?*

"Many people spread their cloaks on the road" (verse 8, NIV). And the people cheered as Jesus rode into Jerusalem.

Lord, I can see! As we move forward, people will join us by spreading their cloaks on the road, and You'll receive the praise of Your people!

Are you looking for direction? Study God's Word to hear Him speak.

DON STARLIN

GOD'S MIGHTY DEEDS

Prepare for God's arrival! Make the road straight and smooth, a highway fit for our God. Isa. 40:3, Message.

At Tuesday evening prayer time I shared the revelation of Mark 10 and 11 with Adventist World Aviation's staff and board members. We made a list of all the evidences of God's hand at work, knelt, and committed the Blackwell airport project to Him.

God immediately began to fulfill His promises. Within 24 hours 75 percent of the tools needed to equip the maintenance shop were donated to AWA. Cloak number one!

Four weeks later an airplane to be used for flight training was donated. Cloak number two!

Five weeks after placing our cloaks on the back of the colt, a contract was signed, insurance bound, and a movement of material and staff began toward Blackwell. A computer-based flight-training device was donated. Cloak number three!

The airport authority purchased new lighting fixtures, an epoxy floor system, corrugated siding to brighten the interior, and electrical materials for new power wiring for the hangar—all of which we installed. Cloaks four, five, six, and seven!

Glass display cases, a riding lawn tractor, and other miscellaneous items were donated. Cloaks eight and nine!

A donor flew to Blackwell and dropped off a check to build a hangar in Dillingham, Alaska, and promised to find an airplane that could be used in ministry among the more than 30 native villages in the area. Blessings are beginning to flow through Blackwell to other projects!

The firstfruits are already being harvested. Six months from the commencement of training, the first missionaries to receive flight training in Blackwell were scheduled for deployment to Guyana.

"He has made everything beautiful in its time. . . . I know that everything God does will endure forever; nothing can be added to it and nothing taken from it. God does it so that men will revere him" (Eccl. 3:11-14, NIV).

Don Starlin

OCTOBER 7

PAINSTAKING EXCELLENCE

His master commended him: "Good work! You did your job well."
Matt. 25:23, Message.

"All labor that uplifts humanity has dignity and importance and should be taken with painstaking excellence!" said Martin Luther King, Jr.

Pete flew to Denver for the sole purpose of calling on one client. Time was of the essence. A spotless cab pulled up. George, the cab driver, rushed to open the passenger door and made sure Pete was comfortably seated before he closed the door. George mentioned that the neatly folded *Wall Street Journal* next to him was for Pete's use. He then showed Pete several CDs and asked, "What kind of music do you enjoy?"

Pete looked around to see if he was on *Candid Camera*. I mean, wouldn't you? The service he was receiving was unbelievable.

"Obviously, you take great pride in your work," Pete said to the driver. "You must have a story to tell."

George began, "I got tired of thinking my best would never be good enough, fast enough, or appreciated enough. I decided to find where I could feel proud of being the best I could be. I knew I would never be a rocket scientist, but I love driving cars, being of service, and feeling as though I have done a full day's work and done it well. After some serious evaluation, I decided to become a cab driver . . . not just a regular taxi hack, but a professional cab driver!"

He continued, "To be good in my business, I could simply meet the expectations of my passengers. But to be great in my business, I'd have to exceed the customer's expectations. I like being 'great' better than just getting by on 'average.'"

We can learn a lesson from this cab driver. So many times we run into people, whether behind the post office counter or at the dry cleaners or in the beauty salon, that are just putting in their time. Don't all of us wish that there were more Georges in this world? It can start with you. Your committed, cheerful labor could spark a revolution!

"By this all will know that you are My disciples, if you have love for one another" (John 13:35, NKJV).

JOEDY MELASHENKO

IN THE DOBERMANS' DEN

*And these signs will accompany those who believe: . . .
they will pick up snakes with their hands; and when they drink deadly poison,
it will not hurt them at all. Mark 16:17, 18, NIV.*

Some years ago I met a family who wanted to study the Bible. I agreed to meet with Peter and Mary each Friday evening, where we would gather around the fireplace with cups of hot chocolate to discuss God's great message. It was a rewarding time, and I enjoyed responding to the questions and observations that they had gathered through the week.

Because it was a rural setting, Peter had fruit trees and enough room to house and train his Doberman dogs. They were truly beautiful animals, but Peter cautioned me not to go around to the back of the house unless he was with me. These dogs were guarding his property to repel intruders (there had been some recent burglaries in the area).

I arrived for the weekly study and knocked on the door. Receiving no response, I went around to the back. I walked right by the Dobermans without them stirring a muscle. However, when I knocked on the door, they leaped toward me. There was a tremendous amount of barking and baring of teeth. Peter jumped out of the shower and flung open the door, expecting the worst. There I stood in the midst of the six Dobermans, who were by now all seated and quiet. "I thought you were dead," he said. "I don't understand why they didn't attack you."

Jesus said to them, "Go into all the world and preach the good news to all creation. . . . And these signs will accompany those who believe: . . . they will pick up snakes with their hands; and when they drink deadly poison, it will not hurt them at all" (Mark 16:15-18, NIV).

Admittedly, these are unusual words, and we do well not to deliberately put ourselves in harm's way. But if in honest fulfillment of the Great Commission to share the gospel we find ourselves in difficult circumstances, God assures us we are not there alone. "I am with you," He says.

K. Lance Tyler

OCTOBER 9

A PERSONAL GOD

Cause me to hear thy lovingkindness in the morning; for in thee do I trust: cause me to know the way wherein I should walk; for I lift up my soul unto thee. Ps. 143:8.

"Lord, why have I been delayed for two days in New Delhi? This is going to upset so much of my itinerary. Have you forgotten that I'm here in India, not Australia just now?"

This was a most frustrating delay for me, with no apparent reason. When I finally was able to get a flight to take me to Cairo, it was via three other places rather than direct.

One of those places was Dubai, where an Egyptian boarded the plane and sat next to me. After introducing himself and telling me that he was a dermatologist, he asked about me. When I told him that I was a Christian, he shared that he had a friend who had given him a Bible about a year before. He had read it and had lots of questions that he wanted to ask someone about. For the rest of the flight to Cairo, he kept plying me with excellent and challenging questions. They ceased only when the plane finally landed at Cairo.

As the plane taxied to the terminal, he thanked me, saying our discussions had given him something to think about. I then told him of my unexplainable delay in New Delhi, and I asked him if he remembered a story in the Bible of how God sent Philip down the road to Gaza to find one man who was trying to understand the Scriptures in Isaiah. He stated that he remembered the story well because he traveled the Gaza road to get home to his family. I told him that I believed that God had brought me all the way from Australia, had delayed me two days in New Delhi, and had put me on a plane to go via Dubai because He saw a man who wanted to understand the Bible. He was deeply impressed and thanked me.

"Cause me to hear thy lovingkindness in the morning; for in thee do I trust: cause me to know the way wherein I should walk; for I lift up my soul unto thee" (Ps. 143:8).

The truth is, my friend, that God loves us and will do all He can to save us—that's why He sent His Son to die for us.

R. E. "BOB" POSSINGHAM

WRITTEN IN THE DUST

O Lord, the hope of Israel, all who forsake you will be put to shame.
Those who turn away from you will be written in the dust.
Jer. 17:13, NIV.

In far-north England as I drove along Hadrian's Wall westward to Carlisle, I burst out laughing. My fellow traveler drove a lorry (delivery truck) covered in dust and dirt. Someone had drawn with a finger in large letters on the filthy roll-up door: "Also available in white." The joke was that the lorry was painted white underneath the grime.

"O Lord, the hope of Israel, all who forsake you will be put to shame. Those who turn away from you will be written in the dust because they have forsaken the Lord, the spring of living water" (Jer. 17:13, NIV).

To write in the dust is to know that the words and the people or actions the words symbolize are impermanent. It's a contrast to carving your legacy in stone, as people have done since prehistoric times.

Often people say they feel as though they're wandering in a dry, dusty wilderness, alone and without hope. Any gust of wind could vaporize them. Even in mature Christians, this is an experience we sometimes go through, especially after trauma.

If you feel alone and comfortless, I encourage you to seek out Christian companionship in your local church or Bible study group. Let the arms of God enfold you through His body, the church. Let the people of God minister to your dry and barren life. Let down the projection that you have everything together all the time, and allow yourself to be vulnerable. The Lord will work for you through His people.

Jesus said that He would never leave us nor forsake us. No matter what we feel, we must trust that Jesus is close by, longing to be in communion with us. Don't turn away from Him. Turn toward Him, and He will give you living water to quench your raging thirst (John 4:14). He begs you to come, lay your burdens on Him, and rest. He loves you, and He is preparing an eternity of joy and love for you.

So let Jesus wash away that dust with His living water. In fact, dive into that river and rejoice in His gifts. He will bring you through.

Christy K. Robinson

HONORABLE CONDUCT

When they speak against you as evildoers, they may, by your good works which they observe, glorify God in the day of visitation.
1 Peter 2:12, NKJV.

The fighting had been fierce, and at day's end there were wounded and dying men scattered across the battlefield. It was the Battle of Fredericksburg in Virginia during the Civil War, and the Union offensive had suffered greatly.

With artillery fire still coming from both sides, it was impossible for either side to get to their men. Amid the thunderous roar, the cries of the men could be heard, "Water! Water!"

But as the guns fell silent, Sergeant Richard Kirkland of the Confederates hastened to General Kershaw. "General, I can't stand this any longer! Those poor souls out there have been crying all night and day, and it's more than I can bear! I ask your permission to go and give them water."

The general paused for a moment and then replied, "Do you know that as soon as you show yourself to the enemy you will be shot?"

"Yes sir, I know it," he answered, "but to carry a little comfort to those poor dying men, I'm willing to run the risk."

Touched with sympathy over the suffering soldiers, General Kershaw finally replied, "Kirkland, it's sending you to your death, but I cannot oppose such a motive as yours. I hope God will protect you. Go!"

The brave soldier, furnished with a supply of water, stepped over the stone rampart and began his work of Christlike mercy. He knelt by the nearest sufferer, tenderly raised his head, and held the refreshing cup to his parched lips.

For an hour, one after another of the wounded and dying men, Confederate and Union, were given a refreshing drink. Every soldier in the Union line understood the tender mission of the man in gray, and not a shot was fired.

"Beloved, I beg you as sojourners and pilgrims, abstain from fleshly lusts which war against the soul, having your conduct honorable among the Gentiles, that when they speak against you as evildoers, they may, by your good works which they observe, glorify God in the day of visitation" (1 Peter 2:11, 12, NKJV).

Larry Becker

A HOLY EXAMPLE

Jesus Christ might demonstrate His perfect patience as an example for those who would believe in Him for eternal life.
1 Tim. 1:16, NASB.

One does not need to look far among their family or friends to find those who have courageously served their country for the sake of freedom. Regardless of our faith background, we realize that we have the opportunity to live lives that are a holy example. Let us ask the question often, "What do others see in my life?"

In order to become the holy examples God wants us to be, we need to own our influence. You can own your influence in three ways.

First, you can seize opportunities when they come your way just as Sergeant Kirkland did in the Battle of Fredericksburg. "Show the way for others, and you will find honor in the kingdom" (Matt. 5:19, Message).

Second, you need to tend to the small stuff. Randy Newman said, "Influence is as much about little things in life as it is the big moments of confrontation. . . . It's about the way our values and beliefs are expressed in our words and actions each day."

Third, widen your sphere of influence. God calls us to stand up in moments when we can exert our influence for His glory. We need to own our influence if we are to be holy examples. "He who speaks on his own does so to gain honor for himself, but he who works for the honor of the one who sent him is a man of truth; there is nothing false about him" (John 7:18, NIV).

The higher the position, the greater the responsibility. Your influence will spread widely, and you will, more than ever, need to depend on God.

Let God use you today to be His holy example wherever He has placed you.

Larry Becker

THAT WE MAY BE ONE

[I pray] that all of them may be one, Father, just as you are in me and I am in you. May they also be in us so that the world may believe that you have sent me.
John 17:21, NIV.

When I finished the final quilt block, I laid out all the pieces like a puzzle on the floor and stood back to view them. Squinting my eyes, I checked the composition. My daughter, Annika, stood beside me and studied the layout. "That one should be on the top and the top one should be on the bottom," Annika declared.

"The first one is supposed to be on top," I replied. Annika persisted, so we switched the arrangement around. I moved the two blocks, then a few others, and we came up with a much more dynamic composition as a result of our collaboration.

Since medieval times, artisans have joined together in guilds, which not only protect their mutual interests but also provide a forum to exchange ideas, support, and advice. There are guilds for artists and writers, as well as piano technicians, automotive restorers, bread bakers, and handcrafted soap makers.

On the occasions when I am struggling by myself to master a new skill or agonizing over various compositions, I feel the void of a quilting community in my life. Sometimes I develop a new technique that I would love to share with others. Many times, though, I am too busy to notice what I am missing. Lucky for me, my daughter, Annika, has a good eye for design.

I can create impressive quilts on my own. But imagine how much more amazing my work could be if I had the support of a like-minded community. Think of the beginners that I could help through their struggles if I made the effort to join a guild.

We don't have to stand alone in whatever we do. Quilters have guilds, and Christians have churches where they support and encourage one another. This was Jesus' prayer for all believers: "[I pray] that all of them may be one, Father, just as you are in me and I am in you. May they also be in us so that the world may believe that you have sent me" (John 17:21, NIV).

When Christians join together with each other and the Lord, there is nothing they can't do!

LAURA WEST KONG

RANDOM ACTS OF KINDNESS

Whatever you did for one of the least of these brothers of mine, you did for me.
Matt. 25:40, NIV.

Lavonne, an eighth-grade student, worked with her six brothers and sisters in their family-owned hardware and furniture store in a small North Dakota town. All the children started working in the store by doing odd jobs, such as dusting, stocking shelves, sweeping floors, and eventually serving customers. As they worked and watched, they learned that making a living was more than making a sale.

It was shortly before Christmas, and Lavonne was working one evening, straightening out the toy section. A little boy about 6 years old came in the store. The boy looked poor—too poor to afford to buy anything. He looked around wishfully at all the toys in the toy section, picking up this item and that, then carefully putting them back in their place. Lavonne's dad, Frank, came down the stairs and walked over to the boy.

"What can I do for you, son?" Frank treated this little 6-year-old customer with the same respect as any adult.

"I'm looking for a Christmas present for my little brother Jimmy."

"Take your time. Look around." After about 20 minutes, the little boy carefully picked up a toy airplane and walked up to Frank.

"How much for this?"

"How much you got?"

The little boy held out his hand and opened it. It was creased with wet lines of dirt from crunching his money: two dimes, a nickel, and two pennies—27 cents.

"That'll just about do it," Frank said as he closed the sale.

After she wrapped the gift, and the little boy walked out of the store, Lavonne did not notice the dirty coat or the straggly hair. What she saw was a radiant child with a treasure.

Every day of our lives, we have the privilege of living out the "Matthew 25:40 principle." I challenge you to conduct an RAK (random acts of kindness) today. Try it! You'll like it!

JOEDY MELASHENKO

October 15

MAKING MUSIC

For I desire mercy, not sacrifice, and acknowledgment of God rather than burnt offerings.
Hosea 6:6, NIV.

Recently I had the opportunity to sit in the piano teacher's chair at the treble end of the keyboard and listen to Calvin Taylor give me a miniconcert of his own arrangements from a newly published book I had just purchased.

I've played from Taylor's other books for 20 years, in churches of many denominations and in other countries. The scores are not always easy to sight-read: some are in six flats, have unusual chords, and feature the melody switching between the right and left hands. Some chords require quite a hand span to attain their full wealth of sound. (Taylor's fingers are at least an inch longer than my long fingers!)

One of his arrangements, "My Lord, What a Mornin'," has a chord progression that I've always played dramatically, milking the chords and melody for every exquisite vibration. However, when Taylor played it for me, he raced through the gorgeous bit to get to the treble arpeggios and end the song. As I sat in the piano teacher's position, I asked him to play that line and just hold the B7(♭9) in a fermata until I said it was time to launch the arpeggios. He played it three times, and just wouldn't do it right. You know—my way.

Who really knew best what to do "correctly" in that situation? The arranger, concert pianist, and doctor of musical arts, or the local church keyboardist? But it's just a matter of taste, after all, not a moral issue of right or wrong. As musicians, even though we sometimes disagree on the interpretation, it's not the music or our ability to play flawlessly that matters. It's what comes from our hearts that God accepts and is pleased with. Whether I play a contemporary praise song or a Bach chorale prelude, God accepts my music-making if it's offered with a loving heart. As long as he is making a "joyful noise," don't we forgive a friend if he's a half-step off? And isn't God's heart infinitely more forgiving than a human's? Oh, yes!

"Do you think all God wants are sacrifices—empty rituals just for show? He wants you to listen to him!" (1 Sam. 15:22, Message).

Christy K. Robinson

GOD SO LOVED

For God so loved the world that he gave his one and only Son, that whoever believes in him shall not perish but have eternal life.
John 3:16, NIV.

There is a reason that this is the most famous of all Christian texts. It tells us all we need to know about the essential qualities of God.

It tells us, for example, that God is a loving being. This is not true of all of the gods that people worship. I remember from childhood hearing mission stories about the dear souls in distant lands who worshipped idols that they had to appease with gifts and sacrifices. In the Old Testament there are stories of people who worshipped the gods Baal and Molech, and one of the things that people thought the gods demanded of them was the sacrifice of their children. What a horrible thing! However, many of the gods people have worshipped were worshipped not in love, but in fear.

People have, of course, done the same thing with the true God of the universe. I've known Christians who have taken all of the very hard, judgmental things that the Old Testament says about God, and said, "Well, that's what God is like." That may have been how He expressed Himself at some times in history, but as a Christian you must read the Old Testament through the lens of the New Testament, and the New Testament is clear that God is love. And any religion that is filled with fear is not a Christian religion, no matter what name it bears.

Sadly, though, that is what passes for religion among some Christians: a religion filled with fear of hell, fear of punishment, fear of failure, fear of being different, fear of end-times. But that's not true Christianity, and we have failed the good name of Jesus Christ if that's the kind of faith we promote.

A religion of fear is not the faith of Jesus. His message was that God loved the world, and because He was, and is, loving, we should be too.

(For Old Testament scriptures proclaiming that God is love, read: Exodus 15:13; Exodus 34:6, 7; Isaiah 43:1-5; Jeremiah 31:3; Jeremiah 31:20; and many, many others.)

LOREN SEIBOLD

OCTOBER 17

CHURCHES AND HOSPITALS

Crowds . . . followed him. He welcomed them and spoke to them about the kingdom of God, and healed those who needed healing.
Luke 9:11, NIV.

Time magazine, in a cover story about faith and healing, reported on people's growing interest in the connection between healing and spirituality. There is a "yearning among . . . patients for a more personal, more spiritual approach" to their ills.

The *Time* reporter then commented, "Not only do [these] patients . . . fail to find relief in a doctor's office, but the endless high-tech scans and tests of modern medicine often leave them feeling alienated and uncared for. Many seek solace in the offices of alternative therapists and faith healers" (June 24, 1996).

Jesus provided the model on how to minister to people, reaching their felt needs. "Crowds . . . followed him. He welcomed them and spoke to them about the kingdom of God, and healed those who needed healing" (Luke 9:11, NIV).

Jesus reached people in other ways. He walked and worked with them. He wept with them. He comforted them. And He gave them hope. His touch is just as much needed today as it was then.

Author Charles Swindoll challenges us, "Churches need to be . . . less like untouchable cathedrals and more like well-used hospitals, places to bleed in rather than monuments to look at, . . . where you can take your mask off and let your hair down . . . where you can have your wounds dressed" (*Dropping Your Guard,* p. 127).

A church open daily, staffed with loving, kind, caring persons ready to welcome and to listen, give comfort, encouragement, counseling, hope, and even just a hug or a touch would bless many people whose problems are largely emotional or stress–based. We need to find ways to be more actively reaching out and serving others. Remember Jesus' words: "All men will know that you are my disciples, if you love one another" (John 13:35, NIV).

AILEEN LUDINGTON

IN GOD'S EYES

For we are God's workmanship,
created in Christ Jesus to do good works.
Eph. 2:10, NIV.

While quilting a recent project, I paused to examine my handiwork. Studying my stitches, I saw nothing but a tangled mass of threads destined for the seam ripper's blade.

With a heavy sigh, I set the quilt down. As I reached across the table to get the seam ripper, I glanced at an open book. It was a how-to manual on machine quilting and was open to the page on how your stitches should not look. The photo was full of loops, tangles, and uneven stitches. I noticed the contrast immediately. Although my stitching was meticulous, when I looked at it I saw only a disheveled mess, such as on that page of don'ts.

I viewed my work in a much different light afterward. Needless to say, I put the seam ripper down and continued quilting with a smile on my face. This quilt, with those same stitches I nearly tore out, won first place in a contest I entered.

Sometimes, even as Christians, we look at ourselves and see only a tangled mess. This, however, is not what God sees. When God looks at us, He sees Jesus' perfection.

"Therefore, since we have been justified through faith, we have peace with God through our Lord Jesus Christ, through whom we have gained access by faith into this grace in which we now stand. And we rejoice in the hope of the glory of God" (Rom. 5:1, 2, NIV).

This grace not only sets us right with God, it sets us free to participate fully in God's plan for our lives. "For we are God's workmanship, created in Christ Jesus to do good works, which God prepared in advance for us to do" (Eph. 2:10, NIV).

If I spend all my days ripping out stitches that were perfectly fine in the first place, I will never finish a quilt, much less win a prize. When I continually worry about my standing with God, I am not allowing God to complete His work in me.

God looks at us with love and acceptance; He sees potential far beyond what we could ever imagine. Why not take another look at yourself, and this time look through God's eyes.

LAURA WEST KONG

October 19

DON'T BELIEVE A LIE

I am the way, the truth, and the life.
John 14:6, NKJV.

While knocking on doors to sell Christian literature and earn my way to college, I began to feel like David when he wrote, "I hate and abhor lying" (Ps. 119:163, NKJV). At one home a small boy came to the door. Smiling, he said, "My mommy said to tell you she isn't home."

What a wonderful little boy, I thought. But his mother—why would she teach her young son to lie?

Approaching another home, I watched a woman run and hide behind a giant washtub. A neighbor stepped up and said, "She doesn't live here anymore." I thanked the woman, walked around the block, came back, and knocked. The woman who'd had her neighbor lie opened the door in surprise, but she paid cash for a set of truth-filled books.

A man looked at my briefcase and said, "Young man, don't waste your time. I don't have any money." Not believing him, I kept on talking until he invited me in and I showed my books. The man, who didn't have any money, paid cash for a complete set of Christian books.

While writing a receipt, I learned that his last name was Bookless. I smiled, "Mr. Bookless, you're going to have to change your name. You can't say you're bookless anymore."

Scripture teaches that "lying lips are an abomination to the Lord" (Prov. 12:22, NKJV). We cannot afford to believe the devil's lies. Paul wrote about people who "did not receive the love of the truth, that they might be saved." In the next verse, he adds, "for this reason God will send them strong delusion, that they should believe the lie" (2 Thess. 2:10, 11, NKJV).

A lot of books would not have been sold if I'd believed everything people said. I'll be lost if I believe the devil's lies. Praise God, I can have eternal life by believing Jesus. He says, "I am the way, the truth, and the life" (John 14:6, NKJV).

Wellesley Muir

THIS IS NOT THAT!

Ask where the good way is, and walk in it, and you will find rest for your souls. Jer. 6:16, NIV.

Poet William Wordsworth had a unique ability to take the human heart and steep it in an atmosphere of deep quietness and peace. Wordsworth had the gift of rest for weary feet.

Our souls long for more permanent repose than any poet can give us in word pictures. The only One who can provide this rest is Jesus.

"Come . . . and I will give you rest" (Matt 11:28, NASB). But "not as the world gives" (John 14:27, NASB). The world provides rest through shorter working hours and weeks. It sends us on a cruise when Christ calls us to a pilgrimage. This is definitely not that!

"Take my yoke." His own yoke! This is not a metaphor for the harness worn by animals plowing a field, but His 10 principles for life. The yoke of the scribes and Pharisees was hard and heavy. For instance, they had more than 500 rules for Sabbath observance while Jesus' law can be summarized in this: "You shall love the Lord your God with all your heart" "You shall love your neighbor as yourself" (Matt. 22:37, 39, NASB).

Jesus said, "I am gentle and humble in heart." The Greek word for gentle, praos, indicated an ointment so strong it could subdue a raging fever or tame a wild horse. Our Savior has tremendous power, and He does not use it for selfish purposes. "Humble" comes from the Latin word humus, for earth or soil. In our world, which idealizes fitness, strength, and force, to be humble is not a sought-after quality, but Jesus was willing to claim this characteristic and be closely associated with us, because this is not that!

He offers us rest for our souls (Jer. 6:16). In our culture, where understanding finds rest in knowledge, wisdom rests in experience, affection rests in love, and satisfaction rests in plenty, our soul can find rest only in Jesus.

On a cruise of the Greek islands we encountered a storm at sea. I was afraid until I learned that the captain's son was on board. I knew he would act to preserve the life of his son, and therefore we passengers would be safe. Similarly, we have the assurance that the Son of God is on board in our lives. So let's relax and find rest for our souls, for this is not that!

Hyveth B. Williams

OCTOBER 21

GOD OPENS PRISON DOORS

The Lord hath anointed me to preach good tidings unto the meek . . .
to proclaim liberty to the captives, and the opening of the prison to them that are bound.
Isa. 61:1.

One February afternoon our music ministry had driven several hours to a prison where we were scheduled to share our message in music. But upon arriving we were told by officials that we would not be able to give the concert or even enter the prison. Several of the employees had called in sick that day, and they didn't have enough security for an event such as this.

We knew it was God's will that we give this concert, so we prayed and left the matter in God's hands. Specifically, we prayed for His intervention. Minutes later one of the guards came back and said, "The supervisor changed his mind. You can come in."

Miraculously, the warden, in a departure from policy, had the guards escort us to a large courtyard located in the center of the four wings. As we began to set up our equipment, the guards escorted approximately 400 inmates from the east and west wings of the prison. Usually the two wings' inmates weren't allowed to mingle.

As I stood up to sing, I felt an evil presence and a choking sensation around my throat. A voice in my mind said, *What are you doing here? They aren't going to like your music or even listen.*

I prayed this silent prayer: *Lord, I know You want me to do this. Please give me Your presence, I can't do this without You.*

I stepped forward and began to sing. My voice, at first weak, gained strength with each note, and I received a tremendous sense of peace. Following my music, we shared a brief message about God's love and forgiveness. By the close of the meeting we had distributed all the Christian literature we had brought with us and enrolled more than 100 inmates in our Bible study correspondence school. God is good!

That day we experienced miraculous events, and lives were changed because we believed in His power to intervene. When you think circumstances are holding you prisoner, step aside and let God open your prison doors and set you free! Will you let Him?

VONDA BEERMAN

THE SECRET

We speak of God's secret wisdom, a wisdom that has been hidden and that God destined for our glory before time began.
1 Cor. 2:7, NIV.

Annika and I returned home from shopping. We sat down to wrap her father's gift, a bottle of cologne, before he came home from work. When he arrived, Annika ran to the door and enthusiastically exclaimed, "Daddy, Daddy, guess what! Mama and I bought you a present. It's some perfume!" In her eyes it was such exciting news that Annika couldn't keep it to herself. How could she hide good news from someone she loved?

God has some extraordinary secrets, secrets that He just can't keep to Himself. "The secret of the kingdom of God has been given to you" (Mark 4:11, NIV). This is a gift for all who take the time to look and listen. Jesus said, "He who has ears to hear, let him hear" (verse 9, NIV). In other words only those who are seeking the secrets of God will discover them.

The apostle Paul knew the secrets of God. "We speak of God's secret wisdom, a wisdom that has been hidden and that God destined for our glory before time began. None of the rulers of this age understood it, for if they had, they would not have crucified the Lord of glory. However, as it is written: 'No eye has seen, no ear has heard, no mind has conceived what God has prepared for those who love him'—but God has revealed it to us by his Spirit" (1 Cor. 2:7-10, NIV).

What amazes me most is not that God has secrets, but that the God who laid the earth's foundation and brings forth the constellations in their seasons is the same God who reaches out to us, reveals Himself, and provides us with understanding (Job 38:4, 32, NIV).

"If you call out for insight and cry aloud for understanding, and if you look for it as for silver and search for it as for hidden treasure, then you will understand the fear of the Lord and find the knowledge of God. For the Lord gives wisdom, and from his mouth come knowledge and understanding" (Prov. 2:3-6, NIV).

"The kingdom of heaven is like treasure hidden in a field. When a man found it, he hid it again, and then in his joy went and sold all he had and bought that field" (Matt. 13:44, NIV).

May we all know the joy of discovering God's secrets.

LAURA WEST KONG

THE RADIO POCKET

How beautiful are the feet of those who preach the gospel of peace, who bring glad tidings of good things! Rom. 10:15, NKJV.

Radios don't have pockets, but it takes pockets full of money to keep religious programming on the air. J. L. Tucker, founder of the Quiet Hour, used to quote the following: "The gospel of Christ is the water of life / And the water of life is free / But it costs for the pipes and the plumbing / That bring it to you and to me" (author unknown).

After being associated with Pastor J. L. Tucker and others in a large evangelistic crusade in Oakland, California, my church asked me to conduct meetings in Hollister, California. A Bible verse kept flashing in my mind. "And how shall they preach unless they are sent? As it is written: 'How beautiful are the feet of those who preach the gospel of peace, who bring glad tidings of good things!' " (Rom. 10:15, NKJV).

Because people were giving to support the gospel, I was sent. Halfway through the meetings I invited Pastor Tucker to visit. He and his son, LaVerne, drove all the way to Hollister to encourage a young minister. Their preaching on Friday and Saturday night filled the hall. No busy pastor would have done this unless he felt a desire to win souls for Christ. And that is what the Quiet Hour has always been about.

The next year I was asked to pastor the Burlingame church. To my amazement, I discovered that half of the members found Christ by listening to the Quiet Hour radio broadcast while commuting to San Francisco to work. Since my church was just across the bay from the Quiet Hour headquarters, I again invited Pastor Tucker to come and preach.

Church members who had been baptized because of Bible messages they heard on the Quiet Hour were thrilled. At the end of the sermon Pastor Tucker announced that he had a "radio pocket." As folks left the worship service they stuffed generous donations into his coat pocket.

Today Quiet Hour Ministries no longer has a radio program, but its evangelism and mission projects reach out to the world with the good news of a soon coming Savior. Generous donations still help thousands find the joy of living for Jesus.

WELLESLEY MUIR

OPEN-HEART SURGERY

Create in me a clean heart, O God, and renew a steadfast spirit within me. Ps. 51:10, NKJV.

"Bob, you need to have your heart valve replaced and a couple of bypasses done," said my cardiologist.

But I wasn't very keen about having open-heart surgery. I had never been admitted to a hospital in all my life, so this was scary. However, circumstances finally forced me to have the surgery.

In the hospital, prior to the operation, the surgeon visited me and assured me that I was in safe hands. He would do all that was necessary to correct my heart condition, and there was nothing I could do to help—except trust him. All he needed was a signature on a hospital form giving him permission to perform the procedure.

When the operation was over, I discovered that all that he had said was true. He worked the miracle without any help from me, and now life has become so much richer and more enjoyable because of it.

The Lord tells us that He is willing to fix our faulty hearts without any help on our part. "I will give you a new heart and put a new spirit within you; I will take the heart of stone out of your flesh and give you a heart of flesh. I will put My Spirit within you and cause you to walk in My statutes, and you will keep My judgments and do them" (Eze. 36:26, 27, NKJV).

There is nothing we can do to help Him, but He does need our permission. If we trust Him enough to allow Him to make the changes needed in our hearts, then our spiritual lives will become so much richer and more enjoyable. So why not say with David, "Create in me a clean heart, O God, and renew a steadfast spirit within me" (Ps. 51:10, NKJV)?

R. E. "BOB" POSSINGHAM

NON NOBIS DOMINE

We don't deserve praise! The Lord alone deserves all of the praise, because of his love and faithfulness. Ps. 115:1, CEV.

In 1989 I dashed home from the movie theater humming the *Henry V* soundtrack theme and its descant repeatedly so that I could reproduce it on my piano and notate it. I never wanted to forget it. I still use that theme when playing softly under a prayer or offertory. The music for *Non Nobis Domine* had a great effect upon me because of its setting in the Shakespeare play.

In the morality play similar to Psalm 115 King Henry V of England was pursuing his ancestral rights to territory in France, but was being rebuffed by the French government. As Anglo-centric William Shakespeare wrote it, the arrogant, godless French depended upon their superior numbers, home advantage, and mercenary muscles to beat the battle-weary, disease-ridden, far-from-home, humble, God-fearing English at the Battle of Agincourt on October 25, 1415. When the battle was over, the French herald gave Henry the news of his victory. Vast numbers of French had died, and only a handful of the English had gone down.

Shakespeare's poetic rendering of King Henry's victory speech was: "O God, thy arm was here; and not to us, but to thy arm alone, ascribe we all! When, without stratagem, but in plain shock and even play of battle, was ever known so great and little loss on one part and on the other? Take it, God, for it is none but thine!" "Come, go we in procession to the village. And be it death proclaimed through our host to boast of this or take the praise from God which is his only." "God fought for us." "Do we all holy rites; let there be sung '*Non nobis*' and '*Te Deum*.'"

In the 1989 movie composer Patrick Doyle begins singing, *"Non nobis, Domine sed nomini tuo da gloriam,"* and gradually the weary, heroic English soldiers join the glorious chorus as they trudge to the nearby church.

The *Non nobis* is Psalm 115:1-3: "Not unto us, O Lord, not unto us, but unto thy name give glory, for thy mercy, and for thy truth's sake. Wherefore should the heathen say, Where is now their God? But our God is in the heavens: he hath done whatsoever he hath pleased."

Christy K. Robinson

ALFRED THE GREAT

Many words rush along like rivers in flood,
but deep wisdom flows up from artesian springs. Prov. 18:4, Message.

Although there's no King Alfred Version, King Alfred the Great of England is the reason that we have Bibles translated into everyday English.

Alfred was born in 849 and spent most of his 50 years of life fighting with Viking invaders. When peace had been accomplished in southern Britain, Alfred finally had time to pursue an education. He compelled his officials, his daughters (who became European queens), and even the clergy to learn to read. As a boy he'd learned to read and write in Anglo-Saxon, or Old English, but now he set out to learn Latin so that he could read the Bible.

Alfred loved the Lord and wanted to know God's wisdom and ways. The first Bibles in English, read in the everyday vernacular to people in the churches, were commissioned and partly translated by Alfred himself. In the fifth century the Latin Vulgate (which hardly anyone could understand 400 years later) quoted Proverbs 18:4: "As deep waters, so are the words of a [wise] man." Alfred put it in English: "A very deep pool is dammed up in the wise man's mind."

He set aside time daily to translate religious works. For the schools he founded, he translated biographies of saints, complete with dragons, miracles, and martyrdoms, action-adventure stories calculated to enthrall the ignorant and bring them back hungry for more. He commissioned the Anglo-Saxon Chronicle, going back to the Saxon invasion of England, and a history that would be kept until the fourteenth century. Alfred compiled laws for his kingdom and based the code upon the Ten Commandments "given by God . . . fulfilled and interpreted by the love and compassion of His Son, the Healer, the Lord Christ; continued in the teachings of the apostles, and thence down the ages by synods of the church and decrees of kings."

Because he was so committed to righteousness for himself and his nation, Alfred created a renaissance of spirituality and enlightenment. He loved and lived God's Word, and he brought God's Word to light the darkness. And we thank God for his amazing vision and energy that gave us the first glimmer of light in our own language!

CHRISTY K. ROBINSON

OCTOBER 27

LESSONS FROM A FLIGHT ATTENDANT

A cheerful heart is good medicine.
Prov. 17:22, NIV.

"Good morning, ladies and gentlemen. Welcome aboard American Airlines Flight 642 direct from Sacramento to Dallas."

Wait a minute! My mind started racing. It was early in the morning, but I was sure this flight was heading to Chicago.

"Now that I have your attention, my name is Dana, and I'll be your head flight attendant today. Actually, we are en route to Chicago, so if you were not planning to go there, now would be a good time to get off the plane."

I chuckled and breathed a sigh of relief as Dana continued. "Safety is important to us, so please take out the safety card and acquaint yourself with it. Come on, everybody, take out those brochures and wave them in the air!"

Most of the passengers were giggling and did as they were told. A few weren't awake yet, and a few were sourpusses.

"In the unlikely event that we mistakenly land in a body of water, a decision must be made. You can either pray and swim like crazy, or use your seat as a flotation device." Those still half asleep started to emerge from their stupor.

"We will be serving breakfast this morning. On the menu we have eggs Benedict, fruit crepes, and fresh-baked cinnamon rolls . . . not really! But they sound so good to me! Actually, we will be serving you a choice of cold cereal or an egg-and-cheese omelet." Now even a few of the sourpusses were venturing a smile. Thanks for an enjoyable flight, Dana.

So many go through life with a terminal case of "sourpuss-itis." If we just pause, we can discover so much to enjoy in this world. To quote the words of a 1940s tune, we need to take time to "eliminate the negative and accentuate the positive."

"A cheerful heart is good medicine" (Prov. 17:22, NIV).

Have you taken your "medicine" today? Better yet, have you dispensed a healthy dose to someone else?

JOEDY MELASHENKO

THE IMAGE OF GOD

God looked over everything he had made;
it was so good, so very good! Gen. 1:31, Message.

When you look in the mirror, what do you see? When you look in your heart, what do you find? Deep below the tarnish of sin and everyday worries, can you see the image of God?

At creation God was not caught up in an impulsive whim when He created us in His image. He deliberately set out to do this. "God spoke: 'Let us make human beings in our image, make them reflecting our nature so they can be responsible for the fish in the sea, the birds in the air, the cattle, and, yes, Earth itself, and every animal that moves on the face of Earth' God created human beings; he created them godlike, reflecting God's nature. He created them male and female" (Gen. 1:26, 27, Message).

Thousands of years of sin and separation cannot erase God's image from our hearts. When we search past all the dirt and the distractions, we can discover a part of God in us, a part that God purposely placed there. It can draw us closer to Him and give us a personal understanding of who God is.

I see in myself a creator. Making wonderful things in paint, fabric, or even words, fills my heart with joy. Through these creation experiences, I better understand God as a creator. "God looked over everything he had made; it was so good, so very good!" (Gen. 1:31, Message).

Because of my love for my own daughter, I can better relate to the way God loves me, His beloved child. "As parents feel for their children, God feels for those who fear him" (Ps. 103:13, Message).

God is also a comforter, a healer, a teacher, and so much more. Which facets of God will you discover in your heart? What new insights will you learn?

As we uncover the image of God in us, we will not only deepen our relationship with Him, but our eyes will be opened to the image of God reflected in our fellow human beings. And if each one of us lets that image shine through freely in our daily lives, think what a welcoming, godly community our church would be, clearly showing the world what God is truly like.

Laura West Kong

CONFESSION

Do not worry about . . . what you will say.
Luke 12:11, NIV.

On occasion I find myself in a situation that I could not have anticipated. Some time later, after the tension of the moment has receded, I recall the words spoken by Jesus in Luke's Gospel, "When you are brought before synagogues, rulers and authorities, do not worry about how you will defend yourselves or what you will say, for the Holy Spirit will teach you at that time what you should say" (Luke 12:11, 12, NIV).

Several years ago I was introduced to a hospice patient by his son-in-law Peter. Jose's reverence for God was apparent as we talked, and he quickly insisted that we pray together. I enjoyed several rewarding and meaningful visits with him.

Then one morning I received an urgent phone call from Peter requesting that I come to the house as soon as possible. Jose was dying and needed to see me. He had wanted to see the priest, but none was immediately available. On arriving at the home, I found Jose in his hospital bed, straining to speak to me. Every move was an effort, and I could see he had something urgent on his mind. I bent closer to him to catch the whisper barely escaping his tense lips. "Can you take my last confession?" was his plea.

No time to think this through now! What would Jesus do? "Yes, the Lord is listening." Jose made a brief, meaningful statement, thanking God for helping him through his life. He lamented that he had not made more of the opportunities he had received and asked for mercy from God for his sins. "That is my confession."

Inspiration gave me the words to say at that moment. "Jose, the Lord has heard your prayer; may His peace be with you." I have never forgotten the look of release and peace that flowed through his body at that moment. Twenty minutes later, he passed into eternity.

Ministry, like art, often means making the best of a difficult and untidy situation. Feeling out of control, racing downhill without any brakes, prepares us to accept the fact that the Lord is fully able to ensure the best possible result for those who are serving in His kingdom. "Do not worry . . ."

K. LANCE TYLER

COOTIES-B-GONE

All of us have become like one who is unclean,
and all our righteous acts are like filthy rags.
Isa. 64:6, NIV.

My late mother said not to use the word "cootie." I'm about to disobey, not for the first time. Cootie is slang for louse, but to every 8-year-old it just means that someone is untouchable, contagiously germy, or emanates uncool vibes. I'm a few decades past 8, but I still use the word. If you greet someone at church with a smile and explain you have cold cooties, they understand the greeting and do not shake your hand.

We knew cootie people in school. They were the class geek whose clothes were dirty, the person with body odor, the one who knew every arcane bit of trivia but couldn't keep a conversation progressing, or the student who played alone because they were shunned by the cool kids. I was not cool, but not cootie-ridden, either. I felt sorry for the cootie kids and treated them kindly but distantly. I'm glad I did, because some cootie people became good friends.

It's still that way. We know loners, social misfits, and nerdy adults at work or church, on the freeway on–ramp, or in our neighborhood or extended family. Horror of horrors, maybe you're a cootie person right now!

You know what? You are. We are. And have been since Adam and Eve tripped over their first bramble. "All of us have become like one who is unclean, and all our righteous acts are like filthy rags; we all shrivel up like a leaf, and like the wind our sins sweep us away" (Isa. 64:6, NIV). Filthy, shriveled, windswept. Definitely cootie-ridden. In Romans 3 Paul said no one is righteous of themselves.

But hear the word of the Lord: we have been given Christ's own robe of righteousness to replace our rags. "This righteousness from God comes through faith in Jesus Christ to all who believe. There is no difference, for all have sinned and fall short of the glory of God, and are justified freely by his grace through the redemption that came by Christ Jesus" (Rom. 3:22-24, NIV).

By creation and redemption, we are doubly children of God and royalty of the universe. Sometimes it's good to be "all washed up."

Christy K. Robinson

MORE!

Pray without ceasing.
1 Thess. 5:17, NKJV.

Some young parents I knew found true joy in learning to know Jesus through Bible study. With thankful hearts, they started the practice of saying grace at meals. They were surprised one day after saying the blessing when their 2-year-old daughter spoke up, pleading, "More please. More!" Almost every night when prayers were said, tiny Marcy chimed in after the "Amen" saying "More! More!"

What a lesson we can learn from this child. We all need to pray more. Jesus says, "Men always ought to pray" (Luke 18:1, NKJV). More praying will mean more answers to prayer. More answered prayer will mean more souls won for Jesus. More souls won will mean the hastening of the coming of Christ.

Pray always! I can pray first thing when I wake up in the morning. All through the day I can pray silently to my Savior. While washing dishes, driving to work, wherever I am or whatever I'm doing, I can pray. Before eating, I will take time to thank Him for my daily bread. I will pray with my family every morning and night. The last thing I will do before I go to sleep is pray. I will pray for Quiet Hour Ministries, with whom I've worked for many years.

Jesus often went up on a mountain to pray. At times He prayed all night. I will pray for my children. I will pray for the Holy Spirit. I can pray for the sick. I will pray for forgiveness. I will pray for my enemies. I will pray that more people become active in evangelism because Jesus told us to pray to the Lord of the harvest to send out more reapers. Inspired words of Paul tell me to "pray without ceasing" (1 Thess. 5:17, NKJV).

Jesus knows my greatest need. He says, "Watch and pray, lest you enter into temptation" (Matt. 26:41, NKJV).

Like little Marcy, I want to pray more.

Wellesley Muir

THE KINDNESS OF STRANGERS

"I will continue to take care of you and your children." So he reassured them by speaking kindly to them.
Gen. 50:21, NLT.

I was at a chain restaurant in the South with my father and grandmother. We had been driving for several hours and were enjoying the opportunity to stretch our legs and share a meal together. Our server, a lovely woman named Chris, had gotten our rather complicated order exactly right and had delivered our food in record time. As she began to refill our glasses before we'd had much of a chance to make a dent in their contents, I cheerfully observed to my father (in her hearing) that we had obviously lucked out and gotten "the best server in the world."

You wouldn't think that a compliment like that could mean very much, but it obviously made an impression. Chris was even more solicitous of our welfare, and in turn, we were more expressive of our gratitude for her thoughtfulness. These exchanges continued throughout the meal, multiplying exponentially.

I was actually moved to tears when I received the bill, and on the back of it, she had written, "Thank you, and may God bless and keep you safe next to His heart!" I told her she'd made my day, and before we left, she gave me a beautiful little angel pin that she said had been a comfort to her and that she hoped would be helpful to me as well.

I was so amazed that one small compliment had multiplied into something much greater than the sum of those little kindnesses we'd exchanged—perhaps even forged a new friendship. But what moved (and shamed) me most was the realization that every day presents countless opportunities to offer a smile or a kind word—which costs me nothing—and yet I so rarely think to give them.

Emmanuel means "God with us." There is no doubt in my mind that God was with us that evening. I saw Him clearly in Chris's kind and generous heart. I believe that if we look carefully, we can see a glimpse of Him in every one of His sons and daughters—our brothers and sisters—here on earth. And if we see Him in others, how can we help treating them differently?

Lorelei Herman Cress

NOVEMBER 2

MORE VALUABLE, MORE LOVED

You are of more value than many sparrows.
Matt. 10:31, NKJV.

Two oriole couples set up housekeeping in Sue's backyard. One couple chose a medium-size palm tree and constructed its well-woven, socklike nest underneath a wide-spreading leaf. Predators would have to be very observant and acrobatic to reach it.

The second set of parents didn't seem so wise. They selected a 40-foot palm tree and built their nest about three feet below the clump of fronds at the top. In a tiny outcropping where old branches had been trimmed away they wedged their nest. It was exposed to hot sun, strong winds, and the view of any passing bird.

Using binoculars, Sue eventually glimpsed movement in the precarious nest. Busy parents repeatedly zoomed in with fat bugs to feed their young. And then, one day when the lawn sprinkler came on, she saw a tiny dark lump at the foot of the 40-foot palm. It was moving. To her dismay, it was an oriole nestling—wet, shivering, and cold.

Placing it in a small box on soft cotton, she was amazed that the little creature began squeaking and opening its beak for food. Using a spoon, she tried feeding it crumbs of boiled egg. Very little got into his mouth. What did, he hardly had strength to swallow. Hours passed. He was warm, and his bright-yellow breast feathers were dry. But he was weakening. The next morning he opened his mouth once or twice and then remained very still. By evening he was gone.

Wrapping him in a white tissue, Sue placed him in a narrow opening she dug beneath the palm tree, surprised at her own grief. She was grateful to recall Jesus' words: "Are not two sparrows sold for a copper coin? And not one of them falls to the ground apart from your Father's will. But the very hairs of your head are all numbered. Do not fear therefore; you are of more value than many sparrows" (Matt. 10:29-31, NKJV).

KIT WATTS

LISTEN TO THE VOICE

Be still, and know that I am God:
I will be exalted among the heathen, I will be exalted in the earth.
Ps. 46:10.

The day started in blessed communion with my Best Friend through prayer and Bible study. I continued to listen to His Spirit, and He was able to use me to touch a life.

My family found seats for the 11:00 a.m. church service. I glanced back to see a visitor slip into the seat behind us. She was a beautiful and elegant woman. She exuded self-confidence.

I heard a strong voice in my mind say, *Turn around and greet the woman.* I thought, *I will when it is more convenient.* Then I heard the command again. In awkwardness or embarrassment, I continued to resist. Again I heard the voice say even stronger, *Turn around now; don't wait.* Finally I realized this was the Holy Spirit.

I turned around and whispered, "Hi, I'm Vonda, so glad you came to join us this morning. Where are you from?" She gave me a look of disbelief and then told me she was Joan and lived nearby. She passed me a note that said, "Thank you for acknowledging me; you don't know how God used you this morning." Then, before the sermon started, she quietly slipped out of the church.

Finally I was fully in tune with the Holy Spirit, and immediately I obeyed the impression to follow her. In the lobby I asked if she was all right. With a tear in her eye she explained that she had been watching an evangelistic series on TV and that God was revealing many new truths to her. She had visited this church once before, and no one had acknowledged her presence. And until I introduced myself to her, no one had said a word to her this morning, either. In her discouragement she had prayed, "Lord, if You want me here in this church, please show me by impressing someone to speak to me."

Joan is a baptized member of our church today!

Friend, are you listening? Every moment in life is precious—don't let those small moments pass. If you listen and obey the Holy Spirit in the small things, He will use you in a big way!

VONDA BEERMAN

FRIENDSHIP EVANGELISM

Go out and train everyone you meet,
far and near, in this way of life.
Matt. 28:18, Message.

"Why should I pray when I am not sure yet if there is a God? I need to learn first," said Mary, a young girl who was preparing to eat her meal at a popular restaurant and was asked to bow her head.

"Before I became a Christian, the concept of God was the most difficult part for me to accept," said a youth pastor.

"There is no place for the concept of a god in my belief," stated Moises, a young Rwandan who came to our evangelism meetings.

I grew up knowing that there is a God. Many times He had answered my prayers, and I found joy in worshipping Him and including Him in my daily life.

Yet through experience I realize that one of my greatest challenges is sharing God with those who are not Christians. What does a Christian do when coming face to face with a person whose worldview is radically different from the biblical view? Even in a Christian-dominated community there are many people searching for the meaning of life and wondering who God is. In my neighborhood there are Muslims, Buddhists, Jews, and some Hindus. They are wonderful people, created by God. And because many of them don't know God, it is my job to share His love and grace with them by daily living for God.

My next-door neighbor, a beautiful Muslim woman from the Philippines, was drawn to my family by kind words, friendly smiles, and home-baked cookies. Watching my teenage sons catch baseballs with her children, she became interested in our Christian lifestyle.

I am so thankful to God for placing in my life people who are searching for Him, because it makes me more mindful of my relationship with Him.

"Go out and train everyone you meet, far and near, in this way of life, marking them by baptism in the threefold name: Father, Son, and Holy Spirit. Then instruct them in the practice of all I have commanded you. I'll be with you as you do this, day after day after day, right up to the end of the age" (Matt. 28:18-20, Message).

CHARLENE HILLIARD WEST

ENJOYING LIFE?

Pay careful attention to your own work,
for then you will get the satisfaction of a job well done.
Gal. 6:4, NLT.

The story is told of a rich industrialist from the North who was horrified to find a Southern fisherman lying lazily beside his boat, whittling away at a piece of driftwood, and chewing on some smoked fish jerky.

"Why aren't you out fishing?" asked the industrialist.

"Because I have caught enough fish for the day," the fisherman replied.

"Why don't you catch more?"

"What would I do with them?"

"You could earn more money. Then you could buy a motor for your boat and go into deeper waters and catch more fish. Then you could make enough money to buy nylon nets that would allow you to catch even more fish. More fish equals more money! Soon you would have enough money for two boats . . . maybe even a fleet. Then you would be a rich man like me."

"What would I do then?" asked the fisherman.

"Then you could really enjoy life."

"What do you think I'm doing right now?"

Wow! This story says so much! Think back to a time in your life that things weren't so complicated. Think back to a time that you were happy, even though you may not have had all the "stuff" that the world tries to tell you that you need to be happy.

Too many of us look beyond the simple joys that surround us every day, because we are told by the advertising gurus that in order to be happy we need to accumulate the bigger, better, and faster stuff. If the truth were told, most people spend a good percentage of their lives accumulating the "latest and the greatest" gadgets in the hopes that they will bring more happiness and joy, only to find that the accumulation of stuff has nothing to do with happiness.

How is it with you? Right now, today, this moment—are you really enjoying life? That joy can come whether you are rich or poor, great or small. It has everything to do with knowing what real wealth is all about.

JOEDY MELASHENKO

DIG AROUND IT

I'll dig around it and fertilize it.
If it bears fruit next year, fine! If not, then cut it down.
Luke 13:8, 9, NIV.

When it comes to gardening, I'm all fingers and no thumbs—green or otherwise. I'm like the man who said, "My tomato plants refuse to grow, so I'm going to show them some pictures of luscious tomato plants with the hope that they'll get really jealous and grow."

The neighbor smiled and said, "Did you ever think of watering them first?"

When I moved to California in 1996, I was blessed with several fruit trees growing on my property. They were all in good shape except an old withered apricot tree that my gardener suggested I cut down. I gave him permission to remove the tree, but after removing some large limbs, he was called away to an emergency and postponed the completion for the next year. My friend relocated to California, and she definitely is blessed with 10 green thumbs. She asked if she could work on the apricot tree. She told me that if it did not respond after a year of special treatment I should then cut it down.

During that year we noticed a few new branches, but no fruit. In the next months she dug around the tree, spoke gently, and sang lovely tunes to it. The next season resulted in the appearance of six apricots, which the birds quickly ate. The following year the produce was doubled.

As I reflected on the parable Jesus told in Luke 13:1-9 I thought of my apricot tree and my own blighted life, which Jesus carefully cultivates. Just as God nurtures His people, represented by the tree in this parable, so He has called us to be witnesses of His grace in our sphere of influence. If we should fail to produce the expected results, Jesus, the Great Gardener, will dig around us and fertilize us. The Jewish leaders in the time of Jesus sold sacrificial animals' coagulated blood as fertilizer. Jesus was saying that His blood, or life, is the source of our sustenance and growth. Then we will produce fruits like my apricot tree, which provided so many baskets of bounty this year, I was able to share with people and birds!

If you are going through a time of unexpected blight, take courage and consume the heavenly fertilizer provided in the Word of God. You will be amazed by the amount of fruits to come.

Hyveth B. Williams

THE PARABLE OF THE WEEDS

Then the righteous will shine like the sun
in the kingdom of their Father.
Matt. 13:43, NIV.

Last July I took out some really big weeds growing behind the vegetables. These weeds were huge—they were like trees. Their stems were an inch across, and they were woody. They topped the six-foot fence. I pulled and tugged and perspired heavily while swatting away gnats. When the roots wouldn't loosen from the east side, I dived through the thick green pine needles to get to the west side. I pulled from that direction and finally finished the job. However, it was too late to prevent the weeds from dropping their seeds and creating more weeds that I needed to pull. The seeds were almost invisibly tiny, borne on the wind with white cottony fluff.

When I first moved here, I planted a blue morning glory vine. It was truly beautiful, but it took over the yard and climbed the fence, as if making for the Canadian border. It can grow a meter a day on every runner! It invaded the avocado tree, stunted the pine tree, and choked out other plants. So I tried to eradicate it. I killed the main stalks, but the runners have taken hold everywhere, coming up 30 feet away from the source. It's a never-ending job. I can't pour poison on the vine or pull it up without killing the desirable flowers and food-bearing plants that coexist in the yard. Until now! This is harvesttime for the annual plants, and like Jesus' harvesters, I let the plants and the weeds grow together; then I collect the weeds to be destroyed. (Unlike Jesus' field, my weeds will be back next year, but for now, it looks clean and orderly, and the winter sun can reach the soil and prepare it for the spring plants.)

Jesus said that the weeds, which symbolize the sons of the evil one, are pulled up and burned in the fire, but the good grain and fruits, representing the sons of the kingdom, are harvested by the angels. "As the weeds are pulled up and burned in the fire, so it will be at the end of the age. The Son of Man will send out his angels, and they will weed out of his kingdom everything that causes sin and all who do evil. . . . Then the righteous will shine like the sun in the kingdom of their Father" (Matt. 13:40-43, NIV).

Even a city kid like me understands that parable! Won't it be wonderful when Jesus comes to collect us in His grand harvest and glorifies our bodies to fit His kingdom? He is faithful to fulfill the promises He has made.

CHRISTY K. ROBINSON

A PRAYER FITLY SPOKEN

A word fitly spoken is like apples of gold in pictures of silver.
Prov. 25:11.

I was barely coping with receipt of some very bad news. But, as the pastor's wife, I answered the phone with a resilience cultivated over years of handling the task.

On the other end was the voice of a woman with limited English-speaking skills whom I had never met. She asked for my husband, and I explained his absence. I informed her that there was slim chance he could call her back that evening, because he'd be coming home late and already had several phone calls to make.

She listened politely. I was speaking slowly because her heavy accent suggested that she might have difficulty understanding me. She understood my elaborate explanation perfectly. "Do you have a minute?" she asked. "I'm calling," she finally had a chance to put in, "because I'm on the prayer committee."

"Maybe you can talk to some staff member at the church tomorrow about it," I suggested, aware of my husband's busy schedule the next day.

"You and the pastor," she persisted, "are on my list. I'm in the L's. I called to pray for you." Convinced of my husband's unavailability, she added, "Is it all right if I pray with you?"

In a very small voice, I assented. I needed the prayer. This servant of the Lord could have called at no more propitious time. I don't recall telling her that her prayer came in what could be called the worst week of my life. I hope I did. (I have since attended her funeral, where I recounted the occasion to her husband.)

I know that when I returned the receiver to its cradle, I wept. But it was a thanks-be-to-God weeping. The prayer reminded me that God would be with me through the pain.

Upon reflection, and reminder in Scripture, I can smile (in embarrassment) at the pain, which is now subsided, and at my own behavior: "To answer a question before you have heard it out is both stupid and insulting" (Prov. 18:13, NEB).

EDNA MAYE LOVELESS

YEARS OF BLESSINGS

Incline your ear, and come to Me. Hear, and your soul shall live.
Isa. 55:3, NKJV.

In 1970 my wife, Jean, and I left California and began 18 precious years of missionary work. It was in the Philippines that I first experienced the encouraging help of the Quiet Hour. We were assigned as professors at Mountain View College, a missionary school. Each weekend students and teachers would hike to distant villages to assist in worship services and conduct public and personal evangelism.

A letter was written to the Quiet Hour requesting help with transportation for the evangelistic outreach. What a wonderful day it was when LaVerne Tucker arrived to dedicate the six used military weapons carriers that had been converted into buses for evangelism. During the six-year period the students planted 40 new churches with the help of those buses.

The church grew when the entire membership was involved in sharing Jesus with their community. Often the members went into the jungles to cut trees for construction. The Quiet Hour frequently provided sheets of metal for roofing. It was a joint effort.

Then there was the day that the Manobo tribal chief asked for teachers to come to his village. What a blessing when funds from Quiet Hour supporters made it possible to send teachers into several remote jungle villages. Today there are more than 3,000 of these people who are followers of Jesus.

Following my six years at Mountain View College, I spent three years as a professor at the theological seminary near Manila. The most effective type of training is by demonstration, so a citywide evangelistic program for Manila was organized, but we needed Bibles. A letter was once again written to the Quiet Hour. "Can you help us with 100,000 Bibles?"

Church members in Manila prayed for those Bibles, which were to be used in the outreach. The day the letter arrived at the Quiet Hour headquarters, a special prayer was offered for Bibles. Before the day was over, a Quiet Hour supporter pledged $50,000 for Bibles. What a wonderful day when church leaders in Manila unloaded the hundreds of boxes containing the 100,000 Bibles. On the final day of the public meeting, 1,500 people were baptized. In the weeks that followed, hundreds more were baptized, and 11 new churches were formed.

J. H. ZACHARY

BORN CRIPPLED

If we confess our sins, He is faithful and just to forgive us our sins and to cleanse us from all unrighteousness.
1 John 1:9, NKJV.

"Look at you, you dirty grub!" These were the words I spoke to my 3-year-old mentally and physically challenged daughter when I found her in our garden as I was returning from work.

Roanne was born with spina bifida with hydrocephalus. Because she couldn't walk, we put little overalls on her with padding on the knees so that she could play outside in the sunshine and fresh air.

As I carried her up the stairs that day, she replied, "I's sorry, Daddy, I's sorry."

I replied, "It's all right, honey, Daddy understands. You were born with a disability."

No sooner were those words out of my mouth than I heard the Spirit's voice saying, "That's how it is with you and your heavenly Father. You dirty your life with sin, and when you tell Him that you are sorry, He says that it's all right—you were born with a disability in your spiritual life. He remembers the pit from which you are dug."

When I took my little girl inside and bathed her, washed her hair, and put her clean pajamas on, there was nothing left to show what she had been like.

Then I understood the real meaning of 1 John 1:9: "If we confess our sins, He is faithful and just to forgive us our sins and to cleanse us from all unrighteousness" (NKJV).

When I tell God that I'm sorry for my sins, He says that He knows we were born with a disability, with a bent to sin, and He willingly forgives us. More than that, He takes us and washes us in the blood of Jesus, puts the clean clothes of Christ's righteousness upon us, and there isn't any evidence left of what we were. As one Christian writer stated: "We stand before God as if we had never sinned." Glory be to God!

R. E. "Bob" Possingham

THE LOADED RIFLE

Pray to thy Father which is in secret;
and thy Father which seeth in secret shall reward thee openly.
Matt. 6:6.

A loaded rifle pressed to the head should surely bring one to fervent prayer. But this time the finger pressing tighter and tighter on the trigger was my own. A distraught Vietnam soldier with seemingly nothing left to live for, I searched for just one glimmer of hope before the bullet fired. There was nothing. A family disrupted by divorce, emotions roaring, friends protesting the war, riots boiling back home, meaningless and merciless killings, a "Dear John" letter from my girlfriend, together with the general poor morale and rampant drug abuse among the GIs, all added up to enormous disappointment and despair.

I had decided to reevaluate life, at the wise age of 20, and see if there were any threads of hope. I even pondered hijacking a native fishing boat and crossing the South China Sea to Japan. But then there would be shame as a deserter. No, I could fathom no way out. I simply couldn't endure such daily anguish.

I walked down the boardwalk at dark with my loaded rifle. The decision was made, and I was committed. The stars were bright against the black Southeast Asian night, and the flash suppressor of my M-14 was placed against my right temple, finger putting pressure on the trigger. "Is there anything worth living for?"

At that moment a voice came clearly, somewhat surprisingly, into my totally unreligious mind. *Have you tried prayer?*

The thought stunned me at first, but then challenged me. Returning to the barracks, I knelt beside my bunk, surrounded by noisy, laughing, cursing guys, and said a prayer I remembered, the Lord's Prayer, which took more courage than flying into a hot zone as gunner.

"Our Father in heaven, reveal who you are. Set the world right; do what's best—as above, so below. Keep us alive with three square meals. Keep us forgiven with you and forgiving others. Keep us safe from ourselves and the Devil. You're in charge! You can do anything you want! You're ablaze in beauty!" (Matt. 6:9-13, Message).

Those four words—our Father in heaven—saved my life. Thank You, Father.

TIM DAVIS

IN EVERYTHING SAY "THANK YOU"

Blessing, and glory, and wisdom, and thanksgiving, and honour, and power, and might, be unto our God for ever and ever. Amen.
Rev. 7:12.

I had the privilege of sharing Christ and His love in central Russia in the city of Salavat. Here were people, many of whom were Muslims or nonreligious, many having never seen a Bible, who kept saying, "Thank you for giving me hope," "Thank you for bringing Christ to me," or "Thank you for all you have done for us here."

These expressions are a direct result of the Holy Spirit's working in the person's life. What a joy it was to witness the life changes of individuals and their expressions of thankfulness.

Yet some may not feel too thankful due to hardship, trial, or tragedy. Remember that God knows the circumstances, and He understands what is being experienced.

George Matheson, the well-known blind preacher of Scotland, once stated, "My God, I have never thanked Thee for my 'thorn!' I have thanked Thee a thousand times for my roses, but never once for my 'thorn'; I have been looking forward to a world where I shall get compensation for my cross as itself a present glory. Teach me the value of my 'thorn.' Show me that I have climbed to Thee by the path of pain. Show me that my tears have made my rainbow."

We are challenged by Paul, who in spite of his personal "thorn" was able to declare, "In every thing give thanks: for this is the will of God in Christ Jesus concerning you" (1 Thess. 5:18).

You ask, "How can we thank God for accidents, death, and sin?" We don't; that is not what the Scripture means. Thank God for His presence and power as we walk through such trials. In Christ Jesus there is victory and triumph over all. Therefore, in everything, not for everything, thank God for the victory He has given us through Christ Jesus.

"Blessing, and glory, and wisdom, and thanksgiving, and honour, and power, and might, be unto our God for ever and ever. Amen" (Rev. 7:12).

BILL TUCKER

SING WITH THE LORD!

Rejoice in the Lord always: and again I say, Rejoice.
Phil. 4:4.

As a child in Christian school I loved to sing the canon based on Philippians 4:4, "Rejoice in the Lord always: and again I say, Rejoice." Most people think it a cheerful song and a cheerful sentiment.

The Message Bible translates Philippians 4:4, 5 as: "Celebrate God all day, every day. I mean, revel in him! Make it as clear as you can to all you meet that you're on their side, working with them and not against them."

Here, the Greek word for "rejoice" is not the word for exultation *(agalliao)*. This rejoice is *chairete,* meaning joy, delight, gladness, gift, and grace. Our modern words charity and charisma (gifts and gifted) stem from the root *charis*. The passage in Philippians is really about being gifted and giving. Give joyfully in the Lord always. Again, give! Paul says that by general prayer and specific petition, and with thanksgiving, we should present our requests to God, who gives us everything, even transcendent, unimaginable peace. God gives us the ability, in Christ Jesus, to be true, noble, right, pure, lovely, and admirable.

In verse 10 Paul *echaren* (rejoices) greatly in the Lord, because his converts love him in such a tangible way through their gifts of love and fellowship. He's learned to be as satisfied as a calf in deep pasture, whatever the circumstances or situation, because he's resting in God's strength to accomplish everything. He thanks the Philippians for their generosity (their donations—not *charis*) in supporting the gospel ministry.

It's facinating to trace, with a Greek Bible and excellent reference books, the word *charis* through Philippians, where Paul uses it so often. It gives us a colorful way of seeing God's Word anew.

Today, as you will inevitably be singing that pretty round, think about all the ways you can give joy to the Lord, in gratitude and love, for all He has graced you with and given to you. And listen carefully for the ways He antiphonally responds with the second part of the round, "Rejoice! Rejoice! And again I say rejoice!"

CHRISTY K. ROBINSON

FAITH OF A CHILD

Assuredly, I say to you, unless you are converted and become as little children, you will by no means enter the kingdom of heaven.
Matt. 18:3, NKJV.

One day while cleaning house, I decided to give my two parakeets a break from their cage. I let them perch on our floor-length wicker mirror. Delilah climbed down to the bottom and sat gazing into the mirror, serenading herself. Samson stayed at the top, singing at the top of his lungs.

It was always entertaining and enjoyable to hear them sing, but this particular day I heard more than singing. As I was going about my duties upstairs, I heard a shriek like I had never heard before. It was Delilah screaming for her life. My dog had happened upon the festivities and decided it was time for lunch! By the time I removed her from the jaws of death, Delilah was in terrible shape. Her tail feathers and part of her back end were missing, and she had a gaping wound on her chest.

In our human judgment we thought there was no hope for this poor bird. The kids and I were all crying, but Kaylie, my 7-year-old daughter, was sobbing pitifully! Between the wails of grief, my husband said that in mercy we should put her out of her misery. That's when Kaylie piped in, "No, Daddy, God can do miracles. I know He'll do it. Daddy, let's pray!"

So the whole family knelt in a circle. "Father, You said in Your Word to become as little children. I believe You meant for us to trust You as little children do, so we are going to trust You as Kaylie trusts You right now. In the name of Jesus, we ask You to heal this bird. We thank You for it now. Amen."

We prepared a shoebox with padding and some food and water. Kaylie said, "I'll put a stick across the top of the box. In case she feels better in the night, she may want to stand on it." The next morning Delilah was perched on the stick, her chest wound completely closed, and her back end totally healed!

God honored our faith that day. He delights to give good gifts to His children when we come to Him in faith, believing as a child. He will carry out what you've asked according to His will. Have a faith-filled day!

Vonda Beerman

STANDING IN THE GAP

I searched for a man among them who would build up the wall and stand in the gap before Me for the land.
Eze. 22:30, NASB.

My friend Gabriella has seen more trouble in the last year than you or I have in a lifetime. I met her at a women's retreat. At that time she was nursing a broken heart, for the love of her life had decided to move on. Upon her return from the retreat, she received notice that she had a virulent brain tumor. She began treatment, and a few months later when her student visa expired, immigration officials demanded that she return home at once. She interrupted her treatment and flew back to Germany in the hopes of returning to the United States. While in Germany, old sibling rivalries escalated into open animosity. As she prayed her way through that, her mother became ill, and my friend was forced to move from her mother's home into an apartment by herself. She recently called and told me that her mother had passed away and that her cancer was not in remission, but it had become even more aggressive.

After I hung up, I began to think of how seldom I give thanks for good health, a safe haven, and God's grace and blessings on my life and ministry. I thought of my friend's valor in the face of these adversities and afflictions, especially that she spent most of our conversation praising God, underscoring His faithfulness and never-ending mercy. I was humbled. As I looked for something to make me feel better about my attitude of carelessness with God's will for my life, my Bible fell open to Ezekiel 22:30, which says, "I searched for a man among them who would build up the wall and stand in the gap before Me for the land, so that I would not destroy it; but I found no one" (NASB).

Instead of weeping like John the Revelator (Rev. 5:4), I fell on my knees and cried for joy that God has provided me with His Son to stand in the gap for me. My friend demonstrates that she stands for Jesus no matter the cost. She stands, though pressed beyond her limits. And because she is so brave, I am deeply encouraged.

Lord, if you are still searching for someone to stand in the gap for our land, call Gabriella. She will not let you down, and I pray that because of her friendship, neither will I. Amen!

HYVETH B. WILLIAMS

WE HAVE ACCESS

By whom also we have access by faith into this grace wherein we stand, and rejoice in hope of the glory of God. Rom. 5:2.

As we neared Buckingham Palace, we saw people standing in a long line that stretched for nearly a mile, waiting to enter the home of the queen of England. For the first time in history, the palace doors were being opened to the general public, but only the very patient and persevering would be able to enter through those huge ornate doors and view the beautiful interior. As my family and I viewed the long line of people, we discussed how we wanted to use the few hours of layover time between planes. We agreed that seeing the queen's palace was not worth the wait or the effort. It would take hours of waiting and being checked by security guards to enter the royal palace.

It takes a special code to enter some offices or industrial buildings. And it takes passwords to get into a computer. But with God we have full and easy access to His presence.

Having access to places and people is important. In the life of a Christian, having access to God is essential! Through Jesus Christ, we have access to God. "For through him we [all] have access by one Spirit unto the Father" (Eph. 2:18).

Jesus Christ throws open the doors so that we may enter into the presence of God, the Sovereign Majesty of the universe. During any hour of our busy day or at any moment of night, we may access God, our Abba Father. "By whom also we have access by faith into this grace wherein we stand, and rejoice in hope of the glory of God" (Rom. 5:2).

How comforting! It doesn't really matter if I see the queen's palace, enter a skyscraper, or obtain computer information. But my salvation depends upon my having access to the throne of God, and the sacrifice of Jesus Christ has made this possible.

"Having therefore, brethren, boldness to enter into the holiest by the blood of Jesus" (Heb. 10:19). Without the blood of Jesus Christ, we would not have access to God. How wonderful and how thankful I am that through the blood of Jesus, which was shed for us, we indeed have access!

BILL TUCKER

PERSISTENCE WITH GOD

Because of his persistence he will rise and give him as many as he needs.
Luke 11:8, NKJV.

Apple strudel and international flights make an incredible combination. Our KLM flight attendant had just brought us some amazing apple strudel. My friends and I loved it! We discussed how we could get some more apple strudel.

"Tatiana, tell him to bring us more apple strudel."

"Actually, Joelle should! She wants some." Tatiana didn't give in easily.

"No, Tatiana, you do it!" I protested. She was the most outgoing in our short-term mission group, so she would make the perfect candidate to ask for more strudel.

When the flight attendant returned with coffee and tea service, he asked our group if we wanted any. Tatiana (the one who was supposed to ask for apple strudel) said, "No, thank you, but may we have some orange juice?"

The flight attendant may have thought we were nuts, but he sweetly brought our group glasses of orange juice. Then Tatiana asked, "Oh, one other thing. Do you have any more of those apple strudels? Some of us would like them." (Several rows of passengers, the expectant friends, looked up brightly and hopefully.)

The flight attendant said, "You guys are hilarious! First you want orange juice when I bring around coffee, and now you want apple strudel!" But he dutifully fetched more apple strudel for us, and we thanked him profusely for his kindness.

Sometimes we don't want to ask God for something because we think it's silly. Or we think that asking just once is enough (though sometimes it is). Jesus tells a parable about a man who knocks on his friend's door in the middle of the night, asking for three loaves of bread to feed guests. The friend says that he can't because he's in bed. But Jesus says, "I say to you, though he will not rise and give to him because he is his friend, yet because of his persistence he will rise and give him as many as he needs" (Luke 11:8, NKJV).

God loves to hear and answer our specific, persistent requests!

JOELLE MCNULTY

VOICE OF VICTORY

He is a rewarder of them that diligently seek him.
Heb. 11:6.

During my service to God as a musician, I have had the privilege of visiting several faraway lands. This is an experience of faith and answered prayer.

In October 1999 I traveled with the Quiet Hour to Papua New Guinea to participate in an evangelistic crusade. It was like being in a different world—a world filled with a level of crime and poverty that I had not dreamed possible. I witnessed a people with a tremendous hunger for the truth and hope. And once accepted they were full of tremendous faith and devotion to God.

One evening while Pastor Bill Tucker was preaching, it began to rain in torrents. The rain was so loud and so strong it was difficult to even hear Bill's voice. The ground became so wet they could not sit. They stood there in the pouring rain listening to every word of hope they could catch. Realizing the rain was not going to stop, Pastor Tucker asked the audience, "Do you want me to quit?" In unison we heard 20,000 people say, "NO!"

The next day I contracted a terrible cough. By evening I was coughing every few seconds, and, at times, I was coughing uncontrollably. As the time of the meeting approached, I prayed, "Lord, I know You didn't bring me around the world to just watch; I want to sing for Your glory!" Just before the meeting began, the local pastors gathered around me and prayed.

Then, in faith, I joined the team leaders on the platform. Not a single cough came out of my mouth the entire time I was up there. As soon as I stepped off the platform, I began coughing again. This miracle happened for several successive nights until I gained full recovery. This was tangible evidence that God was miraculously at work for His glory.

"But without faith it is impossible to please him: for he that cometh to God must believe that he is, and that he is a rewarder of them that diligently seek him" (Heb. 11:6).

Remember how the Israelites had to step into the water first before God parted the Red Sea? Today, take a greater step of faith!

VONDA BEERMAN

TRIBUTE TO GODLY PARENTS

You were there for our parents: they cried for your help and you gave it; they trusted and lived a good life.
Ps. 22:3, Message.

Many times we choose Father's Day or Mother's Day to express our love and appreciation for our parents and what they have done in our lives. Today, I am choosing to share my gratitude, my words of thanksgiving for my parents.

We live in a society in which parenting and raising kids has almost become a lost skill. Many parents have lost their moral strength when it comes to raising families. Secular pressures have nearly destroyed many families.

If you were raised in a family with parents who cared enough to say no, who taught you life skills when it would have been easier to do those skills themselves, who taught you moral values when it was inconvenient or even hurt, who let you see the emotions in their countenances, and who showed their own human weaknesses and were strong enough to ask your forgiveness, then count your blessings. Many of the ills of our society could be mended if the foundation stones of a family were based on some of these "old-fashioned" building blocks.

I thank God every day for my godly parents. Yes, there were times as a teenager when I hated them because I thought they were being too strict and old-fashioned. Ironically, when I became a parent, I realized that I was being more strict with my children than my parents had been with me. The light came on in my heart, and I saw my parents differently.

After reciting a beautiful poem during a church program, my mother was asked by a church member, "Do you do any writing?"

"Yes, I am writing five books," Mother replied.

"What are their titles?" asked the surprised church member.

"Lonnie, Joedy, Dallas, Eugene, and Rudy. My greatest desire is to write on the minds and hearts of my five sons the lessons they will never forget."

JOEDY MELASHENKO

NOVEMBER 20

THANKFUL FOR WHAT?

Don't worry about anything, but pray about everything.
With thankful hearts offer up your prayers and requests to God.
Phil. 4:6, CEV.

My tearful face was unsettling my surgeon, who was also my friend. But this was serious business. I thrust my arm out like a signal for a left turn. "Look at this fat arm," I sobbed. "Why? Why now, after all this time? I've been perfectly normal, even healthy, for a whole year. I . . . I don't understand. . . ." Tears dribbled down my chin.

"Sometimes it happens this way after breast cancer surgery." His voice was calm and kind. "It can happen even after two, sometimes three years. But it's a circulation problem, and it's not fatal." He looked at the arm. "Besides, it's hardly noticeable."

"Hardly noticeable! Well, I notice it. It bothers me all the time, I can't keep my mind off it."

"Cheer up, girl! You'll get used to it." He was smiling.

"GET USED TO IT! You mean I have to carry this ugly, uncomfortable thing around for the rest of my life?"

I walked to my car filled with visions of an arm swelling bigger and bigger, turning purple, then black, then gangrenous. I knew better, but I couldn't help it. I grieved. I pounded the pillows. I considered investing in Kleenex stock. This was harder to take than the lump in my breast. At least that was something I could get rid of.

Pieces of scripture eddied about my mind. "Do not be anxious . . . in everything . . . thanksgiving" (Phil. 4:6, NIV).

It finally occurred to me that I did have another option. My surgeon could cut the thing off. I looked at the offending arm with new eyes. It was all there, working just fine. Actually, I was quite attached to it.

"Hey, praise the Lord! I have a usable arm!"

Yes, I have gotten used to it. And it hasn't gotten bigger or purple or gangrenous.

"Thank You, God. This is a wonderful arm."

AILEEN LUDINGTON

SHOESHOP WISDOM

It's better to enjoy what we have than to always want something else, because that makes no more sense than chasing the wind.
Eccl. 6:9, CEV.

For 11 years I'd patronized Joe's shoe repair. I'd watched his two sons become teenagers. Working with Dad after school, they speak only if spoken to. Joe's wife, a fixture behind the counter, takes money and makes change.

Joe has no prestige, no status. But he's genial to customers. When I give him a deadline for a shoe repair because I'm going on a trip, he'll ask where I'm going. Sometimes he speaks of living in Lebanon. I've assumed he's Lebanese. But last Tuesday when I went to pick up my shoes, Joe said, "Do you have a couple of minutes? I want to tell you something."

My husband is waiting outside with the motor running, but my husband is a patient man; I decide to give Joe two minutes.

"I come from Turkey," Joe says. "Mother, Father born in Turkey. But they are Armenians. In Turkey that means this," he says and draws his hand across his throat. "We go to Syria, Lebanon," Joe says. "I meet my wife there. We have nothing. Eight to 10 people live in one room. Two beds—10 people in two beds. One bowl. Eat [gestures]. One room. We have nothing. But we thank God.

"Now in America, everyone trying—trying to have two cars, buy . . . buy everything—and no thanks to God. Never think of God. Is too bad."

That is Joe's story. His wife stands beside him, nodding. A tattered calendar hangs on the wall. Dust has collected on the sneakers and shoe polish in the racks. Joe's hands are stained, his fingernails filled with grime. Joe is a good workman. He spends long days in the shop. He finds it difficult to speak the language. But he has spoken with the wisdom of the wise man: "It is better to be satisfied with what is before your eyes than give rein to desire; this too is emptiness and chasing the wind" (Eccl. 6:9, NEB).

EDNA MAYE LOVELESS

THANKFUL FOR ANNOYANCES

I have learned the secret of being content in any and every situation,
whether well fed or hungry, whether living in plenty or in want.
I can do everything through him who gives me strength.
Phil. 4:12, 13, NIV.

I am thankful for . . .

- ⋆ the wife who says we're having hot dogs tonight because she is home with me and not out with someone else.
- ⋆ the husband who is on the sofa being a couch potato because he is home with me and not out at the bars.
- ⋆ the teenager who is complaining about doing dishes because it means she is at home, not on the streets.
- ⋆ the taxes I pay because it means I am employed.
- ⋆ the mess to clean after a party because it means I have been surrounded by friends.
- ⋆ the clothes that fit a little too snug because it means I have enough to eat.
- ⋆ a lawn that needs mowing, windows that need cleaning, and gutters that need fixing because it means I have a home.
- ⋆ all the complaining I hear about the government because it means we have freedom of speech.
- ⋆ the parking spot I find at the far end of the parking lot because it means I am capable of walking and I have been blessed with transportation.
- ⋆ my huge heating bill because it means I am warm.
- ⋆ the lady behind me in church who sings off-key because it means I can hear.
- ⋆ the pile of laundry and ironing because it means I have clothes to wear.
- ⋆ the alarm that goes off in the early-morning hours because it means I am alive.
- ⋆ too much e-mail because it means I have friends and colleagues who are thinking of me.

ANONYMOUS

THE HABIT OF THANKFULNESS

So thank God for his marvelous love,
for his miracle mercy to the children he loves.
Ps. 107:8, Message.

The other day I was listening to the radio and singing along—I sound my best when alone in the car! It's true that when we know songs, it's easy to simply sing the words by rote. Eventually we don't think anymore about what we're singing; we're just caught up in the moment. This day it was different—God used the radio to get my attention.

"Give thanks, with a grateful heart. Give thanks to the Holy One, Give thanks for all He's given, Jesus Christ, His Son, and now let the weak say 'I am strong,' let the poor say 'I am rich,' because of what the Lord has done for us. Give thanks."

In that moment I was reminded of Jesus meeting the 10 lepers and healing them all. It's easy to imagine the joy and freedom these newly healed men felt as they ran to the Temple to be declared clean and healthy. One, a Samaritan, came back and fell at Jesus' feet, praising God and thanking Him. Jesus' question to him is haunting: "Were not ten cleansed? Where are the nine? Was no one found to return and give praise to God except this foreigner?" (Luke 17:17, 18, ESV).

Oh how I want to be like the Samaritan and remember to give praise and thanks to God! We desperately need to cultivate a lifestyle of thankfulness. At least I do. So now, each day I make it a habit to write down five things that I'm thankful for. When days get hard or relationships trying, reviewing this list helps quiet my spirit and build my faith.

God has given us life and abundance. Focusing on the gifts helps us get through the hard times and builds our faith.

PAMELA MCCANN

THE ONESIMUS FACTOR

Well done, good and faithful [and useful] servant!
You have been faithful with a few things; I will put you in charge of many things.
Come and share your master's happiness! Matt. 25:23, NIV.

It's often said, "I couldn't have done it without you." But I would like to add another sentence to the saying: "Thank you so much for your loving service."

The apostle Paul wrote to his friend Philemon, saying that he was returning the runaway slave Onesimus. (Onesimus' name meant "useful.") Mr. Useful had actually made himself indispensable to the Christian community, and his living testimony of usefulness and willingness to serve inspired Paul to implore Philemon to treat the returning slave not as a criminal, but as a brother in Christ—an equal.

In our society we might apply the principle to professional ministers and the lay Christians who volunteer considerable amounts of time, expertise, and financial resources. The professional clergy and their paid staff, organized ministries, and churches could not function without a community of true believers—believers in the cause of the gospel of Christ.

Jesus said in the Sermon on the Mount that doing the acts of righteousness and giving alms to the needy are godly acts (Matt. 6:1). Because God acts with justice, mercy, compassion, forgiveness, and love, and because we want to be like Him in all things, we are moved to go where we are needed, to liberate those in bondage, and to bring Jesus' healing balm to His children. When we act unselfishly and without expecting reward or payment, we not only strengthen those we serve but ourselves as well, knowing that we have been instruments in the hands of God.

Sign up for an evangelism program—to teach, preach, carry equipment, lay block, or raise a roof. Pray for your local church, denomination, and your favorite ministries regularly.

God doesn't need our money or our muscle to "finish His work." He could just speak the word. But we need to exercise both action and finances to build faith and trust in His providence. Volunteering for God's cause is ultimately for our own good! Simple acts of usefulness really can change the world.

Christy K. Robinson

THE THANKFULNESS CROWD

The Lord hath anointed me to preach good tidings . . . that he might be glorified. Isa. 61:1-3.

Thanksgiving has always been my favorite holiday. It was the time of year that my family would gather together and be grateful for all the blessings that had been bestowed upon us throughout the year. Wherever my family was at that time, food, fun, and football were in the forefront. I always loved these activities.

One Thanksgiving holiday when I was 14 years old, my family traveled downtown to feed the people who lived on our city streets—people who were poor, mentally ill, crushed by drugs and alcohol, rejected, and lonely. As a teenager, I didn't really understand the effect that this would have on the rest of my life. Nothing changed about my liking of food, fun, and football, but my priorities changed forever because of this experience.

Feeding the less fortunate wasn't what changed my mind. My eyes were opened. I realized that I could lend a hand in the restoration of all people. I could be a part of the thankfulness crowd. Truly, blessings may fall on the good and bad, trouble may beset the rich and poor, but giving thanks with a grateful heart was a lesson well learned when I shared my joy with those around me. Great things He has done.

I am thankful that because of the anointing of the Holy Spirit on His people (including me!), I can say with Jesus Christ, and in His name, "The Spirit of the Lord God is upon me; because the Lord hath anointed me to preach good tidings unto the meek; he hath sent me to bind up the brokenhearted, to proclaim liberty to the captives, and the opening of the prison to them that are bound. . . . To appoint unto them that mourn in Zion, to give unto them beauty for ashes, the oil of joy for mourning, the garment of praise for the spirit of heaviness; that they might be called trees of righteousness, the planting of the Lord, that he might be glorified" (Isa. 61:1-3).

BOB MCGHEE

IS "THANK YOU" ENOUGH?

Giving thanks always for all things to God.
Eph. 5:20, NKJV.

The bellhop at the Pickwick Hotel on San Francisco's Market Street picked up my luggage and led me to the elevator. *Pretty nice,* I thought. I was just a country boy, only 20 years old, and I couldn't remember anyone ever helping me like this.

Not only was I young and inexperienced—I'd never been in an elevator before. My church had sent me to attend a youth convention in the city. The only other hotel I'd ever stayed in had stairs to the second floor, and no one had offered to carry my luggage.

This is great, I thought when we landed on the seventh floor. I followed the bellhop to my room. He opened the door, turned on the lights, put my suitcases in place, opened the drapes, and handed me the key to my room.

Scripture says, "In everything give thanks; for this is the will of God in Christ Jesus for you" (1 Thess. 5:18, NKJV). I turned to the bellhop and smiled. "Thank you, sir." He walked to the door, turned around, and stared. Finally he spoke.

"Saying thank you is all right, but thank you doesn't buy food and clothes for my children. It doesn't pay the doctor bills for my sick wife. It doesn't pay rent for our apartment." Suddenly I got the point. Somewhere along the journey of life I'd heard you are supposed to give tips to show appreciation. I reached in my pocket and fished out a couple of quarters.

The lesson I learned at the Pickwick Hotel was worth much more than the stingy 50 cents I gave a man who was struggling to make a living helping others. He was right. "Thank you isn't enough."

Let's paraphrase the words of Jesus in Matthew 7:21: Not everyone who says, Thank you, Thank you, shall enter the kingdom of heaven, but he who does the will of My Father. Yes, we need to say "Thank you," but the best way to thank our heavenly Father for the gift of Jesus is to do His will.

It's His will for us to say thank you by obeying Him and helping others.

WELLESLEY MUIR

MUSINGS ON THANK-YOUS

He kneeled at Jesus' feet, so grateful. He couldn't thank him enough.
Luke 17:15, Message.

There is plenty of room in the drawer I've reserved for positive messages from students. Students take parents and teachers pretty much for granted. They see us as planted THERE for their use. Staying in touch with reality, I don't find the notes building my ego. They actually reveal to me some rather well-bred students.

A thank-you note arrived recently from my granddaughter. I had sent a fruit-of-the-month gift to her dormitory address. I wanted her to know I was thinking about her without spoiling her valiant efforts to avoid junk foods. I can picture her mother reminding her by cell phone to write the note, as I once reminded her mother, and as my mother . . . ad infinitum.

What delighted me about that note was its specificity. Once she sat down to write it, her inner graciousness emerged. She added some cheery words about my recovery from a recent illness, creating some warm moments for me.

A note from a newlywed couple arrived yesterday. It named the gift and described happy plans for using it. It even thanked us for being at the wedding. I marveled that they remembered and took time to mention it.

Another note last month expressed appreciation for the message accompanying the gift, mentioning our wishes for an enduring connection.

At the time of gifting, I'm reminded of the wise man's words: "Like apples of gold set in silver filigree is a word spoken in season" (Prov. 25:11, NEB).

Some people find putting pen to paper an ordeal. I don't keep record of who did and didn't send notes. I know gift cards can get lost. I know some birthday, holiday, and wedding events produce ensuing pain so surprising that coping with the disappointment makes acts of gratitude daunting.

But my heart is warmed by responses bringing significant evidence that from the dutifully performed task emerges a person throwing off self-absorption that accompanies holiday/wedding events. Such messages create a bit of bonding with well-wishers, an ingredient all of us can use.

Edna Maye Loveless

NOVEMBER 28

THANKSLIVING

Give thanks in all circumstances.
1 Thess. 5:18, NIV.

Corrie ten Boom wrote about her experience in a German concentration camp, and she described how the fleas were so awful that she complained bitterly. Her sister, however, told her, "We must thank God for these bugs." Grudgingly Corrie agreed, and they bowed their heads in prayer of thanksgiving for the fleas. Later they learned that the reason the guards did not molest any of the women in their barracks was because of those insects. Corrie became a firm believer of giving thanks in everything!

However, the doubters among us still say, "I just don't see that God would want me to give thanks for everything, even bad things. After all, the verse says give thanks IN everything, not FOR everything."

We squirm and wonder how God expects us to do this.

The apostle says, "Give thanks in all circumstances" (1 Thess. 5:18, NIV).

This probably makes more sense to us. "Give thanks in all circumstances." God isn't necessarily saying that we should thank Him for evil things but that in all situations, no matter how bad they are, we can still find something about which to be thankful. If we get into a mode of daily "thanks-living," we will be able to find something for which to be thankful when times get tough.

The way to be thankful is to talk about thankfulness, praise, and joy. We'd all feel more thankful if we talked more thankfully. Counselors tell us that behavior follows expression. You may not feel the way you want to but if you start talking the way you want to feel, pretty soon you'll feel that way.

God says to pray, ask the Holy Spirit for help, speak to one another about your blessings, and then sing. What a wonderful prescription for thanksgiving!

All you have to do is decide to do it. And that takes conscious effort. You have to decide to look for things for which to be thankful, instead of for things about which to gripe. Then you need to list those items one by one and thank God for each.

BILL TUCKER

HEARING GOD'S VOICE

I'm thanking you, God, from a full heart, I'm writing the book on your wonders.
I'm whistling, laughing, and jumping for joy;
I'm singing your song, High God. Ps. 9:1, Message.

I am so blessed to be editing this devotional book. So grateful to God!

This book is an anthology of many authors' spiritual insights. Planning the content, developing the guidelines, finding the cover art, pushing the authors to meet deadlines, tweaking (sometimes rewriting) their essays—it's all been a challenge, but a positive one. I'm so grateful for the contributions of talent and time by all of the 50 or so *We Shall Be Changed* authors.

But the best and biggest blessing was unexpected. I'm finding God everywhere since I started this book. When I'm walking the dog, cuddling the cat, driving, listening to a song, pruning the garden, watching a secular show on TV—I'm in a mind-set where I see lessons from the Lord.

The miracle is that I hear Him! God is speaking to me in His whisper, His still small voice. And it's my heartfelt prayer that you will hear His voice speaking to you when you're exercising, lying wakeful in bed, waiting for your plane, or doing dishes, but especially while reading this book! He's there, speaking all the time.

"This God says: 'I am God, the one and only. I don't just talk to myself or mumble under my breath. . . . I work out in the open, saying what's right, setting things right. . . . I promise in my own name: Every word out of my mouth does what it says. I never take back what I say" (Isa. 45:18-23, Message).

Thanks be to God for His words to us, whether written, painted in nature, or exhibited in the actions of those around us. Open your eyes and ears—He's got words for you!

CHRISTY K. ROBINSON

November 30

PEPPER

Suppose one of you has a hundred sheep and loses one of them.
Does he not leave the ninety-nine in the open country
and go after the lost sheep until he finds it? Luke 15:4, NIV.

Pepper was a little puppy with curly white hair who came to live with us one Thanksgiving when our kids were young. He was an affectionate little dog, and we quickly fell in love with him.

Pepper just couldn't wait until we would take him for a walk, and if he didn't think we were taking him often enough, he'd figure out a way to go all by himself. This usually involved digging under the fence or sneaking out the door. It's amazing what he would do once he got a taste of freedom.

We live in an area where coyotes often take pets, and large hawks who roost in a tree near our house could easily carry him away. How do you explain to a little dog the dangers of getting lost or winding up as a menu item? When he did escape, our entire family would search for him. Even late at night, we couldn't rest until he was safely home.

Pepper never knew all the trouble he caused us. Whenever we rescued him, my wife would immediately forgive him. Instead of giving him a well-deserved swat, she'd pick him up and hug him and hold him and tell him how much she missed him. Then she'd carry him safely home, clean him up, and feed him a good supper. Pepper loved her.

"Suppose one of you has a hundred sheep and loses one of them. Does he not leave the ninety-nine in the open country and go after the lost sheep until he finds it?" (Luke 15:4, NIV).

I'm so thankful that the Great Shepherd searches for and finds His wayward sheep when we jump the fence, run out of the fold, or idly wander away. He protects and provides, cleans us up, and holds us in His arms—and for no other reason but that He loves us with an everlasting love.

Robert Johnston

POSSESSED WITH JESUS

Submit to God. Resist the devil and he will flee from you.
James 4:7, NKJV.

I was serving as pastor of the Bangkok Mission Hospital. One morning my phone started ringing, and when I answered, an urgent voice said, "We have a patient that's devil-possessed. Please come!"

"I'll be right over, but give me a few minutes to review my Bible and pray." I took another pastor with me to room 418. A glassy-eyed youth with deep scratches on his shoulders and chest screamed, while throwing himself around on the bed. Trying to talk to him, I reached for his hand. "Don't touch me," he yelled.

The other pastor and I prayed. When I said "in the name of Jesus" the young man shouted, "Don't say that name." After talking and praying for two hours, I asked the young man to pray. He started out, "Father, You know how the devil is troubling me." Finally he struggled, sat up, and gasped: "In the name of Jesus, I ask the devil to leave." He fell back exhausted and slept for 24 hours.

Jesus left us with two great promises. First: "In My name they will cast out demons" (Mark 16:17, NKJV). Second: "If you ask anything in My name, I will do it" (John 14:14, NJKV). Jesus reached into the mind of the young man in Thailand, and after a few months he left the area to attend a Christian college.

Our minds control our bodies. Everything we do, good or bad, has its origin in the mind. When Satan gets complete control, he has physical possession. God challenges us to "submit to God. Resist the devil and he will flee from you. Draw near to God and He will draw near to you. Cleanse your hands, you sinners; and purify your hearts, you double-minded" (James 4:7, 8, NKJV). Paul counsels, "Let this mind be in you which was also in Christ Jesus" (Phil. 2:5, NKJV). Speaking of the name of Jesus, the Holy Spirit used Peter to remind us that "there is no other name under heaven given among men by which we must be saved" (Acts 4:12, NKJV).

Devil possession, no! God wants us to be possessed with Jesus. There's power in His name!

WELLESLEY MUIR

OVERSHADOWED BY THE HOLY SPIRIT

The old things passed away; behold, new things have come.
2 Cor. 5:17, NASB.

I thought the Christmas season was the worst time of the year. I hated it, especially the exchange of gifts. About 20 years before my conversion I spent several hundred dollars purchasing gifts for my staff, and the few gifts I received were old bottles around which they had woven simple macramé patterns. That was the last time I sent Christmas cards and gifts.

My attitude and actions didn't change until, after my conversion, I studied theology and discovered this wonderful truth: that the same miracle that the Holy Spirit gave to Mary is also given to everyone in whom Jesus Christ is born anew.

A Christian author once wrote that no one really knows the moment of conversion because of the Holy Spirit's preconversion work of wooing us to our Savior. What we consider to be the date of our new birth is often the cognitive manifestation of something that has been happening for a long time.

In the same way that the Holy Spirit came upon Mary and placed the Christ-seed in her womb, so He now places that holy seed in our hearts. There's a period of gestation described as "wooing"—we begin to think about God, attend church, study the Bible, and practice the instructions from Scripture as to how we should live.

After gestation it is time for the birth. For some, it is easy. For others, it is a painful experience when the enemy attacks even harder than before. Eventually, we are born again. "Therefore if anyone is in Christ, he is a new creature; the old things passed away; behold, new things have come" (2 Cor. 5:17, NASB). We walk and talk differently; we dress and eat with a new understanding; we are new creatures in Christ.

I love what old Simeon said at Jesus' dedication: "My eyes have seen Your salvation, which You have prepared in the presence of all peoples, a light of revelation to the Gentiles, and the glory of Your people Israel" (Luke 2:30-32, NASB).

These are the gifts that God gives to us: a more abundant life here on earth, eternal life, and revelation of His glorious character. Once I understood that, Christmas became a delight and a time to share those gifts with everyone I know!

HYVETH B. WILLIAMS

ONE IN SPIRIT

If you have any encouragement from being united with Christ,
if any comfort from his love . . . then make my joy complete by being like-minded,
having the same love, being one in spirit and purpose.
Phil. 2:1, 2, NIV.

Our first child, Lucky, was born in early December, so his first Christmas was not well remembered by him or his mother as we adjusted to all the changes going on in our home and new family.

The following year we moved to a new city and celebrated as a family there. We visited all the traditional holiday events like Zoo Lights and the mall, where, traditionally, no child escapes without their terror-stricken portrait on Santa's lap!

But the most memorable moment occurred one chilly night, downtown. Every year, the Sunday after Thanksgiving, the residents of our small town gather in the town square to await the arrival of Santa Claus and the lighting of the freshly-cut 40-foot Christmas tree. Apparently this has been a tradition for the past 50 years or so, but it was unlike anything I had ever participated in. People handed out candles for everyone to light, and we huddled together, sipping hot cocoa and trying to keep warm.

Lucky was looking around, and imagine his surprise when Santa Claus arrived amid the flashing lights and sirens of the fire trucks. It became very quiet as Santa ushered in the holiday season by lighting the Christmas tree. Someone in the crowd began to sing "Silent Night," and the song gathered voices and volume as all joined in a variety of Christmas-themed songs. For the first time I experienced how a community could band together to enjoy the simplest of pleasures, forget about differing opinions, thoughts, and ideals, and celebrate like the family that God created us to be.

"If you have any encouragement from being united with Christ, if any comfort from his love, if any fellowship with the Spirit, if any tenderness and compassion, then make my joy complete by being like-minded, having the same love, being one in spirit and purpose" (Phil. 2:1, 2, NIV).

ROBIN HENNESSY MCGHEE

DECEMBER 4

THE HANGING OF THE GREENS

The rich woods of Lebanon will be delivered—all that cypress and oak and pine—to give a splendid elegance to my Sanctuary, as I make my footstool glorious.
Isa. 60:13, Message.

I've been employed as a keyboardist and choir director for other denominations, and they have a wonderful tradition: the hanging of the greens. On the first Sunday of Advent, during the worship service, they bring fresh fir and pine boughs and handmade Christmas ornaments (some antique), and they carry in a fragrant tree for the chancel. The sanctuary decoration is not left to a committee or a person with a design degree.

As they move through the liturgy of praise to God, the choir members, children, couples, singles, and elderly all participate in beautifying God's house and decorating the tree. Carols are sung, candles are lit, scriptures are read, children imperfectly clang the handbells, and Communion is joyfully shared and celebrated. Offerings of greens and ornaments, as well as tithes and gifts of money, are presented to the Lord. In other words, the people fellowship and worship together with their eyes on God.

I hope that you will be blessed by the verses my Christian friends quote and sing in their Hanging of the Greens ceremony:

"But I am like a green olive tree in the house of God: I trust in the mercy of God for ever and ever. I will praise thee for ever, because thou hast done it: and I will wait on thy name; for it is good before thy saints" (Ps. 52:8, 9, KJV).

"I am like a green pine tree; your fruitfulness comes from me" (Hosea 14:8, NIV).

"A green Shoot will sprout from Jesse's stump, from his roots a budding Branch" (Isa. 11:1, Message).

"All your people will live right and well, in permanent possession of the land. They're the green shoot that I planted, planted with my own hands to display my glory" (Isa. 60:21, Message).

CHRISTY K. ROBINSON

JOY IN LITTLE THINGS

From the lips of children and infants you have ordained praise.
Ps. 8:2, NIV.

Since the birth of our daughter, Emmeline, my husband and I have enjoyed observing the eagerness and awe with which she meets each new experience. She loves people and smiles at everyone she meets. Every sensation is exciting—she revels in the prickly feel of grass under her feet, cool water running over her hands, the warm sun on her back, the sweet taste of ripe bananas, the softness of a favorite blanket. She laughs with delight at the sound of music or with relief when she sees the familiar face of Mommy or Daddy upon waking. If she tips over, she simply pushes herself upright again. She goes to sleep drowsy with content, and she always wakes up happy.

We've had fun speculating about what the world would be like if grown-ups behaved like babies. We've giggled ourselves silly imagining adults in a restaurant whining the minute they feel hungry (escalating in volume until the food arrives), throwing a fit if the food is cold, flailing their arms about wildly and clanking silverware on the table, smearing food all over their faces, hair, clothing—you get the idea.

However, there might be some advantages to adults adopting some babylike behavior. For instance, what would the world be like if we smiled at every person we saw? What if we faced each new challenge with eagerness and perseverance? What if we expressed delight at every meal or were filled with wonder at every sunset? What if we laughed with pleasure every time we saw the face of someone we love? What if we were to notice and take joy in every gift with which God has blessed us? What if we allowed ourselves to experience that kind of happiness, wouldn't it overflow into how we lived?

We have a source of joy that Emmeline hasn't yet discovered—the unconditional love and sacrifice of our Savior, Jesus Christ. So be a baby today—smile at everyone you see. Be filled with wonder and delight at the beauty and deliciousness of life. Laugh out loud and love deeply. Allow yourself to be a wellspring of joy, and share it liberally with all the thirsty people around you.

Lorelei Herman Cress

CHRISTMAS CAN CHANGE YOUR LIFE

You are to give him the name Jesus,
because he will save his people from their sins.
Matt. 1:21, NIV.

Do you remember when you were a child and the Advent season, between Thanksgiving and Christmas, seemed like an eternity? Time stood still while you waited for Christmas to arrive. But to an adult, it seems as if Christmas arrives before you finish Thanksgiving dinner!

Something happens as you age. Life seems to speed up, and you're aware that there's no going back to the "good old days." Growing up changes your life forever. In the same way Christmas can change your life forever if you meet the Christ of Christmas.

The Christmas story begins by telling us why Jesus came. An angel instructed Joseph: "You are to give him the name Jesus, because he will save his people from their sins" (Matt. 1:21, NIV).

Jesus' name, Yeshua/Joshua, means "God saves." But a name wasn't a handle or just a proper noun; a name was a prophecy, a memorial, a verb. Everywhere Jesus went, when someone called Him by name, they were saying quite literally in their Aramaic and Hebrew languages, "God saves."

For centuries Jewish priests offered a lamb sacrifice every morning and evening as a symbol of the coming Savior who would take the punishment of sin and separation from God and die in the place of every sinner who had ever lived.

This is what Christmas is really about. It is about a journey beginning in a cradle, continuing in His human life and ministry, and ending in a torturous death. It is about the Shepherd becoming the Lamb-Sacrifice to save the sheep. It is about the innocent taking the penalty of the guilty. And it's about rising victorious from the grave, having completed the work of our salvation, a work that we could never accomplish.

Your life can be changed forever. Have you accepted that greatest of all Christmas gifts? Salvation is full, free, and wrapped in the glorious package of God's love.

BILL TUCKER

EVERY DAY ANEW

They're created new every morning.
How great your faithfulness!
Lam. 3:23, Message.

Three-year-old Annika gleefully skipped down the aisle, eyes darting from one glittering ornament to the next as she carefully selected her favorites: a sparkly glass slipper here, a beaded star there. How beautiful that red and pink heart would look on her Christmas tree!

Once we arrived home, Annika hovered over me as I hung the strings of twinkling lights and then draped the tree with garlands of silvery beads. Finally came the long-anticipated moment to hang the beautiful baubles on the branches. She carefully hung each shiny doodad, some high, some low, all around the tree.

When the tree was adorned with every trinket and ribbon in sight, Annika stood back to admire our handiwork. It didn't matter to her that it was an artificial tree, only six feet high. In her eyes it was a towering sequoia. Daddy, Grandma, Grandpa, aunts, uncles, friends, and neighbors alike were all summoned to marvel at the tree's splendor.

The very next day Annika stripped the tree bare and trimmed it all over again. Every subsequent day was another opportunity to rearrange the tree's finery. Each time she tackled this task with fervor, displaying no less enthusiasm than the very first time. Annika faithfully and joyfully repeated this ritual until mid-January when everything was wrapped and put away for next Christmas. As excited as Annika was about re-creating our Christmas tree that year, the next December she decorated it only a few times.

God, however, never tires of showering us with His love and mercy. "God's loyal love couldn't have run out, his merciful love couldn't have dried up. They're created new every morning. How great your faithfulness!" (Lam. 3:22, 23, Message).

This Christmas season, as you enjoy the festive decorations that make your community and home sparkle, remember God's everlasting love and mercy, which He delights to adorn us with every day.

Laura West Kong

DECEMBER 8

BLESSED ARE THE PEACEMAKERS

Glory to God in highest heaven,
and peace on earth to those with whom God is pleased.
Luke 2:14, NLT.

On Christmas of 1914 the British and the French forces had been in a fierce battle with the kaiser's troops on the infamous Flanders fields. The two armies had dug themselves into cold, muddy trenches six to eight feet deep, facing one another across a no-man's-land as close as 60 yards.

According to those who were there, some German soldiers set up a small Christmas tree outside of their trench and lit it with candles. Then they began singing carols, and though their language was unfamiliar to their enemies, the tunes were not. After a while, the French and British responded with carols of their own. From the German side a signboard went up that said in English, "You no fight, we no fight." Signs popped up on both sides.

The result was a spontaneous truce. Soldiers left their trenches, and met in the middle and shook hands. The first thing they did was to bury the dead. But then they began to exchange gifts. Just things they had on hand, like chocolates, cakes, postcards, newspapers, and tobacco.

According to the official war diary of the 133rd Saxon Regiment, the Brits and the Germans kicked about a soccer ball supplied by a Scot. "This developed into a regulation football match with caps casually laid out as goals. . . . The game ended 3-2 for the Germans."

It didn't last forever. In fact, some of the generals didn't like it at all and commanded their troops to resume hostilities under penalty of court-martial. By New Year's Day bullets were flying.

There is a maxim that peace is harder to wage than war. Although the Christmas Truce of 1914 may seem like a distant myth, it remains a moving demonstration of the absurdity of war: when it comes right down to it, the common people rarely have much to fight about. I think it is wonderful that at least once in history Christmas gave the common people the courage to say, let's have peace on earth, good will toward men—if only for a few days.

LOREN SEIBOLD

WITNESS

Let us now go even unto Bethlehem, and see this thing which is come to pass, which the Lord hath made known unto us.
Luke 2:15.

I once lived in a neighborhood in which, in December's early darkness, candles appeared in one window on eight-branched candlesticks. The silent figures of children moved along the row of tapers inside their picture window. From the street, although I could not hear, I saw the flames shimmering in the children's eyes, and I sensed something of what was in their hearts.

It was Hanukkah, and they were remembering. Remembering a miracle of long ago. Remembering after all these millennia who they were and what they stood for. Remembering a promise they longed to see fulfilled.

On December 25 their windows were dark. Mine and others filled with light. We enjoyed music, embers in the fireplace, and a pine tree exuding a pungent fragrance.

It was Christmas, and we reread the gospel story. Remembering a miracle of long ago. Remembering after all these millennia who we were and what we stood for. Remembering a promise we longed to see fulfilled in a Second Coming. Christmas and its trappings, the feast and its trimmings are neither a matter of conscience nor commandment, although they make a statement of faith to strangers looking on.

So it was with Daniel. No commandment caused him to pray three times a day where everyone could see. But those who knew Daniel and those who passed by came to count on his witness in the window.

In today's world we also need to give witness to the One who is the source of our identity and the foundation of our faith. All of us know what a Christmas without Christ looks like: an ad theme to stimulate the market or showy merchandise in department stores. It ends up being a holiday without a soul. Yet, I believe, Christmas is a day in many corners of the world when the gospel story can be told and when it may be really listened to. Many would come—as I did in my neighborhood on the December evenings of Hanukkah—to look in the window and consider our witness.

KIT WATTS

HANUKKAH DEDICATION

At that time the Feast of Dedication took place at Jerusalem.
It was winter, and Jesus was walking in the temple in the portico of Solomon.
John 10:22, 23, NASB.

There is a festival of lights that pierces the long nights of winter, and it's been celebrated for more than 2,000 years. The festival recalls the 168-165 B.C. Maccabees' revolt against the assimilation of Hellenistic Jews and oppression by the Syrian Greeks who had desecrated the Jerusalem Temple. When the Maccabean Jews reclaimed the Temple, there was only one day's measure of consecrated oil to burn in the large menorah. Because of their prayer and sincere intention to cleanse God's sanctuary, He kept the lamp burning for eight days, until more olive oil could be obtained and ritually purified.

The Hebrew word Hanukkah means "dedication." Jews and some Christians believe that this dedication and purification of the Temple was a fulfillment of Daniel's prophecy of the cleansing of the sanctuary. Today's Hanukkah customs include gift giving and family celebrations. Many holiday foods are fried to commemorate the miracle of the oil.

Jesus celebrated Hanukkah! In John 10 it says that Jesus was at the Temple during the festival of dedication—Hanukkah (verses 22 and 23, NASB). Jesus used this Hanukkah celebration to compare the miracle of extending the life of consecrated oil in a lamp to the heart consecrated to Him. God is all-powerful to grant eternal life or measureless oil. He's more interested in your heart than He is in ceremonies or the accoutrements of worship.

"The Jews then gathered around Him, and were saying to Him, 'How long will You keep us in suspense? If You are the Christ, tell us plainly.' Jesus answered them, 'I told you, and you do not believe; the works that I do in My Father's name, these testify of Me. But you do not believe because you are not of My sheep. My sheep hear My voice, and I know them, and they follow Me; and I give eternal life to them, and they will never perish; and no one will snatch them out of My hand. My Father, who has given them to Me, is greater than all; and no one is able to snatch them out of the Father's hand. I and the Father are one' " (John 10:24-30, NASB).

Eternal life, which no one can snatch from Jesus' nail-scarred hand, is extended to you by God's hand right now, just as you are. Accept your gift!

CHRISTY K. ROBINSON

JESUS IS FOR ALL SEASONS

And he took the children in his arms,
put his hands on them and blessed them.
Mark 10:16, NIV.

Merchants hope the Christmas season will be a prosperous one. Families hope it will be a happy one. All of us hope the busyness of the season will not exhaust us. When you get swept up in the buying of gifts, the sending of cards, the attending of parties and programs, it's easy to forget the real meaning of Christmas. I like the slogan "Jesus Is the Reason for the Season." Jesus is the Man of all seasons. He is the One who brings meaning to every season of our lives, every day of the year.

Have you wondered why Jesus came to earth as a baby? Of His 33 years of life, only three and a half were devoted to public ministry. For 30 of those years He lived no differently from you or me. He began as a dependent baby. He learned to eat, crawl, sit up, walk, and talk. He grew and developed. He weathered the teenage years and entered adulthood. Even at maturity He stayed in His hometown and worked at a daily job. The Son of God did this to give dignity and honor to every stage of life and to show us that He is a Man for all seasons.

The season of babyhood and childhood is important to God. Lots of adults don't seem to think so. The disciples didn't. When parents brought their infants and children to Jesus, the disciples rebuked them. "When Jesus saw this, he was indignant. He said to them, 'Let the little children come to me, and do not hinder them, for the kingdom of God belongs to such as these.' . . . And he took the children in his arms, put his hands on them and blessed them" (Mark 10:14-16, NIV). Jesus was approachable, loving, and accepting.

What kind of God do the children around you see? A forbidding, stern, no-nonsense, unsmiling God? A God who is always saying, "Shhh. Be quiet!" A God who says, "Wait until you're older; you're not ready; you don't know enough to be part of My family"?

Let the children around you see a God who is loving, caring, and interested in their activities. One who hugs them and says, "Come join Me; be part of My family."

You, a member of the body of Christ, can make God special to children this Christmas and in every season!

Bill Tucker

CHARIOTS OF FIRE

So we fix our eyes not on what is seen, but on what is unseen.
For what is seen is temporary, but what is unseen is eternal.
2 Cor. 4:18, NIV.

Occasionally I am surprised by the unexpected twist in a patient's story. I was visiting a woman on the cardiac unit who told me about what had brought her into the hospital on this occasion. As we concluded, she told me of a close call just before Christmas a couple of years ago that caused her to be rushed to the local hospital.

When the initial treatment was concluded, she called her daughter to come and pick her up. A nurse wheeled her to the lobby to wait, and while she briefly scanned a magazine, the chaplain came up to her to say goodbye. It was a happy moment, and the chaplain offered to say a prayer of thanks to God for her excellent recovery from the infection that had made her so sick.

As the chaplain was praying, this woman had a serious heart attack and slumped forward in her wheelchair. She was immediately rushed to the emergency room. All turned out well in the long run, but I commented on how terrible that whole episode must have been for her. I didn't expect her response. "No," she said, "that was the best thing that could have happened. In a few minutes my daughter would have picked me up and we would have been out on the freeway when this happened. I would never have been able to get back to the hospital in time."

We are people of the moment, and we often respond to what we can see and hear. But there are other realities that surround us as illustrated in this verse: "And Elisha prayed, 'O Lord, open his eyes so he may see.' Then the Lord opened the servant's eyes, and he looked and saw the hills full of horses and chariots of fire all around Elisha" (2 Kings 6:17, NIV).

Living life with our mind open to the work of God in our lives is one of the most precious gifts that He can bestow upon us. This is most clearly seen in stories like this that cause us to wonder where the work of His hand will be manifested next.

K. LANCE TYLER

I BRING YOU . . .

I bring you good news of great joy that will be for all the people.
Today in the town of David a Savior has been born to you; he is Christ the Lord.
Luke 2:10, 11, NIV.

The story of the shepherds is my favorite of all the Christmas narratives. When the angel appears to the shepherds, he says to them, "I bring you good news of great joy that will be for all the people. Today in the town of David a Savior has been born to you; he is Christ the Lord" (Luke 2:10, 11, NIV).

I especially like the fact that it starts out with the words "I bring you." They didn't have to go searching for anything. The angel brought it to them. We human beings are always searching for what will make us happy. When we're young, we think toys or candy will make us happy; later, we seek romance, money, authority, or health. And we spend an inordinate amount of time searching for what we think we need. There's a country pop song that goes like this: "Looking for love in all the wrong places. Looking for love in too many faces. Searching their eyes, looking for traces of what I'm dreaming of." Our general approach to finding happiness is to look for it. Search for it. Earn it, somehow. If you aren't happy, it is because you didn't persevere hard or long enough in the search.

What's so wonderful about this story, though, is that the angel brings them the news that gives them joy. Right where they were, into the life they had. The angel simply came and offered it to them.

I doubt very much that their short-term situation changed much. They didn't get rich after they heard this news. Shepherds were very low status—people thought of them as bums—and their status didn't improve. Poor and cold and hungry and bad reputation before; poor and cold and hungry and bad reputation afterward. But this news was something bigger than one would identify in a list of immediate needs. This was a gift that altered the very foundation of their lives—their needs and desires and joys.

God so loved the world that He gave. It was on God's initiative that this happened, not ours. While we were yet sinners, before we knew our need of Him, God brought us a gift.

LOREN SEIBOLD

GOD-WITH-US. ALWAYS!

The Word became a human being and lived here with us.
John 1:14, CEV.

Christmas is the celebration of God-With-Us. In ancient religious systems the gods were localized to certain places or their spirits were confined to a territory or container such as a wooden idol or a stone shrine. When people traveled or emigrated, they worshipped specific gods in specific places or they took their idols with them (Gen. 31). The gods were capricious, vindictive, killed each other in power struggles, cheated on their spouses, and accepted human sacrifices—even infants.

So when, on the exodus from Egypt, the God of hosts traveled with the Israelites, that was remarkable! A first! Here was a God who was personal, involved, protective, nourishing, healing, and compassionate; who fought battles and resolved conflict; who designed and implemented holidays, festivals and rest days for the former slaves; and who cared so much for their comfort that He shaded them from the desert sun by day and warmed and lit the night for them. Unlike the gods who wreaked vengeance upon any whim, this God demonstrated that He was a forgiving God. He promised a present and future of blessings if they remained in His tender care.

Generations later, when the children had rebelled and forgotten, God repeated His plan for reconciliation. To His people in war and exile of their own making, and subject to the "gods" of their exile, He spoke: "Therefore the Lord Himself will give you a sign: Behold, the virgin shall conceive and bear a Son, and shall call His name Immanuel [God-With-Us]" (Isa. 7:14, NKJV).

Wherever God's people were or are, He is God-With-Us. "I am with you always, even unto the end of the world" (Matt. 28:20, KJV). We can't leave Him behind. He won't abandon us when our closest companions do. And He's not done with us in this short life span and at the end of this old world. He promises everlasting life to His children, and His presence continues forever!

"Now the dwelling of God is with men, and he will live with them. They will be his people, and God himself will be with them and be their God" (Rev. 21:3, NIV).

CHRISTY K. ROBINSON

THE BEST GIFTS

Come to me,
all you who are weary and burdened, and I will give you rest.
Matt. 11:28, NIV.

I can still remember with wonder a very early, and maybe my first, Christmas. In Australia, where I grew up, Christmas comes at the hottest time of the year. Sometime in the night I became aware of something at the end of my bed. Crawling down there, I felt a pillowcase that contained a few indiscernible objects. Several times during the night I crept on hands and knees to investigate and try to guess what was in the pillowcase. It was dark—black dark—in my room. We did not have electricity at that time, so there was no way to use more senses than just feeling the objects one by one.

At daybreak I couldn't wait to make another trip to the end of my bed. Now I could see! There were three objects in the bag. The one that interested me was a box with the name Builda-Brix on the side. (My parents helped me to decipher that as I could not yet read.) I think I had more enjoyment out of that box in building houses and skyscrapers than any gift I have ever received since that time. There were paper windows to put in openings and thin metal strips that could support a row of bricks to build an arch. It was a most wonderful gift.

Many years later, when life was hard and darkness seemed to be everywhere, I received another gift. Growing up in the 1960s and 1970s was dominated by fears of "the bomb" and the possibility of being conscripted to go to Vietnam. I did what I could but was unable to determine what the package we call "life" contained.

It was at my seemingly darkest moment that a light began to shine in my life. I heard a voice calling, "Come to me, all you who are weary and burdened, and I will give you rest. . . . For I am gentle and humble in heart, and you will find rest for your souls" (Matt. 11:28, 29, NIV).

I cannot forget the pure joy of opening the New Testament and reading for the first time the story of Jesus, who came and gave everything for me. I treasure that gift.

K. LANCE TYLER

STUCK

Are not all angels ministering spirits
sent to serve those who will inherit salvation?
Heb. 1:14, NIV.

A vanful of teenagers and I had just come back from taking clothes, gifts, and the gospel to a small village in the Sonoran desert in Mexico. It was Christmas time and the Cajon Pass in southern California was full of snow.

As we were making our way through the highest point, I had to pull over to rest a bit. I had been driving for three hours and it was late, yet I was determined to take the kids home on time just as I had promised their parents. As the van came to a stop, I felt the tires settle in the mud and snow on the shoulder. I thought, *Oh no, I hope this is not what I think it is.* But it was. I got out to inspect the tires, and they were half buried.

We rested for about an hour, and then I noticed how other drivers who had the same idea about rest were now fighting unsuccessfully to get out of the mud and back to the road. I thought we had no chance to get out of that mess, but I began to pray earnestly, asking God for a miracle to get us back on our way home.

I put the van in gear and very slowly applied some gas. I held it there while praying, "Lord, You do the rest. You know what we need, and only You can give it to us."

I could feel the wheels grabbing solid ground through all that sleet, and slowly but surely we came right out of it and onto the pavement. I couldn't help visualizing God's angels as they ministered to us and helped us to safety.

Our God cares for us always, even when we get stuck, and He has commissioned His angels to help us and look after us. "Are not all angels ministering spirits sent to serve those who will inherit salvation?" (Heb. 1:14, NIV).

Praise God that He never runs out of ways to care for His chosen!

FRED HERNANDEZ

THE GIFTIE

The Lord Jesus himself said: "It is more blessed to give than to receive."
Acts 20:35, NIV.

In the poem "Ode to a Louse," Robert Burns wrote, "O wad some Power the giftie gie us / to see oursels as ithers see us!"

When I was a child, the excitement of Christmas Day events was matchless. It really did not matter what gift was given to me, it was something I looked forward to with eager anticipation. Beforehand, I spent hours poring over Christmas catalogs, dreaming of and listing what I wanted. I really didn't notice or care what anyone else received for Christmas gifts.

There was a problem with this philosophy: my parents insisted that I shop for my sister, as well. For years I was concerned only about what was under the tree for me, until one Christmas, my parents invited some missionary friends over who were home for the holiday season. I don't remember what country they were from—they were just people with nothing to give to me for Christmas. I had never been with someone before who couldn't give me a gift. Of course, I didn't have anything for them because all I'd had to do was buy something for my sister.

My parents, being wiser than Santa Claus, had done some extra shopping that season. They always kept a few extra gifts for last-minute visitors. Even though the gifts were inexpensive, the guests started crying before opening the packages. They were hugging and kissing me like I had given them a million dollars because the card had my name written on it. Later I found out these people had never before received Christmas gifts. I didn't deserve any praise for giving a gift I didn't buy, but I learned a valuable lesson. (I also learned the blessing of giving in someone else's name, but that's another devotional thought!)

"The Lord Jesus himself said: 'It is more blessed to give than to receive'" (Acts 20:35, NIV). It is now my goal to teach this to my young sons. I appreciate my parents for covering for me until I learned this lesson.

I am glad that Jesus covers me until I fully understand, "Now we see but a poor reflection as in a mirror; then we shall see face to face. Now I know in part; then I shall know fully, even as I am fully known" (1 Cor. 13:12, NIV).

BOB MCGHEE

CHRISTMAS DINING WITH A NEW ACCENT

Go home and prepare a feast, holiday food and drink;
and share it with those who don't have anything: This day is holy to God.
Don't feel bad. The joy of God is your strength!
Neh. 8:10, Message.

When Shirley called five months after her husband's tragic death in a mountain climbing fall, I knew what it was about. With her two teenagers, she was staging a dinner on December 18. Only when we arrived did I discover how extensive her "Christmas" celebration would be. Fifteen guests joined her at a table set with the family's finest china and crystal, sparkling in the candlelight.

"Today is Christmas for me," Shirley said simply. Aware that most of her friends would be deep into seasonal family gatherings the next week, Shirley had collected her friends on this day for a traditional feast. Many years later I still recall the whipped sweet potatoes in beautifully crafted orange rind shells, just one evidence of Shirley's painstaking preparation.

Shirley asked someone to read the Nativity story from her husband's Bible, a ritual he had created during their too-short time together. If she stifled a sob at the family scene observed by the shepherds—"They went with all speed and found their way to Mary and Joseph; and the baby was lying in the manger" (Luke 2:16, NEB)—no one noticed. We were admiring her tree, lit with white bulbs.

I wish I could tell Shirley, now gone to her own rest, what a powerful event that occasion provided for me. I had known her since our dating days in college. I had admired her homemaking skills. I had sat with her when tears of bereavement overcame her. But this was one of her finest moments. She put aside her grief and her expectations of what she deserved, and she found room in the inn for her friends.

Because of that dinner at Shirley's home, I seek to include one or more single, bereaved, or lonely person on my guest list when I'm planning an event or family celebration. My special guests are always grateful to be remembered during this season and throughout the year.

EDNA MAYE LOVELESS

WHERE IS HE?

A Star shall come out of Jacob; a Scepter shall rise out of Israel.
Num. 24:17, NKJV.

Imagine the stir it would create if three or four Middle Eastern ambassadors arrived in Washington, D.C., inquiring, "Where is the baby born to be president of the United States?" Wise Men came to Jerusalem 2,000 years ago inquiring, Where is He that is born king of the Jews?

The people of Israel had been scattered to many countries, taking their beliefs with them. Perhaps these scholars had read the prophecy of Balaam in Numbers 24:17: "A Star shall come out of Jacob; a Scepter shall rise out of Israel" (NKJV).

When they arrived in Jerusalem, they didn't meet other seekers. Nobody else was looking for Jesus! Here was a city full of religious teachers and priests, in the national center for worship. The sacred writings were here. Yet the religious leaders were not seeking a Savior.

Not much has changed in 2,000 years. We're all so busy we don't have time to seek out Jesus. Even religious leaders get so busy doing "the Lord's work" that they forget the Lord. Other times it is our pleasures that keep us from seeking Him. The end result is the same. Jesus is left out of our lives.

Maybe you long for something better and want fulfillment and meaning for your life, but you're not quite sure how to find it. Jesus humbled Himself to make it easier for seekers to find Him. He came as one of us to make it possible for us to get close to Him, and He to us. I doubt if the wise men understood much of this when they came looking for Jesus. But they said something amazing: "We have come to worship Him."

When you find Jesus, you fall on your knees in worship and adoration at the marvelous gift of heaven. When you know Jesus as your Savior, you can't help loving Him and worshipping Him. Knowing that God gave everything makes you want to give back to Him.

Wise men still seek Him, and wise men still give their hearts and their gifts of love to Him. Are you a seeker this Christmas season? If you are, you will find Him when you look for Him with all your heart and with all your soul. And your life will be changed forever.

BILL TUCKER

THE BEST PAYBACK

Christ encourages you, and his love comforts you. God's Spirit unites you, and you are concerned for others.
Phil. 2:1, CEV.

Only a week before Christmas, Richard Osborn, president of Pacific Union College, stood in a long line at Costco. He noticed an old man ahead of him make a purchase totaling $9.52. *This is amazing,* Osborn thought. Seldom does a person leave Costco with less than $100 worth of merchandise.

The poor old man fumbled in confusion because he didn't have cash, he'd failed to bring his checkbook, and because Costco accepts only American Express, his credit card didn't work. Impatient customers waiting in line watched in silence.

Finally, with no sign of annoyance, the cashier reached in his own pocket, pulled out his billfold, and gave the man a $10 bill. The man handed the $10 back and received 48 cents in change. The cashier smiled, "The next time you're in, just pay me back."

The woman just ahead of Osborn looked at the cashier. "That was really nice," she said. The cashier simply shrugged his shoulders and started ringing up her purchases—she had a lot more than the old man who'd been ahead of her.

Reaching the checkout, Osborn said, "You've given the old man a wonderful gift. Will you ever see him again?"

The clerk responded, "It's just money, and the sooner we realize that, the better off we'll all be."

Osborn paid for his purchases and walked out of the huge store with new hope in his heart. There are still people in the world who show the spirit of Jesus. This is what the Christmas season is all about. Remember the words of the Lord Jesus: "It is more blessed to give than to receive" (Acts 20:35, NKJV).

The best payback is the joy of helping others.

WELLESLEY MUIR

AN OLD-FASHIONED CHRISTMAS

Giving, not getting, is the way.
Generosity begets generosity. Stinginess impoverishes.
Mark 4:24, 25, Message.

Throughout December my parents loved to prepare for Christmas. We baked and decorated cookies to give to the neighbors, held a Christmas recital for Mom's piano students, and decorated the house differently each year. One year we thought we'd do the *Little House on the Prairie* sort of decor. We strung popcorn for garlands on the Christmas tree, and we baked gingerbread men and other frosted cookies, pierced their heads, and threaded yarn through them to make dangling ornaments. (Tragically, many cookies broke as we pierced them, and we were forced to eat our mistakes.) When we finally had enough cookies and popcorn to decorate our tree, we went to bed.

The next morning, I went to the living room to admire our work. But wait! What happened to all the cookies and popcorn? Gypsy, our 25-pound miniature poodle, lay behind the tree, looking guilty as sin, with probably two pounds of Christmas treats in her tummy. She'd stood on her hind legs and walked around the tree, eating everything up to 36 inches from the floor. The glass and paper ornaments remained pristine.

Gypsy didn't know the Genesis story about not eating from the tree in the center of the garden or the one about David eating the sacred bread in the tabernacle. She was smart, but she was just a dog with a sweet tooth. "Stolen bread tastes sweet, but soon your mouth is full of gravel" (Prov. 20:17, Message). "Valuables are safe in a wise person's home; fools put it all out for yard sales" (Prov. 21:20, Message).

We should have known that edible decorations would be too tempting for a dog! We weren't angry with our beloved pet. Gypsy had received her Christmas gifts early. And we've had a warm fuzzy family legend since the late 1960s.

Whatever we gave our dog in treats, toys, vet bills, and other expenses, we received back from her in rich measure. That applies to people, as well. Let's invest our tender care, our gentle touch, our careful respect in people. It's the best gift we can give. Material goods pale in comparison to pleasant relationships. We'll all be blessed beyond measure.

CHRISTY K. ROBINSON

HOME FOR CHRISTMAS

Even so, come, Lord Jesus!
Rev. 22:20, NKJV.

The song "I'll Be Home for Christmas" had a special meaning for vocalist Bob Edwards and me on December 22, 1958. As members of the King's Heralds Quartet, we had just finished a full month's journey singing in Spanish for La Voz de la Esperanza (the Spanish Voice of Prophecy). After thrilling meetings in Puerto Rico, Dominican Republic, Haiti, and Jamaica, the tour concluded with a big youth congress in Havana, Cuba. This was B.C. (before Castro!). The big crowds of people were warm and friendly, responding to our songs in every place, but we were homesick and lonesome for our dear wives, Bob's Irene and my Harriet. And in each home there were four children waiting, anxious for us to get home and play with them.

Volkswagen "Bugs" were all the rage then. I had been lucky to buy a low-mileage one from a minister friend to drive home. I was so grateful that Bob agreed to go with me and take turns driving. All the others in our group flew home to California. Starting at Pensacola, Florida, we drove straight through, stopping every 300 miles for gas and food. I would drive while Bob curled up in the back seat to sleep, and vice versa. It was a long 2,800 miles in 54 hours. Our families had no idea we would do this to get home by Christmas.

The song says, "I'll be home for Christmas, if only in my dreams." This was no dream. Our guardian angels were doing their jobs, and we made it home by 8:30 p.m. Christmas Eve. What a joyful surprise when we each walked through the door of our respective home just in time for the opening of Christmas presents!

We are all on a temporary itinerary in our journey for the Lord. For some of us it gets tiresome and lonely. But we look forward with keen anticipation to that soon homecoming, which will be much better than Christmas, when Jesus comes to this earth a second time. We will be with Jesus and our loving family of God. We can open our gifts of salvation and eternal life!

"He [Jesus] who testifies to these things says, 'Surely I am coming quickly.' Amen. Even so, come, Lord Jesus!" (Rev. 22:20, NKJV).

WAYNE HOOPER

WAITING FOR THE CHRIST CHILD

Unto you is born this day in the city of David a Saviour, which is Christ the Lord.
Luke 2:11.

As I awaited the birth of my first child one Christmas, I wondered what it must have been like for Mary as she awaited the birth of Jesus. She was extremely young, and she didn't have the advantages of childbirth classes, regular checkups, and a nearby hospital with state-of-the-art medical care. She couldn't prepare herself for what was coming by reading *What to Expect When You're Expecting or The Girlfriends' Guide to Pregnancy.* Her only source of information was the women of her family who had given birth before, and when the time came for her delivery, she didn't even have them at her side.

When Mary and Joseph made the arduous journey to Bethlehem, she was already heavy with child. The going must have been slow with frequent stops to rest. Perhaps she comforted herself by dreaming of what this Child would be like and wondering how He would live up to the name she and Joseph had been told to give Him: Yeshua, Savior.

When they finally reached overcrowded Bethlehem and found no place but a stable to stay, she was probably just grateful to have shelter and some privacy. And with a blanket and some hay, Joseph could make a reasonably comfortable bed for her.

When the first labor pains came, she must have felt frightened and alone. Perhaps Joseph fetched a local midwife to comfort and assist her in the delivery. As labor progressed, the assurance of the angel's message must have seemed like a lifetime ago, buried in pain. But when the baby was finally born, imagine her joy and wonder as she looked down at the little miracle—the salvation of the world—lying in her arms!

Throughout the advent season, we can relive Mary's anticipation and excitement as we celebrate the birth of the Christ child. In the bustle of the holiday season, set aside quiet time to experience her wonder and joy at the miracle of Emmanuel, God-With-Us. And on Christmas, hear the song of the angels and rejoice! The waiting is over—our Savior, Jesus Christ is born!

LORELEI HERMAN CRESS

UNTO US IS GIVEN

To us a child is born, to us a son is given.
Isa. 9:6, NIV.

I wanted to be a married mother of children. I planned early to be a piano teacher, so that I could be a work-at-home mom. I saved my journals, photos, and favorite toys as a heritage for my children. I worked with my mother on our family genealogy.

The hundreds of children I taught for 15 years, both one-on-one and in classes, are my kids, minus the sleepless nights and diaper duty. It's true that I'm very proud of the lasting effect I've had on their lives and of their progress as adults and musicians. I still get invited to their weddings and grand occasions. They send Christmas letters and pictures of their babies. Through a Christian agency, I sponsor young girls in Indonesia and Uganda. But face it, at the end of the day, students and sponsored children are not my children.

But just as Jesus came to be my Savior and my Brother, and introduce me to our Father, He is Emmanuel, God-With-Us. He gives me membership by birth and by adoption into the family of God. His incarnation means that He is also my Son, my Child, and my heritage. I can share in the promise He gave us in Scripture, that "to us a child is born, to us a son is given, and the government will be on his shoulders. And he will be called Wonderful Counselor, Mighty God, Everlasting Father, Prince of Peace" (Isa. 9:6, NIV).

At my church the pastors are inclusive of childless women and call us "mothers in Israel." They recognize the influence and ministry we have in counseling, teaching, and befriending children who think their own parents are members of any species but human!

As Christian friends are quick to point out, in the new earth I may be a "mother" at last. The Lord comforts me with the promises that I will have sons and daughters (Isa. 65), that I have a future and a hope (Jer. 29). And every time I sing, in Handel's *Messiah,* the chorus "For Unto Us a Child is Born," I get teary, but with joy. I do have a Son, and He can't wait to come back to fetch me.

CHRISTY K. ROBINSON

MADE HIMSELF NOTHING

Christ Jesus . . . being in very nature God,
did not consider equality with God something to be grasped,
but made himself nothing, taking the very nature of a servant,
being made in human likeness. Phil. 2:5-7, NIV.

I've always thought of this verse as a Christmas reading! It speaks of the preexistence of Jesus as God, and the miracle of the Creator taking the form of His created. It speaks of His life and death, His glorification, and His justification before the world—He is Lord of all.

He "made himself nothing." The Creator of the universe, an infinite being, took the form of a microscopic zygote, embryo, and fetus. He developed a spine and tail, large eyes, and gecko-like fingers. His arms and legs lengthened, His heart began beating, His brain made patterns, and He sucked His thumb. He could hear His mother's heartbeat. As He grew larger, He crossed His ankles and drew up His knees. He developed in every way as we did. When He was born, He cried and needed milk and diaper changes.

As Jesus grew, He played with the neighbor kids and scraped His knuckles and shins. He rolled down hills and climbed trees and helped with the harvests and flocks as a day laborer. He learned to read. He apprenticed to the building trade. As He matured, His voice deepened. Fathers thought He'd make a great husband for their daughters. The town knew Him as the kindest, most helpful kid ever.

"By this you know the Spirit of God: Every spirit that confesses that Jesus Christ has come in the flesh is of God, and every spirit that does not confess that Jesus Christ has come in the flesh is not of God" (1 John 4:2, 3, NKJV).

Fully human, fully divine, even as a "nothing." But being made in the image of God, this One reflected the love, compassion, mercy, and forgiveness of the Abba Father, as well the human body and blended DNA of His ancestors going back to Adam and Eve.

Jesus' authority, power, and glory were always there, but He lived His life as one of us, taking no power of His own, but showing us that even as lowly slaves, we can do anything in God's power.

CHRISTY K. ROBINSON

December 26

THE BEST PART OF WAKING UP

Faith makes us sure of what we hope for
and gives us proof of what we cannot see.
Heb. 11:1, CEV.

You have to love that Folgers Coffee commercial in which the good-looking young man returns home to surprise his family on Christmas morning, and three generations awaken in a delightful mood, with perfect hair and no facial pillow marks, to drink coffee in their jammies and celebrate the reunion.

What a scene. We have total recall of that best-of-all Christmas, until we really do wake up and smell the coffee, and realize that, "Hey! That never happened!" The commercial makes you nostalgic and misty-eyed over an experience you never had.

The reality is that your sister's family is broken and her kids are split between households every holiday, your son can't make it because he has to work on Christmas, your mother and her new husband would just like to spend the holiday in a "low-key" way with a restaurant meal and TV specials (meaning without interference from relatives), and your favorite aunt or uncle passed away right around Christmas last year.

Instead of a *Waltons Homecoming* or *Touched by an Angel* Christmas, you got a *Simpsons* or *Malcolm in the Middle* (in other words, horrifying) Christmas. Unrealistic expectations (especially those generated by a marketing firm) can make real-life special occasions seem bitter or sad. But remember the times, both Christmas and every day, when God turned it around: when all your plans crashed, but church members or neighbors invited you to fellowship in their homes and treated you as family. Or you volunteered at the homeless shelter and found peace in acting as the hands of Jesus. Or you just stayed home alone with your Bible and fuzzy robe. God is faithful and has not forgotten you.

"The Lord's . . . compassions fail not. They are new every morning; great is Your faithfulness" (Lam. 3:22, 23, NKJV).

The best part of waking up isn't what's steaming in your cup. It's the brimming heart of God, whose mercy and compassion are new every morning!

Christy K. Robinson

MORE S'MORES

I will . . . make them joyful in My house of prayer.
Isa. 56:7, NKJV.

"I know exactly how to make s'mores, Mama," Annika said. "I'll teach you."

Annika carefully stacked a graham cracker, chocolate, miniature marshmallows, and a graham cracker on top. She tried in vain to make the marshmallows mush down properly. Finally, she just ate it.

"Let's try again," I offered. We laid two graham crackers on a plate, one with chocolate on top, the other with marshmallows and placed it in the microwave. The marshmallows even turned toasty brown on the edges. Annika put the two sides together and the marshmallows mushed satisfyingly out the edges like little bubbles. She ate the "bubbles" first, then opened it and ate the chocolatey marshmallows, the marshmallowy chocolate, and finally the gooey graham crackers. No one has ever enjoyed a s'more more. Annika's hands and face were a mess; there was marshmallow in her hair and chocolate on her leg. Even after the ordeal of washing up and untangling her hair, Annika was still singing the praises of s'mores.

S'mores without a "spark" are disappointing, but with it—amazing and delicious. Sometimes we get caught up in religion, but leave out the "spark": the joy of knowing God. Even in the Old Testament the writers overflow with joy in their relationship with God: "The joy of the Lord is your strength" (Neh. 8:10, NKJV), and "Happy are the people whose God is the Lord!" (Ps. 144:15, NKJV).

From the Wise Men at Jesus' birth (Matt. 2:10) to Zacchaeus (Luke 19:6) to the disciples at Jesus' ascension (Luke 24:52), people were filled with joy after encountering Jesus. The apostle Paul rejoiced even through persecution and suffering (2 Cor. 7:4; Col. 1:24). God rejoices over each sinner who repents (Luke 15:10).

God wants to fill us with joy: "The ransomed of the Lord . . . shall obtain joy and gladness, and sorrow and sighing shall flee away (Isa. 35:10, NKJV). While teaching His disciples, Jesus said, "These things I have spoken to you, that My joy may remain in you, and that your joy may be full" (John 15:11, NKJV).

LAURA WEST KONG

DECEMBER 28

STANDING STRONG

Others, like seed sown on good soil, hear the word,
accept it, and produce a crop.
Mark 4:20, NIV.

Large yellow, orange, and rust marigold blossoms caught my eye. I thought of my outdoor patio. Proudly, I carried my new purchase home. I planted them in pots filled with the best planting mix. They had space. They felt the wind and savored the sun. But there was room in the pots for only half of the flat of plants. What should I do with the others? I planted them closely together in a corner of the garden, like a ground cover.

At first they did well, and then they began to weaken. There was no place to spread and grow. Everywhere was another plant. Roots tangled with each other. Leaves turned yellow, then brown. Flowers withered. Within a few months only a few of the marigolds were alive. "But since they have no root, they last only a short time. When trouble or persecution comes because of the word, they quickly fall away. Still others, like seed sown among thorns, hear the word; but the worries of this life, the deceitfulness of wealth and the desires for other things come in and choke the word, making it unfruitful" (Mark 4:17-19, NIV).

In contrast, the potted marigolds didn't do well at first. With no support from the other plants, they faced the winds alone. Their heads drooped. Their leaves wilted. I watered and fed and hoped. As the days passed, the plants gradually gained strength. Their heads stood up. Their leaves filled out. They were growing! All the time, they'd been strengthening their root systems. Not only did the potted marigolds grow, they flourished and bloomed. "Others, like seed sown on good soil, hear the word, accept it, and produce a crop—thirty, sixty or even a hundred times what was sown" (verse 20, NIV).

It is comfortable to stay in a secure comfort zone, surrounded by the props of family, friends, money, convenience, and church. We may depend on others for our spiritual growth, but often, it's when we strike out alone on some venture or a crisis in our life sets us apart that we forge ahead with our life and learn what God can do for us individually. It's then that we grow, and it's then that we eventually become strong and secure, compassionate and mature.

EDNA MAYE GALLINGTON

A THANKFUL HEART

Let me shout God's name with a praising song,
let me tell his greatness in a prayer of thanks.
Ps. 69:30, Message.

Have you considered lately how much you have to be thankful for? For those of us lucky enough to live in Western society it is easy to forget just how much we are blessed with. I'm not talking about possessions—although most of us are well provided with those. I'm talking about things that truly matter: positive relationships with family and friends, healthy bodies, freedom of expression, access to education, work that provides fulfillment, and the means to live in comfort and safety.

In addition to these immense gifts, there are countless other sources of daily delight—the sweetness of a ripe berry, the splendor of a sunset, and the heady scent of a rose; the cozy fire on a chilly night or an icy beverage on a scorching day; the laughter of children, the spine tingling glory of a pipe organ, and the beauty of a meadowlark's song; the fun of a conspiratorial wink and the reassurance of a loving hug.

Every day there are hundreds of gifts to be thankful for if we would take the time to notice. Instead, we tend to focus on the negative aspects of our lives—possessions we desire and don't have, minor inconveniences of daily life, or others' behavior toward us that we consider undeserved or inappropriate. Our natural inclination is to focus inward and to miss all the blessings waiting for us just outside ourselves.

Making time to meet with God every day is the best way to turn our focus inside out. Even when things seem hopeless, He can give us something to sing about. King David describes the transformation God made in his heart: "You did it: you changed wild lament into whirling dance; you ripped off my black mourning band and decked me with wildflowers. I'm about to burst with song; I can't keep quiet about you. God, my God, I can't thank you enough" (Ps. 30:11, 12, Message).

If we allow God into our lives, He will transform our hearts, and we will not only notice and give thanks for our many blessings—we'll want to share them (and Him!) with others. Open your heart to Him, and He'll fill it to overflowing with joy and praise.

LORELEI HERMAN CRESS

DECEMBER 30

WE SHALL BE CHANGED

*We will all be changed—in a flash,
in the twinkling of an eye. 1 Cor. 15:51, 52, NIV.*

A sign on a church nursery door said, "Listen, I tell you a mystery: We will not all sleep, but we will all be changed." As a teenager, I worked for a Nazarene church on Sunday mornings, where I was in charge of 20 to 30 babies every week. My helpers and I changed every child's diaper multiple times. We learned that even the stinkiest substances wash off with soap. But I don't think that kind of changing is quite what the apostle meant!

Let's go back to Paul's discussion: what happens when Jesus comes. "Listen, I tell you a mystery: We will not all sleep, but we will all be changed—in a flash, in the twinkling of an eye, at the last trumpet. For the trumpet will sound, the dead will be raised imperishable, and we will be changed. . . . But thanks be to God! He gives us the victory through our Lord Jesus Christ. Therefore, my dear brothers, stand firm. Let nothing move you. Always give yourselves fully to the work of the Lord, because you know that your labor in the Lord is not in vain" (1 Cor. 15:51-58, NIV).

It's been quite a year: it's been filled with long hours, events, and projects that came to fruition, accomplishments at church and work, improvements to the home and garden, struggling to live a healthy lifestyle, and challenges in the family.

The important thing to remember, though, is to not lose heart, but give yourself fully to whatever work God calls you to do. All that labor, though it may seem foolish to a secular-minded person, is not in vain. It's not silly to God. He values the efforts we make. Who has not assigned a task to a child or subordinate, and thought, "I could finish this in a tenth of the time it takes me to teach it." God, our Creator, could speak or even think the word and it would be accomplished, but how would we grow or learn, or value the fruits of our labors? The very acts of planning, executing, and following up are the methods God uses to change us.

Change, whether it's lifestyle or attitude, is difficult when we attempt it alone. Trying to be good is completely impossible! But Jesus said, "What is impossible with men is possible with God" (Luke 18:27, NIV).

He can do it in a flash, in the twinkling of an eye.

CHRISTY K. ROBINSON

IN CONCLUSION

Forget what happened long ago! Don't think about the past. I am creating something new. Isa. 43:18, 19, CEV.

The phrase that is guaranteed to wake up an audience: "And in conclusion . . ."

Today is New Year's Eve. Today's news will carry summaries of the big stories of this year, and tomorrow's will be about the first children born in the new year. You may rush to donate to your church or charity before the year's tax-deduction books close. Perhaps you'll finish off the Christmas sweets today, knowing that the diet resumes tomorrow.

This is a significant day. It's the day people remember one year and look forward to a clean start in the next. The Roman god Janus, after whom January was named, was the god of gates and doorways, depicted with two faces looking in opposite directions.

In Isaiah 43 it says: "Forget the former things; do not dwell on the past. See, I am doing a new thing! Now it springs up; do you not perceive it?" (verses 18 and 19, NIV).

The Lord Jesus, who is our true door and gate, inspired that verse. Heaven forbid that we should forget our experiences or the way that God has led us. No, that's why He gave us reason and wisdom, the application of knowledge. He wants us to forget and forgive ungodly actions and imperfect human ways and look forward with joyful anticipation to the work He wants to do in us and through us to humanity. Don't dwell in past glories or miseries—walk by faith into the future.

The future springs up. Could it be a spring of fresh water bubbling up through gravel or the tension in a metal spiral spring? Either way, there's irrepressible energy coming to you from God.

What new thing will God do in you in the coming year? What gift has He given you that He's eagerly waiting to unwrap and set before you? Don't wait for tomorrow—accept it today!

CHRISTY K. ROBINSON

AUTHOR BIOGRAPHIES

SUE ATKINSON, a retired nurse, preached an evangelism program in Guyana for Quiet Hour Ministries. **May 6.**

TODD BAKER is vice president and senior strategist for Grizzard, a fund–raising agency. **May 23.**

RANDY BATES is the chief financial officer for Quiet Hour Ministries. **June 19; Sept. 6, 25, 30.**

HERMAN BAUMAN, an ordained minister and retired past president of the Arizona Conference of Seventh-day Adventists, lives in Sun City, Arizona. **July 5; Aug. 15, 16.**

LARRY BECKER, D.Min., a vocalist and ordained minister, is a senior pastor in Redlands, California. **Oct. 11, 12.**

VONDA BEERMAN, a Christian recording and concert artist, partners with her husband, Merlin, and their children in several ministries, including overseas evangelism with Quiet Hour Ministries. **Oct. 21; Nov. 3, 14, 18.**

PANSY CHAND was Pastor Bill Tucker's administrative assistant before she retired. She enjoys serving God and humanity in various capacities. **Feb. 5.**

LARRY CHRISTOFFEL, an ordained minister, is associate pastor of the Campus Hill Church in Loma Linda, California. **Sept. 8.**

LORELEI HERMAN CRESS is wife to Peter and mother to 4-year-old Emmeline Claire, the delight of her heart. She currently serves as office manager for Medical Student Education at Loma Linda University School of Medicine. **Jan. 9, 13, 15, 19, 31; Feb. 16, 22; Mar. 3, 14, 19, 22; May 1, 8; July 12, 14; Aug. 7, 13; Nov. 1; Dec. 5, 23, 29.**

TIM DAVIS was a nurse at Feather River Hospital in Paradise, California, when he wrote the devotional article. **Nov. 11.**

LLOYD A. DAYES is a retired neurosurgeon and a member of Quiet Hour Ministries board of directors. **Sept. 24.**

DEL DELKER is a retired vocalist who sang for the Voice of Prophecy radio ministry. **Jan. 25.**

IVAN ELA was a ministerial student at the Theological Institute of Bucharest (Romania) when he wrote for this book. **Apr. 8.**

TIM EVANS, a self-employed Web master and graphic designer, contracts with Quiet Hour Ministries for Web master services. **Sept. 22.**

NORMA V. FLYNN is a former trust operations assistant at Quiet Hour Ministries. She is now a stay-at-home mom to three children. **Mar. 23; Apr. 28.**

EDNA MAYE GALLINGTON writes from her patio in Riverside, California. After a 35-year career in public relations, she has put aside the deadlines and is enjoying writing creatively. **Dec. 28.**

STACEY GURGEL, a La Sierra University student at the time, preached an evangelistic series in Ghana in September 2004. Quiet Hour Ministries helped with her expenses. **Mar. 27.**

FRED HERNANDEZ has been the director of information systems (computer guru) at Quiet Hour Ministries since 1980. He is a husband, father, and grandfather. **June 26; July 19; Dec. 16**.

WAYNE HOOPER was a musical arranger for the Voice of Prophecy radio ministry, the King's Heralds Quartet, and *The Seventh-day Adventst Hymnal.* He was also a member of the Quiet Hour Ministries board of directors. He passed away in 2007. **Jan. 5; Dec. 22.**

ROBERT JOHNSTON is a devoted Christ follower, husband, father, and dog lover. **Feb. 7, 25; Apr. 22; May 12; Aug. 5; Sept. 26; Nov. 30.**

LAURA WEST KONG, M.P.H., is Web site specialist and graphic designer for Quiet Hour Ministries. **Jan. 6, 8, 11, 29; Feb. 4, 11, 15; Mar. 5, 9, 12, 26; Apr. 6, 13; May 4, 14; June 4, 14, 20; July 17, 21; Aug. 12, 23; Sept. 4, 25, 28; Oct. 13, 18, 22, 28; Dec. 7, 27.**

EDNA MAYE LOVELESS, Ph.D., is a retired university English professor who is currently an editor/writer for Loma Linda University School of Dentistry. **Jan. 21; Feb. 10; July 2; Aug. 20; Nov. 8, 21, 27; Dec. 18.**

WILLIAM LOVELESS, Ed.D., is a "retired" university church pastor, who operates a counseling practice, teaches university courses, and serves as an ombudsman at Loma Linda University School of Dentistry. **Jan. 23; Feb. 9, 27.**

AILEEN LUDINGTON, M.D., lives in Paradise (California!) with her husband, Harold Clark. She has authored or coauthored six books. **Jan. 4; Feb. 19; Mar. 4, 15, 31; Apr. 11; May 5, 16; June 2, 9, 13; July 30; Aug. 3; Sept. 13, 28; Oct. 17; Nov. 20**

DARRYL LUDINGTON is a freelance graphic designer. **May 28.**

PAMELA MC CANN is president of the McCann Group, a marketing firm in Bainbridge Island, Washington. **Jan. 17; Mar. 7; July 18, 23; Aug. 9, 19, 27, 31; Sept. 3, 5, 20, 23, 27; Nov. 23.**

BOB MC GHEE, an ordained minister, is a youth and family pastor, a musician, and a father. **May 9; June 18; Dec. 3, 17.**

ROBIN HENNESSY MC GHEE, a flight attendant for America West Airlines, is Pastor Bob McGhee's wife and mother of their sons. **Nov. 25.**

JOELLE MC NULTY was a marketing support specialist at Quiet Hour Ministries at the time of this writing. **July 20; Sept. 20; Nov. 17.**

JOEDY MELASHENKO, an ordained minister, is youth ministries assistant director for Quiet Hour Ministries, and he partners with his wife, Judy, in music ministry. **Jan. 18, 24; Feb. 17, 21; Mar. 16; Apr. 10; May 18, 26, 31; June 3, 6, 27; July 31; Aug. 24; Oct. 7, 14, 27; Nov. 5, 19**.

JUDY MELASHENKO partners with her husband, Joedy, in their music ministry and on Quiet Hour Youth Mission Adventure trips. **Feb. 8, 24; Mar. 11; Apr. 10; May 18, 26; June 6, 27.**

DOROTHY MINCHIN-COMM, Ph.D., is a retired university professor of English literature and creative writing. She has authored many books and articles. **Apr. 20; May 7, 10; June 17.**

BARBARA MOEN retired in 2005. Prior to retirement, she worked for Quiet Hour Ministries, Loma Linda University, and the Southeastern California Conference. **Jan. 27; Feb. 20; Apr. 26; July 28.**

WELLESLEY MUIR is a "retired" missionary pastor and church administrator. **Jan. 7, 26; Mar. 30; Apr. 14; June 5; Oct. 29, 23, 31; Nov. 26; Dec. 1, 20.**

JOYCE NEERGAARD, Ph.D., lives in Egypt and conducts health education programs in churches and communities. **Feb. 6.**

JOHANNES NIKKELS is a retired missionary and pastor. **Mar. 29.**

C. ELWYN PLATNER is a retired journalist and periodicals editor. **Apr. 24.**

MICHAEL PORTER is the chief executive officer of Quiet Hour Ministries. **May 19; July 15; Sept. 14.**

R. E. "BOB" POSSINGHAM, an ordained minister, is a "retired" youth and family ministries director for Australia and New Zealand, but he still preaches, teaches, and does chaplaincy work in three public hospitals. **Oct. 9, 24; Nov. 10.**

STEPHEN ROBERTSON is Internet media engineer at Loma Linda University. **Jan. 12, May 15, Aug. 8.**

CHRISTY K. ROBINSON was public relations and marketing director and publications editor for Quiet Hour Ministries at the writing of this book, and she was the editor of this devotional. **Jan. 1, 10, 14, 16, 22, 28; Feb. 1, 2, 13, 14, 23, 26, 28; Mar. 1, 2, 6, 8, 10, 13, 17, 20, 21, 25; Apr. 1, 7, 12, 15, 16, 18, 21; May 2, 3, 11, 13, 17, 21, 22, 24, 25, 29; June 1, 7, 8 10, 15, 21, 22, 24, 28, 29, 30; July 1, 4, 9, 13, 17, 21, 25; Aug. 2, 4, 10, 11, 14, 21, 22, 28; Sept. 7, 16, 19, 21, 29; Oct. 1, 10, 15, 25, 26, 30; Nov. 7, 13, 24, 29; Dec. 4, 10, 14, 21, 24, 25, 26, 30, 31.**

LOREN SEIBOLD, D.Min., an ordained minister, is a senior pastor in Worthington, Ohio. **May 30; June 11, 12; July 3, 6, 26, 27; Aug. 1, 6, 18; Sept. 1, 9, 17; Oct. 16; Dec. 8, 13.**

MARILYN SENIER is a development officer for Quiet Hour Ministries. **Mar. 18, 24; Apr. 5.**

DON STARLIN is president of Adventist World Aviation, a mission pilot ministry. **Jan. 5, 20, 30; Apr. 3, 29, 30; July 8; Aug. 26; Sept. 12; Oct. 2, 3, 4, 5, 6.**

CORDELL J. THOMAS was the executive director for marketing for Quiet Hour Ministries at the time of this writing. **Jan. 2; Mar. 29.**

BILL TUCKER, an ordained minister, is president and speaker for Quiet Hour Ministries. **Feb. 12; Apr. 4, 17; Aug. 29; Nov. 12, 16, 28; Dec. 6, 11, 19.**

JACKIE TUCKER, R.N., is a cohost of Quiet Hour Ministries' *Windows of Hope* telecast, planned giving associate, and ministry relations coordinator. **May 22; Aug. 10.**

K. LANCE TYLER, M.A., is an ordained minister and chaplain at Loma Linda University Medical Center. **July 24; Oct. 8, 29; Dec. 12, 15.**

PHYLLIS VALLIERES, R.N., of Madoc, Ontario, Canada, teaches oncology nursing. She volunteered with Quiet Hour Ministries in March 2005, traveling with the evangelism teams to El Salvador. **Aug. 25.**

KIT WATTS is a retired pastor, communicator, writer, editor, and founding director of the Women's Resource Center at La Sierra University. **Apr. 23; Nov. 2; Dec. 9.**

CHARLENE HILLIARD WEST is executive director for international evangelism for Quiet Hour Ministries. She and her family run West's Archery, a gospel ministry. **Apr. 19, 25, 27; May 20, 27; June 16, 23, 25; Aug. 30; Nov. 4.**

HYVETH B. WILLIAMS, D.Min., was senior pastor of the Campus Hill SDA Church in Loma Linda, California, a book author, and a popular speaker, and now teaches homiletics at Andrews University Theological Seminary. **Feb. 3, 18; Apr. 2, 9; July 10; Oct. 20; Nov. 6, 15; Dec. 2.**

JAMES H. and JEAN ZACHARY have published two books of mission stories based on their more than 50 years of experience. Jim was evangelism director at Quiet Hour Ministries until his passing in April 2004. **July 7, 11, 29; Aug. 17; Sept. 2, 11; Nov. 9.**